MW00561423

THINKING ABOUT GOOD AND EVIL

University of Nebraska Press
Lincoln

Thinking about Good and Evil

Jewish Views from
Antiquity to Modernity

RABBI WAYNE ALLEN

The Jewish Publication Society
Philadelphia

© 2021 by Wayne Allen

All rights reserved. Published by the University of Nebraska Press as a Jewish Publication Society book. Manufactured in the United States of America.

∞

Library of Congress Cataloging-in-Publication Data
Names: Allen, Wayne R., author.
Title: Thinking about good and evil: Jewish views from antiquity to modernity / Rabbi Wayne Allen, The Jewish Publication Society.
Description: Lincoln: University of Nebraska Press, [2021] | Series: JPS essential Judaism | Includes bibliographical references and indexes.
Identifiers: LCCN 2020034113
ISBN 9780827614710 (paperback)
ISBN 9780827618664 (epub)
ISBN 9780827618671 (mobi)
ISBN 9780827618688 (pdf)
Subjects: LCSH: Yetzer hara (Judaism) | Good and evil—Religious aspects—Judaism.
Classification: LCC BJ1401 .A495 2021 | DDC 296.3/118—dc23
LC record available at https://lccn.loc.gov/2020034113

Set in Merope by Mikala R. Kolander.
Designed by N. Putens.

CONTENTS

PREFACE

In 2017 a general invitation caught my eye. The Jewish Publication Society (JPS) was planning to publish a series of books covering essential topics in Judaism for a general yet sophisticated readership and was looking for authors who would take up particular topics in the series. One among many topics that caught my eye was the Jewish approach to good and evil.

As a congregational rabbi with thirty-five years' experience, I was confronted, more often than I liked, by questions of "why." People who were grieving asked me: Why did someone so young (or so innocent or so good) die? People with illness asked: Why am I suffering?

I had been trained to listen and to offer solace in the affirmation of their feelings, but the core questions lingered.

From the earliest years of my rabbinic career, I had been interested in the answers to such questions, and the more definitive the better. The few texts I studied in seminary that bore on the subject were useful but insufficient, and the few courses on theology that were part of the curriculum only whetted my interest in the subject. And the more I read, the more I needed to read.

Teaching modern Jewish thought at California State University, Long Beach, impelled me to crystalize my thinking, in particular, on how to conceptualize the Holocaust. That thinking was clarified while I was teaching the theology of the Holocaust at the University of Waterloo. In writing my doctoral thesis on the origins of morality, I was compelled to examine the ways in which people came to judge good and evil. All this drew me to respond positively to the JPS invitation.

This book is the cumulative product of study, teaching, research, and experience from which I hope readers will benefit. During the process of writing it I have been compelled to review everything I thought I knew on the subject. Re-evaluating the texts and sources has refined my thinking and afforded me new insights. I encourage readers to be open to the same possibilities.

ACKNOWLEDGMENTS

I need to acknowledge those people, past and present, who have been instrumental in the writing of this book. Professor Israel Knox (d. 1979) first exposed me to the discipline of philosophy when I was an undergraduate at New York University. He was instrumental in changing my thinking about faith in the face of tragedy. Professor Sidney Hook (d. 1989), above all else, demanded of me the intellectual rigor that I believe is reflected in this book. Rabbi Dr. Seymour Siegel, of blessed memory, introduced me to theology and, in particular, the challenge of grappling with God in the aftermath of the Holocaust. Rabbi Dr. Neil Gillman, of blessed memory, was almost responsible for rejecting my rabbinical school application to the Jewish Theological Seminary of America (JTS) but in the end proved to be a valuable mentor who challenged me to look at Jewish sources with a different perspective. We also share a Canadian American identity.

I entered JTS only a few months before the untimely death of Professor Abraham Joshua Heschel, of blessed memory. Even though I did not have the opportunity to study under him in class, I still consider him to be one of my most influential teachers, particularly in the way I try to understand God.

At JTS I had the merit to study with four renowned scholars who were awarded the Israel Prize, but one in particular requires special mention. For four years I learned at the feet of Professor David Weiss Halivni, a singular intellect and inspiring personality whose heroic history and rare genius will forever serve as my model of *Torah im derekh eretz*, scholarship and human decency.

I first discussed taking on this project with Rabbi Barry Schwartz, director of The Jewish Publication Society, and I am grateful for his ideas and his encouragement. Joy Weinberg is most responsible for readying this book for publication. Her intuitions, editorial skill, diligence, and perceptiveness are nonpareil. Always aiming toward improving the clarity of the text and making it more accessible to the reader, Joy's persistent questioning has resulted in a final product far better than I had imagined. The first book of Samuel (25:25) states that a person is very much like the name by which a person is called. That is Joy. My gratitude also extends to the editing staff of the University of Nebraska Press, particularly Debra Hirsch Corman and Elizabeth Zaleski for their attentiveness to detail and considerable expertise.

I also wish to thank the University of Nebraska Press for co-publishing this book and for their commitment to supporting Jewish scholarship.

My wife Patti's ongoing support enabled me to complete this project. I am especially grateful to her. To paraphrase the book of Proverbs (31:12), she is good to me all the days of her life.

Finally, I thank God for all the blessings I have received and for allowing me the opportunity to explore matters that reside at the highest levels of human concern.

INTRODUCTION

As a participant in a 2009 roundtable discussion on religion and mathematics, the noted philosopher, author, and public intellectual Dr. Rebecca Newberger Goldstein explained her perspective on faith:

> I am an atheist. I am not wishy-washy on this question. Not only do I think the arguments for God's existence don't work, I think that this, more importantly to me, does not look like the kind of world empirically that is created by a good and caring and powerful God. It just—to me there's just too much empirical evidence against it. Suffering of children is my number one complaint. And the amount of work that one has to do, that philosophers have done, that theists have done to answer the question, the problem of evil—you know, free will, and that works for only some of them, and the Holocaust was, okay, the Nazis had to have the power of absolute evil in order for them to be free, so a certain amount of suffering had to take place—that even that only goes so far. There's a lot of suffering that can't be answered that way. Soul making, you know, this is a place where a lot of virtues can only be induced, we can only come to them because of suffering, that doesn't really seem to be to explain the suffering of children.[1]

Goldstein expressed the same sentiment in abbreviated form in an interview with the *Harvard Crimson* in 2010. When asked about the most compelling argument against the existence of God she responded, "I think for me the strongest argument is I just find it too difficult to reconcile suffering, especially suffering of children, of innocence [sic] with the notion of a transcendent God who cares about us. I just think if you look at history and look at the world, if you read today's paper, to me it's impossible."[2]

Coming from Goldstein, raised in an Orthodox Jewish home, a graduate of the Bais Yaakov high school for girls, and author of 36 *Arguments for the Existence of God*, this admission is both surprising and ironic. But it reflects the seriousness of the theological problem: How can a believer make sense of a world in which God is supposed to be all-loving and all-powerful and yet evil and suffering are pervasive? Absent a compelling explanation, believers may cease to believe.

The outcome of consideration of good and evil has substantial and profound practical consequences. Contemporary philosopher John Hick calls the problem of justifying the existence of an all-powerful and benevolent God in the face of evil and suffering the single most serious challenge to a belief in God.[3]

Goldstein correctly notes that the problem is not new: it has vexed philosophers and theologians for millennia. And she also alludes to some of the proposed solutions, though deeming them inadequate and unconvincing. Some thinkers have argued that given a world in which people are volitional creatures—that is, operate with free will—people may choose to act cruelly toward other people, and as such, the evil that results from the exercise of free will is a human problem and not a divine one. That is to say, torture, for example, has everything to do with humanity's barbarity and nothing to do with God's goodness or power. Other thinkers have argued that suffering is an inevitable part of human existence—and, moreover, through enduring suffering, human beings develop character. Yet as much as these proposed solutions may be partially successful, their inadequacy is exposed by the evils of the Holocaust, particularly when one and a half million Jewish children (among others) were barbarically murdered. Both the suffering of innocents and the scope of the Holocaust appear to render these proposed solutions dubious at best.

Many readers can sympathize with Goldstein. And, indeed, her hesitations and reservations mirror the sources all the way back to the Bible. Why do innocents suffer? Why do the wicked prosper? Can God be expected to intervene, and when? What qualities constitute a righteous person or an evil one? What is the nature of good and evil? Can evil be overcome? These and other questions surface in the Bible and in the writing of Jewish thinkers thereafter.

Good and evil in Judaism conceptually begins with an understanding of the nature of the universe and the moral development of humanity. These elements are first encountered in the Torah. Hence, before considering how the prophets and later writers refined their thinking, a look at the sources from which their thinking is mined is in order. Furthermore, the prophetic view of good and evil finds both support and qualification in the subsequent biblical and Apocryphal texts. As is their method, the early and later Rabbis will further discuss and debate the texts, contexts, and subtexts of Scripture, proceeding to the more theological ruminations of the medieval Jewish philosophers. The cumulative efforts to better understand the nature of good and evil are later tested by modern thinkers and confronted by the singular problem of the Holocaust.

In This Book

My objective in writing this book is not to offer an exhaustive presentation of Jewish sources on the subject of good and evil or a conclusive solution to the problem. The former would be unfeasible and the latter impossible: the problem of good and evil in Judaism has proved to be both intractable and insoluble. Instead, *Thinking about Good and Evil* offers readers a guided tour through selected important sources in the Jewish tradition that explore good and evil. The work will familiarize readers with paradigmatic passages related to the problem and its various attempted solutions.

Having briefly described what this book is, let me also make clear what this book is not. This is not a book on Jewish philosophers. It is a book about ideas. Specifically, it is a book about ideas relating to good and evil and the sources in which those ideas are located. As such, there is little need to enter into the larger and unsettled discussion of who qualifies as a Jewish philosopher. On the one hand, the influential historian Isaac Husik famously ends his study on medieval Jewish philosophy with the declaration "There are Jews now and there are philosophers, but there are no Jewish philosophers and there is no Jewish philosophy."[4] Contemporary philosopher Daniel H. Frank probably comes closest to explaining what Husik intended by noting that early Jewish thinkers did not consider themselves philosophers, but rather interpreters of Jewish sources in accordance with universal philosophic principles. In effect, "Jewish philosophy" and "Jewish philosophers" are artificial constructs operative only in more recent times.[5] On the other hand, contemporary philosopher Jürgen Habermas was convinced that there was such a thing as Jewish philosophy, determined by the philosopher's ancestry.[6] Jews who wrote philosophy, like Edmund Husserl and Ludwig Wittgenstein, wrote Jewish philosophy, even though there is little or nothing particularly Jewish in their philosophical corpus. In fact, non-Jews like Immanuel Kant probably had more influence on Jewish philosophy than Jews like Husserl and Wittgenstein, even though Kant was neither Jewish nor sympathetic to Judaism. Accordingly, contemporary scholar Kenneth Seeskin observes, "Not every philosopher of Jewish ancestry has made a contribution to Jewish philosophy, and not every person who has influenced Jewish philosophy had Jewish ancestry."[7] Thus the questions "Is Jewish philosophy supposed to be written by, to, or about Jews?" and "Is a given text written by a Jewish philosopher a philosophy of Judaism or a Jewish reflection on philosophical subjects?" remain unresolved. As a result, practically speaking, for the purpose of this volume, any Jewish source or Jewish thinker who contributes to a better understanding of the problem of good and evil might be included.

Why, then, have certain Jewish sources and thinkers been included and others excluded from this book? Here are my guiding principles:

1. *The sources must be relevant.* Thinkers or sources selected are those who contribute substantially to the analysis of the problem of good and evil, either by directly addressing the problem or by providing a special insight into the problem (like Hannah Arendt).

2. *Novel or unique sources or thinkers are included.* Among the thinkers selected are those who offer a singular approach to the problem that is not discernible elsewhere or to the same degree. Samuel Alexander, for instance, abstrusely approaches the idea of God quite independently of Jewish texts, but his thinking yields a novel explanation for the problem of evil. Hence, I include him.

3. *The sources or thinkers are representative.* The sources or thinkers selected are those who offer the best articulation of an approach found elsewhere. In his *Tales of the Hasidim*, modern philosopher Martin Buber identifies 83 Hasidic masters from 1700 to 1859. The list of Hasidic masters compiled by Isaac Alfasi in his more recent encyclopedia is over 2,200.[8] Not all Hasidic masters, of course, have left a literary record, and even among those that have, not all of have commented on evil and suffering. Even so, any attempt to offer a complete picture of Hasidic responses to the problem of evil requires an effort substantially beyond the scope of this book; hence, some selectivity is necessary. I have included the teachings of the masters that in my judgment best represent the fundamental ideas on evil and suffering in the Hasidic tradition. The same selectivity is applied to the biblical, Rabbinic, and medieval sources.

While the selected writings are not exhaustive, they are comprehensive. Readers can expect the explication of texts that span the full range of Jewish history and include the widest variety of sources, many familiar and others less so.

4. *The listing of modern thinkers is intended to be inclusive.* Thinkers selected represent the Reform, Orthodox, Conservative, and Reconstructionist movements. This section also includes female thinkers, notably absent from earlier periods of Jewish history. Martha Nussbaum, like Samuel Alexander, offers nothing by way of interpretation of classical Jewish sources but is included because she offers a unique approach to the message of evil absent a transcendental God, and she is a woman, a convert, and affiliated with the Reform movement.

5. *Redundancy is unnecessary.* Some thinkers straddle different chapters. Rather than duplicate their thinking in more than one chapter, I have chosen what I believe to be the most appropriate placement. For

example, Rabbi Abraham Isaac Kook is a modern thinker and a mystic who bridges the Hasidic and non-Hasidic worlds, and Rabbi Menachem Mendel Schneerson is a modern thinker as well as a Hasid. Both could have been included in the chapter on Hasidism as well as in the chapter on modern thinkers—in fact, Rabbi Schneerson could have also been included in the chapter on the Shoah. However, I have placed these thinkers in the chapter I believe is most apt; readers can construe their respective contributions to other categories of thought. Similarly, Hans Jonas and Emmanuel Levinas (and Jonathan Sacks) are placed in the chapter on the Shoah but could also be included in the chapter on modern thinkers, since their perspectives on good and evil are broader than just that specific focus. Instead, I placed them where I judge their contribution to be most appropriate and allow the reader to extrapolate from there to other problems of suffering and evil.

Each chapter follows the previous chapter chronologically, with the sole exception of the chapter on mysticism, which, because of its ancient roots, should be placed following chapter 1. However, since mysticism is integral to the development of Hasidism (chapter 5) and is its precursor, I have positioned this discussion as chapter 4.

Chapter 1, "Good and Evil in the Bible and Apocrypha," concentrates on Genesis, the Prophets, Psalms, Proverbs, Job, Ecclesiastes, Daniel, and the Apocrypha including Enoch. Chapter 2, "Rabbinic Approaches to Good and Evil," features the Rabbis' novel conceptualization of the evil inclination as well as thirteen disparate approaches to theodicy. The Dead Sea Scrolls and Philo are contemporaneous to the Rabbis and are thus included here. Chapter 3, "Good and Evil in Medieval Philosophy," elucidates the thinking of the philosophers Sa'adiah, Baḥya, Abraham ibn Daud, Maimonides, Gersonides, Crescas, Albo, and Yosef Ya'avetz. Chapter 4, "Kabbalah and the Problem of Evil," turns to the mystical component of Judaism, beginning with *Sefer Yetzirah* and progressing with the contributions of Rabbi Yitzḥak ben Ya'akov ha-Kohen, *Sefer ha-Bahir*, and the Zohar before culminating with Lurianic Kabbalah. Building on the elements introduced in chapter 4, chapter 5, "Hasidic Masters on Evil and Suffering," features the views of the Ba'al Shem Tov and his disciples.

Chapter 6, "Early Modern Thinkers on Good and Evil," explores the contributions of Spinoza, Luzzatto, and Mendelssohn, taking consideration of the problem of good and evil in new directions. Chapter 7, "Modern Thinkers on Good and Evil," considers the work of Hermann Cohen, Samuel Alexander, Martin Buber, Mordecai Kaplan, Hannah Arendt, Eugene Borowitz, Neil Gillman, Harold Kushner, Martha Nussbaum, and Judith Plaskow related to resolving the problem of good and evil. Chapter 8, "The Special Problem of the Shoah," begins with an analysis of names given to the events connected with the Second World War as well as an assessment of the uniqueness of the Shoah. Three specific approaches to the Shoah—traditional, revisionist, and deflective—make up the bulk of the chapter, with a systematic assessment of representative thinkers of each approach. The conclusion to this volume comprises a summation of the thirty-five Jewish answers to why there is evil in the world and the twenty-two reasons why human beings suffer, according to the Jewish thinkers included in this book. While there is no definitive answer, the result of the entire exploration of the subject yields important insights into what is of utmost importance to Jews.

Each chapter is structured to assist readers to grasp the key ideas and texts associated with each point of view. A brief introduction helps the reader contextualize each chapter. Each chapter ends with a summary that includes an evaluation of the thinkers included, through two lenses: "The Nature of Good and Evil" and "Questions of Justice."

Throughout the work, I offer analyses of the individual arguments, to help readers assess their efficacy. Ultimately, though, it remains the prerogative of readers to determine the utility and application of any of these views.

Understanding Theodicy

In any discussion of good and evil, one particular term recurs: theodicy. Theodicy was seventeenth-century philosopher and mathematician Wilhelm Gottfried Leibnitz's neologism, coined from the Greek word for God (*theos*) and the Greek word for righteous (*dike*). In essence, theodicy is a response to what theists—believers in God—see as a flaw in the operation of the universe. Evil, whether understood as a privation or negation of good or as repudiation of a norm, calls into question the believer's trust in the order and structure of the world.

In its formal iteration, the existence of evil is a logical conundrum based on four statements:

1. God is all-powerful (omnipotent).
2. God is all-knowing (omniscient).
3. God is perfectly good (omnibenevolent).
4. Evil exists.

The first three statements assume the existence of an entity identified as God. As well, the first three statements assign certain characteristics to the notion of God. To the believer, any presumed deity would not qualify as God without being omnipotent, omniscient, and omnibenevolent. A powerless and clueless God negates the very idea of God as supreme in power and knowledge, and a God who is not perfectly good would not merit allegiance. The last statement—that evil exists—is the product of observation. It is the least controversial of the four statements, though there are those who make the argument that evil itself is not at all real.

The logical problem is not that any of these statements contradict any other of these statements. God can be both omnipotent and omnibenevolent. Evil can exist even though God knows all. But as a set of statements there is a logical inconsistency. If God were omnipotent, God would be able to prevent the existence of evil. If God were all-knowing, then God would know all about the evil in the world and how to prevent it. And if God were perfectly good, God would want to prevent evil from existing. Hence, if evil exists, either God is unaware of it or ignorant of how to prevent it and must not be omniscient; or God is aware of it but unable to prevent it and thus not omnipotent; or God is aware of evil and could prevent it but does not want to do so and thus must not be perfectly good. (The last is Rebecca Goldstein's position.) In its attempt to harmonize all four statements, theodicy is the defense of God in the face of the existence of evil.

Judaism's Challenges in Addressing Theodicy

In addressing theodicy, Judaism is constrained by one particular handicap: monotheism. Unconstrained by monotheism, other religions have developed alternative strategies. Sixth-century Zarathustra, for instance, taught of one god worthy of worship: Ahura Mazda, the creator of good, truth, and orderliness. While locked in an eternal battle with the evil forces subordinate to Angra Mainyu, the god of disorder and enmity, Ahura Mazda would ultimately prevail. In the Zoroastrian teachings that follow, human beings are the architects of their own fate. Righteous deeds result in blessings for those who perform them, whereas evildoers have only themselves to blame for their demise. Indeed, the object of human life is to maintain *asha*, the equitable law of natural orderliness under which goodness is subsumed, and overcome *druj*, the chaotic nothingness under which evil is subsumed.

The problem of evil in the world befuddles Zarathustra. While not quite the neat dualism that many Western interpreters of Zoroastrianism would claim, Zarathustra nonetheless formulated a coherent strategy that avoided assigning a good God with responsibility for evil. God is not the creator of evil at all. Evil emerges from another source or sources. The evils of this world are products of the malevolent subversion of Angra Mainyu or result from human beings who have succumbed to the temptations of those evils.

The classical Israelite prophets could not assign evil to a competing deity. For Isaiah there is but one God, and thus God creates all—even evil.[9] Hence, Jewish conceptions of good and evil are circumscribed by the monotheism and idealism that fundamentally distinguish Judaism from Zoroastrianism. And herein lies the problem. Absent the possibility of ascribing evil to another power, the classical Israelite prophets were left in the challenging position of trying to account for evil in the world—evil that they regarded as assuredly real.

Saddled by the same handicap, the Rabbis proposed a litany of solutions to the problem of evil and suffering in the world, some more cogent and durable than others. While Jewish mystics would later welcome the scattered approach, favoring the menu of inherited solutions and adding others of their own, medieval Jewish philosophers preferred a more focused approach, emphasizing and defending a select set of solutions. From the seventeenth century onward, Jewish thinkers considered more radical solutions, some of which challenged the Bible's very assumptions. Finally, the scope and magnitude of the Shoah raised a special problem for theologians: justifying radical evil.

Beyond repudiating the idea of assigning evil and goodness to multiple deities, Judaism also holds that assigning moral evil to human genetic predisposition is out of the question: Judaism, from the Torah onward, is predicated on free will. It is not just what the Torah states explicitly ("I have put before you life and death, blessing and curse. Choose life" [Deut. 30:19]), but what the Torah implies. As Maimonides argues:

> If God were to decree that a person should be either good or bad, or if there were in the very essence of a person's nature anything that irresistibly draws that person to a particular course . . . how could God have commanded us through the prophets, "Do this and you must not do that, improve your ways and do not follow your wicked impulse," if that person's destiny had already been decreed . . . or that person's nature draws that person to do something that cannot be avoided? What purpose would there be to the entire Torah?[10]

Were human actions predetermined, then any moral code the violation of which would incur punishment would be absurd. And even today, were someone to argue that human beings are genetically programmed to behave in a certain way, there is still room for people to vary behavior according to sensory input—or else, argues contemporary philosopher Simon Blackburn, there would be point to having these senses in the first place.[11]

And while the solution that evil is part of life does find a voice within Jewish tradition, unlike Buddhism, which sees suffering as an essential feature of life and hence considers it a "noble truth," Judaism sees suffering as a condition to overcome rather than accept.

Some readers might see similarities between Judaism and Christianity in approaching the problem of evil. Some may see similarities with Islam. While this book does not aim to compare or contrast Judaism with other religious traditions, but rather to examine the sources within the Jewish tradition, one basic observation nonetheless obtains. Christian theodicy first begins with proving the existence of God and then analyzing the nature of God's attributes before proceeding to attempt to solve the problem of evil in the world. Judaism presumes the existence of God characterized by certain attributes and thus sees the sole role of theodicy as justification of an all-powerful, all-knowing, and all-good God presiding over a world in which real evil exists.

"That Sore That Will Never Heal"

Notably, most moderns have not been interested in the problem of good and evil—until it affects them directly. Such was the case in eighteenth-century Europe in the midst of the scientific revolution—until suddenly everything changed. An earthquake leveled the city of Lisbon on the eve of All Saints' Day in 1755, claiming several thousand lives, including worshipers. As philosopher Susan Neiman points out, the loss of innocent lives in particular was a theological and moral disaster that "shook the enlightenment all the way to East Prussia."[12] There, a previously unknown minor scholar named Immanuel Kant felt compelled to write three essays for the Königsberg newspaper on the nature of earthquakes. Voltaire and Rousseau quarreled over the meaning of the earthquake. Theologians preached sermons. Poets put feelings to verse, often badly. The six-year-old Goethe, according to some sources, was brought to theological doubt. The severity of the earthquake awakened dormant theological misgivings concerning the goodness of an all-powerful God and the reality of suffering.

In recent memory another seismic event has shaken the European continent, if not the entire world: the Shoah. Philosopher and political scientist Hannah Arendt predicted that "the problem of evil will be the fundamental question of post-war intellectual life in Europe,"[13] and she probably underestimated. The problem of why innocents suffer both natural and human-induced evils remains the intellectual problem facing the entire world—from Biafra to Haiti, from Hiroshima to Hurricane Katrina, from 9/11 to ISIS, from polio to COVID-19. The problem of evil remains that sore that will never heal.

Accordingly, the chapters that follow take readers on an urgent journey of Jewish exploration that will result in a better understanding of the nature of the problem and the range of solutions.

That journey now begins.

THINKING ABOUT GOOD AND EVIL

CHAPTER 1

Good and Evil in the Bible and Apocrypha

The Hebrew word for "good" (*tov*) occurs in the Bible no fewer than three hundred times, with one-third of those references almost equally divided between the books of Proverbs and Psalms. The Hebrew word for "evil" (*ra'*) occurs in the Bible 248 times, with just short of one-fifth of these references in the prophetic book of Jeremiah. The words "good" and "evil" appear in the same verse twenty-four times in the Bible, with six of those references occurring within the first twenty-four chapters of Genesis.

Yet despite the prevalence of the terms and the frequency of occurrence, biblical scholars caution against concluding that the Bible—as a unitary text—has a coherent position on any abstract topic, including this one. First, the Bible is essentially eclectic: it is composed of heterogeneous material from disparate sources with little philosophical cohesion. Second, unlike systematic philosophy or theology typically formulated in propositional sentences and presented through sustained arguments, the Bible presents narratives, dialogues, adages, and poetry that are inimical to deriving philosophical truths or theological explanations. And third, the Hebrew words for "good" and "evil" are multivalent. Sometimes "good" may mean "beneficial" (Gen. 2:18), sometimes "beautiful" (Exod. 2:2), sometimes "proper" (Isa. 65:2), sometimes "sweet" (Judg. 8:2), sometimes "reassuring" (2 Kings 20:19), and other times "cheerful" (2 Sam. 13:28). Similarly, *ra'* can mean "evil" (Amos 5:15), "hateful" (Jer. 42:6), "physically harmful" (2 Kings 4:4), "morally depraved" (Ps. 64:6), "ritually defiled"

(Deut. 23:10–11), or even "sad" (Eccles. 9:3).[1] Moreover, even both words together in the phrase "good and evil" are no assurance of any moral connotation. For example, King David's aging ally Barzillai the Gileadite laments his inability to distinguish between good and evil—that is, his declining sensory perception (2 Sam. 19:36). Without an unambiguous meaning to the words *tov* and *ra'* it is difficult to determine with certainty the precise implications of the words in context.

Nevertheless, there are essential passages and one entire book that frame the biblical conception of good and evil and prepare the way for later Rabbinic and extra-Rabbinic considerations. Five early biblical episodes—the Creation epic, the Tree of Knowledge of Good and Evil in the Garden of Eden, the story of Cain and Abel, Abraham's intercession on behalf of Sodom, and the Binding of Isaac—sketch the contours of the subject for later refinement. The classical prophets apply and amend the earlier precedents. The books of Psalms and Proverbs consider the problem of theodicy broached by the prophets. The book of Job provides a substantially sustained investigation of the singular problem of unjust human suffering. And two Apocryphal texts dispute the origins of immorality. An understanding of the concepts of good and evil in Judaism begins with familiarity with these texts.

Genesis: The Creation Epic

> When God began to create heaven and earth—the earth being unformed and void, with darkness over the surface of the deep and a wind from God sweeping over the water—God said, "Let there be light"; and there was light. . . . (Gen. 1:1–3)
>
> And God saw all that He had made, and found it very good. (Gen. 1:31)

The Creation epic and other primordial stories of early human life pose two separate but equally important questions for readers. To the novice reader, the obvious question is whether the events described in the early chapters of the Torah are true. *Is this what really happened?* The question challenges the veracity of the content and the authority that underlies it. That said, reliance on God's assurance that the stories in the Torah are true is logically problematic. The answer to the question "How do we know the Torah is true?" is answered with the affirmation "Because God says so," and the ensuing question "How do we know God exists?" is answered with the affirmation "Because the Torah says so," which leads back to the original question. The circularity of reasoning is inescapable.

Rather than trying to resolve this logical difficulty (which goes well beyond the scope of this project), we must rely on the approach that sets aside the question of whether the content is true and focus instead on what the text means.

To the more sophisticated reader—the reader aware of the similarities between the biblical epics and those of ancient Mesopotamia—the question is whether the Torah is merely a restatement of earlier Mesopotamian sources, with an affirmative answer thereby denuding the Torah of its originality and even its authority.[2] To be sure, ample evidence suggests that the Bible is closely linked to the ancient Mesopotamian beliefs that preceded it.[3] This, however, does not mean that the Torah is simply a copy of earlier sources. While it does reflect how ancient Mesopotamian material migrated into the consciousness of the biblical authors,[4] it does not suggest that the biblical authors adopted or endorsed the ideas that inhere in that material. By way of analogy, that some homes are decorated with Chinese art and Oriental patterns and motifs is not proof that the residents practice Chinese religion. In fact, readers will note how much the Torah diverges from ancient Mesopotamian beliefs even as the Torah employs Mesopotamian literary motifs.

Thus, as important as what the opening chapters of the Bible say is what they don't say. In contrast to earlier Mesopotamian accounts of the origin of the universe and the emergence of human beings, the biblical account is characterized by what the scholar Nahum Sarna calls "the complete absence of mythology in the classical pagan sense of the term."[5] There is no attempt to offer a biography of God (cosmogony), to describe God's "birth" or origins. There is no cosmic battle out of which the various gods emerge. In fact, there is no affirmative statement in the Bible that God exists at all. The Bible assumes that God's existence is self-evident. In contrast to earlier Near Eastern traditions, the biblical cosmology does not attempt to validate any national ideals or institutions, cultic or otherwise. It tells the story of the origins of the universe detached from any justification for Israel's religious practice. In contrast to its predecessors, the biblical account of Creation does not recognize any primordial realm from which the gods themselves emerge and to which they are subject. Absent is any succession of rival deities.[6] Instead, the biblical account of Creation serves as a prologue for the unfolding historical drama that ensues.

That drama includes at least two essential ideas. First, all of the forces of Creation as well as all Creation itself are totally and unconditionally subordinate to the one supreme Creator. And the supreme Creator can harness both the forces of Creation and all that is created in service to the Creator's will, fulfilling God's intentions in history. Second, the God of Creation is not morally indifferent. Abraham could count on the fact that as judge of all the earth God could not help but be fair-minded (Gen. 18:25). And God's moral concern is expressed in the early occurrences of the word "good."

We find the word "good" seven times in the opening chapter of Genesis: after God created light on the first day (Gen. 1:4); after God creates the sea, land (1:10), and vegetation on the third day (1:12); after God creates the heavenly bodies on the fourth day (1:18); after God creates fish and birds (1:21) and land-based animals (1:25); and, summatively, at the conclusion of the sixth day (1:31). A superficial reading of the text leads to the impression that in each case God is expressing pleasure in God's accomplishment, much like an artist admiring his or her artistry. But this misses the purposeful contrast between the biblical text and other ancient Creation stories. To the ancients, the universe was chaotic, cruel, and unpredictable. As such, human beings had no assurance that life had meaning. Worse still, any attempt to inject meaning was useless. The capricious, unseen, but all-too-real forces that exist above and beyond the visible world into which people were condemned would see to that. The application of the word "good" was intended to disassociate the biblical view from its predecessors. As noted biblical scholar Marc Brettler puts it, to the ancients, the opposite of the created order was something much worse than "nothing." It was an active, malevolent force best termed "chaos." In the ancient Near East, to subdue chaos is worthy of the highest praise.[7]

The biblical view of the world is one of orderliness. It replaces insecurity with optimism. While the Hebrew word "good" (*tov*) in this context has no inherent moral implications, it necessarily leads to them. Moral judgments are only possible in a world devoid of arbitrariness and capriciousness. Understanding precisely this point, the medieval commentator Naḥmanides interpreted "good" as meaning that God desires to make the world's existence eternal, or, in other words, permanent and predictable.[8] And when God declares the entirety of Creation to be "very good" (Gen. 1:31), Naḥmanides, following the Aramaic *Targum Onkelos*, understands the phrase to mean "it is very orderly."[9] Similarly, one of Judaism's premier philosophers, Maimonides, writes that "good" is only used to describe the coming into existence of something stable and permanent.[10]

Thus, within the first chapter, the Bible affirms the basic "goodness" of the universe, offering a revolutionary way of understanding the world and preparing for the story that continues.

Genesis: The Tree of Knowledge of Good and Evil

The Lord God planted a garden in Eden, in the east, and placed there the man whom He had formed . . . with the tree of life in the middle of the garden, and the tree of knowledge of good and bad. . . .

The Lord God took the man and placed him in the garden of Eden, to till it and tend it. And the Lord God commanded the man, saying, "Of every tree of the garden you are free to eat; but as for the tree of knowledge of good and bad, you must not eat of it; for as soon as you eat of it, you shall die." . . .

And the serpent said to the woman, "You are not going to die, but God knows that as soon as you eat of it your eyes will be opened and you will be like divine beings who know good and bad." When the woman saw that the tree was good for eating and a delight to the eyes, and that the tree was desirable as a source of wisdom, she took the fruit and ate. She also gave some to her husband, and he ate. Then the eyes of both of them were opened and they perceived that they were naked; and they sewed together fig leaves and made themselves loincloths. . . .

And the Lord God said, "Now that the man has become like one of us, knowing good and bad, what if he should stretch out his hand and take also from the tree of life and eat, and live forever!" So the Lord God banished him from the garden of Eden. (Gen. 2:8–9,15–17, 3:4–7,22)

The Garden of Eden serves as a foundational allegory cited by later biblical authors. The prophet Isaiah says the promise that the wilderness will be transformed into a garden like Eden is intended to offer comfort to the exiles (Isa. 51:3). Similarly, the prophet Ezekiel foretells how a once desolate land shall become like the Garden of Eden (Ezek. 36:35). The prophet Joel employs a similar metaphor, albeit in reverse. He warns that the land, once as verdant as the Garden of Eden, shall be defoliated by a plague God will inflict on the disobedient.

All of these prophetic references are predicated on the popular familiarity with the story. It is also likely that the allegory of a "garden of God" (Ezek. 36:35) once included embellishments now lacking in the Genesis narrative. For instance, Ezekiel refers to a variety of precious and semiprecious jewels at man's disposal (28:13) in a garden that includes cedar and cypress trees of incomparable beauty (31:8–9). Embellishments are typical in retelling an oft-repeated tale.[11]

The notion of a primeval Paradise was also well known in ancient Mesopotamia. The Sumerian myth of Enki tells of a pure, idyllic island of Dilmun, where both predators and prey live in apparent amity, where sickness and death are unknown, and to which the great hero Ziusudra was sent to repose once he became godlike. To support him with fresh water, the sun god Utu brings it up from the depths and transforms the place into a garden of the gods.[12] And the Akkadian Gilgamesh epic tells of a blissful garden in which the trees bear jewels.

Unlike Ezekiel and the earlier Mesopotamian epics, however, the Genesis narrative never refers to the garden as the "garden of God." Rather, it was a place for human habitation. And in order for human beings to enjoy it, they had to tend it. The Garden of Eden was entirely divested of any magical properties. In fact, the narrative makes the point that while gold and precious gems were embedded natural resources, they were not available on trees. The Genesis narrative is thus a conscious attempt to naturalize an ancient supernatural legend.

Within this setting of the garden, the text introduces the Tree of Knowledge of Good and Evil. It is a tree like all other fruit-bearing trees, except for the effects its fruit will have on its consumers. With perceptible indifference, the initial narrative (Gen. 2:8) has God place the tree in the middle of the garden. But after God instructs the first human being to tend the garden (2:15), he is further warned—upon penalty of death—against eating from this tree (2:16–17). Nothing further occurs until the creation of the first woman (2:18–22). Through the guile of the serpent, the woman—and subsequently the man—eat the forbidden fruit (3:6) and suffer expulsion from the garden as a consequence (3:23). Recognizing that by eating from the forbidden Tree of Knowledge the two have "become like one of us" (3:22), God is alarmed that they may also eat from the forbidden Tree of Life, at which point they would become immortal as well.

What exactly human beings gained by eating from the Tree of Knowledge is open to question. All commentators agree that they did not gain practical knowledge. The scriptural text assumes that the first man had such knowledge prior to the consumption in order to fulfill God's plans for the first human to name the creatures (Gen. 2:19) and tend the garden (2:15). But this is where consensus ends.

Some commentaries explain that by eating from the tree the first human beings gained moral knowledge,[13] but twelfth-century scholar Abraham ibn Ezra, thirteenth-century scholar Naḥmanides, and medieval grammarian and commentator Rabbi David Kimḥi reject this explanation. Ibn Ezra argues that "knowledge of good and evil" cannot refer to moral knowledge, since the expression is connected with being "like the angels" in Genesis 3:5; because angels lack free will, moral knowledge would be useless to them, so the expression must refer to some other kind of knowledge.[14] Naḥmanides argues that defining "knowledge of good and evil" as moral knowledge creates a logical dilemma. The Torah tells that God wished to prevent human beings from accessing the knowledge to be gained by eating the fruit from the Tree of Knowledge of Good and Evil, but given that moral knowledge is surely beneficial to human beings, why would God wish to withhold moral knowledge from humanity? The only way to avoid this absurdity is to conclude that "knowledge of good and evil" must refer to a kind of knowledge other than moral knowledge. For Naḥmanides, that means esoteric or mystical knowledge.[15] Kimḥi argues that "Adam was full of knowledge and it is preposterous to assume he had no concept of what is good and what is evil before he ate from that tree."[16] Furthermore, contemporary scholar Richard Elliot Friedman speculates that "knowledge of good and evil" may mean the ability to discern the qualities that make all things good or bad or the ability to make judgments of good and bad. But it cannot mean moral knowledge in an absolute sense.[17]

These objections are powerful and convincing. It would have been pointless for God to issue a command against eating from the Tree of Knowledge of Good and Evil had the first human beings lacked the understanding that it would be wrong to violate God's command. In fact, the very idea of a command necessitates an appreciation of following the rules, the nature of the consequences of failing to follow rules, and the basic premise that it is right to follow rules and wrong not to. Hence, the text assumes that the first human being understood right from wrong prior to eating the forbidden fruit. The first human beings had an innate moral sense.

Several commentators hold this judgment. Naḥmanides, for instance, explains in his commentary on Genesis 6:13 that the generation of the Flood was doomed to destruction because of the people's violence even though they never received a specific warning against violence, since there was no need for an admonishment against acting in a way that human reason itself would hold to be immoral. Fourteenth-century French rabbi Ḥizkiyah ben Manoah agrees. He writes that "there are a number of commandments that human beings are obligated to observe on the basis of rational opinion" independent of God's command.[18] Twelfth-century philosopher and poet Rabbi Yehudah Halevi writes that the Torah adds further obligations to a moral code already accessible to human beings.[19]

Influenced by Kimḥi's commentary, the contemporary rabbi Robert Gordis suggests that the knowledge gained by eating the forbidden fruit was sexual awareness.[20] Since the text reports that immediately after the consumption the man and woman realize they are both naked (Gen. 3:7), what changed after eating the forbidden fruit was sexual awareness, and therefore the fruit gave them such knowledge. Further, the verb of choice in describing sexual intercourse is the same verb for knowledge (*yd'*). After their banishment from the garden, the first man "knew" (*yada'*) the first woman, who subsequently gives birth to their first child (Gen. 4:1). "Good and evil," then, is an idiom for sexual awareness. This is the knowledge the first couple had lacked until they ate from the Tree of Knowledge of Good and Evil.

Naḥmanides had considered this possibility but rejected it. If "knowledge of good and evil" refers to sexual knowledge, then God's worry in Genesis 3:22 seems ludicrous. God has no sexual urge, so how would "knowledge of good and evil" make human beings "like us"? University of Pennsylvania professor Ephraim Speiser also rejects Gordis's suggestion on linguistic grounds,[21] as well as on the basis of comparison with ancient Near Eastern texts. In the Gilgamesh epic, for instance, Enkidu, after succumbing to the temptation of the courtesan, "now had wisdom, broader understanding,"[22] implying more than sexual awareness.[23]

It is likely that the expression "knowledge of good and evil" is a merism, that is, a figure of speech composed of two contrasting terms representing an entire entity. In common speech today, "night and day" is a merism connoting a twenty-four-hour cycle, and to search "high and low" is a merism meaning everywhere. Merisms are common biblical expressions. For example, that God creates "heaven and earth" means God creates the entire universe. Moses tells Pharaoh that "young and old"—meaning everyone—will leave Egypt (Exod. 10:9). The Israelites are obliged to teach their children to love God "when you lie down and when you get up" (Deut. 6:7), namely, all the time. And the Psalmist asserts that God knows "when I sit down or stand up" (Ps. 139:2), that is, all his actions. Hence, "good and evil" means all that could be known about right and wrong.[24]

By eating the forbidden fruit, the first human beings enlarged the range of their knowledge. They already knew how to distinguish right from wrong and how to function in their environment. The power invested in them by eating the forbidden fruit was the knowledge that comes with calculating consequences.

To explain what this means, two examples will be useful: one from baseball and the other from language acquisition. It is possible for a person to read the entire baseball rulebook and become expert in the rules of the game. But knowing the rules of the game does not assure that one understands the game itself: when to throw behind the runner, when to hit the cutoff man, when to hit and run, how to bunt, etc. Similarly, one can read all the books written on English grammar and every English dictionary, but without knowing which words are appropriate to speak in a given situation, the expert on the rules would be speechless. Academic knowledge—while impressive—is incomplete. Before eating the forbidden fruit, the first couple had a degree of appreciation of right and wrong. They knew the rules and that rules ought to be followed. But only afterward did they fully grasp the consequences of wrongful acts, of violating those rules. Calculating the consequences of actions is a power heretofore reserved for God. Once so empowered, human beings had to be denied the prospect of immortality and thus were banished from the Garden of Eden.

Ironically, knowing the likely meaning of "the knowledge of good and evil" does not shed light on the meaning of the concepts "good" and "evil." But what does stand out is the linkage of "good" with following God's instructions. The prophets of Israel will develop this linkage further.

Genesis: Cain and Abel

And the Lord said to Cain,
"Why are You distressed,
And why has your face fallen?
Surely if you do right,
There is uplift.
But if you do not do right

Sin couches at the door;
Its urge is toward you,
Yet you can be its master." (Gen. 4:6–7)

The quintessential story of sibling rivalry is that of Cain and Abel (Genesis 4). As the narrative relates, following their expulsion from the Garden of Eden, the first man and the first woman start a family, in effect beginning to fulfill the divine command to populate the world. First to be born is Cain, whose name is connected with the Hebrew verb "to acquire." The second child is named Abel (*hevel*). No etiology is offered for this name, though it likely derives from a Semitic cognate root-word meaning "son" (*ablu* in Assyrian). The Hebrew word *hevel* means "breath."

Here the narrative jumps from birth to adulthood, providing no information whatsoever on any factors or experiences that shaped the brothers' personalities. All the reader knows is that the two chose two different occupations. Cain is described as a farmer, and Abel as a shepherd. Ancient Israelites, much less so modern readers, would have been well aware of the signal from the text that the second-born son, Abel, was destined to be favored,[25] as shepherding was the principal occupation of ancient Israelite heroes.[26] Abraham, Isaac, Jacob, Jacob's children, Moses, and David were all shepherds.

At some point in time Cain decides to bring an offering to God, which motivates Abel to do the same. Cain's offering comes from the produce he has harvested; Abel's offering comes from the choicest of his flocks. God solely accepts Abel's offering; Cain is crestfallen—and understandably so. It was his idea to bring an offering to God, his brother copied him, and yet God favors only his brother's offering. To Cain, God's rejection of his own offering is unjust. Aware of his distress, the Torah has God ask Cain, seemingly rhetorically, "Why are you distressed, and why is your face fallen?" (Gen. 4:6). Not waiting for Cain's reply, God says cryptically:

"Sin couches at the door;
Its urge is to you,
Yet you can be its master." (Gen. 4:7)

As is well known, Cain chooses to ignore this advice and instead murders his brother (4:8).

Biblical scholars are unsure of the original meaning of the text in verse 7. However, it is clear that God, here, offers Cain some kind of reassurance. Although his offering has not been accepted, all is not lost. There may be defeats in life, but when faced with equanimity and resolve, ultimate victory will succeed those defeats. Surrendering to one's darkest emotions, however, will end in a form of imprisonment from which there is no escape. As Speiser puts it, "Good conduct should result in exaltation, not rejection."[27]

While readers can intuit the general thrust of God's statement, the particular meaning of the words offers unique insight into the nature of good and evil. The key word in Genesis 4:7 is the verb "couches" (*robetz*, in Hebrew). The use of this particular verb is both grammatically difficult (it appears in the masculine, whereas the associated subject—*hatat*, sin— appears in the feminine, violating the standard requirement of agreement of subject and verb in gender) and mysterious (why this metaphor?). Speiser offers a neat resolution: *robetz* is not a verb but a noun, a loan word from Akkadian meaning "demon." Accordingly, the verse ought to be read as follows: "Surely if you act right, it should mean exaltation.[28] But if you do not, sin is the demon at the door whose urge is toward you; yet you can be his master."

That the Bible invokes an image of a demon does not mean that the Bible accepts or recognizes ancient demonic powers. The Bible merely employs a well-known ancient image that would resonate with its readers. And in the employment of this image of sin as demon, the Bible makes the statement that while sin can be tempting, attractive, and powerful, human beings have the capacity to control and overcome sin. There is no demon that makes human beings behave badly. In short, human beings are not compelled to commit wrongs. The narrative of Cain and Abel thus includes the idea that moral evil is a failure of the will. Human beings may succumb to the temptation of doing evil, but that is their choice. And human beings will be accountable for so choosing. Concomitantly, choosing to do what is good (that is, to "act rightly") brings personal satisfaction independent of what may happen to those who choose evil.

Before proceeding to the next narrative, there is one final point to consider. Why God favors the offering of Abel over Cain's may be explicable to the reader, but not to Cain. From Cain's perspective, bringing an offering to God was his idea, for which he is given no credit. And he had no inkling that what he brought as an offering would matter. God had not provided any particulars on what constituted an acceptable offering. Thus Cain has reason to believe that he has been dismissed unfairly and, furthermore, without a satisfactory explanation. By contrast, before his parents were exiled from the garden, they were given an explicit reason for all that would ensue. Bereft of an intelligible reason justifying God's rejection of his offering, Cain is thereby the first human being to experience divine injustice.

While readers should repudiate his subsequent action, at this point in the narrative Cain is a sympathetic character. The theme of grievances against God for a perceived injustice will repeat in later biblical texts, particularly in the form of the question "Why do the righteous suffer?"

Genesis: Abraham's Intercession on Behalf of Sodom and the Binding of Isaac

Then the Lord said, "The outrage of Sodom and Gomorrah is so great, and their sin so grave! I will go down to see whether they have acted altogether according to the outcry that has reached Me; if not, I will note." ... Abraham came forward and said, "Will you sweep away the innocent along with the guilty? What if there should be fifty innocent within the city; will You wipe out the place and not forgive it for the sake of the innocent fifty who are in it? Far be it from You to do such a thing, to bring death upon the innocent as well as the guilty, so that innocent and guilty fare alike. Far be it from You! Shall not the judge of the earth deal justly?" (Gen. 18:20–25)

The story of Cain and Abel—and to a degree the story of the forbidden fruit—present the concept of good evil within the framework of human conduct. The Abrahamic saga approaches the concept of good and evil within the framework of God's conduct. While the shift need not be intentional, it is nonetheless indicative of the broader view of the biblical author.

The wickedness of the inhabitants of Sodom was well known.[29] The narrative declares, "The inhabitants of Sodom were very wicked sinners against the Lord" (Gen. 13:13). But God's decision to destroy the city comes only after a subsequent investigation (18:21). God decides to share his fateful plans with Abraham, who proceeds to challenge God's decision. Concerned that the wholesale destruction of city might also result in the death of innocents who reside in it, Abraham characterizes the probable annihilation of the innocent as fundamentally unfair ("Will you sweep away the innocent along with the guilty?" [18:23]) and contrary to the very nature of God ("Far be it from You to do such a thing, to bring death upon the innocent as well as the guilty so that innocent and guilty fare alike!" [18:25]). Convinced that the "judge of all the earth" must act justly (18:25), Abraham, with increasing boldness but with consistent respect, demurs. Reducing the number of innocents needed to abort the destruction from fifty, to forty-five, to forty, to thirty, to twenty, and finally to ten, Abraham succeeds in moderating God's plan.

From a didactic perspective, Abraham's daring intercession serves to make him an exemplar of moral character and courage. Significantly, there is no known extra-biblical, ancient Near Eastern parallel to this story. From a philosophical perspective, it seems the text suggests that human morality derives from natural law, a universal standard of right and wrong or good and evil discernible through human reason. Moreover, even God is subject to this standard. The ultimate implication of Abraham's negotiation is God's concession that the Divine cannot act unjustly—a principle that will be affirmed by Jeremiah yet tested in the book of Job.

Appearing, as it does, in close proximity to Abraham's intercession on behalf of the theoretically innocent inhabitants of Sodom, the Binding of Isaac (Genesis 22) serves as a stark contrast. Unlike the earlier episode, here Abraham accepts without objection God's command to offer his son as a sacrifice to God. Readers know what Abraham does not: it is a test.[30] But what kind of test is unclear. It may be a test of Abraham's faith in divine purpose. With Isaac being his favored son (Gen. 22:2), his demise would thwart God's promise to build through Abraham a multitudinous nation (15:4–5). Carrying out God's instructions would demonstrate Abraham's full trust that God's will would prevail, despite reason to the contrary.

The test, however, includes divine instructions that contradict the earlier law that forbids the intentional killing of a human being (Gen. 9:6). So it would appear that God might choose to ignore a rule that God has imposed on humanity. In other words, God is not subject to the same natural laws. In this light, the concession God made to Abraham was false or exceptional. So while the test ends well for Abraham—he demonstrates his willingness to sacrifice his son without actually having to do so—it does not end well for God. God superciliously contradicts God's own standards. While all this is lost in the relief readers experience in knowing Isaac is saved and Abraham is rewarded, the prophets and the Psalmist as well as the author of the book of Proverbs rediscover what is lost on readers and find the arbitrary God unbearable.

As is the case in Genesis 18, the words "good" and "evil" do not appear in Genesis 22, but the concepts of good and evil lurk beneath the surface. Human wickedness is evil, thus making the inhabitants of Sodom subject to annihilation. Right and wrong, good and evil are universal standards that all human beings can discover unaided. Whether God must comply with the standards of good and evil remains as yet undetermined.

Deuteronomy: The Choice of Good or Evil

And now, O Israel, give heed to the laws and rules that I am instructing you to observe, so that you may live to enter and occupy the land that the Lord, the God of your fathers, is giving you. . . .

See, this day I set before you blessing and curse: blessing, if you obey the commandments of the Lord your God that I enjoin upon you this day; and curse, if you do not obey the commandments of the Lord your God. . . .

See, I set before you this day life and prosperity [tov], death and adversity [ra']. For I command you this day, to love the Lord your God, to walk in His ways, and to keep His commandments, His laws, His rules, that you may thrive and increase, and that the Lord your God may bless you in the land that you are about to enter and possess. . . . I have put before you life and death, blessing and curse. Choose life. (Deut. 4:1, 11:26–27, 30:15–16,19)

Life is contingent on obedience to the law. God sets out before Israel a blessing and a curse: the blessing a reward for obedience and the curse a punishment for disobedience. In this matrix, life, good, and blessing are equivalent, with death evil, and curse their opposites. While medieval Italian commentator Rabbi Ovadiah Seforno insists that good and evil in this matrix are not moral categories of right and wrong but conditions — good is the sweetness of this transitory world, and evil is suffering in this transitory world — the predominant view is that these passages intend that good and evil are moral categories and furthermore the outcomes of free will.[31] Thus Naḥmanides explains that life and death, good and evil are determined neither by human coercion (one person compelling another person to act) nor by celestial influence (supernatural forces compelling a person to act). Rather, they are the result of free will: what is in human hands and human power to attain.[32] Similarly, nineteenth-century German rabbi Samson Raphael Hirsch writes that happiness (*tov*) is that which results from general physical and spiritual health, while misfortune (*ra'*) is that which results from its antithesis; it is up to each person to willfully and earnestly choose the way to life and happiness by observing God's laws.[33]

That human will is undetermined from without is essential to the Torah, without which punishment for wrongdoing would be untenable. Only an undetermined will can be responsible for sin. To put it somewhat differently, those who cannot act freely cannot be held accountable for their actions. And the Torah holds wrongdoers accountable. Thus, good and evil in the moral sense assumes freedom to choose between the one or the other: good or evil. It remains the challenge of humanity to choose wisely. Accordingly, the passages in Deuteronomy lay the groundwork for what later philosophers such as Maimonides will call moral evil — evils human beings commit against other human beings as a result of making poor choices.

Friedman connects the act of choosing wisely in Deuteronomy with the earliest biblical mention of good and evil. Deuteronomy 30:19 returns the reader to the story of the loss of the Tree of Life:

> Humans lose access to the tree of life as the price of having gained access to the tree of good and bad. . . . Using knowledge of good and bad and choosing to do good is the path back to life.[34]

In other words, when the earliest humans ate of the Tree of Knowledge, they were banished from the Garden of Eden and thus precluded from eating of the Tree of Life. All humans thereafter are both mortal and morally conflicted. Human beings gained the ability to discern what makes things good or bad, yet they must use that ability wisely. By choosing to do good, human beings recover in part what was long ago lost: a path to life.

The Prophets

The prophetic texts provide no coherent or comprehensive explication of the nature of good and evil. Yet, certain passages offer readers some insights into the topic. For instance, in one of a series of indictments in which the prophet Isaiah condemns those who willfully distort ethical values, we read the following:

> Ah,[35]
> Those who call evil good
> And good evil;
> Who present darkness as light
> And light as darkness;
> Who present bitter as sweet
> And sweet as bitter!
> Ah,
> Those who are so wise —
> In their own opinion;
> So clever —
> In their own judgment! (Isa. 5:20–21)

What concerns the prophet is the intentional corruption of values by the scheming elite. They reject the standard understanding of right and wrong in favor of an understanding that advances their own interests and justifies their own errant conduct. Thus the sin of exploiting the innocent is compounded by the self-congratulatory arrogance of their self-justifications.

However, while the general thrust of the prophet's intent is clear, the precise meaning of his words is not. To be sure, Isaiah asserts that the indicted elite are guilty of making errors in distinction, but what kind of errors? Three types of errors might be possible.[36]

The elite may be making an intellectual error. They simply do not know the respective definitions of "good" and "evil" and thus have confused the two. Underlying this possibility is the notion that the elite act wrongfully out of ignorance. Had they gotten the definitions right, they would have behaved otherwise. So, what appears as "evil" to the public appears "good" to the malefactors.

Alternatively, the elite may be making an error in application. In other words, the elite know what is "good" and what is "evil" in theory—they are aware of the correct definition of each—but they fail to act on the implications of the definition applied in particular circumstances. Three theoretical examples will suffice. The rich man may know that oppressing the stranger by overcharging is "evil" but may argue that a permanent resident of many years is no longer a stranger and consequently is beyond the scope of the rule against overcharging. Or he may defend his actions on the grounds that the amount he has charged the stranger is not excessive; it is comparable to what he would charge anyone. Or he may think that the income he earns from this transaction is useful to society, since he is spending his profits on goods and services that bolster the economy. The error is significant but not necessarily malevolent.

And finally, the elite may be making a judgment error (sweet for bitter). They are aware of what "good" and "evil" are by definition, but they fail to properly identify their actions as evil in this case. Here again, the error is unfortunate but presumably innocent.

In context, however, the prophet lambasts the ruling elite as willful. And this is how the text reads, particularly verse 21, in which Isaiah sarcastically refers to the elites as "wise—in their own opinion" and "clever—in their own judgment." Accordingly, the mistake they make is not accidental at all. In fact, the error has nothing to do with making distinctions. The mistake Isaiah accuses them of making is the mistake of thinking they can get away with their nefarious acts via camouflage. They are now exposed for what they are: scoundrels attempting what German existentialist philosopher Friedrich Nietzsche calls "the transvaluation of values."

With this understanding in mind, readers can infer that for the prophet Isaiah, "good" and "evil" are not subjective terms apt to be interpreted or manipulated to suit the taste of any individual. Yet what precisely "good" and "evil" might be goes unstated.

Nevertheless, Isaiah provides some insight into definitions in another, well-known passage.[37] In chapter 45, as part of a larger body of text devoted to the denial of polytheism, the prophet thus conveys the word of God:

I am the Lord and there is none else;
Beside Me, there is no god. . . .
I am the Lord and there is none else,
I form light and create darkness,
I make weal and create woe—
I the Lord do all these things. (Isa. 45:5–7)

Worldly phenomena cannot be compartmentalized, says the prophet, assigning good works to a good god and evil to another. All phenomena emanate from a single deity. In the affirmation of monotheism, the prophet gives two examples of two disparate—even contrary—phenomena that stem from the same, solitary divine source. The distinction between light and dark is easy enough to comprehend: they are opposites created by the one God. But "weal" and "woe" require some explanation. The respective Hebrew words are *shalom* and *ra'*. While *shalom* is typically rendered as "peace," the Hebrew derives from a root meaning "whole." Since the phrase is syntactically arranged to convey opposites, *ra'* must be the opposite of "whole," that is, "deficient." This is not to suggest that the prophet asserts that God is deficient in any way. Isaiah seems to be saying that just as the one God creates "light" and its opposite "darkness" (two opposite properties), the one God creates wholeness and deficiency (two opposite concepts). Since darkness is the antithesis of light, *ra'* is the antithesis of "wholeness." This leads to the conclusion that *ra'* — commonly accepted to mean "evil" — is the opposite of "wholeness." Moving from the grammatical to the ethical, the evil person is a deficient person. The evil person lacks the qualities that make the good person complete. The prophet Ezekiel lists those qualities:

> Thus, if a man is righteous and does what is just and right: If he has not eaten on the mountains or raised his eyes to the fetishes of the House of Israel; if he has not defiled another man's wife or approached a menstruous woman; if he has not wronged anyone; if he has returned the debtor's pledge to him and has taken nothing by robbery; if he has given bread to the hungry and clothed the naked; if he has not lent at advance interest or exacted accrued interest; if he has abstained from wrongdoing and executed true justice between man and man; if he has followed My laws and kept My rules and acted honestly — he is righteous. Such a man shall live — declares the Lord God. (Ezek. 18:5–9)

Part of chapter 18 of the book of Ezekiel is devoted to outlining the characteristics of the righteous man. Once parsed, verses 5–9 include thirteen qualities. The righteous man "has not eaten on the mountains" (v. 6); that is, he has not joined in the sacrificial meal associated with the worship of idols whose shrines were situated on the mountains. Nor has the righteous man "raised his eyes" (v. 6); that is, he has not prayed to the idols set up high.[38] Second, the righteous man has not committed adultery (v. 6). Third, the righteous man has not enjoyed sexual relations with a menstruous woman (v. 6). Fourth, the righteous man has not committed fraud (v. 7). Fifth, the righteous man ensures that he restores a pledge given as collateral on a loan (v. 7). Sixth, the righteous man never commits robbery (v. 7). Seventh, the righteous man provides bread to the poor (v. 7). Eighth, the righteous man clothes the naked (v. 7). Ninth, the righteous man does not engage in usury (v. 8) or, tenth, in unlawful financial gain (v. 8). Eleventh, the righteous man judges his fellow fairly in court. Twelfth, and more generally, the righteous man follows God's laws (v. 9) and, finally, observes God's rules (v. 9).

It is both interesting and important that all the qualities Ezekiel lists are circumscribed by specific passages in the Torah. The Torah frequently condemns and universally prohibits participating in idolatrous practices.[39] Adultery is specifically proscribed in Exodus 20:13 and Leviticus 20:10. Leviticus 15:19–24, 18:19, and 20:18 proscribe sexual relations with a menstruous woman. Leviticus 19:13 and 25:14 forbids defrauding another. Restoring a pledge is required by Exodus 22:25. The Torah specifically prohibits robbery in Leviticus 19:13 and commands provisions of bread for the poor in Deuteronomy 15:7–11. Clothing the naked is an imperative learned by analogy: God clothes the first man and woman at the time of their expulsion from the Garden of Eden (Gen. 3:21), and thus human beings ought to emulate the same concern for the naked thereafter (Isa. 58:7). Usury is prohibited in Exodus 22:24, Leviticus 25:35, and Deuteronomy 23:20. Unlawful gain (*ona'ah*) is prohibited by Leviticus 25:17. Exodus 23:1–3,6–7 and Leviticus 19:15–17 require judging one's fellow fairly in court. The general requirement to follow God's laws and statutes appears in various passages, among them Leviticus 26:1 and Deuteronomy 7:12 and 12:1. In essence, Ezekiel asserts that what makes a righteous man is adherence to the commandments of the Torah: both those that delineate the relationship between human beings and God and those that delineate the relationship among human beings. Thus, when it comes to human conduct, "the good" is doing what God commands; evil, by inference, is violating what God commands.

It is in this sense that we understand Deuteronomy 17:2. The text admonishes against offering a blemished animal as a sacrifice in that it is "an evil thing" (*davar ra'*) that God detests. Similarly, Deuteronomy 4:25 warns against lapsing into idolatry, which is defined as "that which is evil in the eyes of the Lord your God." Conversely, Deuteronomy 6:18 aligns the "right and the good in the eyes of God" with following all of God's laws and statutes (6:17).

From this perspective, the prophet Jeremiah censures the people Israel for corrupting their ways and abandoning the Torah:

Oh, to be in the desert,
At the encampment for wayfarers!
Oh, to leave my people,
To go away from them —
For they are all adulterers,
A band of rogues.
They bend their tongues like bows;
They are valorous in the land
For treachery, not for honesty;
They advance from evil to evil,
And they do not heed Me
— declares the Lord. (Jer. 9:1–2)

I am going to feed that people wormwood and make them drink a bitter draft. I will scatter them among the nations which they and their fathers never knew; and I will dispatch the sword after them until I have consumed them. (Jer. 9:14–15)

Reminiscent of Isaiah's condemnation of the corrupt elite who distort the truth, Jeremiah condemns the "valorous in the land" who "bend their tongues like bows" (Jer. 9:2). "For treachery, not for honesty; / They advance from evil to evil. / And they do not heed Me / — declares the Lord" (9:2). Those who have forsaken the teachings of the Torah are doomed (9:12). What troubles Jeremiah, however, is not the pervasiveness of evil, but the prosperity of evildoers. Thus Jeremiah questions how the prosperity of the wicked can be reconciled with belief in a good and all-powerful God:

You will win, O Lord, if I make claim against You,
Yet I shall present charges against you:
Why does the way of the wicked prosper?

Why are the workers of treachery at ease?
You have planted them, and they have taken root,
They spread, they even bear fruit.
You are present in their mouths,
But far from their thoughts. . . .
How long must the land languish,
And the grass of all the countryside dry up?
Must beasts and birds perish,
Because of the evil of its inhabitants,
Who say, "He will not look upon our future"? (Jer. 12:1–2,4)

"Why does the way of the wicked prosper?" Jeremiah asks in an accusatory tone (Jer. 12:1). Worse still, the wicked deign to invoke God's name while they hypocritically violate God's laws: "You are present in their mouths, / But far from their thoughts" (12:2). Jeremiah is outraged. But his rage is complicated by his perplexity. Should God fail to punish the wicked, God's justness and power are in question. But when God does punish the wicked—by afflicting the land with infertility, for example (12:4)—then even the innocent are affected with hunger. Punishing the guilty results in the unfortunate but unavoidable consequence of simultaneously punishing the innocent. Readers cannot but wonder how God's response addresses Jeremiah's dual concerns. God, reports the prophet, is said to reply that Jeremiah's current state of confusion, like his personal fortunes, will worsen before they improve (12:5–6). Perhaps knowing that God, who is aware of all, will appropriately right the situation in due course is comfort for the perplexed (16:16–18).

Despite the fact that Jeremiah's question remains unresolved, the prophetic text reinforces the idea that "goodness" is linked to obedience to God and the performance of the commandments and introduces the idea that what remains mysterious now (why the wicked prosper) will be clarified in the future with the eventual punishment of evildoers.

The prophet Micah takes up Isaiah's condemnation of those who willfully act unjustly.

I said:
Listen, you rulers of Jacob,
You chiefs of the House of Israel!
For you ought to know what is right,
But you hate the good and love evil. (Mic. 3:1–2)

In his own denunciation of unethical leaders, Micah accuses them of knowing what is right yet choosing to do wrong (3:2). By acting thusly, they have shown they "hate good and love evil" (3:2). The argument here is that those who fail to choose the good *ipso facto* love evil. Evildoers are not guilty of an error in making distinctions of any kind. Those who choose evil over good make a statement of preference. Micah thereby raises the stakes. The willful choice of evil over good when what is "good" is known is a rejection of the good. And since the "good" is understood to be what God sanctions, the rejection of "good" is a rejection of God. Micah also implies that the right and the good are not beyond human comprehension. Good and evil, right and wrong are accessible concepts; they are clear and distinct ideas. Hence, no leader may excuse misconduct on the grounds of misunderstanding. Good and evil are coherent and familiar terms in human conduct

The Book of Psalms

Psalms approaches the theme of good and evil in two ways. The Psalmist occasionally outlines the characteristics of the noble soul, the person worthy of God's approbation and human emulation. By way of inference, readers can discern what constitutes the virtuous life and what constitutes what seventeenth-century moral theorists quaintly labeled the "vicious" life. At other times the Psalmist engages in a direct consideration of the problem of theodicy, the vindication of divine goodness and fairness given the existence of evil. Specifically, the Psalmist wrestles with the question of why it is that the wicked seem to flourish and the righteous seem to suffer. The book of Psalms exclusively frets over moral evil. The question of natural evil—that is, natural phenomena like earthquakes or diseases that claim human lives indiscriminately—is beyond the ambit of the text.

Psalm 15 is a fine example of the first approach:

A psalm of David.
Lord, who may sojourn in Your tent,
who may dwell upon Your holy mountain?
He who lives without blame,
who does what is right,
and in his heart acknowledges the truth;
whose tongue is not given to evil;
who has never done harm to his fellow,
or borne reproach for [his acts toward] his neighbor;
for whom a contemptible man is abhorrent,
but who honors those who fear the Lord;
who stands by his oath even to his hurt;
who has never lent money at interest,
or accepted a bribe against the innocent.
The man who acts thus shall never be shaken.

The Psalmist lists the traits of the noble individual who, as affirmed in the conclusion, earns God's protection (Ps. 15:5).[40] The list includes eleven items. The noble individual "lives without blame"[41] (v. 2); "does what is right," a very general term for ethical probity (v. 2); acknowledges the truth and speaks no slander (vv. 2–3); never harms a fellow (v. 3) or is held in low esteem on account of his mistreatment of a fellow (v. 3); despises villains and, in contrast, honors those who revere God (v. 4); keeps his vows even when circumstance makes such dependability disadvantageous (v. 4); never commits usury and, relatedly, would never accept a bribe to pervert justice (v. 5).

Upon reflection, readers will surely note fidelity to Jewish ritual practice is nowhere included.[42] That is to say, observance of feasts or fasts, adherence to the dietary laws, or compliance with any of the sacrificial or agricultural laws goes unmentioned. Furthermore, aside from the practice of usury prohibited by Deuteronomy 23:20 and the crime of taking bribes prohibited by Deuteronomy 16:19, the list emphasizes conduct that lies beyond the purview of law. It would seem, then, that from the perspective of the Psalmist, ethical behavior is largely super-erogatory. To put it differently, the good person is not determined as such on the basis of adherence to the law, but on the basis of adherence to a set of moral standards that exist above and beyond the realm of law. Perhaps surprisingly, the Psalmist's implication is that the observant Jew is not necessarily a good Jew, and a good Jew need be more than an observant Jew.

By removing consideration of virtue from complete conformity to the laws of the Torah, the Psalmist further implies that the nature of "good" is independent of God's will. God gives us the law and, to be sure, we are duty-bound to observe it as a matter of theological allegiance. But the laws God gives us do not encompass all that is "good." In some cases, behavior that human beings—in this case, the Psalmist—declare to be good is just that. Remarkably, the Psalmist asserts that God endorses these human-determined standards of good behavior (Ps. 15:1,5).

Examples of the second approach—resolving the problem of theodicy—are Psalms 37, 49, 73, and 94. But prior to considering each in turn, a general observation is in order. In the Psalmist's worldview, God is wholly righteous (Ps. 145:17) and thus loves the upright (146:8) and hears their prayers (34:16, 145:18). God protects the helpless (34:20, 146:9) and allows no evil to befall them (91:10). The righteous shall lack nothing (34:10). They shall enjoy long life (34:13). Yet these expressions of confidence in God's justice are belied by reality. The Psalmist is constantly beset by the wicked to the point of tears (6:7–8), protesting his innocence all the while (7:4). The wicked are incessantly exploiting the upright and needy, thereby challenging God's justice (10:3–4). Further, the Torah itself asserts that "there will never cease to be needy ones in the land" (Deut. 15:11). Unless one is intent on assuming that all needy are wicked—an assumption the Psalmist does not make—confidence in God's justice is undeserved.

Faced with reality, the Psalmist constructs a tiered response. In Psalm 37 he notes that evildoers prosper while the righteous suffer:

Of David.
Do not be vexed by evil men;
do not be incensed by wrongdoers;
for they soon wither like the grass,
like verdure fade away.
Trust in the Lord and do good,
abide in the land and remain loyal.
Seek the favor of the Lord,
and He will grant you the desires of your heart. (Ps. 37:1–4)

Be patient and wait for the Lord,
do not be vexed by the prospering man
who carries out his schemes.
Give up anger, abandon fury,
do not be vexed;
it can only do harm.
For evil men will be cut off,
but not those who look to the Lord—
they shall inherit the land.
A little longer and there will be no wicked man;
you will look at where he was—
he will be gone. (vv. 7–10)

The wicked man schemes against the righteous,
and gnashes his teeth at him.
The Lord laughs at him,
for He knows that his day will come. (vv. 12–13)

Mark the blameless, note the upright,
for there is a future for the man of integrity.
But transgressors shall be utterly destroyed,
the future of the wicked shall be cut off. (vv. 37–38)

The wicked are initially cause for envy (Ps. 37:1). But with steadfastness the Psalmist reassures his listeners that evildoers will ultimately suffer severe punishment meted out by a just God. The victims of the malevolence of the wicked may be envious (v. 1), confused (v. 7), or angry (v. 8), but their victimization will not be permanent. The righteous will only suffer temporarily (v. 24). Until such time that the injustice will be redressed, the righteous must be patient (vv. 7, 10, 34). In the end, the Psalmist reiterates, the righteous will be vindicated (vv. 2, 10, 13, 15, 17, 20, 33, 38).[43]

There is a bit of theological legerdemain here. The Psalmist maintains that since God is just (Ps. 37:28), God will ultimately favor the just (v. 40). But the problem lurking below the surface of the text is that at any given moment up to the point of future vindication, it would appear to the victim that God is unjust (and favors the wicked)—and so might the victim deduce, since the prosperity of the wicked and the victimization of the righteous may persist for a long and indeterminate period of time. So the Psalmist argues that the conclusion that God is unjust based on current experience is premature. Wait long enough and God will set things right. And if things are not yet set right, you have not waited long enough. Apparently believing his resolution of the problem is sufficiently convincing, the Psalmist counsels his listeners to "depart from evil and do good" (v. 27).[44]

In Psalm 49 the Psalmist considers the unfair distribution of wealth. The upper class has exploited the lower class and gained both material wealth and privileged status. Rather than using their substantial means to benefit the poor, the rich hoard their wealth for their own advantage. But rather than invoking the metaphysical solution inherent in Psalm 37, here the Psalmist invokes the ultimate leveler of disparity in wealth: death. It is not the just God who will redistribute wealth that satisfies the Psalmist. Rather, it is the knowledge that wealth cannot save the unprincipled rich from their eventual, natural demise. Here the Psalmist is not intent on establishing the doctrine of remediated fairness (that God will balance the allocation of wealth). Instead, the Psalmist takes a grim satisfaction in knowing that the wealthy will die.

That there is no security in material goods is certainly an emergent theme in Psalm 49. But theologically, the author of this psalm takes a dramatic turn. God is no longer expected to intervene. Death will overtake the wicked in due course. The appropriate response of the victim is not to accuse God of injustice, but to reconsider what is important. While the economic elite consider their wealth important, that is a chimera. Their material goods cannot serve them after death: "For when he dies he can take none of it along; / his goods cannot follow him down" (v. 18). Given this fact, the poor ought to look at their condition differently. Wealth has value, but limited value—not ultimate value. The source of the perceived injustice—the disparity in wealth between rich and poor—is contingent on accepting wealth as the standard of success. However, if that standard is rejected in favor of a more spiritual and enduring standard, the basis of the problem is eliminated. The Psalmist implies that the problem of good and evil is not a problem with God's attributes, but a problem with human perception of value.

Psalm 73 also addresses the problem of the prosperity of the wicked. And rather than giving a solution, it offers a way of living with the problem. The Psalmist almost envies the prosperity of the wicked (vv. 3–5,12) and their resultant sense of immunity (vv. 6–9). His divulging of his own suffering (v. 14) leads to moral confusion (v. 16),[45] so he seeks answers in the Temple, where he goes through a religious experience (v. 17). As in Psalm 37, the Psalmist concludes that the prosperity of the wicked is temporary (v. 19), passing as quickly as a dream upon arousal:

How suddenly are they ruined,
wholly swept away by terrors.
When You are aroused You despise their image,
as one does a dream after waking, O Lord. (Ps. 73:19–20)

Contrary to Psalm 49, here the Psalmist dismisses death as the ultimate leveler (v. 4). Relinquishing his earlier doubts, the Psalmist expresses complete faith in God ("I have made God my refuge" [v. 28]). The revelation the Psalmist claims to have experienced is that there is no satisfactory answer to the problem of why the wicked prosper and the righteous suffer, given a just and all-powerful God. In fact, trying to generate a cogent and plausible solution is "a hopeless task" (v. 16). All one can do is live with trust, faith, and confidence[46] that God in God's infinite wisdom is just, despite the evidence to the contrary. Inevitably, human beings will have their doubts about the persistence of moral evil. But, the Psalmist implies, these doubts should not interfere with the commitment to doing what is good.

Rather than patiently waiting for God to vindicate the victim and punish the wicked as in Psalm 37, and rather than reconfiguring the parameters of the problem (Psalm 49) or accepting with equanimity the persistence of the problem (Psalm 73), Psalm 94 directly appeals to God as divine judge to punish the wicked and avenge their victims:

> God of retribution, Lord,
> God of retribution, appear!
> Rise up, judge of the earth,
> give the arrogant their deserts!
> How long shall the wicked, O Lord,
> how long shall the wicked exult,
> shall they utter insolent speech,
> shall all evildoers vaunt themselves?
> They crush Your people, O Lord,
> they afflict Your very own;
> they kill the widow and the stranger;
> they murder the fatherless,
> thinking, "The Lord does not see it,
> The God of Jacob does not pay heed."
> Take heed, you most brutish people;
> fools, when will you get wisdom?
> Shall He who implants the ear not hear,
> He who forms the eye not see?
> Shall He who disciplines nations not punish . . . ? (Ps. 94:1–10)

The wicked flaunt God's laws: they are arrogant (Ps. 94:4), oppressive (v. 5), and murderous (v. 6). Losing his patience ("How long shall the wicked exult?" [v. 3]), the Psalmist demands immediate recompense. He refuses to concede that God is powerless against evil. What troubles the Psalmist is timing: he urges God to defeat the wicked promptly. Readers may infer the Psalmist's argument that the toleration of evil even for a short time is a challenge to the justice of a good God. As to the essence of theodicy, the Psalmist intimates that a righteous God abhors moral evil and that an all-powerful God can and will defeat evil. As such, the existence of such moral evils as the oppression of the poor is an essential problem demanding effective resolution. But God operates according to a divine—not human—time frame. God will ensure that the wicked become the architects of their own destruction (v. 23), but human beings would be mistaken in trying to predict with any accuracy when that might occur. With regard to the unjustly oppressed:

> They crush Your people, O Lord,
> they afflict Your very own;
> they kill the widow and the stranger;
> they murder the fatherless,
> thinking, "The Lord does not see it,
> The God of Jacob does not pay heed." (Ps. 94:5–7)

The Psalmist asserts that even though the suffering of the victims is undeserved, it still has value:

> Happy is the man whom You discipline, O Lord,
> the man You instruct in Your teaching,
> to give him tranquility in times of misfortune,
> until a pit be dug for the wicked. (Ps. 94:12)

The Psalmist is saying that by enduring unjust suffering, the victim's character is improved. Suffering is a testing and toughening of the righteous man's character. And (in Ps. 94:14), the same is true for the people Israel. (Later on, the Rabbis will explore and expand upon the notion of divinely sanctioned suffering.)

In all of the psalms that constitute the second approach to the theme of good and evil where God is expected to intervene, divine intervention is contingent on the premise that a just God must necessarily thwart injustice—and where injustice cannot be thwarted, it must be corrected. Evil lies in the persistence of injustice, and goodness lies in the eradication of evil. God is just insofar that God acts to defeat injustice and uphold the good. And God is good insofar as God is just. For the psalms that constitute the first approach to the theme of good and evil,[47] what is "good" is identified with exemplary moral character or virtues and sometimes (but not always) is linked to adherence to the commandments. "Evil" is the absence of moral character.

Curiously, the problem of "natural evil"—suffering associated with the natural order—goes untreated, though the psalms themselves make frequent reference to the storm motif. Storms, particularly sudden and violent ones, were common occurrences in the ancient Near East, as were earthquakes. Flash floods would regularly inundate the desert wadis. All these forces of nature could claim human life without regard to one's moral proclivity. Allusions to storms as emblematic of God's power feature in several passages. The Song at the Sea (Exod. 15:1–18) is the earliest and fullest example. Psalm 29 speaks of fear-inducing thunder that reverberates through the mountains, along with fierce winds that can shatter trees. Psalm 89:6–19 imagines the enthronement of God on the flooding waters. Psalm 18:8–16 depicts God as manifesting amid earthquakes, winds, hailstorms, thunder, and flood. Psalm 77:15–20 rehearses the natural upheaval at the Reed Sea. Psalm 114 invokes the image of quaking mountains as celebrating the Exodus from Egypt. Surely the Psalmist was aware that storms and earthquakes resulted in human casualties. People—even innocents—died in these events of nature. Yet the Psalmist chooses to view natural disasters as demonstrations of God's power rather than indications of divine injustice. Later, the Rabbis (to a lesser degree) and the medieval philosophers (to a greater degree) would reconsider the matter.

The Book of Proverbs

Scholars are convinced that while Proverbs is one of three biblical books ascribed to King Solomon—Songs of Songs and Ecclesiastes being the other two—Solomonic authorship is doubtful. More likely, the book is a collective of didactic wisdom spanning many generations.

In relation to the theme of good and evil, the book of Proverbs serves as an adjunct to the book of Psalms. Like Psalms, Proverbs construes God to be wholly righteous. Hence, God protects the upright (Prov. 2:7–8, 17:28). God does not allow the upright to starve (10:3). God blesses the God-fearing with long life (10:27), while cutting short the life of the wicked (10:27). The upright enjoy life, prosperity, and honor (21:21) because they follow after righteousness. On the other hand, God punishes evildoers. The wicked shall suffer for their evil acts (5:22). The upright do not need to envy the wicked, since the wicked will die peremptorily (24:19–20). There is no advantage to joining ranks with robbers and murderers "whose feet run to evil" (1:16, 4:14). In addition, God will not hear the prayers of the wicked (1:28). Given the advantages of the upright over the wicked, it is better to be poor and upright than perverse and prosperous (28:6). A recurrent theme of Proverbs is that retribution for the wicked is assured (1:26, 2:21–22, 11:21–23,31, 13:21, 14:22).

Proverbs furthermore declares that one's actions determine one's character (20:11). Here, Proverbs confirms that right and wrong are not a predetermination of the heart, but a function of human will. Thus the book states that choosing to follow the good path leads to life, while choosing to follow the evil path leads to death (8:35–36).[48] The person of good character operates according to the principle of reciprocal fairness: "Do not withhold good from one who deserves it, / When you have the power to do it [for him]" (3:27). In proclaiming that people have the power to do good and to avoid evil, the text reaffirms God's admonition to Cain.

Like the book of Psalms, the book of Proverbs is concerned with the contrast between the ideal and the real. In the ideal, the upright are under God's protection. In reality, they face hardship and exploitation. In the ideal, the wicked are punished. In reality, the wicked prosper—often at the expense of the righteous. Like in Psalms, when answering the question of why the upright suffer, Proverbs asserts that whatever suffering the righteous endure is for their own benefit: "Do not reject the discipline of the Lord, my son; / Do not abhor His rebuke. / For whom the Lord loves He rebukes, / As a father the son whom he favors" (3:11–12). Also like in Psalms, Proverbs predicts that the prosperity of the wicked will be short-lived.

The Book of Job

The book of Job is the only sustained discussion in the entire Bible on good and evil in general and on suffering as punishment for sin in particular. Some interpreters have characterized the work as a symposium, a dramatic dialogue or debate, where Job and his friends argue about the reason for suffering.[49] But this portrayal is misleading. Ancient Greek symposia were convivial (and often philosophical) discussions following a meal and usually over drink. By contrast, the words Job and his friends/interlocutors exchange are not convivial; often they are angry, accusatory, and antipathetic. The exchanges also take the form of a series of dialogues with no interactions among the discussants. Further, the setting of the exchanges is not a banquet but a house of mourning. Moreover, certain sections of Job—for example, the prologue and epilogue, Job's lengthy soliloquy (chapters 29–31), and the paean to wisdom that is chapter 28—cannot possibly be subsumed under the rubric of a symposium. Instead, the book of Job presents as a failed attempt to console a mourner following the catastrophic loss of his ten children in a common disaster, apart from (and in addition to) the losses of his business empire and his health.

The text begins with the following description: "There was a man in the land of Uz named Job. That man was blameless and upright; he feared God and shunned evil" (Job 1:1).[50] When one disaster after another assails Job, he sees himself as a victim—a good man compelled to cope with undeserved suffering. Readers would agree. All the terrible consequences he is forced to endure seem contrary to the expectation that good men ought to be rewarded. His friends, however, see things differently. Convinced of the truth of the age-old understanding that suffering is God's punishment of the wicked, they view Job's suffering as a clear indication that he is wicked—or at least guilty of some wickedness that has gone unatoned. They implore Job to reexamine his life, discover his wrongdoing, and correct it, since his suffering is proof of his sin. But Job will have none of this. He steadfastly proclaims his innocence. Job does not deny that God metes out suffering; Job insists that God has meted out suffering to the wrong person. Thus, in claiming innocence, Job implies that suffering is independent of sin. The implication is profound. It would then appear that God inexplicably and cavalierly brings evil upon the innocent. Job's wife urges Job to curse God, even if the consequence is death. She intuitively understands that a cavalier God who metes out suffering arbitrarily is a God unworthy of loyalty. But Job will have none of this either. Job insists that as difficult as it may be, humanity must accept evil from God as much as good.

But before going too far ahead, consider the prologue to the events in the story.

> One day the divine beings presented themselves before the Lord and the Adversary came along with them. The Lord said to the Adversary, "Where have you been?" The Adversary answered the Lord, "I have been roaming all over the earth." The Lord said to the Adversary, "Have you noticed My servant Job? There is no one like him on earth, a blameless and upright man who fears God and shuns evil!" The Adversary answered the Lord, "Does Job not have good reason to fear God? Why, it is You who fenced him round, him and his household and all that he has. You have blessed his efforts so that his possessions spread out in the land. But lay Your hand upon all that he has and he will surely blaspheme You to Your face." The Lord replied to the Adversary, "See, all that he has is in your power; only do not lay a hand on him." The Adversary departed from the presence of the Lord. (Job 1:6–12)

Of course, neither Job nor his wife and friends are in on what the reader knows. This is partly what makes the book of Job a literary gem. The reader benefits from the prologue that reveals that Job is the object of a heavenly wager. God boasts that among all human beings Job is exceptional. He is "a blameless and upright man who fears God and shuns evil" (Job 1:8). But the Adversary (*ha-Satan*, in Hebrew) attributes Job's model behavior to his familial and material success. Deprived of his family and property, Job would surely curse God. God and the Adversary agree to put their respective views to the test. God empowers the Adversary to do anything to Job short of killing him. Raiders carry off his cattle and kill the herders (1:15). A mysterious fire destroys his flocks and kills the shepherds (1:16). The Chaldean army steals his camels and slays their attendants (1:17). A gale shatters the walls of the house of Job's eldest son, killing Job's ten children, who are dining inside (1:19). Despite these successive tragedies, Job remains steadfast in his faith, accepting his fate with rare equanimity. "The Lord has given," he says, "and the Lord has taken away; blessed be the name of the Lord" (1:21).

One day the divine beings presented themselves before the Lord. The Adversary came along with them to present himself before the Lord. The Lord said to the Adversary, "Where have you been?" The Adversary answered the Lord, "I have been roaming all over the earth." The Lord said to the Adversary, "Have you noticed My servant Job? There is no one like him on earth, a blameless and upright man who fears God and shuns evil. He still keeps his integrity; so you have incited Me against him to destroy him for no good reason." The Adversary answered the Lord, "Skin for skin—all that a man has he will give up for his life. But lay a hand on his bones and his flesh and he will surely blaspheme You to Your face." So the Lord said to the Adversary, "See, he is in your power; only spare his life." (Job 2:1–6)

Now the terms of the wagers are steepened. The Adversary claims that Job's loyalty is contingent on his health. Deprive the man of his health and he will curse God. Job is subsequently afflicted with a severe, total body inflammation.

Job's wife now urges him to disavow the cruel God that has afflicted him. Yet Job resists.

Upon hearing of Job's predicament, three friends come from afar to offer condolences. For seven days they sit with Job on the ground in silence and in sympathy. Then the serial dialogues begin:

> Afterward Job began to speak and cursed the day of his birth. Job
> spoke up and said:
> Perish the day on which I was born,
> And the night it was announced,
> "A male has been conceived!"
> May that day be darkness. (Job 3:1–4)

Job laments a life of suffering. He argues that it would be better not to have been born than to endure the suffering that comes with living. Thus, while not cursing God, he curses the day he came into the world, exclaiming, "Perish the day on which I was born" (Job 3:3). Contemporary scholar Stephen Mitchell's translation makes the lament more intense: "God damn the day that I was born."

Enter Job's friend Eliphaz, who makes an attempt at consolation. But in place of empathy, he offers only subtle censure. He says, "Think now, what innocent man ever perished?" (Job 4:7). The implication is clear: since no blameless man ever suffers, Job must not be innocent. Eliphaz then dares to argue that suffering is a blessing: "See how happy is the man whom God reproves" (5:17). So Job would do well to accept his suffering without complaint.

Job rejects the words of Eliphaz. Directing his remarks to God, Job insists that he has committed no sin that warrants any punishment (Job 7:20). "Why should you make me your target?" (5:17, Scheindlin's translation), he demands of God.

Enter Bildad, another of Job's friends:

> Bildad the Shuhite said in reply:
> How long will you speak such things?

Your utterances are a mighty wind!
Will God pervert the right?
Will the Almighty pervert justice? (Job 8:1–3)

Can papyrus thrive without marsh?
Can rushes grow without water?
While still tender, not yet plucked,
They would wither before any other grass.
Such is the fate of all those who forget God. (Job 8:11–12)

It is Bildad's turn to speak to Job. He contends that God makes no mistakes. Asking rhetorically, "Will God pervert the right?" (Job 8:3), Bildad argues that God does not punish people without cause. God will punish only those who forget God. Since Job's suffering is presumably an instance of divine punishment, it can only be attributable to some heinous sin of Job's. Yet Job remains adamant, proclaiming, "I am blameless" (9:21). The suffering he endures is unjustified. Professor of Bible Moshe Greenberg has Job say ironically that God "wounds me for no reason"[51] (9:17), thereby unwittingly stumbling upon the true reason for his suffering.[52] In fact, Job insists that he would welcome the opportunity to stand trial so he could prove his innocence. But such a trial would be impossible:

He is not a man, like me, that I can answer Him,
That we can go to law together.
No arbiter is between us
To lay his hand on us both.
If He would only take His rod away from me
And not let His terror frighten me,
Then I would speak out without fear of Him. (Job 9:32–35)

One more friend, Zophar, is next. He rehearses the same theme of his predecessors. Job must be guilty of something, since God is punishing him and "He knows which men are false" (Job 11:11, Scheindlin's translation). Job's failure to admit his guilt demonstrates that he cannot rise above his own self-justifying perspective: "You say 'My teaching is perfect; I was pious,' yes, in *your* eyes" (11:11, Scheindlin's emphasis). Job may think he is innocent, but he is really guilty. Job denies it. "You invent lies," he says to Zophar (13:4). Job goes on to affirm that God is indeed supremely powerful—but that does not excuse making the innocent suffer. "How many are my iniquities and sins?" Job challenges God, certain that he is guilty of none (14:23). "Remove Your hand from me!" he demands (14:21).

Job's friends fail him. They refuse to listen. He faces total rejection ("Who can see hope for me?" [Job 17:15]). He is resigned to the fact that God has ruined his life, while his friends are relentless in blaming him.

A new cycle of dialogues follows. Eliphaz argues that the wisdom of the past teaches that only the wicked are punished (Job 15:18) and that the wicked man "writhes in torment all his days" (15:20). Bildad repeats the argument that only the wicked suffer punishment:

Indeed the light of the wicked fails;
The flame of his fire does not shine.
The lamp in his tent darkens;
His lamp fails him. . . .
He is led by his feet into the net. . . .
The noose tightens on him. . . .
Terrors assault him on all sides. . . .
All mention of him vanishes from the earth. (Job 18:5–17)

Job expresses his disappointment in his ersatz friends ("How long will you grieve my spirit, / and crush me with words? / Time and again you humiliate me, / and are not ashamed to abuse me" [Job 19:2–3]). Again he asserts his innocence and the unfairness of his treatment by God: "Yet know that God has wronged me; / He has thrown up siege works around me. / I cry, 'Violence!' but am not answered; / I shout, but can get no justice" (19:6–7). He also holds out the expectation that one day he will be vindicated: "But I know that my Vindicator lives; / In the end He will testify on earth" (19:25).

Zophar echoes Bildad's argument that those who suffer punishment must be wicked:

Because he crushed and tortured the poor,
He will not build up the house he took by force.
He will not see his children tranquil;
He will not preserve one of his dear ones.
With no survivor to enjoy it,
His fortune will not prosper.
When he has all he wants, trouble will come,
Misfortunes of all kinds will batter him. (Job 20:19–22)

Here Job responds that logically speaking Zophar must be wrong, since there is ample evidence that the wicked prosper: "Their children are with them always, / And they see their children's children. / Their homes are secure, without fear; / They do not feel the rod of God" (Job 21:8–9). Eliphaz now seems to be more sympathetic, agreeing that if Job is indeed innocent, he will be vindicated. However, his vindication is contingent upon repenting of his wickedness ("If you return to Shaddai you will be restored" [22:23]). Job, however, is unyielding in his steadfast denial of committing any wrong (chapters 23–24). He insists that he is innocent of all wrongdoing but will not curse God despite the injustice: "Until I die I will maintain my integrity. / I persist in my righteousness and will not yield; / I shall be free of reproach as long as I live" (27:5–6).

Before the story's denouement, chapter 28—which serves as a kind of dramatic interlude preceding Job's lengthy soliloquy (chapters 29–31)—expresses how difficult it is to acquire wisdom. In three chapters Job bemoans his current condition, sentimentally aches for days long passed, and insists conclusively that he is innocent. He avers, "Let Him weigh me on the scales of righteousness; / Let God ascertain my integrity" (Job 31:6).

Did I ever brush aside the case of my servants, man or maid,
When they made a complaint against me? . . .
Did I deny the poor their needs,
Or let a widow pine away,
By eating food alone? . . .

If I raised my hand against the fatherless, . . .
May my arm drop off my shoulder. (Job 31:13–22)

Job proceeds to list how he has fulfilled every public, moral imperative, including supporting the poor, taking in sojourners, and never succumbing to feelings of pleasure at the misfortune of others. Suddenly, a new visitor appears. Elihu, initially a bystander, now speaks. But rather than offering a new perspective, he reiterates all the previous arguments made by Job's friends. His speech thus serves to summarize the prior dialogues of chapters 32–37.

God now speaks to Job. In a remarkable exchange of roles, Job's demands for answers from God are replaced by a series of unanswerable questions God poses to Job.[53] In the course of those questions, which extend over more than four chapters (Job 38:1–42:6), God says in effect that since neither Job nor any mortal can fathom the scope of God's power, no explanations on such matters may be demanded. Simply put: mortals cannot know the ways of God and thus cannot evaluate them: "Gird your loins like a man; / I will ask, and you will inform Me. / Would you impugn My justice? / Would you condemn Me that you may be right?" (40:7–8). Job had focused on the prosperity of the wicked, thinking this was proof of God's cruelty or indifference. Raising the stakes, God now challenges Job to try to do better:

Deck yourself now with grandeur and eminence,
Clothe yourself in glory and majesty.
Scatter wide your raging anger;
See every proud man and bring him. low . . .
Then even I would praise you
For the triumph your right hand has won you. (Job 40:10–14)

God would applaud him if Job could succeed in being as just as God. The inescapable conclusion, according to Greenberg, is that "no man can comprehend God, whose works defy teleological and rational categories; hence to condemn his supervision of human events because it does not conform to human conceptions of reason and justice is improper."[54] Somewhat differently, Maimonides puts it this way:

> Job abandoned his first very erroneous opinion, and himself proved that it was an error. It is the opinion which suggests itself as plausible at first thought, especially in the minds of those who meet with mishaps, well knowing that they have not merited them through sins. This is admitted by all, and therefore this opinion was assigned to Job. But he is represented to hold this view only so long as he was without wisdom, and knew God only by tradition, in the same manner as religious people generally know Him. As soon as he had acquired a true knowledge of God, he confessed that there is undoubtedly true felicity in the knowledge of God; it is attained by all who acquire that knowledge, and no earthly trouble can disturb it.[55]

For Maimonides, the object of the book as a whole is to caution against falling into the error that God operates along the same patterns of reason and logic as do human beings. This was the error of Job's friends. They believed that good things happen to good people and bad things happen to bad people—an egregiously simplistic and naïve point of view. In Maimonides' view, Job discovers there is no necessary connection between goodness and good fortune or evil and misfortune. "If man knows this, every misfortune will be borne lightly by him."[56] However, later commentators, like eighteenth-century Galician rabbi David Altschuler, reverted to what Maimonides called the "traditional" view, holding that the perception of injustice is due to an insufficiency of wisdom: the inability to recognize that all things occur by providence.[57]

Not surprisingly, God is not angry with Job for voicing complaints. Instead, God is angry with Job's sanctimonious friends for purportedly claiming to understand God's ways (Job 42:7) and thus refusing to surrender their moral certainties.

The epilogue (Job 42:7–17) completes the book. Job prays for his friends. God rewards Job with twice his previous fortune. He fathers ten more children, including three daughters of incomparable beauty. He dies contented at the old age of 140, having been privileged to know four generations of descendants.

What is omitted is striking:

- No mention is made of Job's feelings after his wealth is restored. Does Job feel vindicated—or does he conclude that acquiring new wealth is not altogether different than losing his original wealth, since both are products of the actions of an arbitrary and inscrutable God?
- No mention is made of Job's wife or friends. Whatever they may have learned from Job's experience remains a mystery.
- And no mention is made of the wager that launched the book. The reader, however, might naturally surmise that the Adversary has lost. Despite his unjustified suffering, Job never curses God.

Even with so much left unsaid, some cogent observations bear mentioning.

First, the author takes pains to occlude the time period in which the story is set. Some poetic expressions as well as patterns of thought might suggest an ancient period. But unlike other biblical books in which the setting is clearly identified, no information regarding periodization appears. For the Rabbis, this was an omission that had to be filled in. But no consensus emerged. Job was reputed to have lived during the time of Abraham and the Chaldeans,[58] Jacob[59] and Esau,[60] the tribes who migrated to Egypt,[61] Moses,[62] Judges,[63] Solomon,[64] Ahaseurus,[65] and the Sabeans.[66]

Job could have lived during any of these times. We might infer that the author intended just that: the story could take place at any time. The problem of human suffering and a just God is a timeless problem, one that faces human beings today just as well as in the past. Hence the Talmud can assert that whole story is a parable that transcends time.[67]

Similarly, the author does not state anywhere that Job is a Jew. He is a righteous man for whom things turn out badly. The Talmud asserts that he is a gentile, thereby universalizing the story.[68] The problem of good people suffering is a broad problem.

Second, the book of Job assumes that evil is real. Evil exists in the form of suffering. Suffering is, in fact, a feature of life and the human condition.

Often this reality is unbearable. However, it is the human reaction to the reality of evil that determines character. As Job himself observes (Job 30:26), expectations of fairness are unwarranted.[69] Accepting the bad with the good is the way forward.[70] In the end, it is not the philosophical problem that the book of Job addresses, but the person.

Third, the book teaches that only God has full knowledge and can see the complete picture. Unable to rise up to the state of God's omniscience, the human perspective will always remain limited, and hence life will always seem unfair. All that is left for humanity is the consoling hope that it is not so.

Fourth, complaints are inevitable and useful. Job voices the moral outrage that a reader might feel but dare not express. Job's outcry is thus cathartic. As contemporary scholar Ray Scheindlin puts it, "We read Job not because it provides answers to our questions, consolation for our grief, or redress for our anger, but because it expresses our questions, grief, and anger with such force."[71]

Fifth, as David S. Ariel, president of the Cleveland College of Jewish Studies, notes, the story of Job points to the human capacity to continue life after tragedy and even to grow in compassion and wisdom.[72] Never again will Job expect life to provide him with easy, predictable answers. His experience teaches him to be open to what he might learn from God.

As to the essential question of good and evil, three approaches emerge from the text, each identifiable by way of a syllogism: the argument of Job's friends, the argument of Job, and the argument of the author of the book itself.

Job's friends formulate a classic syllogism from two premises. First, they posit that suffering is punishment for sin. They make this claim on the basis of immemorial tradition. Second, by way of observation they note that Job suffers. These two premises ineluctably lead to the logical conclusion that Job sins.

Job, on the other hand, relies on a contrary syllogism, also based on two premises. First, he asserts that wrongful suffering is unjust. Second, he determines from his own knowledge and experience that God caused him to suffer wrongfully. Accordingly, Job concludes that God is unjust. As Mitchell notes, this may seem blasphemous, but to Job it is undeniably true.[73]

These conflicting syllogisms explain the tension between Job and his interlocutors. Neither Job nor his friends can stray from the conclusion of the syllogism upon which each relies. Because of their irreconcilable differences, the cycle of dialogues must remain repetitive.

Importantly, however, the author of the book presents a third "syllogism." I call this a syllogism even though it lacks the logical rigor the term requires. According to the author's argument, three propositions exist simultaneously. First, Job suffers. On this both Job and his friends would agree, although, crucially, the friends would attribute Job's suffering to a wrong he must have committed. Job and his friends would also agree on the second proposition, namely, all suffering comes from God. But only Job's friends would agree with the third proposition: God is just. Note that this third proposition is not the logical outcome of the first two premises. It exists independently. That God could be just and yet Job still suffer exposes the main idea of the book. There is no effective way to account for human suffering while maintaining that God is just. The relationship between the actions of God and the reality of suffering is beyond human comprehension.

The Book of Ecclesiastes

To the man, namely, who pleases Him He has given the wisdom and shrewdness to enjoy himself, and to him who displeases, He has given the urge to gather and amass—only for handing on to one who is pleasing to God. (Eccles. 2:26)

In my own brief span of life, I have seen both these things: sometimes a good man perishes in spite of his goodness, and sometimes a wicked one endures in spite of his wickedness. So don't overdo goodness and don't act the wise man to excess, or you may be dumbfounded. (Eccles. 7:15–16)

And here is another frustration: the fact that the sentence imposed for evil deeds is not executed swiftly, which is why men are emboldened to do evil—the fact is that a sinner may do evil a hundred times and his [punishment] still be delayed. For although I am aware that "It will be well with those who revere God since they revere Him, and it will not be well with the scoundrel, and he will not live long because he does not revere God"—here is a frustration that occurs in the world: sometimes an upright man is requited according to the conduct of the scoundrel; and sometimes the scoundrel is requited according to the conduct of the upright. I say all that is frustration. (Eccles. 8:10–14)

For all this I noted, and I ascertained all this: that the actions of even the righteous and the wise are determined by God. Even love! Even hate! Man knows none of these in advance—none! For the same fate is in store for all: for the righteous and for the wicked; for the good and pure, and for the impure; for him who sacrifices, and for him who does not; for him who is pleasing, and for him who is displeasing; and for him who swears, and for him who shuns oaths. This is the sad thing about all that goes on under the sun: that the same fate is in store for all. (Eccles. 9:1–3)

I have further observed under the sun that
The race is not won by the swift,
Nor the battle by the valiant;
Nor is bread won by the wise,
Nor wealth by the intelligent,
Nor favor by the learned,
For the time of mischance comes to all. (Eccles. 9:11)

Since the publication of Professor H. L. Ginzburg's *Studies in Kohelet* in 1950, *Kohelet* being the Hebrew word translated as "Ecclesiastes," scholars have generally held that the provenance of the book of Ecclesiastes is more material than spiritual; the physical rather than the metaphysical; the economic rather than the existential. Accordingly, noted historian

Professor Elias Bickerman[74] proposed a subtitle for Ecclesiastes: *The Philosophy of an Acquisitive Society*. On this view, shared as well by professor of Bible Stephen Garfinkel,[75] the author of Ecclesiastes is addressing the newly emergent mercantile class of Jews in the third century and offering the overarching message to "enjoy it while you can," since death is both unpredictable and inevitable. This, however, does not preclude the author from considering the problem of evil, at least incidentally.

Professor of Bible Michael V. Fox, however, sees the book of Kohelet differently. In his view, Kohelet is a book of profound philosophy "about meaning: its loss and its (partial) recovery."[76] Kohelet "is primarily concerned with the meaning of life rather than the value of possessions."[77] Kohelet observes flagrant contradictions in the world. Joyfulness is eagerly pursued (Eccles. 8:15) but remains essentially pointless (2:2). Eating and drinking have both merit (5:17) and demerit (7:2). Yet Kohelet is disinterested in resolving them.

Whether the book of Ecclesiastes is a philosophical disquisition or practical advice, its content on the theme of good and evil bears particular consideration.

Because good men die prematurely and evil men live long, the author of Ecclesiastes reasons that there is no point in excessive righteousness, since goodness does not assure longevity (Eccles. 7:15–16). Further, the author observes that there seems to be no justice in the world. The well-known apothegm that "the righteous will be rewarded and the wicked punished" is challenged by the reality that the wicked prosper with equanimity (8:10–14). Sometimes the wicked are never punished at all. Sometimes God may punish evildoers, but the retribution arrives too late for it to be meaningful. It is not surprising, then, that people believe there is no divine justice at all. As the preeminent medieval exegete Rashi comments on Ecclesiastes 8:10, "Humanity thinks there is neither judgment nor Judge because God does not rush to punish evildoers."[78] Ultimately death claims both the righteous and the wicked alike, again making divine providence inscrutable (9:1–3).

However, the author of Ecclesiastes neither believes nor accepts the idea that evil will always triumph. Otherwise, as Robert Gordis points out, he would not have advised against a life of evildoing.[79] The author is careful to note that *some* upright men suffer the same fate as scoundrels (Eccles. 8:14). And while the author acknowledges that *sometimes* punishment is delayed, he maintains that as a rule, God effects retribution against evildoers (8:11–12). Indeed, early on (2:26),[80] the author affirms divine justice and confirms the teaching of Psalms 37 and 73 as well as Proverbs 13:22 and 28:8, satisfied that whatever fortunes the wicked may amass will be handed over to the righteous.

The moral anomaly of why the wicked prosper and the righteous do not remains logically insoluble. In this the author of Ecclesiastes is in league with the Psalmist. Yet, concomitantly, the author of Ecclesiastes fully expects that divine justice will prevail. In fact, Ecclesiastes seems to anticipate the later Rabbinic doctrine of the dualistic division of body and soul, intimating that reward and punishment await the soul that persists beyond the death of the body. Affirming that "the dust returns to the ground as it was and the lifebreath returns to God who bestowed it" (Eccles. 12:7), the author is explicating Genesis 2:7, where God is described as creating the first human being from the dust and vivifying the earthen creature with the breath of life. In Ecclesiastes, the death of a human being is described as a separation of two elements, which return to their respective places of origin: dust returns to the ground, and breath returns to God. If the Hebrew word *ruah* here is intended to mean "spirit" in the Greek philosophical sense of a nonmaterial soul that preexists the person, enters the body at birth, and departs at death, then this verse in particular and Ecclesiastes as a whole would signal the point of transition of biblical theology into the dualistic anthropology of later Rabbinic tradition (in which the injustices of the world of the body can be redressed in the world of the soul). However, it is more likely that Ecclesiastes 12:7 reflects the worldview of Psalm 146:4, where the departure of *ruah* is synonymous with the permanent cessation of breathing. In its biblical context, Ecclesiastes 12:7 does not introduce the idea of a soul as a distinct entity. *Ruah* is the vivifying catalyst that animates humanity. At best, Ecclesiastes represents what theologian Neil Gillman calls "a way-station" between the biblical view and that of the Rabbis.[81]

At that time, the great prince, Michael, who stands beside the sons of your people, will appear. It will be a time of trouble, the like of which has never been since the nation came into being. At that time, your people will be rescued, all who are found inscribed in the book. Many of those that sleep in the dust of the earth will awake, some to eternal life, others to reproaches, to everlasting abhorrence. And the knowledgeable will be radiant like the bright expanse of sky, and those who lead the many to righteousness will be like the stars forever and ever. (Dan. 12:1–3)

These cryptic verses cry out for an explanation. But Daniel's request for one goes unfulfilled. Instead, "these words are secret and sealed to the time of the end" (Dan. 12:9).

Daniel's vision is ascribed to the mid-sixth century BCE, when King Cyrus of Persia reigned (Dan. 10:1). Scholars, however, are convinced that the book of Daniel was written in response to the Maccabean Revolt of the second century BCE.[82] As such, it was intended to answer the question of how pious Jews could suffer persecution. The Jewish victims of the oppressive policies and actions of Antiochus IV were not sinful but saintly, fighting for God and defending the Torah. Antiochus's persecution of Jews thus presented a severe test of biblical theology. As Gillman puts it, "It was the experience of Job, writ large."[83] In response, the book of Daniel offers a new hope for the martyrs and a warning to evildoers, based on Isaiah 25:7–8 and 26:18–19 and in repudiation of Job 14:12 ("Man lies down never to arise") and Jeremiah 51:39 ("Evildoers will sleep an endless sleep, never to awake"). Leaving alone the nature of the book in reference and the meaning of being inscribed therein, these verses in Daniel speak of the revival of the dead, many of whom will be rewarded, and others punished forever. The Rabbis would later seize upon the idea that injustices of this world will be ameliorated at a future time as a solution to the problem of the suffering of the righteous and the prospering of the wicked. Thus this passage is critical in the evolution of Jewish theodicy.

The Apocrypha

In the thirtieth year after the destruction of the city, I, Salathiel, who am Ezra, was in Babylon, and I was troubled as I lay on my bed, and my thoughts filled my mind, because I saw the desolation of Zion, and the wealth of those who live in Babylon. And my spirit was agitated, and I began to utter devout words to the Most High, and I said: "O Sovereign Lord, was it not you who in the beginning when you formed the earth, and all alone too, spoke and commanded the dust, and it gave you Adam, a dead body? . . . And you led him to paradise and you enjoined upon him your one concern, and he transgressed it, and you immediately enjoined death for him and his peoples; and they sprang from him nations and tribes, people and clans without number. And every nation followed its own will and behaved wickedly in your sight. . . . [And] in time you brought the flood . . . and destroyed them. But you left . . . Noah, with his household and all the upright people descended from him. And it came to pass that when they did what was wrong in your sight, you chose . . . Abraham . . . and you made an everlasting agreement with him. . . . And when you led his descendants out of Egypt . . . you [gave] your command to the posterity of Israel. Yet you did not take from them their wicked heart, so that your law would bear fruit among them. For the first was Adam, burdened with a wicked heart, transgressed and was overcome, as were also all who were descended from him. So weakness became permanent, and the Law was in the heart of the people with the evil root; and what was good departed, and what was evil remained." (2 Esdras 3:1–22)[84]

While there is reason to believe that the adjective *apokrophos* in Greek, meaning "hidden away, kept secret," as applied to books, was first used of writings that were kept from the public because they contained information too profound or too secret to be communicated to any but the initiated, the term came to be applied to texts with the pretension of being sacred Scripture but excluded from the canon (that is, officially approved texts that make up the Bible). Some Apocryphal literature dates back to a time approaching that of some of the later books of the Bible and thus is included in this chapter.

The second book of Esdras, chapters 3–14 is an apocalyptic work written around 100 CE.[85] The word "apocalypse" refers to a vision of the future: what will happen at the end of time or during "the age to come." Ezra—Esdras in Latin—as a scribe, raises serious theological questions that the angel Uriel will answer: What is the origin of suffering and evil in the world? Why does a perfectly just God create humans, who God knows will suffer unjustly or will do wrong and therefore perish? Why do humans possess the mind or reason that makes them conscious of these things? This, incidentally, is reputedly the same Ezra of the eponymous book of Ezra who returned to Jerusalem from Persia in the middle of the fifth century BCE to lead the Jews' Second Commonwealth.

The nomenclature applied to the book of Esdras varies according to differing traditions. The most common modern name is "4 Esdras," but it also appears as "1 Esdras" in the Ethiopic, "2 Esdras" in later Latin manuscripts and the English Bible (and applied here following the translator Edgar Goodspeed), and "3 Esdras" in other Latin manuscripts. Neither the Hebrew nor the Greek version is extant. The second book of Esdras consists of seven visions of Ezra the scribe, the first three of which are of profound relevance to the subject of good and evil.

The first vision is set in Babylonia. Ezra asks God how Israel can be kept in misery if God is just. The archangel Uriel, sent to Ezra to answer the question, responds to him that the human mind cannot fathom God's ways. (Note the similar theme in the book of Job.) Soon, however, the end will come. God's justice will be made manifest. (Note the similar theme of the eventual demise of the wicked in the prophecy of Jeremiah and in the book of Psalms.)

Similarly, in the second vision, Ezra asks why Israel was delivered up to the Babylonians and is again told that humans cannot understand this and that the end is near.

In the third vision, Ezra asks why Israel does not possess the world. Uriel responds that the current state is a period of transition and describes the eventual fate of the wicked and the righteous. Ezra asks whether the righteous may intercede for the wicked—as Abraham did for the inhabitants of Sodom—on Judgment Day, but learns that "Judgment Day is final."[86] All this confirms earlier considerations of the problem of theodicy. Ezra asks God how the misery of Israel can be in keeping with divine justice. Uriel gives him the answer: God's ways are unsearchable, and the human mind cannot grasp them; everything will be clear after the end of this world, which will soon come to pass.

For the Jews of the day, in great distress under Roman persecution, the author of 2 Esdras aims to offer consolation with the assuring eschatological message that ultimately confidence in God's justice will be justified. In the process, the author includes a remarkable perspective of human nature. The very first human being was created without any moral compass—he a "dead body." The "one concern" God commanded Adam to observe (not to eat from the Tree of Knowledge of Good and Evil) was peremptorily violated, resulting in his expulsion from Paradise and the reality of death.[87] Henceforth, disobedience and death are characteristic of humanity. Hence, even though the descendants of Abraham, Isaac, and Jacob are given the Torah, the likelihood that it will transform their lives for the better is remote. As the text says, "Yet you did not take from them their wicked heart, so that your Law might bear fruit among them. For the first Adam, burdened with a wicked heart, transgressed and was overcome, as were all who were descended from him. So weakness became permanent, and the Law was in the heart of the people with the evil root; and what was good departed and what was evil remained."[88] The author thus asserts that it is impossible for Jews to ever be faithful to the Torah because they, like all human beings, are innately incapable of choosing good over evil. The very first human being was "burdened with a wicked heart," a moral disability passed on to all his descendants ("They, too, had the wicked heart" [2 Esdras 3:26]). While later Christian theology conceived the idea that all humanity is born in sin, the author of 2 Esdras claims that all humanity is born inherently evil, which makes sinning inevitable.

This argument was intended to defend against divine retribution in either of two ways. First, while the people Israel may have sinned, they should not be punished, since the Jews had no alternative. The people Israel could not avoid acting wickedly, since they were born to sin. If there is blame to be assessed, it ought to be assessed against God, who created humanity with a wicked heart. Had God wanted humanity to do good and avoid evil, God should have created humanity differently. Second, God's punishment of the Jews is not a theological challenge whereby innocents unjustly suffer. Jews deserved all that happened to them, since they were wicked from the start.

But this defense comes at the cost of free will and logical congruity. Arguing that the Jews had no choice but to do evil renders the Torah's presumption irrelevant. The Torah presumes that human beings have freedom of choice. Otherwise, punishment for the violations of the Torah would be logically inconceivable. No one should be punished for acts they perform under compulsion. As well, God's (aforementioned) advice to Cain assumes that human beings can control their conduct. The evil demon may lurk at the door. But the demon can be subdued.

Ben Sira (also known as Yeshua ben Sirach) anticipated the difficulty of 2 Esdras's argument. Also known as the book of Ecclesiasticus, Ben Sira is a collection of maxims, often utilitarian and sometimes moral in character, mainly secular with occasional religious apothegms, wholly applicable to all conditions of life. Its authorship is still debated, but there is scholarly consensus regarding the date of its composition: before the Seleucid oppression under Antiochus in 168 BCE. While some authorities considered Ben Sira heretical,[89] the book is cited favorably in several talmudic passages.[90]

Ben Sira denies that God causes humanity to sin:

Do not say, "It was because of the Lord that I fell away,"
For He will not do things that He hates.
Do not say, "It was He who led me astray,"
For He has no need of a sinner.[91]

And further:

Life and death are before a man,
And whichever he chooses will be given him.
For the wisdom of the Lord is great;
He is mighty in strength, and beholds all things.
His eyes rest on those who fear him,
And he knows everything man does.
He has not commanded anyone to be ungodly,
And he has given no one permission to sin.[92]

Ben Sira writes, "Life and death are before a man and whichever he choose will be given him" (15:17). Choosing life over death is choosing good over evil (cf. Deut. 30:15,19). Those who choose good earn life. Those who choose evil merit death. God, says Ben Sira, "has not commanded anyone to be ungodly," and "He has given no one permission to sin" (15:20). In contrast to 2 Esdras, Ben Sira articulates the view that human beings are created with unfettered moral freedom. God left each person "in the hands of his own decision" (15:14).[93] Human beings are not wicked from Creation and wicked from birth. Human beings are the architects of their own lives. Consequently, it is entirely proper to expect punishment for improper choices as the Torah describes.

Yet while defending the concept of free will and, concomitantly, rescuing the laws of the Torah from meaninglessness, Ben Sira exposes again the problem of theodicy. Explaining how an otherwise law-abiding Jew might suffer while a law-breaking Jew might prosper is problematic. It will be left to the loquacious Rabbis of the Talmud to try to resolve this problem.

The Book of Enoch

Three versions of this pseudepigraphic (ascribing false authorship) text have come down to us, with the Ethiopic version, called 1 Enoch, the first to be translated and analyzed by Irish biblical scholar Robert H. Charles in his pioneering work *The Book of Enoch*. Hebrew University professor M.

E. Stone calls two sections of 1 Enoch (chapters 72–82 and chapters 1–36) "the oldest surviving Jewish document of religious character outside the Bible."[94] Scholars believe the book of Enoch was compiled prior to the Maccabean Revolt of the second century BCE, thus antedating the book of Daniel by almost half a century.

Much of the book is devoted to Enoch's journey through unseen worlds. Readers of the Bible will recall that Enoch was the seventh descendant of the first human couple who, according to the Genesis narrative (5:24), never died. Accordingly, he was uniquely positioned to gain access to information unavailable to others. Enoch reports extensively on She'ol, the netherworld. The oldest layer of biblical theology and one rooted in ancient Mesopotamian myth had She'ol as the bottom stratum of the cosmos, situated below the earth and the dome of the heavens—a subterranean cavity into which all the dead have been consigned.[95] As the universal repository for the dead, She'ol could not be described as good or bad or its "residents" as good or bad. Thus, Jacob worries that he may descend to She'ol in grief if his youngest son Benjamin meets with disaster (Gen. 42:38). Also, the witch of Endor calls Samuel up from She'ol, where he was consigned (1 Sam. 28:13,15). And Job asserts that rich and poor, kings and sinners, all end up in She'ol upon their death (3:11–19).

The book of Job describes She'ol as dark (10:21), so deep it was set beneath the sea (26:5), chaotic (10:22), and prison-like (17:16). Cumulatively, She'ol is a bleak, forsaken netherworld. But by the end of the sixth century BCE, a notable transition occurs. Contemporary rabbi Simcha Paull Raphael notes the reimagining of She'ol from the repository for all dead independent of earthly conduct to a realm dedicated to postmortem retribution.[96] He ascribes this radical transformation to Jewish reaction to destruction and exile at the hands of first the Assyrians and then the Babylonians. Now She'ol becomes that site of punishment for the earthly kings who have risen against Israel (Isa. 14:9,15; Ezek. 32:18).

This reimagined She'ol is the subject of Enoch's fantastic journey. With a sweeping vision of the end of time, 1 Enoch predicts an eschatological retribution: "In those days She'ol will open her mouth, and [the sinners] will be swallowed up in it and perish" (1 Enoch 56:7–8). In chapter 22 the text goes on to describe the geography of She'ol, an area divided into different compartments. For example, a "division is made for the spirits of the righteous, where there is a bright fountain of water," while another has been "created for sinners" who "when they die and are buried in the earth and judgment has not been executed upon them in their lifetime" are "separated for this great torment . . . forever, on order that [there may be] recompense for their spirits" (1 Enoch 22:9–10). The compartmentalization of She'ol allows for relegating the spirits of sinners to specific realms of punishment, thus providing some degree of satisfaction to the living in knowing that those who exploited others in this world will be requited in the next world.

Thus She'ol now becomes more than a repository for the dead. For the righteous, She'ol is heretofore conceived as a step toward rewarding the discarnate spirit, and for the wicked, She'ol is conceived as the place for eternal punishment of the discarnate spirit. This new conception is revolutionary, or what twentieth-century theologian D. S. Russell describes with regard to Jewish theology as "quite unlike anything that has gone before."[97] The Greek distinction between body and soul, having insinuated itself into Judaism around the third century BCE, now equips Judaism with a way to rehabilitate the one God accused of impotence or indifference.

Summary

The biblical and Apocryphal approaches to the concepts of good and evil and their consequences are eclectic and sometimes contradictory.

The Nature of Good and Evil: At the very outset goodness is framed not in strictly moral terms, but in cosmological ones. In later passages the nature of goodness and wickedness is set aside in favor of consideration of choice in ethical conduct—a matter raised as early as the episode of Cain's rejected sacrifice, but abandoned until Deuteronomy and Proverbs, and later the subject of an intense dispute between 2 Esdras and Ben Sira. To Isaiah, Jeremiah, and Ezekiel, evil is a deficiency—a failure to obey God's commands—and to Micah, evil is the rejection of God. Yet to the Psalmist, the noble soul is one who adheres to a moral code that goes beyond mere obedience to the commandments—a direct challenge to the views of the classical prophets.

Questions of Justice: There is considerable agreement among Jeremiah, the book of Psalms, the book of Proverbs, and Ecclesiastes that evildoers will be punished eventually, because a just and righteous God could not have it otherwise. Yet a God who would demand Abraham sacrifice his son in violation of God's own law that forbids the intentional killing of a human being suggests that God can and does act arbitrarily.

The author of Ecclesiastes, like the Psalmist, observes that the claim that justice cannot be found in the world is the result of human misperception. Justice may be delayed, but justice is inevitable. The author of the book of Job would agree with the claim of human misperception, arguing that only God sees the big picture. But unlike Psalms and the book of Ecclesiastes, the author of Job concludes that there is no reasonable way of reconciling a just God with the reality of suffering. And the Psalmist puts forward the remarkable view that suffering is not the evil people may think it to be, since suffering builds character.

In all, the disparate biblical and Apocryphal outlooks regarding good and evil might come across as incoherent, but they would be better described as "in development." These are the first tentative steps in formulating an approach that can be refined and polished. These early texts serve as the prolegomenon, the necessary introduction—not solution—to the problem of good and evil in Judaism. These biblical passages establish the parameters of the problem. God is not morally indifferent. In ordering the physical universe, God also insists on order in the moral universe. That concern is expressed in the earliest usages of the word "good."

Insisting on goodness, however, puts God—as it were—in a vulnerable position. If God fails to live up to this goodness, God is exposed as hypocritical and the entirety of biblical teaching is thrown into question, if not into outright disrepute. Further, a moral universe is necessarily a just universe. Yet humans experience injustice. How to reconcile a just God with an unjust world is a challenge, particularly when a just God is also an omnipotent one. Hence, the problem of theodicy comes again into focus.

Yet the Apocrypha and even perhaps the book of Daniel offer a way to resolve the problem. By revising the function of the netherworld, third-century BCE texts do not directly answer the question of why the righteous suffer and the wicked prosper, but they do devise a remedy for the injustice.

All in all, as a result, the Rabbis are ready to build upon the foundations laid by the biblical and Apocryphal sources.

CHAPTER 2

Rabbinic Approaches to Good and Evil

According to the Talmud, God honored the three requests of Moses, including "knowing the ways of God" (Exod. 33:13).

> [Moses] said before God: Master of the universe. Why is it that the righteous prosper, the righteous suffer, the wicked prosper, the wicked suffer?
>
> [God] said to him: Moses, the righteous person who prospers is a righteous person, the son of a righteous person. The righteous person who suffers is a righteous person, the son of a wicked person. The wicked person who prospers is a wicked person, the son of a righteous person. The wicked person who suffers is a wicked person, the son of a wicked person.
>
> The Master said: "The righteous person who prospers is a righteous person, the son of a righteous person. The righteous person who suffers is a righteous person, the son of a wicked person." Is it so? Isn't it written: "He . . . visits the iniquity of parents upon children and children's children, upon the third and fourth generations" (Exod. 34:7)? And it is written elsewhere: "Parents shall not be put to death for children, nor children be put to death for parents: a person shall be put to death only for his own crime" (Deut. 24:16), which raises a contradiction between the two verses!

This is not difficult. This verse refers to a case where they adopt the actions of their ancestors as their own. While this verse refers to a case where they do not adopt the actions of their ancestors as their own, as it is stated: "visiting the guilt of the parents upon the children, upon the third and upon the fourth generations of those who reject Me" (Exod. 20:5).

Rather, it must be that God said to Moses as follows:

The righteous person who prospers is a completely righteous person. The righteous person who suffers is one who is not a completely righteous person. The wicked person who prospers is one who is not a completely wicked person. The wicked person who suffers is a completely wicked person.[1]

This text is the single most important talmudic statement on good and evil and, as such, reveals how the Rabbis approached the subject. The passage begins with a question that Moses is imagined to have put to God. In reality, it is a question that troubles the Rabbis, who put the words in Moses' mouth. Note that the question is not the traditional formulation of the problem: "Why do the righteous suffer and the wicked prosper?" The traditional formulation calls into question God's omnipotence and God's goodness. Here, the question is one of randomness. How can anyone explain why sometimes things go as expected (the prosperity of the righteous and the suffering of the wicked) and sometimes things do not go as expected (the suffering of the righteous and the prosperity of the wicked)? This is a broader question, one that addresses the contrast between the orderly world created by God as described in the Bible and the messy world human beings experience. The quintessential evil is moral chaos, and its existence begs an answer. But that question then goes ignored in favor of theodicy, the vindication of God's goodness and power in the face of the reality of the unexpected.

In the first attempt to answer this secondary question, God is imagined to invoke ancestral merit. The actions of one's ancestors enhance or detract from the status of the living. Applied to the problem of the seeming injustices in the world, the righteous who suffer are suffering as punishment for the sins of their wicked ancestors, and the wicked who prosper are being rewarded for the merits of their righteous ancestors. Hence, what the neutral observer may perceive as unfair is entirely justified.

Here it is noteworthy that the good works of the ancestors of the righteous do not gain the righteous any additional benefits, nor do the evil works of the ancestors of the wicked condemn the living wicked to more severe punishment. In such instances, ancestral merit has limited effect.

Yet for the Rabbis, this attempted solution generates a problem: it contradicts the biblical doctrine that each person is held accountable for his or her own sins (Deut. 24:16). Consequently, ancestral demerits should not have any bearing on the prosperity of an otherwise righteous person. To resolve the contradiction, the Talmud suggests that the Rabbis want to uphold both the principle of ancestral merit as well as the principle of individual accountability by distinguishing between two cases: one in which the living persist in the behavior of their ancestors and one in which the living do not. The verses from Exodus, which state that God punishes descendants for the sins of their ancestors, refer to a case where the living adopt their ancestors' actions as their own, whereas the verse from Deuteronomy that states that descendants are not punished for the actions of their ancestors refers to a case where they do *not* adopt their ancestors' actions as their own.

But if the living persist in the actions of their ancestors, their own action is determinative and ancestral merit has no bearing.[2] So a second answer is proposed.

God's response to Moses, the Rabbis reason, must have concerned the thoroughness and consistency of a person's conduct. A completely righteous person does not suffer, and a completely wicked person does not prosper. Any evidence to the contrary means that the person judged was neither completely righteous nor completely wicked.

The implications of this passage are as important as the meaning. The passage implies that the Rabbis, defined as the recognized religious authorities of the Jewish people in Israel and in Babylonia from the first to the sixth centuries of the Common Era, were sensitive to the seeming unfairness in life as they observed it. This passage also implies that the Rabbis' concern required postulating answers. Even second-century Rabbi Yanai's statement in the Mishnah, "It is not in our power to explain either the prosperity of the wicked or the affliction of the righteous,"[3] is an answer. Rabbi Yanai, much like the message of the book of Job, holds that God's decisions are above and beyond human understanding.

This opening passage also reveals two principles in Rabbinic methodology. First, the Rabbis, as the heirs of the biblical tradition, see themselves as scriptural loyalists; that is to say, they feel compelled to uphold the teachings of the Bible and defend the integrity of the text. That does not mean to say that the Rabbis are bereft of new ideas. To the contrary, the Rabbis introduce novel ideas—among them an immortal and immaterial soul, an afterlife, chastisements of love, and the evil inclination—but fit them into scriptural text. Hence, much of Rabbinic theology is rooted in textual interpretation. Second, the Rabbis eschew discursive philosophy or theology in favor of dialectics out of which practical resolutions to specific problems emerge. And more than any other problem, as will be demonstrated below, the Rabbis were preoccupied with theodicy.

As a consequence of the dialectical method, in Rabbinic literature consensus is rare. A plethora of opinions and a general absence of resolution make it difficult to conclude which opinion is probative and which sequacious. Nonetheless, by examining a wide range of Rabbinic sources, it is possible to observe what in particular concerned the Rabbis about good and evil and what approaches the Rabbis took to address those concerns. Thus, this chapter is a "guided tour" through a spectrum of Rabbinic sources that examine the specific problem of explaining how a perfectly good and all-powerful God can allow the righteous to suffer and the wicked to thrive. It is a diachronic tour, a presentation of the issue as debated in the sources over time, as well as a synchronic tour, a consideration of some specific sources in the time they were formulated. The end result illustrates how the Rabbis, building on earlier textual precedents, both broadened and narrowed the scope of the discussion on good and evil.

Thirteen Rabbinic Approaches to Theodicy

If numbers alone are a valid indicator, the fact that the Rabbis generate thirteen approaches to theodicy is proof of their "preoccupation." But what motivated Rabbinical interest and turned it into a preoccupation needs clarification.

Any Jew who accepts the authority of Scripture would understand Jeremiah's statement that God "observe[s] all the ways of men, so as to repay every man according to his ways, and with the proper fruit of his deeds" (Jer. 32:19) to mean that God scrutinizes the conduct of each and every human being, holds each accountable for his or her conduct, and dispenses justice accordingly. Commenting on the verse "Is it not at the word of the Most High / That weal and woes befall?" (Lam. 3:38), "Rabbi Elazar said: From the time that the Holy One, praised be God, declared, 'See, I have set before you this day life and prosperity [tov], death and adversity [ra']' (Deut. 30:15), good has not come to doers of evil and evil has not come to doers of good. Only good has come to doers of good and evil to doers of evil, as it says: 'May the Lord requite the wicked for their wickedness' (2 Sam. 3:39)."[4] But human experience seems to prove otherwise. The Jerusalem Talmud reports that second-century Rabbi Elisha ben Avuya lost his faith when he observed a fellow who escaped divine retribution altogether even though he violated Shabbat as well as the command to send away the mother bird before taking the eggs (Deut. 22:6–7).[5] Yet later, he observed another fellow who observed both commandments and was bitten by a snake and died after he descended from the tree. The injustice was demoralizing. It was inconceivable to him to remain faithful to God who could not or would not punish the wicked and protect the faithful. If there were "no judge and no justice,"[6] Judaism—which according to the Psalmist upholds the principle that God is righteous in all his works (Ps. 145:17)—would be existentially threatened. Hence, the Rabbis were constrained to find some way to account for the suffering of the righteous and the prosperity of the wicked, given the conviction that God is omnipotent, compassionate, and just. Thirteen different approaches emerge from disparate sources in the canon of Rabbinic literature.

1. Refine Definitions

According to third-century CE Rabbi Yoḥanan, people can be divided into three categories: the wholly righteous, the wholly wicked, and those in between.[7] At the time of annual judgment, the wholly righteous are sealed for life, the wholly wicked are sealed for death, and the middling have their judgment suspended until Yom Kippur, giving them an opportunity to tip the scales in their favor or against. By adding to the number of good deeds accumulated, the middlings enter into the category of righteous and, presumably, are sealed for life.

This conception becomes the basis of the popular mythology that infuses the liturgy for the Days of Awe. However, there does not seem to be any obvious, observable correlation between righteousness/life and wickedness/death. To the random observer, and contrary to expectation, wicked people do not merely live but flourish while the righteous die. A way to avoid the contradiction between fact and conviction is to alter the assumption that what the random observer notes is, in fact, accurate. The operative strategy requires redefining what righteousness and wickedness respectively mean.

This strategy can be implemented in different ways. For instance, one may deny that "righteousness" means being nearly or completely sinless or that "wickedness" means being nearly or completely evil, as the second answer in this chapter's opening passage maintains. Explaining the extensive hospitality of Abraham, Rabbi Elazar says, "From here we learn that the righteous say little and do much, whereas the wicked say much and do not do even a little."[8] By this example, righteousness is measured differently than what was supposedly thought. It has to do with humility and industry rather than moral probity—and its opposite, wickedness, has to do with boastfulness and idleness. On the basis of these redefinitions it is conceivable to observe a person who is morally deficient yet still falls within the ambit of "righteousness" and another person who is morally upright but boastful and idle. The suffering of this person is entirely justifiable on the basis of the new definition of "righteous." What the observer had believed to be an instance of injustice is not one at all.

Again, in a passage from the Babylonian Talmud, the early second-century rabbi Yosi the Galilean is reputed to have taught, "The good inclination rules the righteous, as it is stated: 'And my heart is pierced within me' (Ps. 109:22). The evil inclination rules the wicked, as it is stated: 'Transgression says to the wicked; he has no sense of the dread of God' (Ps. 36:2). Middling people are ruled by both as it is stated: 'Because He stands at the right hand of the needy, to save him from those who would condemn him' (Ps. 109:31)."[9] According to Rabbi Yosi, "righteousness" and "wickedness" are defined as tendencies rather than as absolutes or actions subject to quantification. A righteous person is one who tends to act properly most of the time. A wicked man is one who tends to act improperly most of the time. The random observer is not equipped to make any judgment about tendencies. The random observer only has information about a particular act or acts at a particular time or within a confined period of time. Thus, what the random observer sees as good behavior and worthy of reward may actually be out of character for the person who is generally wicked and worthy of punishment. The random observer perceives an injustice, but in reality, what happened to the agent perceived as righteous is actually consistent with that agent's tendencies.

Alternatively, "righteousness" and "wickedness" may connote inclusiveness whereby the absence of one element in the category compromises being included in the category altogether. For example, a fourth-century teacher explains the meaning of a grammatically puzzling verse in Isaiah:

Rava continues: On a similar note, it is written: "Woe to the wicked man, for he shall fare ill; / As his hands have dealt, so shall it be done to him" (Isa. 3:11). And is there a wicked man who is evil and is there one who is not evil? Rather, one who is evil toward Heaven and evil toward people is an evil wicked person; and one who is evil toward Heaven and not evil toward people is a wicked person who is not evil.[10]

In denouncing the "evil wicked one," Isaiah implies that there might be a "wicked one" who is not evil. Hence, "evil" and "wicked" are not the same. Rava suggests wherein the difference lies. Wickedness and evil may have two different targets: God and humanity. To qualify as fully wicked requires wickedness toward both God and humanity. However, those who are wicked only toward God, that is, committing sins that do not impinge on people, are not fully wicked.[11] Only those who are fully evil are subject to divine retribution. Hence, Rabbi Elisha ben Avuya should not have expected any punishment for the Sabbath violator who failed to send away the mother bird. His sins were committed against God alone.

A variant of this strategy of redefinition appears in the passage of the Babylonian Talmud opening this chapter.[12] In an understandable act of psychological projection, the talmudic midrash has Moses pose the question the Rabbis want to ask but are reluctant to utter: "Moses said before God: Master of the universe. Why is it that the righteous prosper, the righteous suffer, the wicked prosper, the wicked suffer?" It seems as if all that happens to people is random, contradicting the conviction that God rewards the good and punishes the bad. The answer is instructive and thus worth repeating:

[God] said to him: Moses, the righteous person who prospers is a righteous person, the son of a righteous person. The righteous person who suffers is a righteous person, the son of a wicked person. The wicked person who prospers is a wicked person, the son of a righteous person. The wicked person who suffers is a wicked person, the son of a wicked person.

Here, the anonymous teacher is not merely speaking of ancestral merit. Ancestral merit alone is insufficient to warrant reward or to prevent punishment. In order to secure divine reward, two prerequisites must be fulfilled: first, an agent must act righteously, and second, an agent must have ancestral merit. A righteous person without ancestral merit—that is, with ancestral demerit—is susceptible to suffering an account of the unatoned demerits of his or her predecessors. To put the matter somewhat differently, the definition of "righteousness" is a condition in which a moral agent has both individual merit and ancestral merit to his or her credit. Likewise, in order to be subject to divine retribution, two failings must be operative: first, an agent must act wickedly, and second, an agent must bear the effects of ancestral demerits. Accordingly, "wickedness" is defined as a condition in which a moral agent lacks both individual merit and ancestral merit. A wicked person of righteous lineage will not suffer, confounding the expectations of the random observer who judges wickedness only on the basis of evil deeds performed. Seeming injustices in the world are thus harmonized in accordance with the revised definition.

Yet another instance of redefinition appears anonymously in *Bereshit Rabbah* 34:10: "The wicked are ruled by their passions . . . while the righteous rule over their passions." The difference between the righteous and the wicked is the power of self-control. The righteous person is not necessarily defined by the performance of good deeds but by restraint and discipline. Restraint and discipline are necessary for controlling the urge to commit sins, but they are not prerequisites for doing good deeds. By this definition, a person would qualify as righteous on the absence of criminality alone. Conceivably, the person in question performs no identifiably meritorious acts, all the while never yielding to transgression. The suffering of a non-criminal so described would not be overly troubling, since this agent is technically "righteous" but undeserving of the appellation.

One final instance of redefining "wicked" appears as a complement to the observation of fourth-century *amora* Rav Yosef in the Babylonian Talmud. Rav Yosef was of the view that those who observed the entirety of the Torah would be destroyed along with the wicked, in accordance with the prophecy of Ezekiel 9:6. The Gemara explains how this is possible: "Since they had the power to protest and did not protest, they [are considered] righteous people who are not completely [righteous people]."[13] In other words, to be considered righteous a person must be more than personally observant. To be considered completely righteous and therefore under God's protection, a person must also actively deter others from committing sins. Without this additional characteristic, the partly righteous are susceptible to suffering as well.

All of these examples of refining the definition of "righteousness" are attempts to vitiate the problem raised by the gap that exists between expectation and observation. But changing definitions in an argument is what logicians call the "fallacy of equivocation." Redefining what righteousness and wickedness respectively mean is a form of equivocation.

2. Resort to the Inexplicability Factor

The main lesson of the book of Job is that while the question of why the righteous suffer is profound, any answer is elusive. That same admission appears in the Babylonian Talmud.[14] Rav Ami is reputed to have said, "There is no death without sin and there is no suffering without iniquity," to which the Talmud appends proof texts:

> There is no death without sin, as it is written: "The person who sins, he alone shall die. A child shall not share the burden of a parent's guilt, nor shall a parent share the burden of a child's guilt; the righteousness of the righteous shall be accounted to him alone, and the wickedness of the wicked shall be accounted to him alone" (Ezek. 18:20). And there is no suffering without iniquity, as it is written: "Then I will punish their transgression with the rod and their iniquity with strokes" (Ps. 89:33).[15]

The Talmud quotes a verse from Ezekiel that each person is held accountable for his or her actions. Serious violations are punished with death. The ineluctable conclusion is that death follows sin, which is Rav Ami's first point. The verse from Psalms states that God, who is purported to be speaking, punishes evildoers for "their transgression," implying that suffering follows iniquity, Rav Ami's second point. In the course of the talmudic dialectic, Ecclesiastes 9:2 is cited as a challenge to Rav Ami's position: "All things come alike to all; there is one event to the righteous and to the wicked; to the good and to the clean, and to the unclean; to him who sacrifices, and to him who does not sacrifice; as is the good, so is the sinner; and he who swears, as he who fears an oath." This verse intimates that death is not contingent on sin; death is a feature of human existence. All humans are mortal, and thus death is indiscriminate. The Talmud parries this challenge by linking Rav Ami's position to that of an earlier tannaitic teacher, Rabbi Shimon ben Elazar, who held that readers must infer from Numbers 20:12 that Moses and Aaron died on account of their sins. That Moses and Aaron died of their sins, however, proves that their cases were exceptions. The general principle is that death is independent of sin. The talmudic passage concludes with Rav Ami's opinion "conclusively refuted" and the observation that "there is a death without sin, and there is suffering without iniquity." The statement that an opinion is "conclusively refuted" is strikingly rare in talmudic discourse and as such lends additional gravity to the conclusion.

Now if death and suffering are not contingent on human conduct, then asking questions such as why the righteous suffer or why the wicked prosper is pointless. There is no connection between conduct and consequences; the vagaries of chance affect the righteous and the wicked alike. Hence, this passage indicates that the Talmud sanctions the view that the death and suffering of the righteous and the prosperity of the wicked remain outside the purview of moral theology. There is simply no compelling way to explain the seeming injustices in life or God's seeming acceptance of them.[16]

A variant of this approach is the assertion that God alone knows the reasons for the suffering of the righteous and that information is not accessible to human beings. The Talmud, explaining the antiquity of the decorative crowns that appear on seven Hebrew letters, tells the following etiological story that also explains the delay in the giving of the Torah:

> Rav Yehudah said in the name of Rav: When Moses ascended on high, he found the Holy One, blessed be He, engaged in affixing crowns to the letters. Moses said: "Master of the universe, who prevents You?" He [i.e., God] answered: "There will arise a man at the end of many generations, Akiva ben Yosef is his name, who will expand upon each serif by adducing heaps and heaps of laws." Moses said: "Master of the universe, allow me to see him." He [i.e., God] replied: "Go forward in time."[17] Moses went and sat down in the eighth row.[18] Not able to follow their arguments, he was ill at ease. But when they came to a certain subject and the student said to the teacher [i.e., Rabbi Akiva]: "Whence do you know it?" and he [i.e., Rabbi Akiva] replied: "It is a law

given to Moses at Sinai," he [i.e., Moses] was comforted. Thereupon he returned to the Holy One, blessed be He, and said: "Master of the universe, You have such a man and You give the Torah through me?" [God] said to him: "Silence! I have my reasons."[19] [Moses] said to him: "Master of the universe, you have shown me his Torah, show me his reward." [God] said to him: "Go forward in time!" He saw that they were weighing his flesh in the butcher shops.[20] [Moses] said to Him: "This is his Torah and this is his reward?" [God] said to him: "Silence! I have my reasons."[21]

Twice God is imagined to have said to Moses that there are reasons for God's actions that cannot be shared or understood by human beings, not even those of the caliber of Moses. A casualty of this story and approach is God's depiction as imperious, arbitrary, and even capricious. Saying that "God chooses to do what God chooses to do" brings us no closer to resolving the question of why the righteous suffer. In fact, arguing that there is no reasonable explanation for the suffering of the innocent merely highlights the problem rather than solves it.

3. Propose the "Chastisements of Love"

Rava, and some say Rav Ḥisda, said: If a person sees that suffering has befallen him, he should examine his actions, as it is stated: "We will search and examine our ways, and return to God" (Lam. 3:40). If he examined his actions and found no transgression, he may attribute his suffering to neglect of Torah, as it is stated: "Happy is the man whom You discipline, O Lord, the man You instruct in Your teaching" (Ps. 94:12). And if he did attribute his suffering to neglect of Torah and did not find this to be so, he may be certain that these are afflictions of love, as it is stated: "For whom the Lord loves, He rebukes, / As a father the son whom he favors" (Prov. 3:12).[22]

No later than the fourth century CE, the Rabbis coined an entirely new expression, loosely based on biblical precedents, to justify the suffering of the righteous: *yisurei ahavah*, or chastisements of love.[23] In the best-known source for this expression, *Berakhot* 5a, the authority cited, either Rava or Rav Ḥisda, begins with the standard view that suffering is a result of misconduct. Through self-reflection, a Jew can discover what transgression was committed and, by redressing it, eliminate the suffering. When self-reflection reveals that no transgression was committed, suffering can be attributed to a lack of devotion to Torah study (Torah study was held to be the preeminent religious duty). However, in such cases where self-reflection reveals that no transgression was committed and no neglect of Torah study occurred, then one must presume that the suffering is a sign of God's love. Such sufferings, the passage goes on to say, "purge all the iniquities of man. As the salt cleanses meat, so chastisements purify the sins of man."

The expression "chastisements of love" also appears in a fifth-century midrash:

> "Happy is the man whom You discipline, O Lord, the man You instruct in Your teaching" (Ps. 94:12). How can such a man be happy? Rabbi Yehoshua said: If when sufferings come upon you, you can still study Torah, then your chastisement is a chastisement of love. If you cannot study Torah, it is a chastisement of rebellion, as it says: "discipline . . . instruct." There is no man in the world to whom suffering does not come. If his eye or his tooth pains him, he cannot sleep. Yet if he is wakeful all night long and can study Torah, he is happy.[24]

In this midrash the neglect of Torah is not a reason for chastisements of love. Instead, the study of Torah is a benefit consequent to chastisements of love. It would appear, then, that chastisements of love ought to be welcome, because they may result either in the study of Torah or in rejoicing in the special attention God's favorites receive.

But this is not the case. The Rabbis of the Talmud are not sanguine about their suffering. For instance, when Rabbi Ḥanina falls ill and Rabbi Yoḥanan visits and tries to comfort him by reminding him of how suffering brings great reward, Rabbi Ḥanina reputedly responds that he prefers "neither the suffering nor their reward."[25] When Rabbi Yoḥanan falls ill and Rabbi Ḥanina comes to visit, Rabbi Yoḥanan reputedly gives the same response.[26] Suffering, it seems, is unwelcome. And, it seems, advising others of the rewards of suffering is far easier than accepting that advice for oneself.

While the practical value of chastisements of love may be suspect, the theological value is significant. The Rabbis, however, refuse to be distressed over the suffering of the righteous, assuming it is unfair. Instead, the Rabbis see chastisements of love as offering comfort by seeing suffering as special recognition. Suffering is not a reward. Suffering is an award.

Even so, suffering is an award that few, if any, will relish. Hence, chastisements of love are lacking as a compelling response to the problem of unjust suffering.

4. Assume Astral Influence

The Talmud reports that Rabbi Yehoshua ben Levi possessed a notebook that charted a person's character in accordance with the day that person was born. Rabbi Ḥanina disagreed:

> Rabbi Ḥanina said to his students: Go and tell the son of Leiva'i:[27] It is not the constellation of the day that determines; rather, it is the constellation of the hour that determines.
>
> One who was born under the sun will be a radiant person; he will eat from his own [resources] and drink from his own [resources], and his secrets will be exposed. If he steals, he will not succeed.
>
> One who was born under Venus will be a rich and promiscuous person. What is the reason for this? Because fire was born [during the hour of Venus].
>
> One who was born under the influence of Mercury will be an enlightened and expert man, because [Mercury] is the sun's scribe.
>
> One who was born under the moon will be a man who suffers pains, who builds and destroys, and destroys and builds. He will be a man who eats not from his own [resources] and drinks not from his own [resources] and whose secrets are hidden. If he steals, he will succeed.

One who was born under Saturn will be a man whose thoughts are for naught. And some say that everything that others think about him and plan to do to him is for naught.

One who was born under the influence of Jupiter [*tzedek*] will be a just person [*tzadkan*]. . . .

One who was born under Mars will be one who spills blood. Rav Ashi said: He will be either a bloodletter, or a thief, or a slaughterer of animals, or a circumciser. Rabba said: I was born under the influence of Mars and I do not perform any of those activities. . . . It was stated that Rabbi Ḥanina says: A constellation makes one wise and a constellation makes one wealthy, and there is a constellation for the Jewish people.[28]

The difference between Rabbi Yehoshua ben Levi and Rabbi Ḥanina is a question of wherein planetary influence abides. Rabbi Yehoshua ben Levi believes that the constellation of the day determines a person's character, whereas Rabbi Ḥanina holds that the constellation of the hour is the determining factor. Both agree that heavenly bodies affect a person's character and conduct. While in the continuation of this passage Rabbi Yoḥanan disputes Rabbi Ḥanina, stating that "there is no constellation for the Jewish people," he seems to accept the fact that the planets influence other nations. Along these lines, Rava proclaims that "children, length of life, and prosperity do not depend on merit but upon planetary influence [*mazzala*]."[29] The earlier *tannaim* held similar views. Rabbi Meir, for example, believed that eclipses were evil omens.[30]

Astrology itself was not considered a religion or religious doctrine. It was, rather, a worldview that held that heavenly bodies were not merely astronomical phenomena but possessors of abstract powers reflective of enduring laws that controlled all existence. As such, some Jewish authorities gave it credence, despite the fact that it compromised free will.

Still, the idea that astronomical phenomena influenced humankind was not universally accepted. *Sifra Kedoshim* 6:2 includes astrology among other banned modes of divination. The Talmud also forbids consultation with the Chaldeans, reputed experts in astrology, on the grounds that doing so violates the command to be "wholehearted with God."[31]

According to the distinguished Israeli scholar Ephraim Urbach, the matter remained unresolved, since "the Tannaim and Amoraim were divided in their views."[32] Those who found astrology convincing also found astrology useful in defending against the charge that the innocent suffer without cause and the wicked prosper without merit. To them, prosperity and suffering were determined less by one's actions and more by planetary influence. The righteous person who suffers and the wicked person who prospers do so because of the constellations under which they were born.[33] Consequently, what appears unjust to the neutral observer is, in effect, entirely explicable by means of astral influence. It might appear that a given righteous man suffers unjustly, but his suffering is attributable to astral influence, and not to an impotent or unjust God.

But with one problem solved, another emerges. Astral influences seem to imply that there are supernal powers at work that are independent of and perhaps rival God—a position that the Rabbis are loathe to contemplate (see below, "The Evil Inclination").

5. Compensate Injustice in the Afterlife

Rav Naḥman bar Ḥisda interpreted: What is the meaning of Scripture: "Sometimes [asher] an upright man is requited according to the conduct of the scoundrel; and sometimes the scoundrel is requited according to the conduct of the upright. I say all that is frustration" (Eccles. 8:14)? Happy [ashrei] are the righteous, to whom it happens in this world according to the experiences of the wicked in the world to come, and woe unto the wicked, to whom it happens in this world according to the experiences of the righteous in the world to come. Rava said: Are we, then, to object if the righteous enjoy both worlds!? Rather, Rava said as follows: Happy are the righteous, to whom it happens in this world according to the experiences of the wicked in this world, and woe to the wicked, to whom it happens in this world according to the experiences of the righteous in this world.[34]

The author of Ecclesiastes voices the frustration that comes with witnessing the suffering of the righteous and the prosperity of the wicked.

A similarity of expression (*asher–ashrei*) allows Rav Naḥman to make the homiletical connection that while the righteous may endure suffering and the wicked enjoy prosperity in this world, the righteous happily know that the reverse will be true in the next world. For Rav Ḥisda, all injustices will be remedied in the afterlife, where the righteous who suffered will receive their reward and the wicked who enjoyed prosperity will suffer punishment.

Rava, who does not dispute the existence of the world to come, would prefer matters to be otherwise. He hopes for reward for the righteous in this world as well as in the world to come, and punishment for the wicked in both worlds. For Rav Ḥisda, Rava is an optimist. A midrash expands on the purpose of the world to come:

Whomever God has afflicted in this world—the blind, the deaf, the lame—is healed in the world to come, as it says: "Then the eyes of the blind shall be opened, and the ears of the deaf shall be unstopped, then the lame shall leap like a deer" (Isa. 35:5–6).[35]

The anonymous teacher interprets Isaiah's prophecy of the future as referring to the afterlife. The afterlife will remedy such injustices as a righteous man who suffers from physical disability or a baby born with birth defects (what later philosophers would term "natural evils"). As to the seemingly inexplicable success of the wicked, another Rabbinic source has God offering reassurance:

Says the Holy One, praised be God: "If you see the lamp of the wicked burn brightly, do not envy him, for it will go out in the world to come, as it is written: 'The lamp of the wicked goes out' (Prov. 24:20)."[36]

The contours of this afterlife are admittedly amorphous, even obscure. According to *Sifrei Devarim* 356, "All Israel gathered before Moses and said to him, 'Our master Moses, tell us what good things the Holy One, blessed be He, has in store for us in the future.'[37] He replied: 'I do not know what to tell you. Happy are you with that which is prepared for you.'"[38] But that is to be expected of a concept that emerges in the Rabbinic period with little introduction or prefatory comment.[39] To flesh out the concept, the Talmud offers this description: "In the world to come there is no eating or drinking or procreation or commerce or jealousy or enmity or rivalry. But the righteous sit with crowns on their heads and enjoy the radiance of the Divine Presence."[40]

While this brief description emphasizes the spiritual nature of the afterlife, the fact that only the righteous are seated there is significant. Apparently, the wicked are excluded. Further, the purpose of the afterlife is to serve as postmortem judgment, both for nations[41] and for individuals.[42] And since the kinds of activities associated with human existence in this world are absent in the world to come, it is not a place of residence for physical bodies. It is an entirely spiritual realm—the realm of souls.

The concept of a soul is generally conceived as an intangible entity that exists separate from the body, though animating it, and survives after its death. One Rabbinic text describes the soul this way: "As God fills the whole world, so also the soul fills the whole body. As God sees but cannot be seen, so, too, the soul sees but cannot be seen. As God nourishes the whole world, so too, the soul nourishes the whole body. As God is pure, so too, the soul is pure. As God dwells in the innermost part of the universe, so too, the soul dwells in the innermost part of the body."[43]

Some social scientists have postulated that the concept developed organically as human beings became more self-aware. Dutch historian and religious philosopher Jan N. Bremmer, for one, has claimed that those early human beings who embraced the concept of a soul earned a distinct cognitive advantage, allowing them to look behind appearances and enable creative discovery.[44] And psychologist Vera Pereira et al. suggest that the cluster of beliefs regarding an afterlife, including the concept of a soul, might have originated as an intuitive religious concept connected to the experience of the Self as somehow independent of the body.[45] The implication of these views is that the concept of the soul is quite ancient. However, the literary record shows that the concept emerged no earlier than the late fifth century BCE. Theology professor Neil Gillman,[46] among others,[47] pinpoints its emergence to ancient Greece, particularly in the dialogues of Plato,[48] from which the concept was exported. Plato, like some of his pre-Socratic predecessors,[49] believed that the physical world is in constant flux. With everything in the world ever changing, nothing can achieve stable and permanent being, and human beings cannot possess sure knowledge about ever-fluctuating realities. Nevertheless, he realized, human beings do have exact knowledge of some matters that are constant and unchanging, such as mathematical and moral truths. To account for this anomaly, Plato theorized that there must be some way by which human beings gain access to eternal truths, even as they remain hampered by the limitations of the human body, which only has unreliable sensory tools for knowledge acquisition. Plato further theorized that these eternal truths inhere within each person. Through engagement with the physical world or in social interactions, people unconsciously recall to mind those ideas stored within and apply them. Plato called the repository of these eternal truths the "soul."

That the soul possessed unobscured truths led Plato to conclude that the soul must be distinct from the body that can only acquire tendentious information. Hence the soul, as essentially separate from the body, must both preexist the body and survive after the body decays.[50]

Plato's concept of the immortality of the soul enabled the Rabbis to identify the "going out" of the *ruah* or the *nefesh* as in Genesis 35:18, or God's "taking away" the *nefesh* as in 1 Kings 19:4, or God's "calling back" the *neshamah* as in Job 34:14 as a reference to the soul. Having now rooted the concept of the soul in biblical texts, the Rabbis could then easily justify the existence of an afterlife.

The concept of the afterlife is another arrow in the Rabbinic quiver for bridging the gap between expectations and reality. The injustices observed in this world are real and painful, but in the next world, all will be made right. Yet while the promise of future recompense is reassuring, the projection of an afterlife is a tacit admission that the world human beings experience is unjust and that God is either incapable or unwilling to change it.

6. Ascribe Evils to the Trials of the Righteous

"The Lord seeks out [yivḥan] the righteous man, but loathes the wicked one who loves injustice" (Ps. 11:5). Rabbi Yonatan said: A potter does not detect defective vessels, because he cannot give them a single blow without breaking them. Similarly, the Holy One, praised be He, does not test the wicked but only the righteous. Thus: "The Lord tests the righteous man. . . ." Rabbi Yosi ben Rabbi Ḥanina said: When a flax worker knows that his flax is of good quality, the more he beats it the more it improves and the more it glistens; but if it is of inferior quality, he cannot give it one knock without splitting it. Similarly, the Lord tests only the righteous, as it says: "The Lord tests the righteous man. . . ." Rabbi Elazar said: When a man possesses two cows, one strong and the other feeble, upon which does he put the yoke? Surely upon the strong one. Similarly, the Lord tests only the righteous, hence: "The Lord test the righteous man. . . ."[51]

Elsewhere (Pss. 94:12, 119:71) the Psalmist asserts that afflictions are beneficial in that they bring the sufferer closer to God and Torah. Here, the Psalmist asserts that even though the evil perpetrator of injustice merits punishment, the righteous man is the one who suffers.

This is certainly counterintuitive. The expectation is that the wicked, not the righteous, are punished. Attempting to explain the difficulty, three Rabbinic authorities employ common examples from a pre-industrial society. Rabbi Yonatan compares God to a potter who tests the durability and strength of his wares by striking them. The potter knows not to test the faulty vessels because they will surely break; consequently, only the higher-quality vessels absorb the potter's blows. Thus, God afflicts the righteous—that is, people of higher-quality character. But the analogy is not exact. If the quality of the potter's wares is unknown, then all his wares should be tested. If the quality of his wares is already known, then there is no need to test the high-quality ones.

Rabbi Yosi compares God to a flax worker. In his comparison, the beating of the high-quality material improves the final product. Hence,

Rabbi Yosi asserts that the testing—that is, the suffering the righteous man endures—improves his character. That the experience of suffering improves character is assumed but unexplained.

Rabbi Elazar compares the righteous to the sturdy ox harnessed to ably serve the farmer (God). Why God would insist on service through suffering also goes unexplained.

Though the reasoning behind the entirety of this midrash is not convincing, the midrash nonetheless presents another approach for explaining the suffering of the righteous, namely, the opinion of Rabbi Yosi. By enduring undeserved suffering, the righteous man is better for it.

The idea that suffering is a test is already intimated in the Bible. Moses reminds the people Israel that their forty-year trek through the wilderness was intended as a test of character—to determine the extent of their devotion to God (Deut. 8:2,16). The book of Judges (3:3–4) refers to a similar test of devotion. Likewise, an anonymous mishnah delineates ten trials undergone by the paragon of righteousness: Abraham, the founding patriarch of Judaism. "With ten trials our father Abraham was tried, and he stood firm in them all," but with a different outcome: "to make known how great was the love of our father Abraham."[52] Perhaps the way to understand this assertion is to consider the example of the parent whose continual and difficult demands on a child may seem excessive and even cruel but actually demonstrate great love and concern for the child's future. Alternatively, a teacher who overloads a particular student with additional assignments may be perceived as unjust but in reality may be endeavoring to develop a talented student's potential.

Yet there is a further problem to be addressed in this mishnah. Since God is omniscient, God would most certainly know Abraham's character and the outcome of any such test in advance. Why, then, subject Abraham to the trials? Contemporary scholar and author Rabbi Morris Schatz suggests that the simple answer to this question was anticipated in the last words of the previous mishnah.[53] Abraham is reputed to have "received the reward" of all ten generations that preceded him. Had he not been tested ten times, he would not deserve the reward. Alternatively, the phrase "how great was the love of our father Abraham" refers not to

God's love for Abraham (and the source of the difficulty), but rather to Abraham's love for God. The trials of the righteous are not a test or trial in the sense of determining whether Abraham loved God, but rather a demonstration of the love Abraham had for God that would serve as an example for others.[54]

While the trials of the righteous seem conceptually similar to chastisements of love, the Rabbis distinguish between them. Chastisements of love do not result in any change in the sufferer's praxis, such as neglect of the study of Torah or of regular prayer.[55] The same is not assumed for the righteous who undergo trials. Further, the trials of the righteous are intended to better their character or strengthen their resolve. There is no such expectation from chastisements of love, which are expected to be accepted with equanimity, if not joy.

Suffering as a trial for the righteous to endure was both a troubling and evolving idea for the Rabbis. Rabbi Akiva, for example, seems to have changed his view. The Jerusalem Talmud reports that Naḥum of Gamzu delayed giving charity to a needy man who subsequently died before Naḥum could provide the assistance. Admitting his "sin," Naḥum welcomed punishment and, according to the story, suffered blindness, loss of his hands, and broken legs. When visiting, Rabbi Akiva pitied him, but Naḥum reprimanded his colleague. By Naḥum's reasoning, his punishment was deserved and Rabbi Akiva's pity suggested that he denied the benefits of suffering as a trial.[56] Yet the midrash has Rabbi Akiva advocating the opposite view. In examining the proposition that "one should rejoice more in chastisement than in prosperity" because "if one is prosperous all his life, no sins of his will be forgiven," the midrash concludes that suffering brings forgiveness of sins. To illustrate, the midrash reports how Rabbi Akiva visited Rabbi Eliezer, who fell ill, and alone of all the Rabbis, Akiva was able to lift his spirits by claiming that suffering atones for sin.[57]

Since, some of the Rabbis say, God "rewards" the righteous man by hardening his resolve or deepening his faith through suffering,[58] consequently the suffering of the righteous should not trouble observers. What the neutral observer perceives to be unjustifiable punishment, the more thoughtful observer would perceive as beneficial treatment.

7. Assert the Usefulness of the Continued Existence of the Wicked

It is forbidden for a person to pray for the demise of the wicked [literally, that "they disappear from the world"] for were it the case that God removed Teraḥ from the world since he was an idolater, Abraham would not have been born.[59]

The multitude of biblical verses that speak of the demise of the wicked whose existence offends God suggests that they will be eradicated quickly. When the wicked endure and flourish, it seems contrary to God's stated choice and a challenge to God's power or justice. However, this late midrash[60] argues that there is value in allowing the wicked to live on. Since the righteous may descend from the wicked, the demise of the wicked would foreclose that possibility.

In the one example included in this midrash, Teraḥ, the father of Abraham, is named an idolater.[61] Idolatry is inimical to Judaism. Logically, the eradication of idolaters ought to be welcome. However, the midrash argues that the death of Teraḥ would make Abraham's birth impossible. Since this midrash assumes that prayer is efficacious, a prayer for the demise of the wicked that would result in their death would thwart a larger purpose: bringing a righteous man into the world. Of course, the righteous man need not be the son of the wicked, but even a later descendant.

A statement attributed to Rabbi Yoshiyah in *Kohelet Rabbah* (7, 15, 1) reinforces the idea that the wicked survive in the present to allow for a better future: "Rabbi Yoshiyah said: For three reasons God is long-suffering to the wicked: perhaps they will repent, or perhaps they will fulfill some commands the rewards for which God may grant them in this world, or perhaps some righteous sons may issue from them." If the wicked can generate the righteous, there are grounds for tolerating their wickedness.

This midrash advises a reconsideration of human thinking about the question of why the wicked live on. It is not the case that the wicked deserve to live or that God is powerless to eliminate them or indifferent to their wickedness; instead, God sees the lives of the wicked as necessary for the propagation of a later, righteous generation. Human beings can only assess this retroactively and only after the passage of much time. In the meanwhile, the endurance of the wicked seems wrong.

However, this midrash does not answer the question of why the wicked prosper. Even if we accept the explanation of why God allows the wicked to live, it is hard to explain why God allows the wicked to flourish. Hence, the theodical applicability of the explanation is marginal.

8. See Early Death as a Benefit to the Righteous

"Sometimes a good man perishes in spite of his goodness, and sometimes a wicked one endures in spite of his wickedness" (Eccles. 7:15). They asked Samuel the Younger the meaning of this verse. He said: God, at whose word the world came into being, knows that the righteous man will inevitably at some time falter. So the Holy One, praised be God, says: "While he is still in his righteousness I will remove him from the world."[62]

Shmuel ha-Katan (the Younger or Small), a scholar who lived at the end of the first century CE, applies the book of Ecclesiastes to the question of why the good die young. Since all people are imperfect, eventually all of them will sin.[63] Even the righteous will inevitably succumb to transgression. So, out of love for the righteous, God claims their lives while they are still in the state of righteousness.

This explanation complements the view of Rabbi Yoshiyah on the endurance of the wicked and thus appears in the same midrashic passage. Notably, Shmuel does not rank sins. It is unclear whether the sin that warranted the death of the righteous was great or small. The plain meaning of the text suggests that Shmuel refers to *any* sin, and therefore he holds that *any* sin is sufficient to remove a person from the category of "righteous" and thereby expose him or her to death.

But if this is so, a subsequent question emerges. How does the death of a person who commits a relatively insignificant sin—however defined— solve the problem of God's seeming injustice? It would seem to merely substitute one theological dilemma (why should a person who commits a minor wrong receive such a severe and permanent punishment?) for another (why should the righteous die young?). Moreover, Shmuel does not indicate at what point God should take the life of a would-be sinner. It could be at the moment immediately prior to commission of the wrong. If so, the preemptive death might be justifiable. But it also could be earlier. If it is earlier, then Shmuel justifies the death of children, even infants—something equally problematic, even unconscionable.

Finally, Shmuel's explanation of the death of the righteous, even if plausible, leaves a more terrifying proposition in its wake. If the good die young, then all those who are old must be sinless or evil. Since, as already established, no one is sinless, it must be the case that all those living are evil. And this is preposterous.

Despite the minimal efficacy of this approach to theodicy, it nevertheless stands as an alternative Rabbinic approach to solving the problem of why sometimes the righteous die prematurely.

9. Claim That Prior Assumptions Are No Longer in Force

The Rabbis also propound the view that in an era when the number of righteous Jews is few, their collective merits are insufficient to protect the many. Talmud professor Yaakov Elman calls this "historicization."[64]

The midrash on Psalm 71 is the classical source for this approach. The Psalmist, an innocent man in distress, appeals to the righteous God for vindication. The midrash cites an auxiliary text, Isaiah 50:10, "Who among you reveres the Lord and heeds the voice of his servant?" that gives assurance to the righteous. But reality seems to be otherwise:

When Israel enters into synagogues and study halls and says before the Holy One, blessed be God, "Redeem us!" [God] says to them: "Are there righteous men among you? Are there God-fearing men among you?" And they say: "In the past there were: in the days of our ancestors, in the days of Moses and Joshua, and in the days of Samuel and Saul, and David and Solomon." [God says to them]: "You once had righteous men." But nowadays, because of our sins, "the righteous man perishes and no one considers; [pious men are taken away and no

one gives thought that because of evil the righteous was taken away]"
(Isa. 57:1). And we have no one on whom to rely.[65]

The underlying assumption is that the vindication of the righteous applied only in a past age when there was a critical mass of righteous men. However, that period has expired, such a mass no longer exists, and thus the expectation of rewards for the righteous is unwarranted.

Unlike various other explanations we have considered, this source does more than "sidestep" the question of the undeserved suffering of the righteous.[66] It answers it directly: God's protection of the righteous no longer applies.

However, this answer contradicts the contextual reading of the various biblical verses on the subject. For instance, the Psalmist (Ps. 92:13–15) avers that the righteous shall "bloom like a date palm," "thrive like a cedar in Lebanon," and "flourish in the courts of our God," connoting their unceasing enjoyment of divine protection. And the book of Proverbs goes further, asserting, "The righteous will never be shaken" (Prov. 10:30).

10. Interpret the Suffering of the Righteous as Vicarious Atonement

Rabbi Guryon, or some say, Rabbi Yosef the son of Rabbi Shemaiah said: When there are righteous men in the generation, they are taken for the sin of the generation. When there are no righteous men in a generation, schoolchildren are taken for the generation.[67]

In this remarkable passage attributed to either of two tannaitic authorities, the death of the righteous—and, in their absence, the death of young children—is conceived as a remedy for the sins of the generation. Flaunting the widely held view that each person is held accountable for his or her own sin, the author makes the shocking claim that innocents die as a kind of compensation for the sins of others. On this principle, innocents are sacrificed for the greater good of the people. Thus, for example, if the righteous die, the deaths may be unwarranted, but they are not in vain. Likewise, the death of a child from a debilitating disease is attributable to a grander and justifiable purpose: the salvation of a generation in the absence of righteous men.

However, the principle of vicarious atonement leaves many questions unaddressed. How many must die in order to satisfy God? Must innocents suffer before they die, or is death alone sufficient? And why does God require the death of innocents in the first place?

Indeed, this approach leads to questions as serious as those it attempts to resolve.

11. Recognize Evil as a Universal and Regular Phenomenon

"None of you shall go outside your door until morning. For when the Lord goes through to smite the Egyptians, He will see the blood on the lintel and the two doorposts, and the Lord will pass over the door and not let the Destroyer enter and smite your home" (Exod. 12:22–23). This tells us that when permission is granted to the Destroyer to destroy, he does not distinguish between the righteous and the wicked.[68]

This midrash addresses the question of why Scripture insists that no Israelite leave the house at night when the tenth plague strikes. Surely the righteous would be protected from harm. Yet they, too, it seems, are included in the general restriction to remain indoors.

The midrash answers that the righteous are not protected in all circumstances. At times when a danger is ubiquitous, the righteous cannot expect special treatment. The Babylonian Talmud cites the same midrash in the name of fourth-century Rav Yosef, with the addendum that in such times of universal danger, the righteous actually suffer first, as in Ezekiel 21:8 ("and I will wipe out from you both the righteous and the wicked") where mention of the righteous precedes mention of the wicked. Another midrash supports the view of Rabbi Yonatan: "Calamity befalls the world only when the wicked are in the world but begins first with the righteous."[69] Since there can never be a time when there are no wicked in the world, Rabbi Yonatan is saying that the righteous are always going to suffer—or, to put it somewhat differently, it is the way of the world that innocents suffer. The Talmud goes on to list times or calamities for which the righteous may expect no protection—night, plagues, war, and famine—thereby implying that the righteous should not expect to be spared from natural catastrophes like plagues and famine. These phenomena are indiscriminate in the evil they cause. Even warfare, presumably a human-caused evil, is indiscriminate in the suffering it causes.

This approach reduces the question of why the righteous suffer to a triviality. Most of what happens in the world is a result of universal phenomena for which there is no special protection for the righteous. Hence the question of why the righteous suffer is of little substance.

12. Apply the Concept of "God's Wrath" to Explain Suffering

Rabbi Yoḥanan further said in the name of Rabbi Yosi: How do you know that we must not try to placate a man in the time of his anger? For it is written: "My face will go and I will give you rest" (Exod. 23:14). The Holy One, blessed be God, said to Moses, "Wait until My face of wrath [za'am] shall have passed away and then I will give you rest." But is anger then a mood of the Holy One, blessed be God? Yes. For it has been taught: "God pronounces doom each day" (Ps. 7:12).[70]

In this talmudic passage, what begins as a helpful recommendation on how to interact with an angry acquaintance becomes a statement about divine character. The Gemara is incredulous that God would ever be thought to be angry, since the existence of divine anger is incompatible with a God understood as perfect. Yet, on the basis of the Psalmist's declaration, the Talmud concludes that God can indeed be angry, attempts to limit God's anger in duration and timing notwithstanding.

Another passage even tries to deny the claim in part:

Rabbi Ḥama, son of Rabbi Ḥanina, raises a contradiction between the following verses. It is written: "Fury [hemah] is not in Me" (Isa. 27:4), and it is written: "The Lord is a jealous and furious God" (Nah. 1:2). This is not difficult: here, it is speaking with regard to the Jewish people, whereas there, it is speaking with regard to the nations of the world. Rav Ḥinnana bar Pappa says in explanation of the verse: "There is no anger in Me: / If one offers Me thorns and thistles, / I will march to battle against him, / And set all of them on fire" (Isa. 27:4). "There is not anger in Me," as I have already taken an oath that I will not destroy the Jewish people; "would that I" had not taken this oath, since then I would be active "as the briars and thorns in flame! I would with one step burn it altogether."[71]

God's fury only exists when applied to the nations of the world, says Rabbi Ḥama. But with regard to the Jewish people, God has no anger. But Rav Ḥinnana disagrees. God's anger applies equally to the Jewish people. Accordingly, all people can expect suffering as a result of God's disappointment with humanity. Furthermore, the only reason that Jews persist as a nation is that God forswore their destruction. Had God not taken a vow, as it were, not to destroy Israel, God would have done so out of anger. Individual Jews, however, are likely to suffer no matter their merits. On Rav Ḥinnana's account, the suffering to which Jews and non-Jews alike are subject is a consequence of God's wrath. Talmudist Yaakov Elman sees "God's wrath" likened to the operation of natural law: God allows the world to function with disdainful indifference.[72]

Rather than dispute the existence of the "wrath of God," fourth-century Babylonian authority Rav Naḥman was resigned to its operation. In fact, he saw it as having supreme value. "With regard to any anger like this, let the Holy One, blessed be God, express that anger upon us and let God redeem us, if that is the process necessary for redemption."[73] If suffering is necessary for redemption, then suffering is welcome.

Rav Naḥman's perspective was a necessary accommodation, since "God's wrath" is unavoidable. The Tosefta asserts, "So long as there are wicked men in the world, there is wrath [ḥaron] in the world. When they depart from the world, retribution and wrath disappear from the world. It is not just that the righteous uphold the world only while alive but even after death."[74]

According to Rav Yosef, a contemporary of Rav Naḥman, the "wicked men" refer to thieves.[75] But this association was only intended to fit with Deuteronomy 13:18, cited in context ("Let nothing ... stick to your hand").

Thieves, however, are just one example of wicked men, not an exhaustive identification. Now, since it is the widely held view that the world will always have its sinners, it must also be the case that God's wrath is perpetual.

Consequently, two ideas emerge. First, turning the principle of "God's wrath" into a positive characteristic is essential in preserving the positive perception of God. Second, since the wrath of God is perpetual, evil in this world, even that which befalls the erstwhile righteous, is inescapable. Hence, when the righteous seem to suffer, it is because of God's general anger with humanity. Such a conception bypasses attributing to God any inability or injustice. Yet, concomitantly, it calls God's mercy and forbearance (Exod. 34:6) into question.

13. Be Resigned to the Inevitability of Injustice

Linked to the previous approach is the acceptance of injustice as a feature of an imperfect world. Commenting on Abraham challenging God's inclination to destroy the cities of Sodom and Gomorrah with the argument "Shall not the judge of all the earth deal justly?" (Gen. 18:25), Rabbi Levi has Abraham making the following observation: "If You [i.e., God] desire the world to endure, there can be no absolute justice. And if You desire absolute justice, the world cannot endure. Yet You want to hold the cord at both ends: the continued existence of the world and also absolute justice. Choose one of them. Unless You forgo a bit of absolute justice, the world cannot endure."[76]

Rabbi Levi imagines God thrust into a dilemma. The twin cities of evil are to be destroyed on account of their wickedness. But if wickedness is grounds for destruction of Sodom and Gomorrah, it should also be grounds for the destruction of all civilization. The world is fundamentally unjust. God cannot have a world that is perfectly just if there is to be a world at all. Thus, Rabbi Levi implies, given that the world exists, even God must come to accept the basic injustice that characterizes it. This being the case, the suffering of the righteous and the prosperity of the wicked should not be surprising. Even so, Rabbi Levi's opinion is challenged by a contrasting talmudic view that holds that God cannot be suspect of any injustice.[77]

This first leg of a "guided tour" through Rabbinic literature demonstrates how preoccupied the Rabbis were with justifying the problem of evil in the world. There is no subject in all of Rabbinic literature that merits as much attention as the problem of theodicy. That the Rabbis propound thirteen different approaches to the problem attests to both the seriousness of the subject and the inadequacy of the answers. Had the subject been of little importance, there would not have been a need for thirteen approaches. Had any of the approaches been thoroughly convincing, there would have been no need for any other.

The next leg of the "guided tour" is through the Rabbinic conception of human nature.

The Evil Inclination

More than any other approach to theodicy, the distinctive Rabbinic concept of the "evil inclination" is a way of explaining human nature. Yet as a consequence of adducing the concept, the Rabbis came to introduce an alternative explanation for moral evil.

The concept did not arise mature and complete. It was the outcome of a process of internalization that shifted thinking about evil as an independent power rivaling that of God to an inner desire over which human beings could exert control. Early Israelite religion, though never accepting the demonology of ancient Mesopotamian religion, could not help but live under its influence. Evil was personified because ancients thought it to be a deliberate malignancy that intrudes upon human beings from outside themselves.

The idea that good and evil remained in perpetual struggle, each personified by divine forces, reached its apotheosis in the ancient Near East with the emergence of Zoroastrianism shortly before 600 BCE. Zarathustra, also known as Zoroaster, the reputed Persian founder of Zoroastrianism, held that evil is not and could not be a manifestation of the Divine; it proceeds from a wholly different source. Thus, Zoroastrian dualism had Ahura Mazda, the good god, in constant battle against Angra Mainyu, the evil one. By the onset of Rabbinic Judaism, from the first to the sixth centuries of the Common Era, in Israel and in Babylonia, both Manichaeism[78] and Christianity[79] also included the personification of evil, albeit in an attenuated form. In the pre-exilic Israelite religion, however, an independent evil power simply did not exist. All things came from the one God. Thus the prophet Isaiah relates that God declares, "I am the Lord and there is none else; Beside me there is no god . . . there is none but Me. I am the Lord and there is none else, I form light and create darkness, I make weal [*shalom* = peace] and create woe [*ra'* = evil] — I the Lord do all these things" (Isa. 45:5–7). As professor of medieval studies Jeffery Russell comments, "Since the God of Israel was the only God, the supreme power in the cosmos, the orderer of all things, no deed could be done unless he willed it."[80] Israelite monotheism left no room for competition.

On Russell's reconstruction, the concept of the evil inclination in Rabbinic Judaism developed organically from the pre-prophetic emphasis on ritual taboos to the prophetic concern for ethical conduct and human responsibility. As a result of this shift, evil was now seen as a consequence of being human. In this context, "the Hebrews wondered how it was that God, all powerful and all knowing as he was, would permit humanity to sin. The corrupt will of human beings seemed insufficient to explain the vast and terrifying quantity of evil in the world."[81] But rather than surrender entirely to the notion that a malevolent spirit "whose power to offend was greater than that of mere mortals"[82] instigated the evil in the world—a notion that directly contradicted biblical theology—the Rabbis, instead, chose to internalize the evil spirit, making it a manifestation of human desire.[83]

This pivot was necessitated by the events of the second century BCE. The inexplicable suffering endured by many pious Jews under Hellenistic repression required a theological response, which itself took the form of various apocalyptic writings characteristic of the period. Chief among this genre of influential theological literature was the book of Enoch, which introduced the idea of an afterlife in which the good are rewarded and the evil punished (see chapter 1 of this volume). The book of Enoch also introduced the idea of fallen angels as evil beings led by an essentially evil master with the power to do great harm.[84]

Yet this Enochian innovation was eclipsed by the ideas embedded in other literary works of the same period. For instance, in the *Testament of the Twelve Patriarchs*, a Hellenistic book dated to sometime in the late second century BCE, the author posits:

> God has granted two ways to the sons of men, two mind-sets, two lines of action, two models, and two goals. Accordingly, everything is in pairs, the one over against the other. The two ways are good and evil; concerning them are two dispositions within our breasts that choose between them. If the soul wants to follow the good way, all of its deeds are done in righteousness and every sin is immediately repented.

And in Ben Sira 15:14–15:

> It was God who made man in the beginning,
> And left him in the hands of his own decision;
> If you will, you can keep the commandments.
> And acting faithfully rests on your own good pleasure.

In other words, each person has within the ability to follow a disposition toward good or a disposition toward evil, precisely as the Rabbis are going to argue.

The origins of the Rabbinic concept of an evil inclination is traceable to the Bible. The Hebrew word *yetzer* appears in Genesis 6:5 and 8:21 to mean "a devising of the mind"; in Deuteronomy 31:21 as "an impulse"; in Isaiah 26:3 as "purpose"; and in 1 Chronicles 28:9 and 29:18 as meaning "thoughts of your heart." Urbach sees the common strand for *yetzer* as the power of thought or, better, human desire.[85] The operation of the *yetzer* in making choices between good and evil is intimated in Deuteronomy 30:15, Joshua 24:15, and Jeremiah 21:8–14. Ultimately, the Rabbis came to interpret biblical verses to conform to the concept they invented. Thus Psalm 35:10, "You save the poor from one stronger than he, the poor and needy from his despoiler," was not held to declare that God saves the needy from exploitative villains, but from the evil inclination: "The spoiler is the evil inclination. How does the good inclination strive [to do right], and then the evil inclination comes and causes loss! There is no brigand stronger than the evil inclination. But God delivers Israel from the evil inclination."[86]

As a human desire, the evil inclination has its benefits. Commenting on God's overview of Creation, declaring it to be "very good" (Gen. 1:31), the midrash cites the following opinion on what, precisely, God does declare to be very good:

> Rav Naḥman ben Shmuel said: That is the evil inclination. But is the evil inclination very good? Yes! For if it were not for the evil inclination, man would not build a house, or take a wife, or beget a child, or engage in business, as it says: "All labor and skillful work comes of a man's rivalry with his neighbor."[87]

According to third-century *amora* Rav Naḥman, the evil inclination is tantamount to human ambition and competitiveness, without which people would not be motivated to act. Religious historian and talmudist Daniel Boyarin stresses that the evil desire (in fact, all desire) is composed of constructive and destructive forces within.[88]

Yet despite the virtue of being motivational, the Rabbis considered the evil inclination to be malignant. According to second-century *tanna* Rabbi Yanai, "He who listens to his evil inclination is as if he has practiced idolatry, as it says: 'You shall have no foreign God [within you]' (Ps. 81:10)."[89] The evil inclination, being "within you," is compared to idolatry, the single most reprehensible evil. The evil inclination is also dangerous. An anonymous opinion in the Talmud warns, "If you do not occupy yourself with the study of Torah, then you will be delivered into the power of the *yetzer*, and all its activity will be against you."[90] The evil inclination is deceptive, too. "If the evil inclination says to you, 'Sin and God will forgive you,' do not believe it."[91] The evil inclination is seductive as well. It is like "putting fire next to flax."[92]

The evil inclination grows increasingly more powerful. According to an early midrash, "Rabbi Akiva said, 'At first it is like a spider's silk and in the end it is like a rope of a ship.' Rabbi Yitzḥak said, 'At first it is a visitor, then a lodger, and finally, the master of the house'" (*Bereshit Rabbah* 22:6). In fact, the evil inclination becomes so powerful that the Rabbis imagine that even God regrets having endowed humans with it. "So God said: It was I who put the bad leaven in the dough, for the *yetzer* of the heart of man 'is evil from his youth' (Gen. 6:5). The words refer to man's heart, not God's. God grieved over man's heart."[93] Commenting on the same verse, the fourth-century *amora* Rav Aibu imagines God to have said, "I made a mistake that I created the evil inclination in man, for had I not done so, he would not have rebelled against me" (*Bereshit Rabbah* 37:4). The *amora* Rabbi Ḥana bar Aḥa relays a teaching from the academy of Rav: "There are four things that God regretted to have made: the Exile, the Chaldeans, the Yishmaelites, and the evil inclination."[94]

Yet despite the power of the evil inclination, humanity is not impotent to fight against it. "In the Academy of Rabbi Yishmael it was taught [with regard to the evil inclination]: If this abomination should meet you, drag it to the House of Study: if it is as hard as stone, it will be crushed; if is it as hard as iron, it will be broken in pieces."[95] Study of Torah is the antidote to the evil inclination. The words of Torah are the elixir of life that protects the student from the harmful effects of the evil inclination.[96] Fasting is similarly efficacious.[97] According to the third-century *amora* Rabbi Shimon ben Lakish, in the battle against the evil inclination the first line of defense is to resist it with the good inclination. If that proves insufficient, the study of Torah may subdue it. If the study of Torah cannot ward it off, then the recital of *Shema* reminding one of the yoke of heaven and punishment for sinners might avail. If none of these tactics work, then remembering one's mortality may provide the motivation to resist.[98]

If the study of Torah is a potent weapon in the fight against the evil inclination, one would think that the Rabbis themselves were well armed.[99] Surprisingly, however, this is not the case:

The evil inclination attacks scholars most of all. Abaye once heard a man say to a woman, "We will go together," as their destination was the same. He [Abaye] thought, "I will go and prevent them from sinning." He went after them for some distance[100] along a meadow. When they separated from one another they said, "The journey has been long, our companionship has been sweet." Then Abaye said, "If he who hates me [i.e., the evil inclination] had similarly encountered me, I could not have withstood it." Then he leaned against the door of his house and mourned. An old man came and said, "The evil inclination is greater in him who is greater than his neighbor."[101]

After making a general observation that the evil inclination has even greater power over rabbis, the Talmud tells the story of a fourth-century *amora*, Abaye. While Abaye hopes that his watchfulness can prevent a couple from illicit intercourse, apparently his presence is unnecessary, since the couple remain nothing more than travel companions. Abaye, however, remains troubled by his own weakness of character. Unhappily, he reflects that were he that man, he would have given in to the evil inclination and had relations with that woman. Had the story ended here, the reader would probably have concluded that Abaye lacked self-control, but the continuation of the story comes to support the initial talmudic claim. The old man offers consolation to Abaye by way of a formula: the strength of the evil inclination is directly proportionate to one's knowledge of Torah.[102]

Sometimes the power of the evil inclination is so great, there is no recourse but to submit. In this case, the Talmud offers a strategy:

Rav Ilai[103] said: If a man finds that his evil inclination overpowers him, let him go to a place where no one knows him, wear black clothing, and act as his passions direct him, but let him not profane the name of God in public. Does this not contradict the teaching that it is better that he who does not spare the honor of his Creator should never have been born? (Rav Yosef interpreted this to refer to a man who sins secretly.)

No! The latter teaching [i.e., Rav Yosef's] refers to a man who could control his evil inclination; the former refers to a man who could not.[104]

Strikingly, the Talmud conceives of a case in which a person has no alternative but to sin. But sinning someplace where others might see the act would be devastating. To mitigate the damage of profaning God's name in public, the person lacking self-control must go in disguise to a place where he cannot be recognized and there commit the sin.

There is no mistaking that the concept of the evil inclination is yet another Rabbinic approach to solving the problem of evil in the world, yet it is qualitatively different from the previously identified thirteen. In essence, by introducing the concept of the evil inclination, the Rabbis shift the discussion of evil from theology to psychology. In making this shift, the question is no longer how to account for evil in the world, but why people themselves make poor decisions. Such argumentative legerdemain seems to enable the Rabbis to evade the essential and most troubling question, by substituting for it a far more soluble one. On account of the evil inclination, the Rabbinic answer to the question of why evil exists is that so long as there are people in the world, there will also be the possibility of evil in the world. Thus the existence of evil is not a challenge to God's power or goodness, but rather a consequence of human nature. Accordingly, for the Rabbis, the evil performed by people is of greater consequence than the perceived evil in the nature of the universe.[105]

Yet, generations later, the medieval authorities saw this as a lacuna that had to be filled with a compelling explanation (see chapter 3).

The Dead Sea Scrolls

Since their discovery in Qumran in 1947, the Dead Sea Scrolls have proved to be a watershed for scholars studying Rabbinic Judaism and early Christianity. This treasure trove of texts, written mostly in Hebrew and sometimes in Aramaic between the third century BCE and the end of the first century CE, has shed much light on the religious beliefs of this period. Who authored these texts is still subject to scholarly dispute. The standard view, mainly based on the attestation of the ancient historian and

Jewish apologist Josephus, holds that most were written and preserved by a Jewish sect called the Essenes.[106] In any event, leaving the question of authorship undecided does not detract from the importance of the texts themselves.

Good and evil play a prominent role in the thinking of this community. The two are understood as opposing powers that govern the world. Humanity awaits the outcome of a cosmic battle between the Sons of Light and the Sons of Darkness. Sometimes sin is personified as an angel (of Darkness), represented as Belial, in conflict with the angels of God or the Prince of Light, or the angel Michael. In *The War Scroll* the battle is described in detail: "The first attack of the Sons of Light shall be undertaken against the forces of the Sons of Darkness, the army of Belial."[107] Earthly troops join the forces of Belial, among them biblical Israel's traditional enemies, as well as "those who have violated the covenant."[108] In the end, "There shall be a time of salvation for the People of God, and a time of dominion for all the men of His forces, and eternal annihilation for all the forces of Belial."[109] The "great hand of God shall overcome [Belial and all] the angels of his dominion, and all the men of [his forces shall be destroyed forever]."[110]

After the great apocalyptic victory, the leaders of the forces of light recite a blessing in which they say to God:

> You appointed the Prince of Light from of old to assist us, for in [His] l[ot] are all sons of righteous[ness] and all spirits of truth are in his dominion. You yourself made Belial for the pit, an angel of malevolence, his [dominio]n is in darken[ss] and his counsel is to condemn and convict. All the spirits of his lot—the angels of destruction—walk in accord with the rule of darkness, for it is their only [des]ire. But we, in the lot of Your truth, rejoice in Your mighty hand. . . . You appointed for Yourself a day of gre[at] battle . . . to [sup]port truth and to destroy iniquity.[111]

Ultimately, the forces of evil will be vanquished, and with their defeat comes the end of sin.

The "Last Days" is a topic of considerable interest to the Qumran community. Thus, another text comments on Psalm 6:1–4, in which the Psalmist, presumably King David, appeals to God for relief from torment. The text asserts that "this refers to the Last Days."[112] In his fury Belial planned to destroy the righteous, "but the angel of God's truth will help all the Children of Light from the power of Belial [text damaged] and to scatter them[113] in a dry and desolate land"[114] so that "[they shall perish] forever"[115] while the Children of Light will be saved.[116] During this cosmic battle, the righteous will endure great torment but only "to test them and purify them."[117] The implication here, that suffering is a trial for the righteous, is, as noted above, a Rabbinic idea as well.

The Qumran community appears to have felt confident that one day the evils of the present would become a distant memory. The eschatological vision of the victory of good over evil resonated, particularly during a time of Hellenistic persecution.

Until that victory occurred, however, some practical approach to confronting evil was necessary. The Qumran community developed two approaches, both of which the Rabbis had considered. Accepting the notion that heavenly bodies have influence on a person's character, the community married that notion to the ancient pseudoscience of physiognomy. Each person's character—his or her spirit—is a combination of various proportions of light and darkness. This spirit transfuses the body until it reaches a place where its nature will become manifest. The person's birth sign determines the place where the spirit will lodge. By examining a person's features and knowing the person's birth sign, the expert can identify any person's character. For example:

[And] anyone [whose] eyes are [text damaged] . . . whose thighs are long and slender, whose toes are slender and long, and who was born during the second phase of the moon: he possesses a spirit with six parts light, but three parts in the House of Darkness. This is the birth sign under which such a person shall be born: the haunch of Taurus. He will be poor. This is his animal: the bull.[118]

By rule, the person here described will be poor, despite the fact that he has twice as much light as darkness. This would mean that even if this person were righteous, in terms of patterns of religious behavior, this person would suffer poverty.

To be clear, the Qumran community did not have as an objective the resolution of the problem of why the righteous suffer. On most accounts, the Qumran community believed that the great cosmic battle was imminent, rendering any temporary theodicy unnecessary. Nevertheless, the implications that emerge from this literature are applicable to the problem of the seeming injustices in the world. At Qumran, fate is detached from conduct and linked to the stars.

A second approach invests evil spirits with the power to corrupt humanity. In one manifestation of this approach — seen, for example, in *The Testament of Amram*[119] — the evil inclination itself leads humanity to sin. Hence, the initiate in the teachings of *The Secret of the Ways Things Are* is counseled, "Do not let a thought from the evil impulse deceive you."[120] In another manifestation, demons, under the direction of the chief of the evil spirits, Mastemah, leads people to wickedness. In the *Songs of the Sage*, the faithful, led by one of their officials, recite an incantation for protection from the power of the demons:

> And I, the Instructor, proclaim His glorious splendor so as to frighten and to te[rrify] all the spirits of the destroying angels, spirits of the bastards, demons, Lilith,[121] howlers, and [desert dwellers . . .] and those which fall upon men without warning to lead them astray from a spirit of understanding.[122]

This teaching that demons are the source of evil in the world contradicts the Rabbinic view. As we saw, the Rabbis rejected the idea because it invests an alternate entity with powers assigned exclusively to God.

Along similar lines, the Qumran community set the battle between good and evil as a cosmic struggle, whereas the Rabbis saw the battle of good against evil as a continuous internal human struggle. And for its part, the Qumran community advocated a life of abstemiousness, strict rules of conduct, regular immersion in water (symbolic of the washing away of sins),[123] and reliance on God's grace rather than any human action for salvation,[124] all of which placed the Qumran sect closer to early Christianity than to the Rabbis.

In general, however, the Dead Sea scrolls do support the Rabbinic view that while humanity has a propensity to sin, humanity may achieve atonement and mercy through the study of Torah. The scrolls also share the Rabbinic idea that evil can result from the operation of the evil inclination. Further, the scrolls rely on planetary influence as a determinant of human conduct, a view that finds acceptance among some Rabbis.

Philo

Whereas theodicy preoccupies the Rabbis, the ontology of evil generates little attention. The question "How can evil emanate from a perfectly good God?" receives no more than a perfunctory answer: "Rabbi Elazar ben Pedat said in the name of Rabbi Yoḥanan: God's name is not mentioned regarding evil but only in connection with good."[125]

Rabbi Yoḥanan seems to be saying that God cannot be the source of evil in the world (presumably because God is good). But Urbach cautions against drawing this conclusion.[126] Rabbi Yoḥanan's wording is intentionally precise. He is not saying that God does not create evil. He only says that God's name cannot be associated with evil. If Urbach is correct, then this terse statement fails to address the question, let alone provide an answer for the existence of evil.

Yet even if Urbach's warning is set aside and Rabbi Yoḥanan's statement is read at face value, it raises another question: if God is not responsible for evil, who or what is? As we saw, the Rabbis rejected dualism, so evil cannot emanate from an evil god just as good emanates from a good God. Hence the source of evil itself remains elusive.

Philo of Alexandria attempts to identify the source.

Much is still unknown about Philo. His dates of birth and death are guessed at around 25 BCE and 45 CE. Scholars still debate his awareness of Jewish sources. Christian scholar Kenneth Schenk points out that Philo neither quotes nor even mentions any books of Apocrypha or

Pseudepigrapha.[127] Twentieth-century scholar Samuel Sandmel asserts that "there is no persuasive evidence that [Philo] clearly knew and abundantly utilized Palestinian exegesis."[128] Even his knowledge of the Hebrew language remains undetermined. While most scholars are unwilling to champion Philo, as the eminent classicist Harry A. Wolfson did in 1947 as the thinker responsible for laying the foundations of religious philosophy in Judaism, Christianity, and Islam, the consensus is that Philo did produce an original synthesis of Judaism and Greek philosophy that influenced many thinkers thereafter. His synthetic approach to religious philosophy set a pattern that all three major Western religions would follow throughout the Middles Ages.[129]

With regard to good and evil, Philo takes a dual approach. He wants to account for the existence of evil altogether—the ontology of evil. He also wants to solve the problem of theodicy. For the first approach, he relies on Greek philosophers ranging from Plato to the Stoics. For the second, he finds common ground with ideas that would later emerge in Rabbinic texts.

Philo is the first known thinker to refer to God as "incomprehensible by any idea"—that is, essentially unknowable.[130] Human beings, according to Philo, can only know *that* God is but not *what* God is. The only statement knowably true about God is that God is "the perfectly pure and unsullied Mind of the Universe, transcending virtue, transcending science, transcending the Good and the Beautiful."[131]

To Philo, God's transcendence implies that God could not have been directly responsible for creating the world that would have insinuated God in "limitless chaotic matter."[132] This would be beneath the status of a transcendent God. So God has created the world indirectly, through "incorporeal powers."[133] These incorporeal powers are associated with what Philo calls *Logos*.[134]

When out of that confused matter, God produced all things, God did not do so with God's own handiwork, since God's nature, happy and blessed as it was, forbade God to touch the limitless chaotic matter.

Instead, God made full use of the incorporeal potencies denoted by their name of Forms[135] to enable each kind to take its appropriate shape.[136]

Philo explains that while God is the power behind all things, God is not the direct agent of anything. Thus, any evil in the world that has come into being from deficient matter is not God's doing. Consequently, God cannot be blamed for the existence of evil.

While some later thinkers will adopt this approach, it is not without its flaws. First, while God may not be blamed for the existence of evil, God can still be blamed for the persistence of evil. Surely an omnipotent and good God would want to eliminate evil no matter its source. And second, according to this approach God still causes evil, albeit indirectly. Besides, a transcendent God is also a disinterested God, making it more difficult for humanity in general and Jews in particular to feel any personal relationship with God.

Perhaps recognizing the inherent flaws in his ontology of evil, Philo gives his attention to the experience of evil. In his treatment of Providence, the character Alexander poses a question:

> Are you alone ignorant that to the worst and vilest of men good things in abundance come crowding in, wealth, high repute, honors paid to them by the masses, authority . . . while those who love and practice wisdom and every kind of virtue are, I may almost say, all of them poor, obscure, of little repute and in humble position?[137]

In the course of his writings, Philo gives four different answers to the question of why good people suffer and wicked people prosper.[138] Each of the four finds expression in Rabbinic sources as well.

The righteous person who suffers, Philo explains, really may not be righteous at all. "It does not follow if certain persons are considered good by us, they are so in reality, for God judges by standards more accurate than any which the human mind employs."[139] An observer may sense an injustice when a seemingly righteous person suffers illness or financial setbacks. However, Philo asserts, what the observer sees is not what God knows. The observer's judgment is in error, not God's.

Alternatively, the "good" that the wicked enjoy is not the "real" good. Real good, Philo argues, is not any material good, but the good of the soul. The "wealth of Croeses," the muscular "strength of Milo," or the "beauty of Ganymede" cannot compare with the true goodness of spirit.[140] Real goodness is the domain of the virtuous.[141] Elsewhere, Philo, in commenting on the verse in Deuteronomy (7:12,15) that speaks of the removal of sickness from those obedient to God, writes:

> If some infirmity should befall [the righteous] it will come not to do them injury but to remind the mortal that he is mortal, to humble his over-weening spirit and to improve his moral condition.[142]

If the righteous are to be protected from illness, why is it sometimes the case that the righteous take ill? Philo invokes the concept of "trials of the righteous." Suffering is a benefit to the righteous. The righteous person who suffers is not enduring unjust punishment but receiving character improvement. Similarly, Philo argues that the success of the wicked should not be surprising. Just as loving parents indulge their rebellious children, God coddles the wicked. "So God also . . . takes thought even for those who live a misspent life, thereby giving them time for reformation."[143] By excusing the wicked from a deservedly immediate death, God allows them an opportunity to repent. Finally, God may allow the wicked to prosper or the righteous to suffer on account of ancestral merits or demerits.[144]

In concert with both Plato and the Stoic philosophers,[145] Philo distinguishes between the emotions and Reason. To Philo, the emotions are "a battery of destruction to the soul,"[146] the "vilest thing,"[147] "a fountain of all evil"[148] that "must be done away with or brought into obedience to the guidance of reason."[149] His commentary on the Ten Commandments states that "while each of the other . . . [emotions], coming from the outside and assaulting from the outside, seems to be involuntary, desire alone derives its origin from ourselves and is involuntary."[150] Inborn in every person is passion that assaults the soul but is also the means of taming it. "For the soul of every man from the first, as soon as he is born, bears in the womb twins, namely, good and evil, having the image of both of them."[151] In other words, Philo conceives of two internal influences upon human conduct, one good and one evil, similar to what the Rabbis call the good and evil inclinations. And, like the Rabbis, Philo holds that some emotions are good and useful. For example, "righteous indignation," particularly against kidnappers, is laudable.[152] So is "hatred of evil."[153] But even the destructive emotions can be controlled, and once under control by Reason can be rendered a virtue (eupathy).[154] The means of controlling the destructive emotions is through the practice of virtue that Philo identifies with Torah.

In assessing the relationship between Philo and the Rabbis, Sandmel concludes that there is considerable overlap, but the overlap does not necessarily signal dependency.[155] It is more likely that Philo and the Rabbis independently developed their own responses to the problem of good and evil under the influence of the ideas extant in their day.

Summary

The Rabbis, explicating the biblical tradition they inherited, had little concern with the origin of evil or the existence of evil in the natural world, but had great concern with human suffering. A measure of that concern is attributable to historical circumstance: victimization under Roman rule. But much of their concern transcended the events of their day. It expressed a worry over justifying how evil can exist in a world ruled by an all-powerful and exclusively good God. This worry was not restricted to the Rabbis. Contemporaneous sectarians and Hellenistic philosophers mused the same problem and sometimes found solutions common to the Rabbis.

The Nature of Good and Evil: Like their biblical precursors, the Rabbis were less concerned with the broader ontology of good and evil than in the practical consequences of good and evil. One Rabbinic approach insists that moral evil is directly attributable to sin, and sinners will be punished for their poor choice of conduct. But unlike the earlier biblical sources such as Isaiah, Jeremiah, Ezekiel, Micah, and even the Psalmist, the Rabbis were generally averse to ascribing evil to a failure of human will. Instead the Rabbis invented and proposed a range of novel ideas as possible solutions to the problem of the existence of evil, among them ancestral merit, chastisements of love, astral influence, vicarious atonement, and especially the afterlife and the evil inclination. Even so, two strains of Rabbinic thought held that evil is either a regular feature of the world or that injustice is simply inevitable, a consequence of the nature of the universe.

Questions of Justice: The sheer number of approaches to theodicy generated by the Rabbis leads to two conclusions. First, the Rabbis were preoccupied with the problem of human suffering. Because human suffering was a problem of the highest order, the Rabbis had to devote their creative efforts to its resolution. Second, none of the proposed solutions to the problem of suffering was adequate. Had any of the various solutions been sufficiently compelling, there would have been no need for any other.

Among the various solutions are those that follow biblical precedent and those that shatter biblical assumptions. Like the psalms, one Rabbinic approach to injustice maintains that suffering builds character. But another Rabbinic approach to injustice that propounds that evil is inexplicable directly repudiates the biblical assumption that God cannot act arbitrarily. And another that propounds the idea that all things happen by chance challenges the biblical assumption that the created world must be orderly and not random.

And so, what began as a few appetizing biblical offerings for addressing the issues of good and evil would in time grow into an entire Rabbinic menu. It would then become part of the mission of medieval Jewish philosophers to select the options they believed to be most satisfying and systematize them.

CHAPTER 3

Good and Evil in Medieval Philosophy

The biblical and Apocryphal sources provide the raw material, as it were, for fashioning a construct of good and evil. The Rabbinic sources and sources contemporaneous with the Rabbis drew from the earlier raw material to produce more than a dozen approaches to the problem of good and evil. The medieval philosophers selected from those approaches, developing them further.

Medieval Jewish philosophy properly begins with the North African Jewish physician Isaac Israeli, whose life spanned the mid-ninth to mid-tenth centuries.[1] Yet his largely composite (and derivative) Neoplatonist philosophy adds little to the consideration of the topic of good and evil and, accordingly, is not discussed in this chapter. For the same reason, the work of Solomon ibn Gabirol—which, like that of Israeli,[2] had greater influence on non-Jewish philosophy[3]—is also excluded. It is in the writings of Sa'adiah ben Joseph al-Fayyumi, better known simply as Sa'adiah Gaon, that a substantive treatment of the problem of evil emerges.

Sa'adiah

I . . . begin this book . . . with an exposition of the reason why men, in their search for Truth, become involved in errors, and how these errors can be removed so that the object of their investigations may be fully attained; moreover, why some of these errors have such a powerful hold on some people that they affirm them as the truth, deluding themselves that they know something. . . .[4]

We see the godless prospering in this world, while believers are in misery therein. There can, therefore, be no escaping the belief that there exists for the former, as well as for the latter, a second world in which they will be recompensed in justice and righteousness.[5]

As head (ga'on) of the academy of Sura in Babylonia, Sa'adiah ben Joseph al-Fayyumi (892–942) was the guardian of the Jewish intellectual tradition that began with the Bible and was developed by the talmudic sages. Circumstance thrust him into controversy both within the Jewish community of his day and without. Within the Jewish community, his resolution of a calendar dispute with a prominent authority in Israel established the general preeminence of the Babylonian authorities over their Palestinian counterparts. In addition, his polemics against the Karaite sect and defense of the imaginative Rabbinic readings of biblical texts helped fix the boundaries of Jewish belief and practice. At the same time, the emergence of Islamic philosophy compelled him to distinguish between its claims and those of Judaism, resolving the confusion among Jews by clarifying the differences. As a result, Sa'adiah produced polemical works, translated the Bible into Arabic, wrote a commentary on the Torah, and developed a philosophy of Judaism that fit with the most authoritative scientific and philosophic opinions of his time. His philosophical treatise, in which his treatment of good and evil appears at length, is called *Emunot ve-De'ot, Beliefs and Opinions*.

Sa'adiah was the first Jewish philosopher to approach the problem of theodicy systematically. Part of his larger project was to expose the errors into which he declares human beings have lapsed. Principal among those errors is the thorny problem of why it seems that the righteous suffer and the wicked prosper.

That God observes all human action is axiomatic for Sa'adiah, as is its corollary that God will hold all human beings accountable for their actions, rewarding the good and punishing the evil:

God has also informed us that during our entire sojourn in this work-aday world He keeps a record of everyone's deeds. The recompense for them, however, has been reserved by Him for the second world, which is the world of compensation. . . . There He will requite all of them according to their deeds.[6]

Sa'adiah cites Ecclesiastes as justification.[7] But how and where the settling of scores takes place is more complex. Sa'adiah is of the view that distinct from this world (what he terms "the World of Action"), it is in the future world (what he terms "the World of Reward") that the final and appropriate settlement will occur. This is not to say there is no judgment whatsoever in this world. Yet the rewards the righteous enjoy and the punishments the wicked suffer in this world are a mere "hint" of what awaits them in the time to come:

God requites people in this world for the minority of their deeds and leaves the majority for the next world.[8]

Sa'adiah maintains that the difference between the righteous and the wicked is the sum total of the type of deeds performed. The righteous are not sinless, and the wicked are not without merits. The righteous are those "in whose conduct good deeds predominate."[9] He cites King Ḥizkiyah and King Yehoshaphat as examples.[10] And because the majority of the deeds performed by the righteous are good, whereas the majority of the deeds performed by the wicked are evil, God has accordingly

arranged the retribution for the class of deeds which are in the minority to be meted out in this world, in the way in which He has explained[11] that the total sum of good deeds of a pious man is stored up for the Future World, whereas the few good deeds of an impious man are rewarded in this world.[12]

The result can often be jarring to the neutral observer:

It often happens that a pious man who has committed a fairly large number of sins incurs punishment throughout the greater part of his life, and a wicked person who has performed a fairly large number of good deeds is privileged to enjoy well-being for the greater part of his life.[13]

Seeing the punishment absorbed by the righteous and the successes enjoyed by the wicked leads the neutral observer to conclude that God is unjust. But, Sa'adiah notes, the neutral observer fails to take into account that in the future, the righteous will enjoy eternal reward, while the wicked suffer eternal punishment. As the rabbi and philosopher Alexander Altmann notes, Sa'adiah holds that the sins of the righteous are expiated by suffering in this world such that the righteous will only enjoy eternal reward in the next.[14] And the merits of the wicked that result in success in this world will only be followed by their eternal punishment in the next.

Of course, a person may change. Taking account of a person's possible transformation in character, Sa'adiah qualifies what he believes is God's calculations. "If one who has a great number of good deeds to his credit regrets having done them, he loses all his merits on account of his regret."[15] And correspondingly, "If one who has committed a great number of evil deeds feels remorse for them and carries out all the conditions of repentance, he has thereby removed them from his soul."[16] Thus, he would no longer be subject to punishment in the Future World.

Sa'adiah thereby imagines the following scenario. By his righteousness, a man is destined to enjoy eternal reward for the merits accumulated in this world. At the same time, the righteous man is subject to endure a small degree of punishment in this world for the number of misdeeds he committed. However, now that the righteous man has regretted all his merits and turned to evil ways, his eternal rewards are canceled. This also results in the cancellation of his punishment in this world, since that will be reserved for the future. Instead, he will enjoy success in this world as compensation for the good that he had done.

Here, again, what the neutral observer sees is troublesome, but Sa'adiah warns against being "led astray" by appearances: "The well-being which he now enjoys is not due to his adoption of an irreligious life, but is payment to him, in this world, of the happiness that was reserved for him in the Future World, and is now thrown in his face."[17] The same consternation would befall the neutral observer in the case where a previously wicked man abandons his evil ways and becomes completely rehabilitated, only to suffer:

> People may observe that immediately upon his turning away from sin he was visited with grief and affliction, and they will be at a loss to understand it, not knowing that the suffering which has befallen him is not the result of his fresh start in life, but it is the legacy of the past which he relinquished.[18]

Sa'adiah argues that what appears to be evil in the world—unjustified human suffering—is a misperception. In actuality, God administers both success and suffering in this world and beyond according to a reasonable and ascertainable formula.

Yet according to Sa'adiah's understanding of the process he describes, the suffering of the righteous in this world ought to be minimal, since the number of transgressions committed by the righteous must be a minority of their actions. However, experience shows that the suffering of the righteous is often substantial. Moreover, the class of innocent sufferers—like children who are not held accountable for their actions—goes unaddressed.

Consequently, Sa'adiah adds another justification for suffering in this world: "a visitation from God" in order to "test" the righteous.[19] The test or trial is customized for the benefit of the righteous on the basis of what they are able to tolerate so that the

> incipient trials with which God tests them, when he knows they are able to withstand them, only in order to compensate them for their trials later on for good.[20]

Suffering as a test comes with two qualifications, according to Sa'adiah. The first is that God always compensates the righteous for their suffering at some later time. Thus the suffering of the righteous is never in vain. The second is that the suffering administered as a test is never greater than the endurance of the sufferer. For Sa'adiah this second qualification is logically obvious, since no useful purpose would be served through excessive suffering. Sa'adiah adds that aside from "trials," sometimes the virtuous endure "penalties for slight failings."[21] As for the wicked, "the godless may be permitted to linger on earth merely in order that his punishment be made more severe."[22]

Unlike suffering as punishment when God, if asked for a reason, would reveal it,[23] God does not tell the sufferer the reason for the suffering when suffering serves as a test. Sa'adiah explains that in the former case, "telling him the reason of his suffering will have the good effect of making him depart from his sins."[24] However, when suffering is a test, not revealing that suffering is meted out for this purpose serves the objectives of dissuading people from concluding that (1) the only reason the righteous endure it is in anticipation of the reward, or (2) that suffering is something easy.[25]

Sa'adiah is powerless to explain why little children suffer, but he is certain that they will be compensated for it; he compares the suffering to strong medicine or parental discipline administered for the benefit of the child. Of course, Sa'adiah's assurance ineluctably leads to the question of why such suffering is necessary at all, even if it is to be compensated. If God wanted to bestow happiness on innocents, God could have done so without inflicting any suffering! Here, Sa'adiah relies on a distinction between gifts—what Altmann calls "grace"[26]—and rewards. Both are benefits allotted by God. Gifts, however, are bestowed independently of any "work" performed. In contrast, rewards are allotted on the basis of the "work" performed. Sa'adiah claims that since rewards are earned, it is eminently reasonable to conclude that rewards are of a superior status than gifts. Applied to the suffering of innocents, Sa'adiah holds that suffering earns a reward and that the benefit is "more abundant" than if it was gifted. In effect, Sa'adiah implies that the suffering of innocents is good.

Maimonides, as will be shown, objects to Sa'adiah on three counts. First, Maimonides contends that a world to come is an inadequate device for overcoming the problem of suffering in this world. Second he calls Sa'adiah to task for blaming the sinner for his suffering—which, Maimonides argues, only makes the problem worse. Third, Maimonides maintains that the suffering of innocents is never good.

Before considering the ways Maimonides diverges from Sa'adiah, a short detour to the Spanish scholar Baḥya ben Yosef ibn Pakuda (ca. 1050–1120) is warranted. Although Rabbenu Baḥya has as his main intent the formulation of Judaism as an ethical system, he does include some important observation about the problem of good and evil.

Baḥya

A person might say: "The world does operate justly. If the world operated along the principle of justice, the wicked would not prosper and the righteous would not suffer."[27]

The life of Baḥya ben Yosef ibn Pakuda largely remains a mystery. Near the end of his life, he felt compelled to write the first Jewish system of ethics in order to counterbalance what he considered a preoccupation with practical Judaism (what he called "duties of the limbs") by the rabbis in his day, to the near exclusion of the philosophical requirements of Jewish belief. His book, written in Arabic under the title *Al Hidayah ila Faraid al-Kulub* (Guide to the duties of the heart), was translated into Hebrew some twenty to thirty years later under the title *Hovot ha-Levavot* (*Duties of the Heart*), by which it is known today.

Baḥya divides *Duties of the Heart* into ten sections he termed "gates," corresponding to the ten fundamental principles that, according to his view, constitute man's spiritual life. He does not directly address the problem of evil, but the alert reader can discern the elements of Baḥya's approach in how he addresses three particular gates.

In Gate 2, "The Gate of Reflection," Baḥya insists that reflecting on the greatness and goodness of God, as manifested throughout Creation, is the highest duty of humanity. However, most people fail in this duty. Among the reasons Baḥya cites are humanity's insatiable longing for pleasure, which deprives it of the sense of gratitude ("all those who achieve much always want more"); humanity's having been spoiled by success ("like a baby raised in comfort cannot appreciate what it was accustomed to have"); and people's dissatisfaction or disappointment with life.

With regard to this last factor, Baḥya mentions that "when people suffer setbacks, whether a physical or monetary loss, they fail to understand how beneficial these are for moral instruction."[28] Thus the Psalmist writes, "Happy is the man whom You discipline O Lord, the man You instruct in Your teaching, to give him tranquility in times of misfortune" (Ps. 94:12). The metaphor Baḥya goes on to employ is that of the householder who is given useful instructions by the master of the house but, by ignoring them, fails to take advantage of all the good things that would have served him well, suffers terribly as a result, and ends up bitterly complaining against the master of the house, calling him the author of his suffering. Taken with his description of humanity's ingratitude to God, Baḥya implies that humanity (or certainly Jews) are the architects of their own suffering when they refuse to follow the teaching of divine law.

Yet even those who follow divine law may still suffer. Still, this suffering is not unjust. The suffering of the righteous, as the talmudic concept of "trials" taught, helps improve their character. Besides,

the suffering, whether an evil applied or a good denied, may be imposed as a punishment by which your sins are absolved or the initiation of a divine trial so that God may enlarge your reward . . . [and] ought to be willingly accepted.[29]

Further, in Gate 8, "The Gate of Taking Spiritual Account," Baḥya goes on to say that when the wise person calculates the suffering he deserves, he will come to realize that the actual degree of suffering he endures is far less than what God should have meted out,[30] thus encouraging that person to repent. Hence, rather than complaining about the unjust suffering absorbed, the righteous person should be thankful for the amount of suffering absolved.

In Gate 5, Baḥya introduces into his philosophy the concept of good and evil inclinations. The evil inclination, Baḥya asserts, is one of the reasons why people fail to attribute all things to God's unity:

The deceptions of the evil inclination lead people away from what they ought to embrace in this world and thus distance people from attaining their rewards in the world to come.[31]

Only when the evil inclination is tamed can a person merit his or her ultimate reward. And it is the study of Torah that tames the evil inclination. Baḥya tells the following illustrative story with the appended advice:

One should take account with his soul regarding the conditions imposed upon him by his status as a stranger in the world. He should regard his position as that of one who came from a foreign country where he knew none of the inhabitants and none knew him. The king of the country had compassion on him because of his being a foreigner and instructed him on how to improve his condition there. . . . Therefore, my brother, voluntarily assume the obligation of the status of a stranger in the world, for you are indeed a stranger therein.[32]

Consistent with his division of the duties of the limbs with the duties of the heart, Baḥya contrasts the outer life of a person with the inner life. The evil inclination resides in the soul, and it is in the soul that the conclusive battle will be fought.

In one telling passage, Baḥya links together the competing inner dispositions, the battle between body and soul, and the route to overcoming the evil dispositions and gaining salvation:

It is clear to you [the intellect tells the Soul] and firmly fixed in your mind that you are pledged to your Creator for His goodness and belong to Him because of the multitude of kindnesses and His favors. . . . If your longing proceeds from a clear realization [of] how great is your obligation to God, how little it is in your power to fulfill it, and that your neglect of it involves your ruin, while your endeavor to fulfill it will secure your salvation, your longing is genuine and your desire urgent; if not, it is false. . . . The reprehensible dispositions in you are many. But the root and stock from which they spring are two. One of them is love of physical pleasures. . . . This disposition you have acquired from your neighbor, the body. The second disposition is love of domination and superiority—pride, haughtiness, jealousy. . . . This disposition you have acquired from your associates among whom you have grown up.[33]

Baḥya was also an exegete. In his commentary on the book of Exodus (5:22) he writes that sometimes people suffer on account of their sins. At other times, however, he says that people may suffer "chastisements of love." By invoking this talmudic concept, Rabbenu Baḥya adds another element to his approach toward good and evil.

Baḥya trims the manifold Rabbinic responses to evil from more than a dozen to a mere five. Even so, the question remains: why are five responses necessary if any one of them is sufficiently compelling? Moreover, when it comes to the chastisements of love, the same critique leveled against the Rabbis who introduce it may be leveled against Baḥya, who cites it: suffering is an award that few, if any, will relish. Moreover, what moral instruction the righteous gain through suffering is unstated and unclear. It would seem that the morally upright could add to their virtuousness in ways that would not require affliction.

Abraham ibn Daud

Abraham ibn Daud (ca. 1110–ca. 1180) was a rough contemporary of Maimonides. In matters of Jewish law, ibn Daud was Maimonides' fiercest critic. In matters of philosophy, ibn Daud was Maimonides' precursor.

Like Maimonides, ibn Daud was born in Cordova and forced to flee from impending Islamic persecution. While Maimonides left for North Africa, ibn Daud settled in Toledo. His historical *Sefer ha-Kabbalah* (*The Book of Tradition*) remains an important source for tracing the development of Jewish law; his philosophical book, *Emunah Ramah* (*The Exalted Faith*), was eclipsed by Maimonides' *The Guide of the Perplexed*. The Arabic original of ibn Daud's philosophical work is no longer extant, but a Hebrew version has been preserved.

The historian of philosophy Isaac Husik maintains that ibn Daud was the first Jewish philosopher who shows an intimate knowledge of the works of Aristotle and makes a deliberate effort to harmonize the Aristotelian system with Judaism.[34] Concomitantly, Husik holds that ibn Daud composed the entire book for the express purpose of considering the problem of evil and human freedom.

To understand ibn Daud, a short excursus into Aristotelian thought is necessary. Aristotle makes a distinction between matter and form.[35] All things in the universe (with one exception, as will be noted) are composed of the two. A chair, for example, is made of wood, its substance (substance here defined as the stuff that makes up any material item in the universe), but it is also designed so that person may sit upon it, its form. Note that form, while subject to the perception of the senses, is not the shape of an object, and it is not material. Form determines an object's properties because form inheres in the object itself—form *is* its essence. Thus, the form of a chair would dictate that it would have at least three legs, its properties, to fulfill its essence: to serve as a stable seat.

What is true with inanimate objects is also true for living things. A plant, for example, is a material thing, a substance with both matter and form. Plant matter is the stuff of which it is made (cellulose, etc.), and form is the arrangement of its matter (stem, leaves, etc.) as well as all its functions (nutrition, growth, reproduction) that are inseparable from the actual plant. Likewise, human beings are a composite of matter and form. Aristotle held that there is only one thing in the universe that can have form and not be made of matter: God.[36]

Proceeding from Aristotle, ibn Daud asserts that God is exceptional in several ways.

First, God is "actuality," while all material things in the universe are in various stages of "potentiality." All defect and evil are assigned to potentiality, since God is perfect. So it follows that the farther a thing is situated from "actuality," the more likely it is to be defective; and the closer a thing is to "actuality," the freer a thing is from defect.

Second, because God is essentially perfect, it means that God's knowledge is perfect, since God is exclusively form. From this it follows that matter is inimical to knowledge. Thus, inanimate objects that are situated as the most extreme outlier on the potentiality scale have the least "knowledge." Having perfect knowledge also means that God alone knows God's essence.

Third, part of God's perfection is God's willingness to extend God's knowledge and perfection, "communicating" of God's self to all other things. By contrast, while human beings have a significant degree of knowledge, they do not know their own essence. However, on account of God's willingness to extend God's knowledge to human beings and human beings absorbing this knowledge, godliness is incorporated into their essence.[37]

Given this architectonic, ibn Daud can now explain good and evil. First, ibn Daud claims (as do Maimonides and Gersonides) that the evils observed in the world are relatively few and insignificant in comparison with the overwhelming good. Second, evil is not a product of God's creation; it is not something that God has made. Evils are "privations"—that is, they are negative in character. Poverty is a privation: the absence of wealth. Illness is a privation: the negations of health. These and similar privations, being negatives, are not "made" in and of themselves; they are the result of an absence of something else that is made. Thus, God cannot be held accountable for the evils observed in the world.

Third, ibn Daud argues that evil is a defect. Defects cannot come from God. To him, this is not just a claim; it is a consequence of logical reasoning. Two contradictory ideas cannot apply to the same unitary subject simultaneously. An object, for instance, cannot be said to exist and not exist at the same time. Hence, since God is a unitary being, God cannot be the source of both good and evil. To imagine that God were the source of both good and evil would require an illogical upholding of two contraries at once. Alternatively, because human beings are not unitary but composite creatures comprised of both reason and desires, they can be the source of both good and evil. That is, reason leads human beings to good, while desires lead human beings to evil. Now if the same were said about God, it would make God no different from human beings, and that would be preposterous.

Ibn Daud may indeed be correct: the evils observed in the world may be few in number compared to the overwhelming good. But the number of evils is not at issue. Even one instance of unjustifiable evil is sufficient to challenge the power and goodness of God. And while ibn Daud is a superb metaphysician and logician, the existence of evil is not a mental conundrum to be solved through reasoning, but an observed phenomenon that requires a practical, not theoretical, solution.

Maimonides

I have called this Treatise "The Guide of the Perplexed." I do not say this Treatise will remove all difficulties for those who understand it. I do, however, say that it will remove most of the difficulties and those of the greatest moment.[38]

In his wide-ranging assessment of Maimonides (1135–1204), the contemporary philosopher Moshe Halbertal notes, "Medieval Jewry had its share of great thinkers and halakhists, but Maimonides was the only one who attempted to bring about, simultaneously, two such profound and far-reaching transformations, one in the domain of *halakhah* and the other in that of philosophy."[39] For his part, Husik claims that with Maimonides we reach "the high water mark of medieval Jewish philosophy."[40] An argument could be made that with Maimonides we reach the high water mark of all Jewish philosophy. Since his death in 1204, it has been impossible to engage in any serious discussion of Jewish philosophy without reference to his writing. Employed as the court physician to the caliph in old Cairo (Fustat), he wrote on medical theory and practice. His book on poisons and their antidotes was a medieval bestseller. Yet his scientific knowledge extended well beyond the art of medicine. He was expert in mathematics, astronomy, chrononomy, metaphysics, Greek philosophy, and logic. Given that, coupled with his expertise in the breadth and depth of Rabbinic literature, both his supporters and his detractors recognized in him the "master mind."[41] He has left as a legacy a significant written corpus.

However, as the philosopher and classicist Leo Strauss has observed, his philosophical magnum opus, *The Guide of the Perplexed*, where we find most of his analysis of good and evil, is largely an esoteric book.[42]

Maimonides' *Guide* is predominantly a work of exegesis. As such, his interpretation of the key biblical passages regarding good and evil is the proper starting point for understanding his thinking on the subject.

Returning to one of the first biblical texts to use the expression "good and evil," recall that the serpent tempts the first woman by assuring her that eating from the fruit of the Tree of Knowledge will result in her (more broadly, humans) becoming like "*Elohim*," "knowing good and evil." Assuming *Elohim* is translated as "God," the reader is inclined to think that knowing good and evil—that is, moral awareness—is a god-like quality. Maimonides, however, argues in the very first chapter of the *Guide* that the godlike quality associated with humanity's being created in God's image is the human capacity for the highest level of intellectual apprehension and contemplation:

> Now man possesses as his proprium[43] something in him that is very strange, as it is not found in anything else that exists under the sphere of the moon,[44] namely, intellectual apprehension. . . . Because of the divine intellect conjoined with man, it is said of the latter that he is in the image of God and in His likeness, not that God, may He be exalted, is a body and possesses a shape.[45]

Maimonides worries that a reader of the Bible could make two fundamental errors. The first would be imagining that since human beings have a physical body and humans are created in God's image, it must be the case that God has physical body. Maimonides dismisses this claim as outrageous. There is a vast difference between asserting that man is created in God's image (the view of the Torah) and claiming that God is created (or imagined to be created) in man's image (the error).

The second error is in believing that "being like God" means the ability to make moral distinctions. Anticipating this error, Maimonides launches the entire treatise with a lexicographical discussion. Some Hebrew words are ambiguous and equivocal. *Elohim* is one of them. *Elohim* can mean "God"; it can refer to the angels; and it can also mean "governing rulers." Mistaking *Elohim* for "God" is the source of the confusion. If, in context, *Elohim* means "God," then the assumption that knowledge of good and evil is moral awareness is justified. But, Maimonides argues, the correct contextual meaning of *Elohim* in this verse must be "rulers."

Maimonides terms the capacity to distinguish between good and evil — that is, what is generally thought of as the ability to make moral distinctions — "the noblest of the characteristics existing in us."[46] But, according to the biblical narrative, this asset is only gained through disobedience. Only after eating from the forbidden fruit do the first human beings gain this capacity. Yet how could it be that the first human beings are greatly rewarded for violating God's instructions? The only way to avoid this difficulty, Maimonides determines, is by rejecting the equating of knowledge of good and evil with the ability to make moral distinctions.

Maimonides' explanation rests on more than logic alone. Maimonides assumes that at the time of Creation, humanity must have existed in the highest possible state of perfection.[47] "It was because of this" — here Maimonides is referring to God's endowment of human beings with intellect — "that it was said of him that he was created in the image of God."[48] As such, "he had no faculty that was engaged in any way in the consideration of generally accepted things, and he did not apprehend them."[49] In this pristine state, human life was devoted exclusively to intellectual contemplation. Accordingly, the first man and the first woman were naked but not ashamed, since they had no apprehension of nakedness as a moral concern. Nonetheless, being endowed with intellect enables human beings to be open to commandments, "for commandments are not given to beasts and beings devoid of intellect."[50] Yet human beings are also corporeal creatures. Human beings are not pure intellect, but intellect housed in physical bodies subject to desires and the free will to follow them.[51] When the first human beings disobeyed the commandment not to eat the fruit from the Tree of Knowledge of Good and Evil, it was because of an inclination "toward his desires of the imagination and the pleasures of his corporeal senses."[52] The results were catastrophic: "he was punished by being deprived of that intellectual apprehension."[53] Only then is humanity "endowed with the faculty of apprehending generally accepted things,"[54] thus absorbed in judging things "bad or fine."[55] A contemporary interpreter of Maimonides, Marvin Fox, is quite correct when he observes that for Maimonides, "acquiring a concern with the realm of moral judgment is not an advancement for man but a tragic mark of deterioration."[56]

This brings Maimonides around to the true meaning of the serpent's statement meant to seduce the woman into eating the forbidden fruit. It is not a promise of great reward. Rather, it conveys the inevitable consequence of yielding to humanity's baser nature. By violating God's command, humanity will descend from a life of the intellect to a life subject to passions and desires. Human beings will become like earthly rulers (*Elohim*), who set for themselves standards and conventions that respond to the desires of the corporeal senses.

In essence, the serpent offers humanity an alternative to the contemplative, godlike life of the intellect. The serpent is correct when he says that eating the forbidden fruit will not result in actual death. But herein lies his deceit. Eating the fruit will deprive them of intellectual life, which, from the divine perspective, is a kind of death.

Maimonides, to his own satisfaction, refuted an erroneous understanding of the biblical narrative. In doing so, he also propounds a well-formulated axiology. Intimated by Maimonides is a value system in which the *summum bonum* (the supreme good to which humanity aspires) is the contemplative life of the intellect, which was lost by Adam and Eve but is possible for their descendants to recover. For Maimonides, moral rules are noncognitive, meaning that determinations of good and evil are not properly objects of the intellect, since good and evil cannot be either true or false. "Through the intellect," says Maimonides, "one distinguishes between truth and falsehood, and that was found in [Adam] in its perfection and integrity."[57] All ethical distinctions are conventional. In the realm of the passions—that is, the world in which we live—all rules are arbitrary. They are the products of social convention or positive law. Hence, without knowing what objectives are intrinsically good, it is often the case that human beings, urged on by their passions, will pursue whatever happens to strike them as pleasing. This is precisely why the teachings of the Torah are necessary: to prevent people from falling victim to their own warped desires.

While Maimonides might be satisfied that he has disposed of an erroneous understanding of Scripture, he leaves room to suggest that he is guilty of the same misreading. In his code of law he writes the following:

> Free will is granted to every human being. If a man wants to follow the good path and be righteous, he has the power to do so; if he wants to follow the evil way and be wicked, he is free to do so. It is written: "Indeed, man has become like one of us, knowing good and evil" (Gen. 3:22). That is to say, the human species is unique in the world, there being no other species like it in this respect, namely, that man, by himself, using his own intelligence and reason, knows what is good and what is evil, without anyone preventing him from doing good or evil as he pleases; in view of this, "he will perhaps put forth his hand and take also from the Tree of Life."[58]

It certainly seems as if Maimonides understands Genesis 3:22 to mean that the first human being is capable of using his own intellectual powers to make moral distinctions, contradicting what he says in the *Guide*. Here, it appears, good and evil are objects of the intellect and can be cognitively determined.

However, if what Maimonides writes in his code is read in conjunction with what he says about this verse in his *Guide*, the difficulty disappears. For Maimonides, the word "good" in both the Creation story and the expulsion story conveys something that conforms to God's purpose.[59] As Maimonides explains, God only says that God brought every part of the world into existence and that its existence conformed to its purpose.[60] "Good" has no moral connotations whatsoever. Indeed, if "good" meant ethically correct, God's declaration that all God created was "very good" would make no sense. There can be no moral sense attached to the description that God found the birds "good." Instead, "the meaning of the words, 'that it was good,' is that the thing in question is of externally visible and manifest utility for the existence and permanence of that which exists,"[61] or, as Fox puts it, is useful and effective in achieving some specified purpose.[62] Thus, Maimonides is telling his readers that human beings are endowed with practical reason, the ability to choose from among the options available to them that will appropriately serve their ends. In this sense human beings may become, as God says, "like one of us."

As serious as the textual problems associated with the terms "good and evil" may be, even more serious is the problem that results from living in a world in which theological expectations are challenged. As previously noted, the conceptual problem regarding good and evil involves four propositions that cannot be affirmed simultaneously—namely, that God is all-powerful, that God is omniscient, that God is all good, and that evil is real. If evil exists, then God cannot be all good and all-powerful. If God were all good and all-powerful, then God would have both the inclination and the means to prevent evil. Hence, God must be indifferent to evil or, alternatively, unable to prevent it. The truth of either alternative would challenge the fundamental assumptions of ethical monotheism. The only way to avoid this challenge is to deny the existence of evil. But such a denial would run counter to human experience. Disease, infant mortality, famine, and earthquakes are all very real and palpable. Moreover, even newborns who have not sinned and the righteous who have performed only acts of goodness are not protected from the deleterious effects of natural disasters.

To address these and other concerns, Maimonides employs a dual strategy. First, constrained by the philosophical thinking of his predecessors, Maimonides attempts to demonstrate that evil does not really exist. Then, perhaps unhappy with the cogency of this argument, Maimonides goes on to minimize, but not eliminate, the problem of evil. This second strategy conforms to what Maimonides promised at the outset of his treatise. He may not be able to remove all difficulties, but he will remove most of the difficulties of the most severe problems.

Maimonides sees a bifurcation between natural evil and moral evil. Moral evil, the result of human beings' inhumanity toward other human beings, is easily attributable to a failure of free will.[63] People wronging other people is a consequence of human choice, not God's. But the suffering of innocents as a result of earthquakes, for example, cannot be similarly dismissed. The problem of natural evil lies with God alone.

Here, Maimonides comes to the same conclusion as Plato—namely, that evil cannot really exist. His argument is based on a metaphysical definition of matter. Matter has no definite nature or actual being. In Greek thinking, matter is formless. Evil, being formless, is a "privation": it is an absence of something real. Light is real. Darkness (the absence of light) is a privation. According to Aristotle, who Maimonides admits to owing much, darkness has no efficient cause (that is, no creator), only a deficient cause. Only a positive thing can be made. A negative thing, like a privation, cannot. Hence, God cannot be the creator of evil. God produces only the good, while evil is the result of a defect in the thing itself.

A Karaite critic of Maimonides, Aharon ben Eliyahu of Nicomedia (ca. 1328–69), exposes the weakness of this argument. Exonerating God from responsibility for evil by arguing that evil is merely a "privation" should likewise result in exonerating human beings from responsibility for evil for the same reason. Logical consistency would thus result in never holding human beings responsible for their wrongs. Since this position is contrary to the Torah, it must be rejected.[64]

A modern interpreter of Maimonides, Moshe Halbertal, also exposes the weakness of this argument but frames it differently. Defining evil as a privation is a semantic argument. To the sufferer, pain "can hardly be described as an absence, for it is real, extant, and scorching."[65] Further, defining evil as a "privation" seems to be a "kind of casuistic logic game that contributes little to an understanding of the question."[66] Were this scholastic denial of evil the only explanation Maimonides could offer, the problem of evil would persist.

Fortunately—perhaps intentionally—Maimonides develops an alternative approach, one that does not deny the existence of evil absolutely but instead lessens the potency of the problem. The evils that befall humanity fit into three categories. The first kind of evil—one that is sometimes called natural evil—is that which exists by virtue of the fact that human beings are physical creatures:

The first species of evil is that which befalls man because of the nature of coming-to-be and passing away, I mean to say because of his being endowed with matter.[67]

As physical creatures, human beings are subject to all the maladies that would affect a material body, from illnesses to which people might succumb to environmental factors that cause people harm, what Maimonides calls "corruption of the air." Illness, disease, and death are inevitable consequences of human life. When faced with such evil, people often demand that it be otherwise. But this would be foolish, even contradictory. To demand that a flesh and blood creature not be subject to such evil is tantamount to saying a human being should not be a human being:

> He who wishes to be endowed with flesh and bones and at the same time not be subject to impressions . . . wishes to combine two contraries.[68]

To put it somewhat differently, to complain about natural evils "entails an expectation of being something other than what we are. . . . And hoping for [bodies made of matter] to be perfect and eternal is like hoping for a square to be circular."[69]

The second kind of evil is moral evil: the wrongs committed by human beings against other human beings. As relatively frequent as these evils (wars, crimes, various forms of discrimination) may be,[70] they are no challenge to God's goodness and power. God has endowed human beings with free will. In exercising free will, some human beings commit great evils, including murder—but these are not God's doing, and God is not to blame for the crimes. Introducing his categorization of evils, Maimonides notes, "We suffer because of the evils that we have produced ourselves of our free will; but we attribute them to God."[71]

The third kind of evil is self-induced. In Maimonides' estimation, "This is what happens in the majority of cases . . . [which are] much more numerous than those of the second kind."[72] By making poor choices, human beings bring this evil upon themselves. In today's milieu, God cannot be blamed for the harm resultant from a person's abuse of drugs or alcohol or from smoking or overeating. Through self-indulgence and bad habits people put themselves in jeopardy.

Maimonides has now shown to his satisfaction why the problem of theodicy is not as severe as imagined. Nevertheless, people still believe that the world is characterized by injustice. Maimonides theorizes on why this is so. The problem of why the righteous seem to suffer, says Maimonides, is rooted in a fundamental misperception:

> Every ignoramus imagines that all that exists exists with a view to his individual sake; it is as if there were nothing that exists except him. And if something happens to him that is contrary to what he wishes, he makes the trenchant judgment that all that exists is an evil. However, if man considered and represented to himself that which exists and knew the smallness of his part in it, the truth would be clear and manifest to him.[73]

Only in humanity's self-centeredness does evil emerge as a problem. If, instead, people could look beyond their own condition, they would recognize God's beneficence and what was heretofore labeled "evil" would shrink in comparison to the great good humanity enjoys. As Halbertal puts it, "The key to confronting the problem of evil . . . is to be found in a change of human consciousness."[74]

Of course Maimonides realizes that the misperception is not baseless, given the fact that observation of the human experience shows that the righteous sometimes really do suffer and the wicked sometimes do prosper. Yet Maimonides disavows the possibility that God could be unjust:

> It is in no way possible that He . . . should be unjust, and that all the calamities that befall men and the good things that come to men, be it a single individual or a group, all of them are determined according to the deserts of the men concerned through equitable judgment in which there is no injustice whatsoever.[75]

What human observers perceive as an injustice is only an inadequate grasp of the facts:

> Thus if some individual were wounded in the hand by a thorn, which he would take out immediately, this would be a punishment for him, and if he received the slightest pleasure, this would be a reward for him—all this being according to his deserts. . . . But we are ignorant of the various modes of desert.[76]

And further:

> An obedient individual receives compensation for all the pious and righteous actions he has accomplished . . . and . . . he is punished for all evil acts committed by him.[77]

Even so, Maimonides is fully aware that the incontestable justice of divine providence is compromised by the Rabbis' admission that sometimes the righteous suffer undeservedly. Here Maimonides adopts the classic Rabbinic explanation that these are either "sufferings of love"[78] or imposed on the righteous "in order that his reward should be greater."[79]

What Maimonides does not do is blame the sufferer or posit an afterlife where the disparity between desert and reality can be corrected—that is, where the righteous who have suffered can be appropriately rewarded and where the wicked who have prospered can be justly punished.

Blaming the sufferer entails accepting the idea that while it may not be readily apparent to the observer or even to the sufferer, the sufferer must have committed some wrong. This was the opinion of Job's visiting friends, who urge him to undergo self-examination, determine his sin, and atone for it, at which point his suffering will disappear. Maimonides rejected the opinion that Job was to blame.[80] Blaming the victim makes things worse and leaves the problem in place.

Maimonides does not reject the concept of the afterlife. He objects to the strategy of using the afterlife as a device for rectifying injustices, for two reasons—one logical, one conceptual. Logically, it makes little sense to posit an afterlife for leveling injustices. Had God wanted to add to the reward of the righteous, God could have done so without having to make the righteous suffer. Conceptually, for Maimonides the afterlife is not intended for meting out rewards and punishments. Says Maimonides, "In the World to Come, there is nothing corporeal, and no material substance; there are only the souls of the righteous without bodies."[81] Further, "since there is nothing corporeal, there is no eating or drinking, nothing of any of the kinds of things that bodies would need in this world; and nothing occurs to bodies [in the world to come] that occurs to bodies in this world."[82] This would make rewarding the righteous commensurately in the next world virtually impossible. To compensate for their poverty in this world, the righteous cannot be rewarded with sumptuous meals in the next world, since there is no eating there. Likewise, punishing the wicked in the world to come would be impossible, for a different reason: the wicked are denied access to it altogether. As Maimonides puts it:

> The reward of the righteous is that they will attain bliss and abide in this state of happiness; the punishment of the wicked is that they will not attain this life but will be cut off and die.[83]

To Maimonides, the bliss that the righteous will enjoy is basking in divine splendor, communing with God by virtue of attaining supreme knowledge.[84] There is no higher reward.[85] Thus, all of Rabbinic literature that suggests otherwise must be read as parables.[86]

All said, Maimonides thoroughly rejects the idea that the world to come could possibly be the place for delayed gratification of bodily pleasures. The proper—and the only—place for compensation for good deeds and punishment for bad deeds is in this world.

Two further observations round out the picture Maimonides paints in order to solve the problem of theodicy. First is the role played by the attainment of knowledge of God. Knowledge of God is the noblest human pursuit. If attained—and it is indeed possible for the descendants of Adam and Eve to attain it—human beings gain ultimate happiness. As Maimonides writes, "True happiness, which is the knowledge of the deity, is guaranteed to all who know Him and . . . a human being cannot be troubled in it by any of all the misfortunes in question."[87] In other words, once acquiring the happiness that comes with attaining knowledge of God, any calamity that is suffered may be inconvenient but not unsettling. The person with knowledge of God is able to bear any misfortune.[88]

Second is the connection between the problem of theodicy and Maimonides' view of providence. Maimonides holds that "divine providence watches only over the individuals belonging to the human species and that in this species alone all the circumstances of the individuals and the good and evil that befall them are consequent upon their deserts."[89] Even so, divine providence is unequal. "Providence is graded as their human perfection is graded."[90] Prophets merit a high degree of divine care owing to their aptitude for perceiving the Divine—what Maimonides calls "this measure of the overflow of the divine intellect that makes the prophets speak."[91] Below the prophets are the "excellent and righteous men," who merit divine protection proportionate to their excellence in what they know. And below the "excellent and righteous men" are the ignorant and the disobedient, who, because of their "despicable state," earn no divine protection whatsoever. They are no different than animals, for which God offers no care, leaving their fate to chance.

The implications are significant. Maimonides has attached the benefit of divine care to knowledge of God and not to obedience to divine law. Hence, individuals who would generally be called "righteous" because they dutifully follow their religious obligations may still not qualify for divine care if they lack knowledge of the Divine. Accordingly, their suffering cannot be construed as a challenge to God's justice. In like manner, individuals who might generally be called "wicked" because they flagrantly violate religious obligations may still prosper under God's care because they have attained knowledge of the Divine. Since it is impossible for an observer to ever know what knowledge of the Divine a given person may have attained, it would be wrong to draw any conclusions about God's justice from common observation of human circumstance. As such, the problem is no longer theological but linguistic. Calling someone "righteous" or "wicked" as a consequence of observed behavior is misleading, since that has no bearing on whether this person merits divine care. (Of course, Maimonides would hope that one who has attained divine knowledge would ineluctably be drawn to observing God's laws.)

On the timeline of Jewish philosophy, particularly regarding the problem of good and evil, Maimonides is heir to both Sa'adiah and ibn Daud, sometimes in agreement with them, most times not. Like Sa'adiah, Maimonides sees the problem of good and evil largely as a problem of perception. Both would agree that the problem retreats to a mere triviality when seen with the proper perspective. For Sa'adiah, the misperception is rooted in ignorance of the full inventory of a given person's deeds as well as the direction (toward good or evil) in any given person's life. For Maimonides, the misperception is rooted in ignorance of a given person's knowledge of the Divine. More fundamentally, for Maimonides, the misperception lies in judging good or bad egoistically. A person prepared to see the manifold goodness of God in this world will have a different outlook than a person who sees only what is good to me or good for me. Moreover, Maimonides was too sharp a thinker to define "righteous" and "wicked," as does Sa'adiah, solely on the preponderance of deeds in each category. For Maimonides, it is not the quantity of deeds that matters but their quality. Some deeds are so profoundly evil that they outweigh the totality of good a person has performed, and some deeds are so breathtakingly noble that they outweigh all the wicked deeds a person has performed.[92] Only God can make the correct assessment.

On the matter of good and evil, Maimonides also departs from Sa'adiah in four other significant ways. First and foremost, unlike Sa'adiah, Maimonides does not assume that the world to come is the place for redressing injustices. Further, by holding that the rewards or punishments absorbed in this "World of Action" are "hints" of what awaits a person in what he calls the "World of Reward," Sa'adiah seems to be saying that the world to come features physical rewards and punishments, which Maimonides entirely rejects. Second, Sa'adiah suggests that except for the limited cases of "visitations" and "trials," each person is accountable for the punishments he or she receives. In effect, Sa'adiah argues that people are to blame for their state, and Maimonides rejects the idea of blaming the sinner.

Third, Sa'adiah claims that while the "trials" a person might endure are undeserved, they result in a greater reward later, whereas Maimonides points out that the idea that "God sends down calamities upon an individual, without having been preceded by a sin, in order that his reward be increased" is a "principle . . . not at all mentioned in the Torah in an explicit text."[93] Instead, Maimonides says, "trials" are meant to serve as a model of behavior to be imitated and followed.[94] Thus, for example, by sending false prophets,[95] God allows the Israelites to test the extent of their religious commitments and remain faithful, a course of action all Jews need to follow. Finally, Maimonides maintains that the suffering of innocent children is never acceptable.

Like ibn Daud, Maimonides holds that the evil observed in the world is exceedingly small in comparison with goodness. And like ibn Daud, Maimonides invests considerable space in demonstrating that evil is attributable to the imperfection of matter. But while ibn Daud begins and ends with this attribution, Maimonides goes much further, setting the stage for reactions by his successors.

Gersonides

Doubt arises on a given matter when we have contrary views concerning it; but when the inquiry will be completed and the true will be sifted out from the false, the doubts in this matter will vanish. Since there have been many false opinions among our predecessors on these matters, and we have [therefore, in our] investigation contended with them in order to refute these views in every possible way, and yet everything that we have been able to demonstrate is the view of the Torah, we have accordingly entitled our book "The Wars of the Lord." For we have fought the battles of the Lord in so far as we have refuted the false views of our predecessors.[96]

To claim the capacity to refute all rivals, discover the truth, and dispel all doubt seems to be astonishingly boastful were the claim to be made by any ordinary writer. But Rabbi Levi ben Gerson (1288–1344) was far from ordinary. He was the most prolific Jewish author of the Middles Ages and a true polymath, writing in Hebrew treatises on astronomy, zoology, medicine, mathematics, biblical exegesis, Jewish law, and philosophy, all subjects in which he had expertise. As such, his writings on good and evil, which appear in books 4–6 of his *Wars of the Lord* on divine providence, are of particular interest.

To Gersonides, as he is called, the context for any analysis of the problem of why the righteous suffer while the wicked prosper is God's relationship to human beings. If God does not care for human beings in any individual way but only generally as a species, then there is no problem at all, since the fate of each individual is left entirely to circumstance. But if God cares for human beings in some kind of individual way, then the appearance that good people suffer while wicked people prosper runs counter to the principle of justice by which we expect that God must operate. If God monitors the lives of every single person and notes their actions, then God should ensure that those who act righteously should be rewarded and those who act wickedly should be punished. Humanity would expect no less from an omnipotent and omnibenevolent God. Thus, Jews are faced with a dilemma. Jews cannot maintain that God holds no interest in any particular individual, since Scripture is replete with examples that teach otherwise. And Jews cannot comfortably assert that God takes an active interest in each individual while also observing general injustices in the world that hurt the righteous as much as the wicked.

To navigate through this dilemma, Gersonides distinguishes between two types of providence. The first type is embodied in nature, like the light and warmth of the sun. God manifests care for the world by creating the sun, which provides a uniform, universal, and predictably regular blessing. (To Gersonides, the regularity of nature is the surest proof for the existence of God.) Within the framework of natural providence, the wicked can prosper. The wicked—no less than the righteous—benefit from the sun's rays and from mineral-rich soil. The earth does not withhold its bounty from a farmer who cheats on his taxes. Nature has no favorites. A contemporary interpreter of Gersonides, Seymour Feldman, calls this phenomenon the "promiscuous profit" of living in the natural world.[97] Accordingly, no one should be troubled by the material success of criminals. As Gersonides puts it, "It does not follow that it is impossible for the sinners to receive benefits that are determined by the heavenly constellations. Indeed, we do maintain that they are left and abandoned to those accidents that are ordered by the heavenly bodies."[98] For Gersonides, natural providence emanates from God indirectly, through the instrumentality of spheres and constellations. Conceptually, this means that God has delegated the task of providing for humanity through nature rather than through taking a personal interest in people. Whatever happens to people as a result of "those accidents"—that is, the natural order—is entirely unrelated to merit.

The second type of providence emanates directly from God, the "Agent Intellect," whereby human beings, alone among all of God's creatures, are subject to God's concern, particularly for their spiritual perfection. This type of providence applies to individuals. Accordingly, God rewards and punishes human beings in direct proportion to the level of each person's spiritual perfection. Gersonides puts it this way:

> Some men never go beyond the disposition with which they are endowed as members of the human species and do not try to attain perfection so that they could become close to the Agent Intellect— indeed, some of them increase their imperfections, which they have been born as members of this species—such people are obviously not within the scope of divine providence except in a general way as members of the human species, for they have no individual [perfections] that warrant [individual] providence. Accordingly, divine providence operates individually in some men [and] in varying degrees and in others it does not appear at all.[99]

Like Maimonides, Gersonides holds that reward and punishment vary according to the intellectual excellence a given person has achieved. All people are born with two capacities, what Gersonides calls "dispositions." By virtue of being members of the human species, all people are born with imperfections. Those willing to pursue improvement and thereby develop a closer relationship with God can remedy these imperfections.

Those unwilling to pursue improvement will only see their imperfections increase. Even so, they will still enjoy the providence that applies to all members of the human species. The capacity to benefit from general providence is the first disposition. All people are also born with the potential to perfect themselves through the development of a closer relationship with God. This is the second disposition. Those people who choose never to develop this potential will not enjoy individual providence. Those who choose to develop their potential somewhat will gain a modest measure of individual providence. Those who develop their potential moderately will gain a moderate measure of individual providence. Those who develop their potential maximally will gain a full measure of individual providence.

However, virtue and excellence are not easily sustainable by human beings. So when the righteous stray, as Ecclesiastes insists they will, they are subject to the "arrows of fortune" which, as imagined, could include being victimized by the nefarious intentions of the wicked. When "these righteous people . . . have pursued sensual pleasures," for instance, "the bond and union between them and God . . . has been loosened."[100] In that moment of disunion, the righteous disconnect themselves, as it were, from God's protection, and they are "forsaken and abandoned to . . . evil."[101]

In fact, straying from righteous conduct not only makes the righteous susceptible to misfortune, but also makes the righteous deserving of misfortune:

> Anybody who does not endeavor to perfect his intellect according to the proper mode so that his providence will be connected with him should not complain if these evils fall upon him, for it is his fault that they have occurred.[102]

Alternatively, the suffering endured by the righteous following the suspension of individual providence is a warning to return to the proper direction—the warning being a sign of God's concern:

> His providence with respect to individual men consists [precisely] in informing them of the good or evil that is to come upon them,

so that they will avoid the evil and pursue the good. . . . This kind of [providence] and the like are called by our rabbis (may their memory be blessed) "visitations of [divine] love."[103]

Like Maimonides, Gersonides insists that the evils observed or experienced by humanity occur infrequently.[104] Consequently, the actual challenge to God's justice is minimal. Further, Gersonides goes on to offer a defense of God's justice that competes with Maimonides. He gives four reasons why "the occurrence of . . . evil among the virtuous" does not constitute "a moral defect in God."[105] First, what observers see as an unjustified evil may be the result of the righteous straying from the path of intellectual perfection and pursuing "sensual pleasures":

In such an eventuality they are forsaken and abandoned to the evil deriving by accident from the patterns determined by the heavenly bodies. If they then suffer these evils . . . this is not a moral defect in God.[106]

Second, "it is possible that these righteous men suffer evil from the time of their birth because of the great misfortunes suffered by their fathers, which can be avoided only with difficulty by their offspring."[107] It sometimes happens, Gersonides explains, "that the offspring, [even though] they are righteous, are caught up in these evils so long as they have not attained that level of intense union with God" that frees them from these evils.[108] Third, "it [sometimes] happens that God dispenses evils to the righteous in order to save them from greater evils that have been ordained to befall them from the heavenly constellations. . . . Since this kind of evil is really an expression of beneficence and graciousness to the good man, it is obviously not a moral defect [in God]."[109] Finally, "it [sometimes] happens that God brings evil upon the righteous because of His providential desire to save them from that minor sin they are about to be implicated in."[110] In each of these cases, it is impossible for the observer to discern the justification for the evil the righteous endures. So, like Maimonides, Gersonides maintains that the benefits of individual providence, being entirely variable, are not readily perceived.

Now Gersonides is able to explain Job's apparent suffering. It could be that Job's afflictions were the result of a temporary suspension of individual providence for a momentary lapse—a test of faith. Or, alternatively, Job's sufferings are afflictions for which Job will be greatly compensated in the world to come. Or, alternatively, Job's afflictions are perceived to be serious, but in the scheme of things they are minor, since the greatest happiness is not contingent on physical rewards. True reward, writes Gersonides, "consists of the acquisition of spiritual happiness . . . and not the pursuit of good food and sensual objects."[111] Hence, Job gained spiritual happiness despite being deprived of his wealth and health. Similarly, when the renegade Rabbi Elisha ben Avuya observed his student being executed by the Romans and doubted God's justice, he confused reward with material benefit and physical protection. True reward, however, is to be found in communing with the Agent Intellect—something that his student, through the study of Torah, surely attained.

Gersonides' comprehensive system is not without weakness. Like Maimonides, Gersonides appears to be overly idealistic in claiming that observed evils are infrequent. In truth, injustices seem to be far more evident than what both would admit. Gersonides also contends that the perceived suffering of the righteous is attributable to a temporary lapse in their connection with God, which Maimonides rejects on the grounds that blaming the victim only exacerbates the problem. Furthermore, to ascribe suffering to the possibility of inherited evil seemingly requires an explanation far beyond what Gersonides offers. Moreover, there is the problem of proportionality. A minor and temporary lapse would appear not to merit a severe punishment. Even were it the case that Job committed a minor sin (which he denies), how is it fair for him to suffer such major afflictions? And to consider the suffering of the righteous as a warning assumes that God has no better way to communicate than through meting out pain. This seems incompatible with the idea of a compassionate God.

Perhaps the most troublesome aspect of Gersonides' theodicy is the fact that it has only rational adults in mind. That is to say, Gersonides assumes that the suffering of the righteous is the result of poor choices. But certain classes of evil are not contingent on personal choices made by rational adults. Gersonides seems to ignore the concept of natural evil that can encompass a range of catastrophes that afflict the righteous indiscriminately, like landslides and famines, as well as those that afflict non-volitional agents like children. The suffering an innocent child endures on account of a debilitating disease or a birth defect cannot be ascribed to a bad choice.

Yet professor of philosophy Seymour Feldman believes that Gersonides is in fact able to find an answer for cases like this within his philosophical system.[112] In book 4 of *Wars of the Lord* Gersonides argues that even though God created nature, it is in good measure an autonomous agent. And in book 6 Gersonides claims that nature, being created from shapeless matter, is the cause of all natural imperfections. The "necessity of matter" is the cause of "a surplus of limbs among some individuals,"[113] or, in other words, birth defects. The imperfection of shapeless matter is an idea familiar to readers of Maimonides and ibn Daud. Yet for Gersonides, God is responsible for even an autonomous "nature." As such, ascribing evils to nature does not relieve God of responsibility, and the problem still remains. In addition, it can be argued that an omnipotent and omnibenevolent God should have created nature in a way that would, in the words of eighteenth-century philosopher David Hume, "secure the happiness and welfare of the creature in the most unfortunate concurrence of circumstance."[114] A nature inimical to human happiness exposes an "Author of Nature" who is "inconveniently powerful."[115]

Instead of relying on autonomous nature as the solution for why innocents suffer, perhaps Gersonides would argue that children are not yet able to fulfill the disposition with which they are endowed—namely, to commune with the Agent Intellect. So until the time that children can realize their potential and gain individual providence, they remain exposed to the arrows of fortune.

Finally, as Feldman contends, it is true that Gersonides differs from Maimonides on whether God can "know particulars as particulars."[116] Maimonides, according to Feldman, claims that God has knowledge of "particulars as particulars," that is, specific awareness and knowledge of all people and all events, while Gersonides rejects this idea. That is to say,

Gersonides claims that God has no knowledge of Moses or pharaoh as individuals whose good deeds are rewarded and whose misdeeds are punished; God only knows them as members of the species called humanity. At the end of his treatise, Gersonides maintains that God's knowledge is of "the general order [of events] in this world" and not "the accidents that will happen to this man."[117] Maimonides seems to agree, arguing that God "only knows the permanent and immutable things."[118] Maimonides makes an exception only in the case of those who have gained true knowledge of God. However, Maimonides further asserts that God must have knowledge of all things God creates, including particulars.

Applied to the problem of good and evil, by rejecting the idea that God knows "particulars as particulars," it would seem that Gersonides ought to claim that the problem of why bad things happen to good people disappears, since God does not take notice of particular human activities. That Gersonides develops an elaborate system involving two types of providence suggests that his rejection of God's knowing "particulars as particulars" is not a complete rejection. Indeed, Husik places Gersonides' theodicy between the possibility that God knows "particulars as particulars" and God cannot know "particulars as particulars." God knows the universal order and knows the particulars insofar as they inhere in the universal order.[119]

In sum, Gersonides' work is not entirely "the fresh philosophical treatment" claimed by Feldman.[120] Certainly, though, it is a modification and expansion on Maimonides.

Crescas

Hasdai ben Abraham Crescas (1340–1410) was an intellectual irredentist who aimed to liberate Jewish thinking from the grip of Aristotelianism and Platonist thought and restore it to what he considered its purer ideas. His restorative project, a book he called *Or Adonai*, or *Light of the Lord*, takes issue with ibn Daud, Maimonides, and Gersonides.

Crescas does not differ from his predecessors on all matters. For instance, he sides with Maimonides against Gersonides on the matter of God's knowledge, asserting that God does know particulars as particulars.

To think otherwise would limit God's knowledge and thus stand opposed to the Bible.

Since God's knowledge is total and complete, God must know all the individual things God creates. In fact, to Crescas nature itself attests to this view. Plant and animal life and their respective powers of growth, movement, and reproduction reveal God's providence. That said, Crescas submits, God sometimes exercises providence directly and sometimes indirectly, through an intermediary. An example of the direct exercise of providence is God's role in redeeming the Israelites from Egypt. At other times and in other cases, God's providence may be effected through angels or prophets or even the heavenly bodies.

Crescas divides providence into different kinds. General providence governs all of nature, including all the various species of plants and animals, including human beings. General providence has nothing to do with a person's merits or demerits. General providence is entirely a function of the influence of the stars. The Jewish people enjoy special providence, a consequence of divine election. And, within the Jewish people, even more special providence obtains for males and even more so for the priests and Levites. Finally, individual providence is contingent on personal conduct, with rewards and punishments effected on the basis of each individual's actions, but with some qualifications: reward and punishment in the next world are entirely determined by conduct in this world, but reward and punishment in this world are not entirely so determined. This distinction helps explain why, in this world, the righteous sometimes suffer.

Still, asserting that this is the case does not explain why it is the case. There must be some reason that explains why the righteous undeservedly suffer.

Crescas rejects both Maimonides' and Gersonides' claims that evil emanates from imperfect matter. He further rejects the theories that material goods do not measure prosperity, that rewards are conferred on the basis of intellectual perfection, and that heavenly bodies influence good and evil. Crescas, instead, advocates a return to pure Rabbinic doctrine. God metes out reward and punishment on the basis of loyalty or disloyalty to God's commands. Though it appears that sometimes the righteous suffer while the wicked prosper, that seeming injustice will be recompensed in the afterlife. Further, the seeming injustices of this world are explained by redefining good and evil, or by inherited merits, or by evil as a regular phenomenon in the physical world—all traditional Rabbinic approaches.

With regard to resolving the problem of good and evil, Crescas's importance lies not in his originality, but in his staunch traditionalism and his anti-Aristotelianism, which served as a kind of restorative in medieval Jewish philosophy. Yet Crescas's theological recidivism only serves to reassert approaches characterized by their inherent weaknesses (as described in chapter 2).

Albo

> What is required of every person of faith in God to believe is that God supervises all people and notes the details of their conduct in order to reward and punish each person accordingly. This is fundamental to all divine faiths. . . . Yet what brings people into denial of providence . . . is the apparent violation of the expected order of the world in which the righteous should be rewarded and the wicked punished. This is what caused Job to doubt divine providence and think that there is no difference in treatment of those who do good and those who do evil. . . . It is very difficult [to think otherwise] when people see with their own eyes the profound evil committed by the wicked who worship idols, commit acts of sexual depravity, murder, commit violent and infamous crimes without the fear of God yet, nonetheless, they prosper.[121]

One can agree with Husik that Joseph Albo (1380–1444) was "of little importance as a philosopher,"[122] merely rehashing the ideas of Maimonides and Crescas, yet find within his principle work, *Sefer ha-Ikkarim* (Book of essential principles), new, if not novel, approaches to theodicy. It was Albo's contention that there are merely three principles fundamental to Judaism, namely, first, the existence of God; second, providence and reward and punishment; and third, revelation. Within his discussion of the second of the three principles, Albo addresses the problem of why the righteous suffer and the wicked prosper.

For Albo, the suffering of the righteous is less a problem than the prosperity of the wicked, "since everyone knows that there is no righteous man on the earth who does only good and never sins, whether much or a little. So if troubles afflict the righteous it is not strange for them since they will think that they committed some wrong unobserved."[123] An example of such a wrong, according to Albo, would be blasphemy or any sin related to thought.[124] To the observer, it would appear that the suffering is undeserved. But upon reflection, assigning the suffering to punishment for sin is plausible.[125]

The prosperity of the wicked is not so easily dismissed. Hence, Albo devotes an entire chapter for explanation.[126] Underlying the chapter as a whole (and a point to which Albo frequently returns) is the difficulty in assessing who is really righteous and who is really wicked. Unlike Sa'adiah, Albo implies that the criteria for making such a judgment are unclear. Of course, if convincing criteria are lacking for rendering a moral judgment on the status of the sufferer, the problem of theodicy is lessened if not eliminated. What one person may see as a mostly wicked person prospering, another may see as a partly righteous person being rewarded—and no one can know whether the wicked person has repented. Albo holds out the possibility that the problem may be one of identification rather than theology by adding the qualifier *rasha b'emet*—a *really* wicked person, as opposed to a presumably mostly wicked person.

Assuming that what the observer sees is actually the case, there are four reasons for the apparent prosperity of the wicked, according to Albo. First, the prosperity of the wicked may be subsumed under the blessings that an entire class of people is to enjoy. So, for instance, all Jews are to be blessed with peace, tranquility, and success. Isaiah foretells a time when "you shall be safe from oppression / And shall have no fear; / From ruin, and it shall not come near you" (Isa. 54:14). Jeremiah prophesies that the Israelites returning from exile will prosper: "Radiant . . . / Over new grain and wine and oil, / And over sheep and cattle. / They shall fare like a watered garden, / They shall never languish again" (Jer. 31:12). Micah (4:4) describes how "every man shall sit / Under his grapevine and fig tree / With no one to disturb him." These blessings accrue to all Jews, irrespective of the individual merits of any Jew.

Second, a wicked man may enjoy personal prosperity on account of some good he has done. Albo emphasizes that a just God cannot withhold reward for an act performed even though the same agent may have performed other despicable acts. Each act must be fairly requited on independent grounds. Albo further sees the reward the wicked receive for some noble act as a kind of punishment. The wicked will now see what they will be losing if they persist in their wickedness.

Third, the wicked may enjoy prosperity as an indirect consequence of affiliation. Albo gives several biblical examples. Jacob merited blessings. Laban grew wealthy on account of the blessings Jacob deserved. So even though Laban was wicked, he grew prosperous by way of his meritorious son-in-law. Similarly, the House of Potiphar thrived because of the blessings that Joseph deserved. Again, Lot was redeemed from captivity on the strength of the merits of Abraham. In each case, the ostensibly wicked prospered indirectly, not because of any merits of their own, but because of the merits of the righteous person with whom each was connected. In a like manner, the wicked may enjoy success through the merits of their righteous ancestors, or wicked parents may enjoy success through the merits of righteous children. The possibility also remains that the wicked man amasses much wealth in order to pass it on to his (righteous) son and the wicked man lives a long life in order to produce righteous offspring.

Fourth, Albo imagines that the prosperity of the wicked has a beneficial outcome on both the wicked and the righteous. The wicked, seeing themselves succeeding, obstinately refuse to change their ways and thus open themselves to the penalties imposed on those who fail to repent. To put it somewhat differently, the wicked enjoy gain now only to suffer more intense pain later. Alternatively, observers will reason that the only reason the righteous maintain their righteousness is out of fear of the punishment they would receive identical to the punishment the wicked receive. Since the wicked are seemingly not punished, the righteous persist in their righteousness out of love of God and love of the good rather than out of fear of punishment.

In focusing exclusively on the evils people commit against each other, Albo fails to offer a complete explanation of natural evil. But even with regard to moral evil, Albo's approach is less than compelling, arguing as he does in part that observers simply do not have all the facts. To do so requires suspending reliance on what one observes to be so for faith in what one can only hope to be so.

Yosef Ya'avetz

Rabbi Yosef Ya'avetz (d. 1507) was a victim of the expulsion from Spain in 1492 who was welcomed by the Jews of Mantua, Italy. Aside from serving as one of the leading rabbis of his generation, he was an exceptional scholar, preacher, and prolific writer. As a communal leader he was faced with the daunting task of providing some explanation for the event that ended a more than seven-hundred-year period of remarkable Jewish history. Being committed to the talmudic principle that there is no suffering without sin, Rabbi Ya'avetz was compelled to identify the sin that led to this catastrophe. Accordingly, he pioneered a strategy that will later characterize some Jewish respondents to the Holocaust.

In one of his books, *Or ha-Ḥayyim* (*The light of life* or *The living light*), he claims that while the exiles had mechanically studied Torah, they did not apply the teachings of Torah to their lives. He connects this claim with a variation on another talmudic concept. As noted earlier, the Talmud includes the statement that leaders who fail in reprimanding the sinners of their generation cause the entire generation to perish. Rabbi Ya'avetz argues that the leaders of the generation of the expulsion had such serious flaws that they were unable to protect them from God's wrath.[127]

Apart from the strategy of blaming the victim, Rabbi Ya'avetz proposes an alternative response to catastrophe:

> The Almighty, may He be blessed, has placed us in exile because He wishes to forgive our sins, thereby enabling us to maintain the yoke of His kingship over us. When He, may He be blessed, sees our strong love toward Him—that we bear so many hardships for the sake of His name with love—He will cover our sins and will fulfill His covenant with

us. . . . [God will say] just as they uphold My divinity, so will I uphold them. It turns out that exiles are the reason for the maintenance of our souls before God; and they are an absolute good.[128]

Exile, what any objective observer would adjudge to be evil, is actually a good. In fact, it is an "absolute good." For Rabbi Ya'avetz, exile is a trial. By enduring the trial of exile with equanimity—even with love—sins are forgiven and Israel's close relationship with God will be restored.

Rabbi Ya'avetz speaks only of a communal catastrophe. It is clear enough that his view also applies to individuals. The righteous person who suffers undergoes a trial through which his soul is purged, as it were, and his character is tempered, emerging the stronger in the end. But readers will be left wondering whether suffering is the only way to strengthen the character of innocents.

Summary

After the Rabbis had vastly expanded the range of solutions to the problem of human suffering, the medieval philosophers focused on a select few.

Fairness and Justice: Chief among the conceptions is the idea that God operates according to principles of fairness and justice. Therefore, God protects the innocent and punishes the wicked. If that does not seem to be true, it is not because of divine failing, but because of human misperception. This position is affirmed by Sa'adiah, confirmed by Maimonides, and reaffirmed by Gersonides.

The Nature of Good and Evil: Some medieval philosophers, like ibn Daud, Maimonides, and Gersonides, return to the idea of the cosmological origins of evil, an idea introduced in Genesis but later set aside in favor of concentrating on moral evil. Maimonides and Gersonides consider the imperfection of matter as the source of evil in the universe. Further, ibn Daud, followed by Maimonides, introduces the concept of "privations" as another way of explaining the existence of evil.

Questions of Justice: Sa'adiah, Baḥya, and Ya'avetz champion the idea that the innocent suffer trials or setbacks that benefit them: gaining greater reward in the afterlife, absolving them from sin, or receiving moral instruction that improves character. Sa'adiah also sees the afterlife as a remedy for the injustices perceived in this life, a position Maimonides rejects. Sa'adiah, Maimonides, Gersonides, and Albo take the approach that God's justice is faultless provided that people correctly identify "righteous" and "wicked," "good" and "evil." These thinkers adopt and expand the talmudic defense of God's justice on semantic grounds. Baḥya resists surrendering the notion of the evil inclination and chastisements of love, though they do not appear in the repertoire of other philosophers of this period. Baḥya also adds a new idea: whatever suffering a person endures, it is most certainly less than what that person should receive. Such is the compassion of God. Gersonides also adds a new dimension to the problem by proposing two kinds of providence, with the loosening of personal providence as an explanation of individual suffering.

Hence, the medieval period was a time for both contraction and expansion of the problem of good and evil.

CHAPTER 4

Kabbalah and the Problem of Evil

Some scholars consider the phenomenon of mysticism too complex to define.[1] However, one could argue that it is less important to define mysticism than to understand its function. Almost all religions begin with some epiphanic experience whereby an individual or a group feels a direct, personal, intimate, and transformative encounter with the Divine. The spellbinding effect of the experience is aptly expressed by the chronicler, who urges the affected to "seek his presence constantly" (1 Chron. 16:11). Yet two phenomena conspire against that possibility, expelling the newly inspired individual or group from the sublime, heavenly domain and into the earthly domain: time and the exigencies of life. Over the passage of time, the initial transcendent experience dissipates, remaining only a memory. And the quotidian activities of daily living absorb so much attention, they leave little space for the spiritual.

Religion introduces a regimen or praxis intended to recapture that peak experience by legislating moments for spiritual engagement as well as imbuing the mundane activities of daily life with divine significance. Religious practice is not introduced willy-nilly; it is introduced thoughtfully and gradually. Yet the more formalized and institutionalized the regimen becomes, the more distant adherents feel from the Divine. To put it somewhat differently, the greater the emphasis placed on rituals and the more detailed they are, the more mechanical and the less inspiring rituals tend to become. Thus, ironically, the organized efforts to retain a sense of communion with the Divine thwart the very achievement of that goal. Mysticism is the attempt to bridge the gap between formalized religion and the initial experience upon which that religion is based.

Jewish mysticism falls into this schema. The events at Sinai were transformative. But even after encountering God, the Israelites still had to cook dinner. And after Sinai, that dinner had to be kosher. From Sinai forward, Israelites and then Jews were preoccupied with which animals to eat, how they were to be slaughtered and prepared, what other foods could be eaten in tandem, and what needed to happen if some accidental admixture occurred. The descendants of those who stood at Sinai inherited the worry over "pots and spoons" but were disconnected from the communion with God experienced by their ancestors. Not just in matters of diet but in all areas of life, laws grew in number and complexity, while the initial experience of the Divine upon which all the laws were intended to preserve grew historically distant and spiritually remote. As the historian of mysticism Joseph Dan puts it, "Jewish religious law seemed to decide one's level of religious attainment solely on one's physical and bodily behavior, and not on any spiritual element."[2] Thus, to paraphrase Gershom Scholem, over time Judaism came perilously close to losing the living God. Kabbalah—Jewish mysticism—set out to preserve God.[3]

To express in words the substance of an inner, mysterious experience,[4] mysticism resorts to the use of highly imaginative, evocative, symbolic, ambiguous, and sometimes erotic language. Even then, any clear and accurate communication is useless. Likewise, logic is inapplicable, since mysticism ventures into the hidden, unknown, and indescribable realm. The truth is beyond verbal expression. At best, mystics can provide only a vague and incomplete picture of reality. Mysticism includes, in part, a return to the mythical lore characteristic of biblical and Apocryphal literature.

Mystics also introduced deeply theosophical layers into the rational writings of Jewish philosophers, initiating new terms in the process. For instance, mystics refer to God as *Ein Sof*. This is not to say that God ought to be described as the "Infinite One" or the "Unlimited One," as the term can be conceived, because the essence of the Divine defies human description. In essence the term holds no particular significance; it is equivalent to a mathematical variable. *Ein Sof* is thus a placeholder suggesting something far beyond what might be expressed through human language. However it is to be understood, mystics maintain that the supreme Godhead is both the source of all things and essentially unknowable. Further, contact with the *Ein Sof* is unattainable, no matter the mystic's efforts.

Elements of Kabbalah are traceable to the Apocrypha and mysterious passages in the Bible, like Ezekiel 1, which describes a four-sided chariot (*merkavah*), and Isaiah 6, which describes God's heavenly throne room (*hekhal*). According to 2 Esdras 15:45–46, seventy books of esoteric knowledge remain hidden, accessible only to the initiates. The book of Enoch describes the angels and demons insinuated in the creation of the world. The book of Jubilees describes the four classes of angels who preside over Creation and the phenomenon of fallen angels. Both Enoch and Jubilees discuss the primal elements necessary for cosmogony, all of which are strikingly different from those in the Genesis account. *Sefer Hekhalot*, also known as 3 Enoch or the Hebrew book of Enoch, introduces Metatron, initially a human being encountered by Rabbi Yishmael in his ascension to the celestial world. Metatron seems to be a rival of God, raising the thorny problem of demiurgic dualism, two competing divine powers. Scholem disputes this understanding of the nature of Metatron.[5] But if it is correct, then an early kabbalistic source offers an explanation of the existence of evil in the world that resembles Gnostic mythology: evil is the work of Metatron, not God.

Mystical knowledge is esoteric. Mystical knowledge was controversial. Mystical knowledge was also dangerous. Ben Sira (3:22) warns against having any business with "secret things." The Rabbis of the Mishnah forbade such teachings in public or to the non-adept.[6] Even scholars are not protected from the perils of mystical pursuits. Of the four sages who engaged in such speculations, Ben Azzai died, Ben Zoma went insane, and Rabbi Elisha ben Abuya became a heretic. Only Rabbi Akiva emerged unscathed.[7]

Because of the dangers associated with mystical knowledge, the guarded attitude mystics took toward the tradition they received (Kabbalah), and the controversial mythology of mystical speculation, much of mysticism went underground for some eleven centuries. It only resurfaced in the thirteenth century, under the influence of German Jewish pietism and asceticism and in reaction to the tribulations following the Crusades. And when it reemerged, the question of the origin and nature of evil became a principal concern.

Sefer Yetzirah

The earliest surviving book devoted entirely to hidden knowledge is the compact *Sefer Yetzirah*, best translated as *The Book of Formation*. Both authorship and date are uncertain. Some have ascribed its origin to the patriarch Abraham, others to Rabbi Akiva.[8] It was already widely known in tenth-century Italy.[9]

If the account in the Talmud is accepted as fact, *Sefer Yetzirah* served as the instruction manual for the creation of life.[10] Even if the talmudic account is deemed fanciful, *Sefer Yetzirah* was important enough for ninth-century Sa'adiah Gaon to write a commentary on it. But it was the thirteenth-century commentary of Rabbi Yitzḥak ben Ya'akov ha-Kohen that transformed the text into a kabbalistic classic.

Sefer Yetzirah introduces the concept of *sefirot*, or emanations, which will later become a given in kabbalistic literature. Ostensibly a mystical commentary on the Hebrew word *m'saprim* as it appears in Psalm 19:2 ("The heavens declare [*m'saprim*] the glory of God"), *Sefer Yetzirah* begins with the declamation:

In thirty-two mysterious Paths of Wisdom did Jah, the Jehovah of hosts, the God of Israel, the Living Elohim, the King of ages, the merciful and gracious God, the Exalted One, the Dweller in eternity, most high and holy—engrave his name by the three Sepharim—Numbers,[11] Letters, and Sounds. Ten are the ineffable Sephiroth.[12]

The text continues:

The Ten ineffable Sephiroth have ten vast regions bound unto them; boundless in origin and having no ending; an abyss of good and of ill;

measureless height and depth; boundless to the East and the West; boundless to the North and South; and the Lord the only God, the Faithful King rules all these from his holy seat, for ever and ever.[13]

Out of these ten *sefirot* come the ten numbers, the first of which is "the Spirit of the God of the living,"[14] from which the elements of air, water, fire, height, depth, east, west, south, and north proceed.[15] As Rabbi Yitzḥak ben Ya'akov understands it, all of creation is the process of emanation or outflow from the ten divine attributes.

The concept of emanations (*atzilut*, in Hebrew) is predicated on the idea that all things necessarily and automatically descend from an immutable primary source. The further downward a secondary thing is from the primary and perfect source, the more flawed it must be. As a concept, emanations debut in the Apocryphal work the Wisdom of Solomon, in which, under Hellenistic influence, the author describes wisdom as "the breath of the power of God and a pure influence flowing [*aporrhia*, in Greek] from the glory of the Almighty." Philo of Alexandria, building on the Neoplatonist system, talks of the flow from the One to all beneath it, or from the Nous (Intellect) to the Logos (word).

Gnostics developed this Neoplatonist idea into a mature mythology. To the Gnostics, the material world is the consequence of a primordial mistake. Atop the cosmic hierarchy, called the pleroma, sits the One Beyond Being, the supreme God. The pleroma, meaning "fullness," is much like the "boundless abyss" mentioned in *Sefer Yetzirah*. A series of emanations or *aeons* ensues. The final emanation is Sophia (wisdom), also known as Logos. Sophia is hypostatized as a kind of supra-cosmic being. Sophia's pretentious and careless quest to "know" the transcendent God leads to the appearance of the Demiurge, an ignorant but powerful creature who creates the material world and proclaims himself to be its master. The Demiurge is responsible for all the imperfections in the earthly world.

Even without accepting the dualistic system of the Gnostics, who ascribe evil to a power separate from God, the concept of emanations ineluctably leads to the advent of evil. Consider an analogy to radiating heat. Radiating heat dissipates over distance even if the heat source is constant. As a person moves farther and farther from a heat source, the colder that person becomes. At some point that person will not feel any heat at all and will suffer from cold. Similarly, at some downward point along the course of emanations, a person will be so remote from the primary source that the influence of that primary source will no longer be felt. Evil, therefore, is the inevitable outcome of the distancing of a creature from God as a result of the process of emanations.

This concept of emanations premieres in *Sefer Yetzirah* as enlarged by Rabbi Yitzḥak ben Ya'akov and becomes the standard of thirteenth-century Kabbalah. Thus, for example, the unknown author of a little known but important kabbalistic work of the late thirteenth century, *Ma'arekhet ha-Elohut*, argues that evil has no objective reality. The origin of evil is humanity's inability to adequately receive all the influx from the *sefirot*.

Rabbi Yitzḥak ben Ya'akov ha-Kohen, Sagi Hahor (the Blind)

In the second half of the thirteenth century, Rabbi Yitzḥak ben Ya'akov ha-Kohen (precise dates unknown) wrote *A Treatise on the Left Emanation*, the "left emanation" being a synonym for evil. The book is now recognized for a number of "firsts." It is the first comprehensive kabbalistic presentation on the concept of evil. It is also the first datable Jewish work in which the evil angel Samael and the mythological demon Lilith are described as husband and wife, united in the realm of satanic power.[16]

Rabbi Yitzḥak accounts for evil in three different ways, or in one way but in three stages. At the outset, he invokes the myth of the destroyed worlds. These worlds existed prior to our own but could not endure. From a "curtain" below the third emanation in the system of *sefirot*, the first evil powers emerged. The three excessively evil worlds that resulted were destroyed by means of reverse emanation. The currently existing world endures despite the evil embedded in it because, unlike the prior worlds that were totally evil, the evil in the existing world is moderated by some measures of goodness.

In chapter 6 Rabbi Yitzḥak explains:

The reason which evokes hatred and jealousy between the heavenly powers and the powers of the supreme host is one form that is destined for Samael, and it is Lilith, and it has the image of a feminine form, and Samael is in the form of Adam and Lilith in the form of Eve. Both of them were born in spiritual birth as one, similar to the form of Adam and Eve, like two pairs of twins, one above and one below. Samael and the Eve the Elder, which is called the Northern one, they are emanated from below the Throne of Glory, and this was caused by the Sin.[17]

The disastrous "Sin" is that of Adam and Eve in the Garden of Eden, which caused the sexual "awakening" among the two pairs of twins, Samael and Lilith above and Adam and Eve below, in which the serpent as the tempter took part. As a result, Evil came into the world, symbolized by the virulent serpent. Samael is also identified as "the Great Demon" who sexually defiles Lilith (Eve the Elder).

In chapter 19 Rabbi Yitzḥak details the struggles between Asmodeus and Samael over the younger Lilith, which resulted in Asmodeus's victory, his union with the younger Lilith, and the ensuing birth of eighty thousand destructive demons, with their leader Alpafonias, "whose face burns like fire," ruling over them. Rabbi Yitzḥak concludes the chapter with a teaching he calls "a wonderful, unknown thing":

Evil Samael and Wicked Lilith are like a sexual pair, who . . . receive an emanation of wickedness, one from the other, and emanate it onwards. I shall explain this relying on the esoteric meaning of the verse (Isa. 27:1): "In that day the Lord will punish, / With His great, cruel, mighty sword / Leviathan, the Elusive Serpent— / Leviathan, the Twisting Serpent"—meaning Lilith—"He will slay the Dragon of the sea." As there is a pure leviathan in the sea and he is called a serpent, so there is a great impure serpent in the sea, in the usual sense of the term. And it is the same above [in the divine world], in a secret way. And the heavenly serpent is a blind prince, who is like an intermediary between Samael and Lilith, and his name is Tanin-iver (Blind Serpent) . . . and he is the one who brings about the union between Samael and Lilith.

If he were created in the fullness of his emanation he would have destroyed the whole world in one moment.[18]

Evil enters the world through the process of emanations, possibly triggered by human sin. But evil will not persist. From the same process that produced Alpafonias, the evil destroyer, another prince, Meshiḥiel, was born. At the time of God's choosing, this messianic savior will unsheathe his sword and destroy evil.

Mystical texts were not intended to be held up to analytical scrutiny. Thus there is no point in trying to tease out the differences between the various accounts or to reconcile them. What does emerge, however, is a description of all existence in terms of the struggle between antagonistic powers: Asmodeus and Samael, the Older Lilith and the Younger Lilith, the destructive power of Alpafonias and the redemptive power of Meshiḥiel. These pairs remain in continuous conflict. Rabbi Yitzḥak's stark dualism and demonological mythology are vehicles to express two fundamental themes: one descriptive and the other apocalyptic. Evil is an integral part of the world humanity inhabits, and yet it can — and will — be overcome.

Sefer ha-Bahir

The most influential kabbalistic works of the thirteenth century, by far, are Sefer ha-Bahir[19] and the Zohar.[20] Sefer ha-Bahir — translated as The luminous book, The book of illumination, or The book of brilliance — simulates a midrashic commentary on the opening chapters of the book of Genesis that describe Creation. The name of the book might be derived from Job 37:21, "And now they do not see the light, it is brilliant in the skies." The text spread from southern France at the beginning of the thirteenth century. Scholem identifies it as the first work to contain kabbalistic symbolism.

It contained short paragraphs, presented as a dialogue between master and disciples, filled with many enigmatic parables. Neither the original manuscript nor the subsequent printed editions had any systematic divisions, so in his translation, Scholem arranged the book into 130 sections.[21]

The author attributes Creation to a combination of matter and spirit. The divine pleroma is conceived as a tree with ten branches, one below the other. The ten *sefirot* as understood in classical Kabbalah are presented here for the first time. Also for the first time the *Bahir* (as *Sefer ha-Bahir* is also known) portrays the *Shekhinah* as *bat ha-or*, "the daughter of light,"[22] in exile from the source of light, but nonetheless a feminine divine power, setting the scene for the sexual symbolism characteristic of later Kabbalah.

Section 161 presents a myth in which the *Sefer ha-Bahir*'s theory of evil is subsumed. Along the route of the Exodus from Egypt, Moses and the people Israel reach Marah but are unable to drink the bitter waters (Exod. 15:23). God shows Moses a tree that, when put in the water, makes the water potable. The *Bahir* explains that the tree of this episode is none other than the Tree of Life of Genesis, removed by Satan and hidden away. Absent the presence of the Tree of Life and any life-sustaining water, the people would be led to sin, and God would have no recourse but to destroy them. But God shows Moses the tree, foiling Satan's plans. The warning that follows (Exod. 15:26) is a warning not to be deceived by Satan, a point reinforced by a parable that begins section 162:

> What is this like? A king had a beautiful daughter, and others desired her. The king knew about it but could not fight those who wanted to bring his daughter to evil ways. He came to his house and warned her, saying, "My daughter, do not pay attention to the words of these enemies and they will not be able to overcome you. Do not leave the house, but do all your work at home. Do not sit idle, even for a single moment. Then they will not be able to see you and harm you."

The grand message is a worthy one: evil can be avoided with due diligence. However, portraying Satan as a force independent of God and at odds with God would situate this book within the problematic Gnostic tradition. So *Bahir* retreats. Satan is not an independent force of evil but an attribute of God:

> The Blessed Holy One has an attribute whose name is Evil. It is to the north of the Blessed Holy One, as it is written (Jer. 1:14), "From the

north will Evil come forth, upon all the inhabitants of the earth." Any evil that comes to all the inhabitants of the earth comes from the north.

Historically, any invader would have to assault Jerusalem from the north, since the city is otherwise geographically secure. Hence, the "north" symbolizes evil forces that aim at the destruction of Israel and, by extension, all evil and destructive powers in the world. According to *Bahir*, it is God who creates a universe in which evil serves God's divine plan. These evils in the created world are described as the hand of God, called "evil evil" (*ra' ra'*), with the fingers symbolizing the variety of ways ("messengers") in which evil is manifest in the created world. To cement the idea that these evils are subordinate to God, *Bahir* links evils to the left hand of God. Given that most people are right-handed, the left hand symbolizes the weaker hand:

And why is it placed to the left? This is because it does not have any authority any place in the world except in the north.

Evil is real but its power is limited. It can enter only where people allow it:

This is the meaning of the verse (Gen. 8:21), "Since the devisings of man's mind are evil from his youth." It is evil from his youth, and it does not incline [in any direction] other than the left, for it is already accustomed to be there. It is regarding this that the Blessed Holy One said to Israel (Exod. 15:26), "If you heed the Lord your God diligently, doing what is upright in His sight, giving ear to His commandments" — and not to the commandments of the Evil Urge — "and keeping all His laws" — and not the decrees of the Evil Urge — "[then I will not bring upon you any of the diseases that I brought upon the Egyptians] for I the Lord am your healer."

The lure of evil can be overcome by the faithful who would then enjoy God's protection. And by overcoming evil, people are made stronger. This message is conveyed in section 164 through *Bahir*'s application of the parable of a royal clerk who sends messengers to tear down weak houses in order that they be replaced with stone.

Human confrontation with evil is inescapable, since evil is inherent in Creation. Near the outset of *Sefer ha-Bahir* the author explicates the verse in Ecclesiastes (7:14) to mean that Creation can be described as a series of antinomies: "One opposite the other was created by God." Principal among them is *tohu va-vohu*. Evil derives from *tohu* (chaos) and peace encompasses *vohu* (desolation).[23] The existence of evil is embedded in the architecture of Creation, and its lure is tantalizing. It is not surprising, then, that humanity would be drawn to evil. What is surprising is the penalty for succumbing to evil.

Sefer ha-Bahir postulates that the souls of every new generation are those of the previous one:

> "The Lord shall reign forever, your God, O Zion, from generation to generation" (Ps. 146:10). What does "from generation to generation" mean? Rabbi Pappias said: It is written: "A generation goes and a generation comes" (Eccles. 1:4). Rabbi Akiva said: [The meaning of "a generation goes and a generation comes" is that] it has already come.

In this passage, *Sefer ha-Bahir* introduces the concept of the transmigration of souls. As Joseph Dan notes, the concept is introduced "without any qualification or hesitation, as a well-known traditionally accepted truth."[24] However, this is the first appearance of the concept in all of Jewish literature.[25] It is a process through which the soiled souls of the dead are purged and returned to new bodies. The operative parable appears in section 122:

> What is this like? A king had slaves, and he dressed them with garments of silk and satin according to his ability. The relationship broke down, and he cast them out, repelled them, and took his garments away from them. They then went on their own way. The king took the garments and washed them well until there was not a single spot on them. He

placed them with his storekeepers, bought other slaves, and dressed them with the same garments. He did not know whether or not the slaves were good, but they were [at least] worthy of garments that he already had and which had been previously worn.

The consequence of the transmigration of souls does not emerge until section 195:

Why is it that one righteous person prospers and [another] righteous person suffers? This is because the [second] righteous person was wicked previously and is now being punished.

In ordinary circumstances, the righteous should prosper. God rewards the righteous and punishes the wicked. So observing a righteous person who suffers is both contrary to theological expectations and a challenge to the goodness of God. Since souls are replanted in new bodies, the solution is obvious. The righteous person who suffers is suffering for sins committed by his soul while inhabiting a previous body. The *Bahir* employs an apt metaphor to explain the "replanting" of used souls in new bodies in the name of a certain unidentified Rabbi Rahumai:

What is this like? A person planted a vineyard and hoped to grow grapes, but instead, sour grapes grew. He saw that his planting and harvest were not successful so he tore it out. He cleaned out the sour grape vines and planted again. When he saw that his planting was not successful, he tore it up and planted it again.

Based on Psalm 105:8, *Sefer ha-Bahir* concedes the replanting could continue for a thousand generations! Moral evil, it seems, is punished over successive transmigrations over extended time. Thus, what appears to be a theological challenge is actually a just resolution. The apparently good and decent person suffering unfairly is, in reality, a body punished for the earlier evil committed by the soul now inhabiting its current body.

The uninformed observer witnesses a terrible injustice, but the kabbalist knows otherwise.

Presumably, the inverse is also true, although it is nowhere stated explicitly in the *Bahir*. The apparently wicked person who seems to prosper is enjoying prosperity on the merits of reward due the soul in an earlier life.

Zohar

The highly regarded authority on mysticism Arthur Green calls the Zohar "one of the most important bodies of religious texts of all times and places."[26] It presents as a commentary on the Torah following the standard Torah-reading cycle but, according to Green, is best described as "a work of sacred fantasy"[27] and "the highest expression of Jewish literary imagination in the Middle Ages."[28]

The name of this compendium of esoteric knowledge derives from the book of Daniel (12:3) in which Daniel's eschatological vision includes a prediction of the revival of the worthy who have died yet "will be radiant like the bright [*zohar*] expanse of sky." The text made its debut in Castile, Spain, toward the end of the thirteenth century. Even though it has been ascribed to Rabbi Shimon bar Yoḥai,[29] a somewhat mysterious recluse of the second century CE, scholars are convinced that it could not have been authored any earlier than the end of the thirteenth century, since it refers to events in the years following 1270.[30]

Scholem emphasizes that "the Zohar supplies no completely unequivocal answer" for the metaphysical cause of evil.[31] Even so, its various approaches to the existence of evil are valuable. For instance, one passage advances the notion that what is perceived as evil is all part of God's plan and, as such, must be accepted:

It is written that "God saw all that He had made, and behold it was very good" (Gen. 1:31), even serpents and scorpions, and fleas, and all things that appear to be pests—all of these are for the service of the world, though men know it not.[32]

Here, the zoharic text addresses the question arising from the Torah's unqualified declaration that all that God created is "very good." Does this include the creatures that harm us, from the dangerous to the annoying? From the human perspective these creatures are not good at all! Anticipating this question, the text responds that all creatures, including the annoying and dangerous ones, serve God's purpose. The problem is not with these creatures. The problem is with human perception. To illustrate, the text proceeds:

> As they went along, they saw a snake crawling in front of them. Said Rabbi Shimon, Assuredly this creature is there to perform some miracle for us. The snake quickly crept in front of them and wound itself around a basilisk in the middle of the path. They then struggled until both were killed. When they came up to them they found them lying dead in the road and Rabbi Shimon said, "Blessed be God for performing for us this miracle, for if anyone had looked upon this creature while it was alive, or had been looked upon by it, he would not have escaped harm, much less if he had approached it. Thus God makes all things His agents and we must not revile anything that He has made."

Like many passages in the Zohar, this passage includes fantastical elements. It presumes the existence of a reptilian creature whose powers exceed those of the mythical Greek gorgon. It is not just the case that any that look at it will die (in the gorgon's case it means being turned to stone); it is also the case that any that the basilisk looks upon will die. The contingent of Rabbis Elazar, Abba, Ḥiyya, Yosi, and Yehudah feel endangered by a venomous snake that lies in their path, but Rabbi Shimon assures them there is nothing to fear: the snake is there in God's service, intended not to cause them harm but to protect them from harm. And such turns out to be the case. A double threat is averted: the threat from both the snake and the basilisk. The stated lesson is that even deadly snakes are "very good." The implication is that a presumed evil may, in fact, be a power for good. And this "evil" comes from God.

Thus in Zohar, Yitro 68, the text asserts that "everything is formed according to a divine pattern and therefore is of some necessity."[33] And in a remarkably familiar scenario, the text relates:

Rabbi Elazar was walking along accompanied by Rabbi Hezekiah when they came across a snake. Rabbi Hezekiah was about to kill it, but Rabbi Eleazar said, "Nay, leave it alone, do not kill it!" Said Rabbi Hezekiah to him, "But is it not a noxious creature that kills people?" to which Rabbi Elazar replied, "It is written: 'If the snake bites because no spell was uttered?'" (Eccles. 10:11). The serpent does not bite unless it be whispered from above and commanded to kill someone, so as to prevent that person from committing some evil; thus the very poison is used by the Holy One in order to perform some miracle. It is, in truth, all in His hands; it is all according to His plan, and if it had no purpose He would not have created it.

Killing the venomous snake would interfere with God's plan. God instructs each creature to carry out specific functions that are necessary for God's grand design. Without knowledge of the grand design, humanity often judges right and wrong or good or bad on the basis of what is subjectively good for those affected. But that would be a mistake. Whatever humanity might adjudge to be "evil" is none other than a necessary part in the fulfillment of God's plan.

Also embedded in this larger idea is the remarkable notion that the death of a person by a poisonous snake is a form of divine intervention, the fatal snakebite being a way to prevent the perpetration of evil by the victim. It is unclear whether all deaths by any means are to be understood as God acting preemptively to thwart would-be evildoers in similar fashion. The passage goes on to reiterate that "it is wrong to despise anything in the world," since everything is in service to God, the proof text being that everything is "very good."

Summing up, the passage ends with this affirmation:

In His creation all are united, above and below, the "Right Side" and the "Left Side," the angel of life and the angel of death: all are a part of His plan, and it is "very good"; it is all part of the same mystic doctrine, apprehended by those who contemplate the mystery of wisdom.

The mystic becomes aware of what the non-mystic cannot grasp: evil, in reality, is not a challenge to God's justice but a manifestation of it. The created world is a harmony of good and evil. That sounds paradoxical, but to the mystic it is eminently plausible. In fact, "there can be no true good unless it proceeds from evil."[34] The perfection of all things first requires a "commingling" of good and evil and then the materialization of good out of evil.[35] Applied to human conduct, God is most glorified when a person enters upon an evil way and then forsakes it. Without the possibility of choosing to act wickedly, human beings cannot attain nobility.

In this context another passage becomes clear. The Torah commands the love of God with all one's possessions (Deut. 6:5), which the Zohar takes to mean with all aspects of one's faculties, including the evil inclination. This in turn raises the immediate question of how it is possible to love God with something evil:

> The answer lies in this, that there can be no greater service done to the Holy One than to bring into subjugation the "evil inclination" by the power of love to the Holy One, blessed be He. For, when it is subdued and its power broken by man in this way, then he becomes a true lover of the Holy One, since he has learnt how to make the "evil inclination" itself serve the Holy One.[36]

Evil, in the form of a psychological disposition, must necessarily exist so humanity can demonstrate an unimpeachable love of God by overcoming it. The self-actualization of human character is possible only when confronted by temptations to resist. Or, as Scholem puts it, since God wants humanity to morally excel, God "ordained the real existence of evil, that he might prove his moral strength in overcoming it."[37] Evil, then—or better, the response to evil—is a test of human character. The possibility of overcoming the evil inclination and the means for doing so are thus recurrent zoharic themes.[38]

As to why innocents suffer, one particular passage in the Zohar offers a relatively lengthy and novel explanation. Based on the verse in Ecclesiastes 4:1, the author imagines the wise King Solomon examining the nature of the kinds of suffering for which no comfort is possible. The author asserts that King Solomon must be referring to babies, "sucklings snatched away from their mothers' breasts."[39] They are "oppressed from all sides: oppressed above in the celestial regions, and oppressed on the earth below."[40] The author surmises that these babies are the product of inherited sin:

> "Visiting the guilt of the parents upon the children, upon the third and upon the fourth generations" (Exod. 20:5). How is this? King Solomon loudly gives the answer when he says, "A man oppressed by bloodguilt will flee to a pit; / Let no one give him support" (Prov. 28:17). Since he is "oppressed with the blood of a soul" (i.e., he has committed some grievous sin), either he or his son or his son's son will be "oppressed" (i.e., wronged) in the "balance"; he shall flee to the pit away from righteousness and none shall stay him; because he has oppressed the blood of the soul he shall himself be oppressed by the other side, or his seed shall bear his oppression of retribution for him on his account.

When a person commits a grave and severe sin, one of two things may occur. Either the sinner may suffer punishment at the hands of the Other Side or, alternatively, the descendants of the sinner may be punished. The author offers no clue about when or why each possibility might apply, though the implication is that if an innocent child is suffering unfairly, it must be due to some grave sin committed by an ancestor for which the child is paying the price. This implication fits the contextual meaning of Exodus 20:5 but flies in the face of the standard talmudic[41] explanation that both Jeremiah (31:29–30) and Ezekiel (18:1–4,20) repudiate the doctrine of inherited sin. The thorny nature of the problem of the suffering of innocents seems to result in the Zohar's resuscitation of the earlier, popular view.[42]

Among the specific classes of babies destined to suffer are children born of an adulterous union. They are—applying the language of Ecclesiastes 4:1—"made" to suffer. The Zohar then gives King Solomon's reaction:

> Solomon reflected on this and said, "I consider the fate of these hapless oppressed ones who have been 'made,' how they shed tears before the Holy One. They complain before Him and make moan, saying, 'When a person commits a sin[43] he must assuredly die. But, Sovereign of the universe, when a child is but one day old, shall he be judged?'"

As wise as Solomon may be, here he is depicted as just as perplexed as lesser intellects with why newborns suffer. While there are grounds to accept the punishment of adults, as severe as those might be, no grounds can justify the suffering or death of a child who has neither legal responsibility nor life experience. Similarly, the *mamzer* (a child of an incestuous or adulterous affair) is consigned to a life "separated from the community of the holy people"[44] despite the fact that he has not committed any sin. Hence he legitimately complains as an adult, "Lord of the world! If my parents have sinned, wherein is my guilt? I have ever striven to do only good works before Thee."[45] The pain that accompanies this complaint cannot be comforted.

Worse than this, however, are the tears of "the sucklings removed from their mothers' breasts." The author admits that the suffering of babies "causes the whole world to weep . . . and say . . . why is it necessary that these poor little ones, who are blameless and without sin, should die? Where is now the true and righteous judgment of the Lord of the world?"[46] Here we find a sympathetic and compelling articulation of the problem of theodicy.

The remarkable zoharic response follows:

> The actual fact is that the tears of these "oppressed ones" intercede for and protect the living, and because of their innocence and the power

of their intercession a place is eventually prepared for them such as even the perfect righteous cannot attain or occupy; for the Holy One does in truth love them with a special and particular love, He unites himself with them, and prepares for them a supernal place, very near to Himself.

The Zohar advances a doctrine of redemptive suffering whereby the sufferer endures the ordeal for the greater benefit of others. In this case, innocent babies suffer for the good of humanity. The power that resides in their tears born of suffering is sufficient to protect others in two useful ways: first, humanity itself is protected by virtue of the potency of innocent tears; and second, the innocents who suffer receive a special reward in the afterlife by way of communion with and proximity to God. This second reward is nonpareil: not even the perfectly righteous can attain it. In answer to the question of why do innocents suffer, this passage would respond by emphasizing the first reward: so that humanity is redeemed. Apparently, the remarkably christological notion that an individual suffers and dies for humanity and ultimately ascends to a revered place with God does not disturb the zoharic author.

A variant of this doctrine appears in another passage:

> When God desires to give healing to the world He smites one righteous man among them with disease and suffering, and through him gives healing to all, as it is written, "But he was wounded for our transgressions, he was bruised for our iniquities . . . and with his stripe we are healed" (Isa. 53:5). A righteous man is never afflicted save to bring healing to his generation and to make atonement for it, for the "other side" prefers that punishment should light upon a virtuous man rather than on any other, for then it cares not for the whole world on account of the joy it finds in having power over him.[47]

Here again the Zohar claims that the vicarious suffering of one righteous man allows the entire ailing world to be healed. Notably, in this passage it is not God but the *sitra aḥra* (the other side) that is responsible for suffering and takes delight in the fact that the suffering of the righteous thwarts what ought to be expected. But if the *sitra aḥra* takes delight in the suffering of the righteous and has the power to impose it, why not make all righteous men suffer? For it is clear to any observer that "we see a righteous man in one place who is sick and suffering, and a righteous man in another who enjoys all the good things of the world."[48] The Zohar explains the seeming contradiction:

> One or two of them is enough, since God does not desire to smite all of them, just as it is sufficient to let blood from one arm; only if the sickness becomes very severe is it necessary to let blood from two arms, and so here, if the world becomes very sinful all the virtuous are smitten to heal all the generation, but otherwise one is smitten and the rest are left in peace.[49]

Ordinarily, God allows for the suffering of one or two righteous individuals in order to heal the world. Only in the rare case when the world is suffused with evil will God sanction the suffering of all the righteous for the salvation of the generation, just as only in extreme cases would a physician apply excessive bloodletting.

As for the righteous selected for suffering, this zoharic passage ends with an addendum:

> When the people are healed the righteous are healed with them, but sometimes all of their days are passed in suffering to protect the people, and when they die all are healed.[50]

Should the vicarious suffering of the righteous result in the rehabilitation of humanity, the righteous should be healed as well. But not always. It may be necessary for the righteous to suffer prophylactically until their death in order to protect humanity.

Alternatively, a righteous person who dies prematurely is compensated by way of the merits borrowed from the wicked.

We have learnt that the good deeds which a man does in this world fashion for him a precious and noble garment wherewith to cover himself. Now when a man has laid up a store of good deeds and then falls into evil ways, if God observes that his bad ways outweigh the good and that he is wicked enough to regret all the good deeds that he did at first, then he is entirely lost in both this world and in the other. What then does God do with the good deeds he performed at first? For though the wicked sinner perishes, the good deeds that he performed do not perish. If, then, there is a righteous man who walks in the ways of the King and is preparing his garment from his works, but before he has completed it he departs from this world, God completes it from the deeds which have been lost to that wicked sinner for him to array himself therewith in the other world.[51]

Each person is recompensed after death in accordance with the good deeds and wicked deeds performed while alive. Consequently, a person who has accumulated an abundance of good deeds will be rewarded. This is the simplest case. In the case where a person has accumulated a substantial number of good deeds but then turns wicked, that person would suffer in this world and in the next, presumably with oblivion. Nevertheless, the accumulated good deeds live on as if they have an existence independent of the agent who performed them. God retrieves and rewards those surviving good deeds to the righteous who died before they had "earned" a sufficient number of "credits" to gain reward in the hereafter. And so, to the observer who worries about the unjust suffering and death of the righteous, the Zohar would offer the reassurance that the righteous will be rewarded in the afterlife and the reward shall come at the expense of the wicked—an original twist on a Rabbinic idea.

From these passages, the zoharic approach to the suffering of innocents can thus be summarized as follows: Innocents suffer as a result of inherited sin. But through their suffering and in their sad predicament the rest of humanity benefits. Ultimately, the innocents themselves are rewarded for their suffering. Similarly, the righteous suffer for the benefit of others in their generation. Usually, the number of righteous people who suffer at any given time is limited to one or two. But at times when humanity is inordinately sinful, all righteous people may suffer. The suffering of the righteous will generally abate when goodness is restored to the world. However, there is an exception to the rule. Sometimes the suffering of the righteous persists so as to keep humanity protected from punishment. The righteous may also rest assured that their final disposition will be facilitated through God's assignment to them of the good deeds lost to the wicked.

The Zohar further explains the cause of evil. According to zoharic doctrine, all elements in the universe ought to exist in an ideal state of harmony, in which each of the divine potencies is in balance. In the symbolic language of the Zohar, God's anger (the left hand) must be in balance with God's mercy (right hand). That is to say, God's anger is held in check by God's mercifulness. But when, periodically, the universe is out of balance—if, for example, God's judgment is no longer in check—evil enters into the world. This was the case on the second day of Creation, when the powers of the left hand grew uncontrollably, resulting in a "separation" from the right.[52]

Rabbi Isaac Luria

Just short of three hundred years after the appearance of the Zohar and as a consequence of the unfathomable expulsion of Jews from Spain, Rabbi Isaac Luria's singular contribution to Kabbalah appeared.

Known as "the Holy ARI" (ARI being the acronym for "Our master and our rabbi, Isaac"), Rabbi Isaac Luria (1534–72) was one of the most important kabbalistic thinkers of the sixteenth century and perhaps one of the most radical Jewish thinkers in history. "Whereas the Zohar may be viewed as a symbolic reading of Scripture," writes the professor of Jewish studies Shaul Magid, "Lurianic kabbala transforms Scripture into a symbolic rendering of the cosmic universe."[53] This approach is unprecedented. Lurianic Kabbalah requires knowledge of events prior to the Creation epic at the outset of the book of Genesis nowhere implied in the text—and cannot be understood without it. Unfortunately, Luria left no writings himself. His thinking can only be accessed through the writings of his disciples.

To understand Luria's complex metaphysical system in relationship to good and evil, a short digression on the kabbalistic view of the origin of evil is in order. As we've seen, there was no consensus among kabbalists concerning how evil enters into the world. Rabbi Yitzḥak ben Ya'akov held that evil first entered the world with Adam and Eve's original sin. By contrast, the Gnostics believed that evil exists independently of humanity and that an element of evil existed prior to human sin. In other words, the sin of Adam and Eve did not activate evil; evil was, to use Scholem's phrase, already "woven into the texture of the world."[54] This seems to be the dominant view of the Zohar, which frequently depicts evil as a residue of "the hidden life's organic process."[55] Just as a tree cannot exist without its bark, and wine cannot be fermented without its lees, the universe cannot exist without the demonic.

An expression of this view is the naming of evil as the *kelipah* (peel, husk, or shell)[56] of the cosmic tree.[57] Even so, the incongruity of kabbalistic thought allows for the use of the term *kelipah* to refer to the form of evil that came into independent being only after Adam's sin.[58] On this view, the demonic realm resides separately from the divine realm in the "crevice of the great abyss" and can only surface through human sinfulness.[59] On the former and the dominant view, the demonic realm is depicted as a series of three or four layers (*kelipot*) wrapped around the Divine. Luria approaches the existence of evil from an entirely different perspective.

On Luria's account, the existence of the world is possible only if God withdraws, as it were, from primordial space. The withdrawal of God is necessary for two reasons. If the prophet Isaiah is correct and "the whole world is filled with His glory" (Isa. 6:3), there is no space for the world to exist. Only by contraction (*tzimtzum*) can a space be made for the birth of the physical universe. Second, God realized that the power of God's judgment was capable of acting disharmoniously with God's mercy. The process of withdrawal was also a process of purification whereby God purged God's self from the elements of judgment. In either case, God is no longer in a place where God had previously been present. God is now in exile. The absence of God allows for the presence of evil.

One way to describe the resultant predicament is a pail of water emptied.[60] Although the water is removed, a vestigial moisture remains. Likewise, while the elements of judgment were largely removed by contraction, some trace (*reshimu*) persists. This remaining residue becomes the source of evil in the world.

Yet even with God's withdrawal, some divine light proceeded from the *Ein Sof* to the vacated space, touching the trace of judgment. The movement of contraction and the subsequent emanation gives rise to the ten *sefirot*. They take the form of a colossal, cosmic human being, *Adam Kadmon*, who becomes a kind of template for the earthly human who appears later.

But the process of forming *Adam Kadmon* is not without incident. A cosmic accident occurs. Before the shape of the primordial form reaches completion, the forces of judgment refuse to cooperate further, and furthermore they withdraw from connection with the lights from *Ein Sof*. Beforehand, these lights had been contained in a series of vessels, but now, on account of their fragility, four of the seven vessels break. The "breaking of the vessels" (*shevirat ha-kelim*) shatters the divine plan of Creation. Everything deteriorates into disorder. The *sefirot* are no longer in their original place. Any subsequent Creation will no longer be in accord with God's original plan. And, just as importantly, the fallen fragments of the broken vessels form an independent realm of evil powers: *kelipot*. The divine sparks no longer contained by the broken vessels become intermingled with the *kelipot*. Thus, divine light is exiled among the forces of evil.

Next comes the most critical phase of both the cosmic process and the Lurianic system: cosmic restoration (*tikkun*). All that was broken and in disorder is to be set right. A stream of divine light emanates simultaneously from the *Ein Sof* and from the forehead of *Adam Kadmon*. In this iteration of the *sefirot*, a pairing of *partzufim*, or divine faces, occurs, one of which becomes responsible for the Creation described in Genesis. The process of restoration depends on God—but only in part. Certain parts of the process are relegated to humanity. As Scholem puts it, "Not all the lights which are held in captivity by the powers of darkness are set free by their own efforts; it is man who adds the final touch ... it is he who completes the enthronement of God."[61] Each commandment fulfilled by Jews accelerates the process of restoration, making humanity partners with God in perfecting the world. In the earthly realm, the appearance of the Messiah parallels the final step in cosmic restoration.

Luria thus provides both a description of the origins of evil and a blueprint for its eradication. Yet Luria says little, if anything, that applies his complex theosophy to the problem of evil in interpersonal relationships. That task was left to his Hasidic successors.

Summary

A brief synopsis of the contribution of Kabbalah to the problem of good and evil shows the following:

The Nature of Good and Evil: More than the Bible, the Rabbis, and the medieval thinkers, kabbalists were determined to explain the origins of evil. *Sefer Yetzirah* describes a process of emanations from which all things derive. The further an element radiates from a primary source, the more flawed it becomes. Since evil enters the world from a flawed source, it is not directly attributable to God.

Evil as the outcome of a process of emanations also plays a role in the kabbalistic view of Rabbi Yitzḥak ben Ya'akov ha-Kohen. *Sefer ha-Bahir* is inclined to revert to the Gnostic belief that evil stands as a power independent of God but moderates that view by subsuming evil under God and making it susceptible to being overcome. Even so, it is a power embedded in the very architecture of Creation.

The Zohar also conceives of evil as a residue of the organic process of Creation, with evil woven into the fabric of the universe—thus minimizing the theory that evil entered the world through the sin of Adam and Eve. And Rabbi Isaac Luria introduces the concept of God's withdrawal to explain how evil enters into the world.

Questions of Justice: As much as the kabbalistic tradition is preoccupied with the origins and nature of evil, some kabbalistic sources grapple with the problem of divine justice. *Sefer ha-Bahir*, for instance, presents a novel explanation based on the transmigration of souls. Since all souls have a history, what appears to be unjust now may actually be recompense for actions during a previous lifetime. Here the Zohar offers a range of justifications from the earlier inventory of ideas, among them the evil inclination, ancestral compensation, resolution in the afterlife, and vicarious punishment, along with new twists on earlier ideas, like prophylactic suffering and the awarding of credits co-opted from the wicked.

As heirs to the mystical, kabbalistic tradition, the Hasidic masters now have additional sources upon which to construct their approach to the problem of good and evil.

CHAPTER 5

Hasidic Masters on Evil and Suffering

Between the times of the destruction of the Second Temple and the failed revolts against Rome and the Shoah, it would be hard to imagine any one-hundred-year period that tested Jewish perseverance more than the seventeenth century. The violent Ukrainian peasant revolt against the Catholic Polish overlords included targeting Jews, whom they also regarded as agents of their oppression. The Chmielnicki Massacres (1595–1630) saw the destruction of many Jewish towns and villages as well as the brutal deaths of thousands of Jews. The Russian and Swedish invasions of Poland inhibited the rehabilitation of the destroyed Jewish communities. Many Jews were reduced to poverty. Persecutors rushed to condemn the Jews for spreading the plague. Blood libels resurfaced.

Within the Jewish community, the gap between rich and poor grew wider. Rabbis, obsessed with demonstrating their own intellectual achievements, spent little time educating the masses. The people increasingly turned to superstition and obscurantism. Jewish minds became preoccupied with amulets, charms, and spirits. Jewish learning became increasingly abstruse. Prayer became mechanical and formalistic. Surrounded by hatred and infected by stagnation, crippling hopelessness gave rise to messianic fervor. Yet the hope for anticipated redemption was crushed when the self-proclaimed Jewish messiahs Shabbetai Tzvi and, later, Jacob Frank were proved to be impostors. Jewish despair deepened.[1]

Hasidism emerged from this sad state of affairs. Hasidism in its essence is a vigorous response to evil.[2]

Rabbi Ya'akov Yosef of Polnoye (1710–ca. 1782), a friend and disciple of Rabbi Yisrael ben Eliezer (1700–1760), or the Ba'al Shem Tov, the founder of Hasidism, wrote one of the first books on Hasidism to appear in print (*Tzafenat Pane'ah* [Revealer of secrets],[3] 1780). The book consists mostly of brief parables and fragments of tales relating to his master, used as examples or illustrations on mystical or doctrinal points that were being integrated into Hasidic thought.[4] In his description of the singular gifts of the Ba'al Shem Tov, Rabbi Ya'akov Yosef makes an essential point about the nature of evil. He argues that the world is full of *kelipot* (shells or husks), that is, forces of evil, as claimed by earlier Gnostics and kabbalists. Were it not for these forces of evil, human beings would have foresight and insight that would bring them closer to God. As Rabbi Ya'akov Yosef puts it, "Were it not for the *kelipot,* one would be able to see from one end of the world to the other and also hear heavenly voices."[5] He goes on to say, "My master is the proof; he could see afar and hear heavenly voices as has been truly proven."[6]

Evil forces permeate the world and prevent ordinary human beings from reaching their spiritual potential. The extraordinary human being can overcome these evil forces. However, those who are not invested with the unique powers of the Besht (as the Ba'al Shem Tov was known) are surrounded by ubiquitous evil.

To Rabbi Ya'akov Yosef, the suffocating presence of evil in the world best describes the ethos of those times. But a real theological danger of dualism emerges if these pervasive evil forces are seen as independent of, and thus in opposition to, the power of God. Hence, Rabbi Menaḥem Mendl of Vitebsk (1730–88) affirms a distinctly monistic perspective on the presence of evil. Evil, he writes in *Peri ha-Aretz* (Fruit of the earth), his commentary on the Torah published in 1814, springs from the divine source. He lays stress on the verses "and You give life to them all" (Neh. 9:6) and "His kingdom rules over all" (Ps. 103:19).[7] The emphasis is on the word "all." All the forces in the universe are under God's control. Evil is not an independent element at war with the one God, but subordinate to God.

Subordinating evil to God addresses the theological danger of dualism but simultaneously raises the problem of how a supremely powerful and exclusively good God can allow evil to exist.[8] The teachings of the Hasidic masters, considered in the aggregate rather than presented chronologically, include seven answers. These answers are not systematic, discursive, or comprehensive. Consequently, they must be teased out of aphorisms, observations, anecdotes, and scriptural interpretations.

1. What Is Perceived as Evil Is in Fact Good

One answer is that what is perceived as evil is, in fact, good, since it is part of God's divine plan. Rabbi Moshe Leib Erblich of Sassov (1745–1807) taught, "If you are convinced that good and evil occurrences are the handiwork of God, you will not be distressed if anything transpires in your own life that is not in accordance with your desires."[9] Rabbi Erblich implies that when one's expectations (e.g., for material gains and safety and security) are realized, people find it easy to believe that their success is attributable to God's goodness. However, in the sad but frequent circumstances in which one's aspirations are thwarted (e.g., wealth is squandered, health is compromised, freedom is lost), people question the power of God. But this ought not to be the case. What people interpret as evil is also the handiwork of God and should be accepted likewise. Thus, attitudinal realignment is necessary. If people accept the idea that everything that happens is part of God's master plan, then evil is no longer considered at variance with it.

Critics, however, might point out that this solution merely results in just as troubling a question: Why is this God's plan? What possible plan would include the suffering of children, for example? Without any defined answer to these questions, this approach would appear to fail.

2. There Is Good in Evil

Several Hasidic masters take a second and different approach, arguing that there is good in evil. The Besht, as an example, intuited that evil concealed a seed of the good.[10] Further, he is reputed to have taught that evil is the basis (kisse, literally, "seat") for good, based on Exodus 14:10

"Pharaoh neared." With the word "neared" in the causative case, it means that Pharaoh caused the Israelites to draw closer to God.[11] In other words, the suffering the Israelites endured at the hand of Pharaoh brought *them* closer to God. The implication is clear: suffering conveys a benefit to victims so that evil is construed as not really evil at all.

Rabbi Levi Yitzhak of Berditchev (1740–1809 or 1810) saw good in evil deeds. Commenting on the verse "But when I make an accounting, I will bring them to account for their sins" (Exod. 32:34), he writes:

> This phrase does not mean that God will consider further sins as second offenses and thus punish the [Israelites] more severely. The opposite is the case.
>
> Who deserves greater approbation for good behavior: a member of an exceptional family or the member of a common family? [It must be] the latter, for certain, since that person has conquered the evil habits he has both inherited and learned and has become a refined gentleman. So when Israel eagerly accepted the mitzvot, God judged their acceptance as the characteristic act of a refined people in whom such obedience has become second nature. No special commendation need be given them for their prompt acceptance.
>
> But when almost immediately thereafter they sinned by worshipping the Golden Calf, it became clear that submission to authority was not a mere habit for them, indicating that their previous acceptance of the Torah was a deliberate action, dictated by their heart and mind. And any inheritance of their good conduct due to noble origin had been long lost due to slavery.
>
> Therefore, God applauded the greatness of their act of accepting the Torah. It demonstrated that they had resisted the evil inclinations they had acquired in Egypt—at least this once. So God promised to always remember this and be lenient toward them thereafter.[12]

The standard interpretation of the Golden Calf incident is that it was a sinful repudiation of the Torah recently given to the people Israel. Sin is a moral evil. But Rabbi Levi Yitzhak sees it entirely differently. The incident of the Golden Calf reveals the noble character of the people Israel. All agree that the people Israel willingly and unhesitatingly accepted the Torah, as is evident in the people's response, "We will do, and we will hear" (Exod. 24:7). There are two opposing ways to explain their enthusiasm: they were either naturally inclined to accept moral authority, or they exerted concerted effort to overcome their natural inclination to do otherwise. The Berditchever, as Rabbi Levi Yitzḥak of Berditchev was known, argues that the second way must be true. The incident of the Golden Calf proves it. The sin reveals that the Israelites were inclined to reject moral authority, as years of Egyptian bondage had obliterated their natural inclination to do good. This means that their acceptance of the Torah was an extraordinary act of moral commitment, earning the people Israel special treatment in the future. In other words, a reputed evil deed—namely, the sin of the Golden Calf—is actually proof of the moral worthiness of the people Israel. More simply put, there can be good in an evil deed.

Rabbi Barukh of Medzhybyzh (1753–1811) sees good in evil people. He argues that no one is truly evil; there is good in all. Commenting on Psalm 37:10, "A little longer and there will be no wicked man; / you will look at where he was— / he will be gone," Rabbi Barukh says, "Even the evil man is not thoroughly bad. There is still a little in him that is not wicked. Look carefully for the goodness within him. You will discover he is not truly evil."[13] To be sure, Rabbi Barukh speaks of evil as a descriptor of character and not about evil as a broader theological concept. As such, he denies the possibility of a thoroughly wicked man. He cleverly plays on the word "little," applying it to character rather than time. Whereas the Psalmist sees the triumph of the truly wicked man as temporary, Rabbi Barukh sees a "little" goodness in the wicked.

Rabbi Naḥman of Breslov (1772–1810) argues that all things happen for the good, and all the more so: "The knowledge that whatsoever occurs to you is for your own good raises you to the heights of living in paradise."[14] The significance of this brief statement becomes far clearer when its content is unpacked. The idea embedded in this statement, namely, all that happens is for the good, is not original. The Talmud credits two mishnaic teachers for having expressed unreserved optimism in God's divine plan.[15] But beyond parroting an earlier Rabbinic text, Rabbi Naḥman expands the idea to a universal ideal. Further, note how Rabbi Naḥman uses the word "knowledge" rather than "belief." He asserts that "whatever happens is for the good" is a matter of fact.

But it is a fact not known by all. No doubt, many would interpret sudden and severe illness or bankruptcy as antithetical to their own good. However, Rabbi Naḥman maintains, once a person becomes aware of the fact that whatever happens is for the good, that knowledge is life changing. Knowing that God wants the best for each person and that each person figures in God's plan is inspiring. It also steels the individual against adversity.

However, how one gains this knowledge that God wants the best for each person remains unexplained. Both experience and observation work against gaining this knowledge. An innocent victim of a life-threatening disease is unlikely to experience an epiphany and suddenly realize that suffering is for the good. As a psychological response to suffering, considering everything that happens as a good may be a useful and even comforting strategy. But as a solution to the problem of evil it is wanting.

3. Evil Does Not Exist

In saying that nothing bad ever happens, Rabbi Naḥman takes the view that evil is illusory. Other Hasidic masters go further. It is not that evil is illusory. Evil does not exist at all. Rabbi Ya'akov Yitzḥak ha-Levi Horowitz of Lublin (ca. 1745–1815) articulates this third answer:

A hasid asked the Seer of Lublin: "To the words in the Mishnah: 'Man should thank God for evil and praise Him,'[16] the Gemara adds: 'with joy and a tranquil heart.'[17] How can that be?"

The zaddik could hear that the question sprang from a troubled heart. "You do not understand the Gemara," he said, "and I do not understand even the Mishnah. For is there really any evil in the world?"[18]

According to the Seer of Lublin, as Rabbi Ya'akov Yitzḥak was known, evil does not really exist. This is not to say that the Seer of Lublin never observed inequity or witnessed suffering. Rather, he is denying the metaphysical existence of evil. Since evil cannot exist in a universe created by a good and loving God, all that occurs must be good.

This approach is reminiscent of that of the Besht in his commentary on Exodus 26:33.[19] Commenting on the curtain that serves as a partition between "the holy and the holy of holies," the Besht recounts a parable of a king who wanted to give a son a delight and made it special by creating the illusion that it was hidden behind a series of barriers. Evil in this world is an illusion. It does not really exist at all. It only appears to exist so that whatever pleasures people enjoy are more delightful. What remains is for people to come to terms with whatever occurs.

Similarly, Rabbi (Meshullam) Zusya of Hanipol (1718–1800) boldly claims that evil cannot really exist since only good comes from God. What appears to be evil to the human observer is merely an earlier stage of what will ultimately prove to result in good.[20] Commenting on Lamentations 3:38, "Is it not at the word of the Most High that weal and woe befall?"[21] Rabbi Zusya said:

> Nothing is evil, for whatever is so in man's estimation, is also good. As it states in *Midrash Tanḥuma* (Bereshit): "Nothing that is evil comes from on High." Even wickedness may serve a man to bring about conversion. While the strands of cause and effect are being unraveled, we grope about, calling things "good" and "evil." But what first appears as misfortune, years later, may be determined as the best outcome and cause for rejoicing. Says the Zohar: "Man does not know the taste of sweets until after the bitter."[22]

Rabbi Zusya makes three related points. First, since God is good, nothing evil can come from God. This is an unequivocal affirmation of theological monism. God has no competitors. Second, while nothing evil can ever come from God, human beings may still mistakenly believe the opposite. This common error is attributable to the human need to interpret events in terms of causes and effects. An illustration may be useful. Marauders destroy a Jewish village, forcing the people to move elsewhere. Naturally, the people would view the destruction and subsequent relocation as an "evil." Accordingly, the victims would search ("grope about") for answers to the question of why this evil befell them. The question would be sharper when posed as a theological challenge: How could a good and all-powerful God allow such evil to happen to innocents? One response might be to assert that the victims were not really innocent. But this is not Rabbi Zusya's response. Rather, he argues that as time unfolds, people will come to realize that what was initially deemed "evil" ultimately worked out for the best. Returning to the illustration: the relocated Jews flourished in their new location. Third, Rabbi Zusya argues that until such time that the "good" can be appreciated, given that this may occur "years later," people can employ what they currently interpret as evil ("wickedness") as a goad for character improvement on the unstated but underlying assumption that there is no punishment without sin. First and foremost, however, is the claim that there can be no independent evil power. That "evil" cannot exist.

A fundamental flaw in this approach as well as in the previous one is that Hasidism tends to blur the distinction between good and evil or claims that evil differs from good only by degree or time. For example, with regard to pain and suffering, Rabbi Naḥman of Breslov declares, "They are not evils at all but great goods. . . . Indeed, there is no evil in the world, only complete goodness."[23] Good and evil are essentially the same. If that is the case, then there is no justifying reason for human beings to shun evil for good. Both are equal. And what may seem evil now will eventually be proven good. Morality, however, is based on recognizing the antipodal relationship between good and evil.

4. Evil Induces Holiness

Separate from denying the existence of evil as noted above, Rabbi Menaḥem Mendl of Vitebsk further argues that evil exists only insofar as an idea to be nullified. The idea of evil is a target for directing human attention. By resisting "evil" and its temptations, human beings can elevate themselves. Hence, Rabbi Menaḥem Mendl generates a fourth answer: evil induces holiness.

In support of his view, Rabbi Menaḥem Mendl uses the parable of the prostitute.[24] She represents the evil inclination sent into the world to strengthen man against submitting to her temptations. According to Rabbi Menaḥem Mendl's account, there is no empty space in the world—there is either purity or impurity.[25] Where holiness isn't, impurity or "evil" is. Evil exists, if only in a theoretical sense, when humanity eschews the pursuit of holiness. The active pursuit of holiness is humanity's weapon against evil.[26]

Rabbi Yisrael Hapstein, the Maggid of Koznitz (1733–1814), similarly sees evil as a temptation intended to lure people away from the good. In his biblical commentary *Avodat Yisrael* (The service of Israel),[27] he writes at length on an interesting aspect of Pharaoh's dream (Gen. 41:4):

> "And the ugly gaunt cows ate up the handsome sturdy cows. And Pharaoh awoke."
>
> Now when Pharaoh related this dream to Joseph he elaborated on this, saying (v. 21): "but when they had consumed them, one could not tell they had consumed them, for they looked just as bad as before. . . ." This was not stated previously when [the Torah] tells of [Pharaoh's] dream. This must be understood as a hint, for all the narratives of the Torah hint at the way we should learn to love God and to serve Him.
>
> "The one no less than the other was God's doing." All the evil inclination and the "Other Side" (*Sitra Aḥra*) have been created to entice man to worldly things and stupid nonsense to lead him on the path to anything but good. He comes to love strange things, to fear others than God, to take pride in another than God, and so with regard to the other qualities. The fool who walks in darkness and allows himself to be enticed by his evil inclination causes, God forbid, the seven qualities of holiness to be devoured by the seven qualities of the other side.
>
> Now the sinner at the time of his sin, and as he daily continues to folly, and for as long as he fails to repent, becomes completely

insensitive to his wickedness, unaware that . . . he weakens the power of the holy. . . . When the sinner bestirs himself to repent of his sins, he is compared to the sleeper awakening from his sleep.[28]

The Maggid identifies the "hint" as how the sinner, through his sin, devours (that is, destroys) the seven qualities of holiness corresponding to seven of the ten *sefirot*, replacing them with seven evil qualities. One way to serve God is to struggle against the evil inclination and be victorious in that struggle. The quality, and the corresponding *sefirah*, associated with this struggle is *netzah* (victory). The Maggid quotes Ecclesiastes 7:14 ("The one no less than the other was God's doing") as support for the kabbalistic view that God makes both the good and evil qualities. Thus, everything in the domain of the holy has its opposite in the allegorical realm of evil. All of these are represented in Pharaoh's dream by the seven handsome cows and the seven ugly cows. So long as the sinner persists in surrendering to the evil inclination, there is no change, like the ugly cows that, even after devouring the handsome cows, look as they did before. The sinner remains asleep. Repentance, however, is an awakening. Once his eyes are opened, "he sees that he has been guilty of the great sin of not even knowing" that the handsome cows had been devoured.

For the Maggid, God can have no equal. Thus all things come from the one God. Whatever appears to be evil is merely an enticement designed by God to strengthen human resolve to do good. Too often, human beings succumb to such enticements without even realizing they have done so. But it is possible for people to awaken and realize the error of their ways.

Rabbi Shne'ur Zalman of Liady (1745–1813) advances a related approach. As the noted scholar on Jewish thought Moshe Hallamish explains, "Rabbi Shneur Zalman . . . maintains that evil does not exist in the metaphysical sense, but that on the cosmic and human plane evil is engaged in a mighty struggle against good."[29] Accordingly, every person, from the wicked to the saintly, is—or ought to be—engaged in the process of resisting evil. Rabbi Shne'ur Zalman imagines this process as a process of conversion. The saintly person converts the "evil" within him to holiness. In particular, the tzaddik devotes his energy to the introspective task of converting the evil within him to holiness.

These approaches are all related to a doctrine that Hasidic thought terms "descent for the purpose of ascent."[30] According to this doctrine, when people fall into evil it is only to rise, improved by the experience. But the critic may ask: Is this trip really necessary? Is it possible to strive for and attain holiness without a descent into evil? The critic's answer would be "Yes." It is indeed possible to attain holiness independent of the existence of evil, thus rendering this doctrine unnecessary.

5. Good Is Appreciated Only in Contrast with Evil

Although "evil" is devoid of reality, it still has value. The Besht taught that the perception of evil leads the good man to rejoice in goodness. He is reputed to have said, "Absolute evil does not exist. When the good man perceives evildoers, he rejoices in his goodness."[31] Evil gains the righteous perspective. The righteous man does not truly appreciate his happy condition until he notes the sad spiritual state of the wicked. Hence, evil has the salutary effect of affirming the good. That good is appreciated only in contrast with evil underlies a fifth answer.

Hence, making a Maimonidean pivot, Rabbi Pinḥas of Koretz (1726–91) takes the view that the good can neither be known nor appreciated without evil:

Said the Koretzer: A man cannot be consciously good unless he knows evil. No one can appreciate pleasure unless he has tasted bitterness. Good is only the reverse of evil, and pleasure is merely the opposite of anxiety.

"And the Lord God said: 'It is not good for man to be alone; I will make a fitting helper for him'" [Gen. 2:18], meaning, there can be no goodness in man while he is alone without an evil impulse within him. I will endow him with the ability to do evil, and it will be a fitting helper to him to enable him to do good, if he masters the evil inclination within him. Without the evil inclination, man could do no evil; but neither could he do good.[32]

Contrast is what makes concepts discernible. Just as there can be no mountains without valleys, no charitableness without poverty, no heroism without peril, there can be no good without evil. Without the one, the other is meaningless.

In a daring and imaginative interpretation of the narrative describing the creation of Adam's mate, the Koretzer takes it to be a description of an internal rather than an external mate. The "fitting partner" to the first man is not the first woman, but the evil inclination. Having such a "mate" is advantageous to the first man because it allows him to identify the good and value it. The presence of the evil inclination is both a danger and a blessing. That a person might surrender to the evil inclination is indeed a real danger with undesirable consequences. However, the very existence of the evil inclination enables a person to determine what is truly worthy and pursue it.

But what is epistemologically true—that is to say, contrasts are useful in gaining knowledge—is not necessarily morally justifiable. A criminal defense that argues that without the perpetrator's robberies the victims would not be appreciative of their property and thus the criminal act was beneficial to the victims would be rejected out of hand. And besides, understanding the difference between what is good and what is bad does not ineluctably lead to pursuing what is good.

6. Evil Allows for the Attainment of Good

The Creation epic finds its way into another Hasidic account of good and evil. Rabbi Elimelekh Weisblum of Lizensk (1717–86) argues that evil—at least in one manifestation—allows for the attainment of good. When the first human being was banished from the Garden of Eden, it was, literally, a godsend, since good deeds cannot be performed in paradise.

The Lizensker explained:

"And the Lord God said, 'Now that man has become like one of us, knowing good and evil...'" (Gen. 3:22) [means that] he acquired the power to desire both good and evil, just as in the supernal world there are holy and unholy spirits. "What if he should stretch out his hand

and take also from the tree of life and eat, and live forever!" (Gen. 3:22) [implies that] he became endowed with the ability to do evil, and thereby to die. On the other hand, he is able to do good and gain immortality for his soul by partaking of the tree of life, namely, by obedience to the Lord's instruction. "So the Lord God banished him from the Garden of Eden, to till the soil from which he was taken" (Gen. 3:23). Since good deeds cannot be performed and self-improvement cannot be achieved in Paradise where there are no evil impulses, the Lord sent him forth from the state of primitive happiness to labor in a world of strife and impulse. "He drove the man out, and stationed east of the Garden of Eden the cherubim and the fiery, ever-turning sword, to guard the way to the tree of life" (Gen. 3:24). Therefore, the Lord placed within man the quest for pleasure and the evil desire that revolves continuously in his brain, inflaming his heart with its intensity and its urgent power. They guard the way and force man to battle them. Over them he must gain victory before he can perform the will of the Lord, and thereby gain the route to immortality.[33]

Underlying the Lizensker's interpretation is the presumption that the universe is divided into two realms: one above (the supernal world of God and the spirits) and one below (the earthly world of human existence). Until the first human beings eat from the Tree of Knowledge of Good and Evil, the man does not realize that there exists an upper world where unholy spirits reside. But once he eats from the tree, he gains not only that knowledge, but also opposing desires: to do good and defeat the unholy spirits as God does, or to do evil and yield to them. Doing good—that is, following God's commands—gains man immortality, but doing evil results in death.

The standard interpretation of this passage is that the exile of the first man from the Garden of Eden was both a punishment and a measure preventing the first man from gaining eternal life and thus threatening God's preeminence. But this is not the way the Lizensker reads it. To him, the exile from Eden is not a punishment but an opportunity. Only outside Eden does Adam gain the possibility of choice. In Eden, Adam was powerless against the evil impulse; hence, Adam had no choice but to comply. Outside Eden, however, Adam can choose to do good and gain immortality or choose evil and suffer death. Choosing to do good results from the suppression of the evil inclination and the person's consequent self-improvement.

The world below is an imperfect world. It is filled with strife: the result of the tenacious and inflammatory workings of the evil inclination in humanity. And yet, it is only in this world that human beings can distinguish themselves. Hence, living in this imperfect world is a blessing.

Critics may note that the Lizensker argues that the first humans had no choice but to follow God's instructions so that expulsion was actually a blessing. But careful readers of the text would offer a rejoinder that the very act of eating the forbidden fruit was a violation of God's instructions. This means that humanity did not require expulsion from Eden in order to gain the possibility of choice. They already possessed it. Moreover, the Lizensker is right: good deeds could not be performed in Eden. But it is not because of an absence of choice. It is because of an absence of other people with whom to interact. Loving your neighbor, for example, can only be performed if one has neighbors.

7. Evildoers Persist as Good Examples

That our imperfect world is a blessing also features in the view of Rabbi Shalom Rokeaḥ, the first Belzer Rebbe (1779–1855). On the subject of whether or not evil is real, the Belzer Rebbe is agnostic. It is not clear that he (as well as other Hasidic masters) conceived of evil as a cosmic problem lacking metaphysical reality or as a real, palpable, and pervasive phenomenon. That said, the Belzer Rebbe concedes that evil people live among us—and, ironically, serve as a good example.

This is a seventh Hasidic answer to the question of how a supremely powerful and exclusively good God allows evil to exist: evildoers persist as good examples. The Belzer Rebbe writes:

Oftentimes we observe the thoroughness with which an evil man plans a deed and the untiring effort with which he executes it. Should we not imitate him when we endeavor to perform a good deed? As the Psalmist (Ps. 119:98) says: "Your commandments make me wiser than my enemies."[34]

The evil person approaches malfeasance with the passion a good person lacks in doing what is right. A thief, for example, meticulously plans his caper and will not allow any hitch to deter him from his goal. Not so the good man. Even a minor obstacle is all that is necessary to dissuade him from performing a good deed. So the evil man should be admired, even imitated—not because of the merit of his actions, but because of the single-mindedness and devotion he dedicates to it. The Belzer Rebbe thus reads the verse in Psalms as if it says, "From my enemies you teach me wisdom." Sinners are living examples of what can be accomplished through resolute determination.

Critics can argue that there are far better ways of learning the value of determination than through evildoers. The book of Proverbs, in contrast, directs humanity to look to the animal kingdom for acquiring virtue. Industriousness and foresight, for example, are learned from the ant (Prov. 6:6, 30:25). And the Talmud teaches that people can learn modesty from cats.[35] Moreover, one could learn self-control, for example, from Joseph, who rejects the advances of Potiphar's wife (Gen. 39:9,12). Tolerating the wicked to learn from their "good" qualities is unnecessary. Tolerating the wicked only to suffer from their bad qualities is shameful.

On Personal Suffering

Apart from the more theological aspects of the problem of evil, the Hasidic masters also had something to say about personal suffering.

The empathy of Hasidic masters was well documented. It was said that whenever Rabbi Moshe Leib Erblich of Sassov (1745–1807) saw anyone suffering, he shared it so earnestly that he made it his own. Once, when someone expressed his astonishment at this capacity to share in another's troubles, the rabbi is reputed to have responded, "What do you mean 'share'? It is my own sorrow."[36] It is further reported that Rabbi Yehudah Tzvi Brandwein of Stretyn (1780–1844), afflicted with painful ulcers all over his body in the last years of his life, explained his forbearance as the result of his prayer that God assign to him the suffering of a sickly person who asked for God's help.[37]

Here, the message appears to be that there is no justification for the suffering of innocents. There is only compassion for their suffering. The best human beings can do when confronted with unjustifiable suffering is to be present for the sufferer and by joining together help ease the burden. It is much like a modern, anonymous story that is not Hasidic but could have been. One little girl sat sobbing disconsolately with a broken doll in her lap. A friend came and sat beside her and offered to help. "Can you help me fix the doll?" the first little girl asked. "No," said the second, "but I can help you cry."

Beyond empathy, the Hasidic masters do seriously consider the question of why the righteous suffer. Thus, the following story is told:

When Rabbi Shmelke and his brother visited Rabbi Dov Baer, the Maggid of Mezerich (1704–1772), they asked him about the following: "Our sages said certain words which leave us no peace since we do not understand them. They are that men should praise and thank God for suffering just as much as for well-being, and receive it with the same joy. Will you tell us how we are to understand this, rabbi?"

The Maggid replied: "Go to the House of Study. There you will find Zusya smoking his pipe. He will give you the explanation." They went to the House of Study and put their question to Rabbi Zusya. He laughed. "You certainly have come to the right[38] man! Better go to someone other than to me, for I have never experienced suffering." But the two knew that, from the day he was born to this day, Rabbi Zusya's life had been a web of need and anguish. Then they knew what it was: to accept suffering with love.[39]

The Maggid conveys the message that suffering is inevitable in life. The only recourse is to lovingly accept it. Unstated but most surely intimated is that suffering is part of God's plan. As such, human beings are duty bound to be assured that it comports with God's best intentions.

Similarly, a story is told about an anonymous tzaddik who, when robbed, did not lament his loss. His family protested his equanimity, but the tzaddik replied, "They have taken by force what was theirs by rights as decreed in Heaven. As for me, the Besht taught: 'Suffering makes for proper insight and compassion.'"[40] Here too, the tzaddik is asserting that God must have intended that he be robbed. Further, God actually assigned his possessions to the robbers, so that the "robbery" was not in fact a criminal deprivation of property, but a restoration of property to the rightful owners.

Another story is told about Rabbi Yisrael of Rizhyn (d. 1850):

A man who was afflicted with a terrible disease complained to Rabbi Yisrael that his suffering interfered with his learning and praying. The rabbi put his hand on his shoulder and said, "How do you know, friend, what is more pleasing to God, your studying or your suffering?"[41]

The lesson here is that suffering may serve to please God. But this is a strange lesson. It seems inconceivable that suffering would please a good and merciful God. More likely, Rabbi Yisrael is suggesting that God is pleased by the loving acceptance of suffering.

Rabbi Menaḥem Mendl Morgensztern of Kotzk (the Kotzker Rebbe; 1787–1859) had a contrasting view of suffering (according to Rabbi Abraham Joshua Heschel). To him, suffering is neither accepted nor welcomed. Suffering is a spiritual test that some people must undergo. Yet Rabbi Menaḥem Mendl never explicitly maintained that suffering is indispensable to a life of faith.[42]

Suffering as a test of character is also the subject of an anecdote reported in the name of the Kobriner. "When a man suffers," he is reputed to have said, "he should not say, 'This is evil!' for the Lord sends no evil. He should rather say, 'I am undergoing a bitter experience.' It is like bitter medicine a doctor prescribes to cure the patient."[43]

In addition, as we saw, Rabbi Naḥman of Breslov holds that suffering leads to nearness to God, a view he derives from Exodus 14:10, "And Pharaoh drew near." While ostensibly the Hebrew means that pharaoh approached, Rabbi Naḥman understands this phrase to mean that pharaoh "drew the people nearer to their father in Heaven because pharaoh pursued after them."[44]

In sum, the few Hasidic masters whose views have been recorded consider personal suffering as part of God's plan. It is either a test of one's character or should be lovingly accepted by the afflicted. In either case, suffering allows the community in which the sufferers are found to manifest empathy and compassion.

But nagging questions remain. For whom is suffering a test? Surely God knows the heart of each individual and no test is necessary.[45] If the test is for the individual, surely there are other challenges than poverty and disease to improve character, particularly when the suffering is unjust. And while marshaling the community's resources in response to suffering is certainly a noble goal, it leaves unanswered the question of why any particular individual is chosen to suffer in order to attain it.

The Suffering of the Collective

All of what is included in Hasidism on the subject of evil is derivative. What is truly original in the Hasidic tradition is consideration of the suffering of the collective.

For example, Rabbi Avraham Yitzḥak of Sadagorda (d. 1883) sat for his midday meal but did not eat. His sister repeatedly asked him what was troubling him. Finally he responded with a question of his own: "Have you heard the reports about the sad condition of our brothers in Russia?" "It seems to me," she answered, "that these sufferings might be the birth pangs that herald the coming of the Messiah." The tzaddik considered this answer with "Perhaps." After due consideration he added, "When suffering is about to reach its peak, Israel cries out to God saying it can bear it no longer, and God is merciful and hears them: he relieves the suffering and postpones the redemption."[46]

In this anecdote Rabbi Avraham Yitzḥak considers two possibilities related to national suffering. One is that suffering hastens the arrival of redemption. The second is that God can eradicate suffering. But the two cannot occur simultaneously. Hence, if national suffering is alleviated, then messianic redemption must be delayed, and if messianic redemption is imminent, then suffering must be endured.

The novelty of this idea is unquestionable. But the source for this idea is unknown. Beyond this, why would God consider a zero-sum outcome whereby only one of two goods is possible at any given time?

Rabbi Menachem Mendel Schneerson (1902–94), the Lubavitcher Rebbe, propounds a different, and surely more controversial, view of collective suffering. He writes:

> It is clear that "no evil descends from Above," and buried within torment and suffering is a core of exalted spiritual good. Not all human beings are able to perceive it, but it is very much there. So it is not impossible for the physical destruction of the Holocaust to be spiritually beneficial. On the contrary, it is quite possible that physical affliction is good for the spirit.[47]

Since God is perfectly good, it is inconceivable that any evil can flow from God. Consequently, even what appears to be evil must have some intrinsic good at its core. Even an event as radically evil as the Holocaust might be understood positively. A helpful analogy is the surgeon's intent to save a life by amputating a limb.

> The Holy One, Praised be He, like the professor-surgeon . . . seeks the good of Israel, and indeed, all He does is for the good. . . . In the spiritual sense, no harm was done because the everlasting spirit of the Jewish people was not destroyed.[48]

The terrible cost of six million Jewish lives, as difficult as it may be to fathom, was a necessary outcome for the greater good ("the everlasting spirit") of the Jewish people. As such, collective suffering is not a theological challenge. To the contrary, it is a demonstration of God's love and beneficence. It is an affirmation of God's providential care.

As one might imagine, when this text was first published in 1980 it generated a considerable stir, and the controversy has lingered. Noted

Holocaust scholar Yehudah Bauer has accused the Lubavitcher Rebbe of justifying the Holocaust.[49] For his part, Rabbi Schneerson offers his ruminations on the Holocaust in the form of speculation ("not impossible," "quite possible") rather than a definitive explanation, which leaves himself and his apologists some wiggle room. What is undeniable is that Rabbi Schneerson, like his Hasidic forerunners, considers suffering of whatever scale as part of God's cosmic plan. As such, it must be accepted—even lovingly—by the sufferers.

However, the ultimate message that suffering should be lovingly accepted is packaged in an analysis that is both insulting to the victims and offensive to survivors. Rabbi Schneerson suggests that somehow the victims deserved their fate and that Hitler was an instrument of God.

One additional figure merits mention: Rabbi Avraham Yitzhak Kook (1865–1935). Born in what is now Latvia, Rav Kook was recognized early on as an intellectual giant who bridged the Hasidic and non-Hasidic traditions. After excelling in his studies at the famous yeshiva in Volozhin, he took up his first rabbinic position in Lithuania at age twenty-three. In 1904 Rav Kook moved to Ottoman Palestine to serve as the rabbi of Jaffa. He wrote profusely and earned a reputation for trying to bring secular settlers closer to Judaism. After his return from Europe at the beginning of the First World War, Rav Kook was appointed the Ashkenazi chief rabbi of Jerusalem and, shortly thereafter, the chief rabbi of Palestine. He also founded a yeshiva that still bears his name and remains influential in the religious Zionist community.

Much of Rav Kook's philosophy regarding good in evil, richly influenced by his Hasidic background (his maternal grandfather was an avid follower of the Alter Rebbe of Lubavitch), is that all of life is in the process of striving toward perfection. As all life moves closer to this ideal, evil disappears and is gradually transformed into the good and the holy. One of Rav Kook's foremost interpreters, Ezra Gelman, succinctly explains Rav Kook's perspective: "Evil is but the good still incomplete, perfection not yet fully realized."[50] Thus, in one representative passage Rav Kook writes:

We see the evil within the individual and in the life of human society. We find that with all its negativity and evil, it has a purpose—a temporary purpose. Evil contains particular power, the might of will and the depths of life. These are necessary components with which to perfect virtue and goodness. And we are assured that in the end, the evil will pass. The individual will be perfected and society will be perfected. Then everything will stand upon the basis of goodness. Evil will evaporate, and the yearning of evil, the wrath, the murder, the coarseness, and all their offshoots, will evaporate like smoke.[51]

And he goes on to say:

The same process applies to the entire world. Without any doubt, this power of evil yearning for evil causes upheaval in the world. It rules and is filled with force, all the days of evil. As long as the world requires the evil upheaval, the universal evildoer yearns, with all his might, to exterminate and destroy, to poison and pollute, to darken and blacken, to separate and explode. And he extends his evil until the final time, until the world will be perfected, until a new spirit, a spirit of pure life, will breathe upon human beings, when holy souls will awaken to the struggle of true liberation, and take refuge [in] the kingdom of supernal holy ones.[52]

In the meanwhile, Rav Kook offers two approaches for coping with the evil that currently exists. The first is philosophical and the second is practical. Philosophically, Rav Kook advises looking at the evildoers in the world as necessary for the elevation of the righteous and the not-yet-righteous:

Just as it is impossible to have wine without the dregs, so too it is impossible for a world to not have wicked people. And just as the dregs preserve the wine and keep it, so too the coarse will of the wicked cause a standing for the flow of life for the intermediate and the righteous.[53]

He also advises considering evil in context:

Within the totality of the world—both this-worldly and spiritual—the
only evil to be found is that which exists in its isolated state. But in the
gathering of everything, everything is good—literally, not because evil
is nullified into the majority (as the desiccated accounting would have
it), but when seen from the perspective of the value that is independent
and ideal. From this, you can understand that to the degree that the
quantity of movement toward wholeness grows, evil decreases and
goodness is revealed. Not only that, but the gathering of evil in all
its parts appears as the depths of a very great goodness, connecting
in the depth of the heat of its yearning to total goodness, with which
evil will not abide.[54]

As all life moves toward perfection, evil makes up a lesser and lesser part
until at last it transforms into a great goodness.

Rav Kook realizes that pain and suffering are real and part of the human
condition. So he offers as practical advice a two-pronged approach for
coping with painful experiences:

There remains only the feeling of pain and sorrow. We ask regarding
this feeling: Why does it exist? Sorrow is ameliorated in two ways: The
first is by accepting suffering with love. That is the level of supernal
consciousness. The second is by attaining a supernal viewpoint that
transcends consciousness of belief in the quality of goodness.[55]

First, human beings who suffer are to accept their suffering with love,
presumably because it is part of God's plan. Second, taking a grander
view—namely, realizing that the world is moving toward goodness—can
serve as a kind of comfort.

As such, instead of voicing a theological challenge that would require a
theodicy, Rav Kook recommends that the afflicted follow what he attests
is the path of the pure righteous:

The pure righteous do not complain of the dark, but increase the light; they do not complain of evil, but increase justice; they do not complain of heresy, but increase faith; they do not complain of ignorance, but increase wisdom.[56]

To Rav Kook, the pure righteous who turn suffering to goodness are the models to be emulated by the rest of us. If we are afflicted, we are to do whatever we can to add to goodness in this world.

Rav Kook provides compelling motivation to improve the world but offers little new on the subject of the nature of good and evil. He is presenting earlier Hasidic ideas somewhat differently, and thus the same questions raised against earlier approaches can be raised here. His novel idea that the world is moving to a better state is more hopeful than descriptive.

Summary

The number and variety of Hasidic responses to the problem of evil and suffering reveal both the depth and the severity of the problem. Not surprisingly, there is no consensus among Hasidic masters. And some Hasidic responses remain problematic; as the eminent rabbi and philosopher of religion Norman Lamm notes, all responses are intended to be existentially viable and psychologically constructive rather than intellectually satisfying.[57]

The Nature of Good and Evil: Fundamental to Hasidism since its inception is the kabbalistic notion that evil forces pervade the world and prevent humanity from reaching its fullest potential. These forces must be subordinate to God, but exactly how they came into existence remains undetermined.

Questions of Justice: Far more than ruminating on the origins of evil, Hasidic masters were absorbed with explaining how an all-powerful and just God can tolerate the existence of evil. Like the Rabbis of the Talmud, Hasidic masters offer a menu of possible solutions ranging from redefining evil as good to denying the reality of evil to seeing evil as possessing inherent value. Personal suffering is a necessary component of human life that should be accepted with equanimity or, alternatively, conceived as a test of human character. Rabbi Menachem Mendel Schneerson goes further, claiming that suffering is, in fact, beneficial. One original approach to suffering in Hasidism links the suffering of the collective with national redemption: the avoidance of suffering comes at the cost of redemption. In a modern exposition of Hasidism, Rav Kook sees pain and suffering as part of the human condition that should be accepted with love on the one hand and defeated with increasing goodness on the other.

CHAPTER 6

Early Modern Thinkers on Good and Evil

The early modern period was a pivotal time in Jewish thought. Both the audience and direction of Jewish philosophy began to shift. Whereas earlier Jewish thinkers were certainly aware of and influenced by secular philosophy, their audience had remained essentially Jewish—Jewish thinkers wrote for questioning Jews—but in the early modern period at least one Jewish thinker, freed from the constraints of theological orthodoxy, turned to writing for a general audience. Furthermore, the early modern period saw a return to the rational philosophy of medieval authorities like Maimonides and Gersonides, even as kabbalists cultivated the buds of mystical Jewish thought.

Barukh Spinoza

Barukh (Benedict) Spinoza (1632–77) was the exemplar of this axial shift. His expulsion from the Jewish community of Amsterdam allowed him, as historian of philosophy Oliver Leaman notes, to take Maimonides and Gersonides "to what he took to be their logical conclusion, and the notion of a personal God largely disappears as a result."[1] Spinoza's project of harmonizing religion and rationality resulted in a radical reinterpretation of familiar terms and a novel solution to the problem of good and evil.

Unlike Spinoza's *Ethics*, which is written as a pedantic series of definitions and propositions, his *Tractatus Theologico-Politicus*, described by one interpreter as "an eloquent plea for religious liberty,"[2] is far more accessible. Written in an expository style, it aims to demystify the universe and expose the elaborate system of dogmas and anthropomorphisms favored by theologians — all based on what Spinoza terms "superstition." In chapter 3 he articulates how he understands God operates:

> The universal laws of nature, according to which all things exist and are determined, are only another name for the eternal decrees of God, which always involve eternal truth and necessity.[3]

Hence:

> To say that everything happens according to natural laws, and to say that everything is ordained by the decree and ordinance of God is the same thing.[4]

Spinoza legitimates identifying nature with God because, as professor of philosophy Steven Nadler explains, "God is the infinite, necessarily existing (that is, uncaused), unique substance of the universe. There is only one substance in the universe; it is God; and everything else that is, is in God."[5] Or, as Spinoza himself puts it, "All things, I say, are in God, and all things that happen, happen only through the laws of God's infinite nature and follow . . . from the necessity of his existence."[6]

The implication of Spinoza's thinking here is that the very asking of the question "Why does God allow the righteous to suffer?" is an absurdity. To ask this question assumes that God is to be conceived as the perfect human — that is, possessing all the virtues ascribed to human beings, with goodness and justice among them — and none of the vices. To ask this question further assumes that God intends that the good be rewarded and the wicked punished. Since it would be a failing for a person to treat another unjustly, it would likewise be a failing for God to tolerate injustice. As such, observing the suffering of the innocent raises the question of God's goodness or power. But Spinoza denies that any such assumption is warranted. In a letter to a friend, Willem van Blijenburgh, Spinoza writes:

To ascribe to God those attributes that make man perfect would be as wrong as to ascribe to a man the attributes that make perfect an elephant or an ass.[7]

God is beyond such ridiculous assumptions. Spinoza returns to this point again in a subsequent letter to another friend, Hugo Boxel. Boxel, like many traditional believers, asserted that God can only be conceived as a supreme being, with supremacy defined by human characteristics. Spinoza rebuts:

When you say that you do not see the sort of God I have if I deny him the actions of seeing, hearing, attending, willing, etc. and that he possess those faculties in an eminent degree, I suspect that you believe that there is no greater perfection than can be explicated by the aforementioned attributes. I am not surprised, for I believe that a triangle, if it could speak, would likewise say that God is eminently triangular, and a circle that God's nature is eminently circular.[8]

Human beings simply ascribe to God those virtues that are most valued by them. But that does not mean that this ascription is in any way valid. As Spinoza contends, God is not some cosmic architect who "directs all things to some certain end"[9] or some heavenly judge who makes things conform to God's purposes by righting all wrongs. Rather, "things happen," Nadler neatly sums up Spinoza's thought, "only because of Nature and its laws."[10] Accordingly, Spinoza is inexorably led to the following conclusion:

For this reason we could not conceive sin to exist in the state of nature, nor imagine God as a judge punishing man's transgressions; but we supposed all things to happen according to the general laws of universal nature, there being no difference between pious and impious . . . because there was no possibility either of justice or charity.[11]

That the righteous sometimes suffer and the wicked sometimes prosper is simply the way things are. This is not an indictment of God but a fact of nature. Babies suffer from birth defects on account of the laws of heredity, not the impotence of God. Illness is a consequence of biological or environmental factors that inhere in the world in which humans live. Floods and tornadoes are entirely functions of climatic and weather conditions irrespective of the moral standing of those who stand in their paths.

Yet human beings are befuddled by a kind of magical thinking in which they assign purpose and intentionality to God rather than submit to the rational laws of nature. Spinoza both describes and mocks this kind of thinking.

> If a stone has fallen from a room onto someone's head and killed him, they will show, in the following way, that the stone fell in order to kill the man. For if it did not fall to that end, God willing it, how could so many circumstances have occurred by chance (for often many circumstances do occur at once)? Perhaps you will answer that it happened because the wind was blowing hard and the man was walking that way. But they will persist: why was the wind blowing hard at that time? why was the man walking that way at that time? If you answer again that the wind arose then because on the preceding day, while the weather was still calm, the sea began to toss, and that the man had been invited by a friend, they will press on—for there is no end to the questions that can be asked: but why was the sea tossing? why was the man invited at just that time? And they will not stop asking for the causes of causes until you take refuge in the will of God, i.e., the sanctuary of ignorance.[12]

Nature is devoid of will, even if people want it otherwise. As Nadler sums up Spinoza, "Whatever is, is in Nature and is therefore brought about by Nature; and because Nature is all there is, there is nothing outside Nature to constrain it to do one thing rather than another."[13]

For Spinoza, there is no question of why there is unmerited evil or, for that matter, why there is evil at all. All that happens in the world is a result of quite specific natural causal factors. Any confusion about what people observe—the innocent suffering, for example—lies inside the human mind, not in God. But, as Leaman voices Spinoza, "Once we perceive the world from the point of view of how it has always been and how it will always be . . . we have to jettison our ordinary moral language in favor of higher intellectual categories of thought."[14] Hence, to gain a better understanding of good and evil, Spinoza reflects on how the human mind works.

In one of his earliest works, Spinoza argues that the human mind is equipped with unique faculties that allow people to comprehend the world on the basis of differentiation:

> Some things are in our understanding and not in Nature, and so they are also our own creation, and their purpose is to understand things distinctly: among these we include all relations, which have reference to different things and we call these *Entia Rationis* [things of reason].[15]

Being part of human nature—let's call it the human mind—this faculty is an inner faculty that does not exists outside of the individual. It allows each person to rationally differentiate among things he or she experiences. *Entia Rationis* (things of reason) stand apart from *Entia Realia* (real things) that exist in nature itself. For Spinoza, these are the only two categories into which all phenomena can be sorted.

> Now the question is, whether good and evil belong to the *Entia Rationis* or to the *Entia Realia*. But since good and evil are only relations, it is beyond doubt that they must be placed among the *Entia Rationis*; for we never say that something is good except with reference to something else which is not so good, or is not so useful as some other thing.[16]

What seems like an arcane, semantic question is actually one with very practical ethical consequences. "Good" and "evil" are relational terms that have meaning only by means of comparisons. Spinoza explains they "are not things or actions which exist in nature."[17] "Good" and "evil" are what Spinoza calls "modes of thought."[18] In the theater of human conduct, we say that a man is bad, only in comparison with one who is better, or also that an apple is bad, in comparison with another which is good or better.[19]

Reminiscent of Maimonides, for Spinoza, the import of the relational nature of good and bad is the realization that for "bad" to be meaningful, good must exist:

All this could not possibly be said if that which is better or good, in comparison with which it [the bad] is so called did not exist.[20]

Yet rather than follow the familiar Maimonidean trail and comfortably conclude that evil does not really exist except as a foil for good, Spinoza goes off in a different direction.

He concludes his analysis of this point by stating that when people call another person "good"—that is, apply their mode of thinking—they intend that the person so identified conforms well to the particular idea they have of him and not to the idea they have of people in general. Spinoza introduces his conclusion with an analogy.[21] The clock that conforms with the clockmaker's specifications to precisely show and strike the correct time is called "good." A clock that fails to conform to the clockmaker's design and shows the incorrect time is "bad." However, a clock that conforms with the clockmaker's irregular design to strike at the wrong times is still "good." The clock striking the wrong time may be judged "bad" from the perspective of those who judge all clocks on the basis of telling time correctly. But from the perspective of the clockmaker's contrarian design, the clock is functioning perfectly.

Human beings typically expect conduct to conform with some universal standard of "goodness." A failure to conform is judged a human vice and a divine weakness. But, in Spinoza's view, this ascribing of purpose to God is symptomatic of magical thinking. All that should be expected is conformity with nature's laws. A human being should only be expected to behave in the way human beings are designed. Hence, a selfish or cruel person is not "bad" or "wicked" or "evil" from the perspective of nature. That person is merely acting on the impulse for self-preservation. A selfish or cruel person is acting exactly as that person naturally does. From the perspective of other people, selfish and cruel conduct might be termed "bad" with reference to most others who are kind and generous. But, Spinoza warns, it is a mistake to substitute moral judgments for what should be an assessment of function. An individual who acts as nature has intended should not be condemnable.

This does not mean that for Spinoza there are no ethics. Indeed, he writes a major work to describe how ethics work. But it does mean that the question of "why do the wicked prosper?" is inapt. The oppressor is no more "wicked" than any of nature's predators.

It would thus seem that to Spinoza there is no difference between "good" and "evil" people, or, in religious thinking, God is unable or unwilling to differentiate between the righteous and the wicked. That would be true if by the terms "good" and "evil" we think of degrees of virtue: "good" people having more virtue and "evil" people less. The mistake here, Spinoza would note, is to assume that good and evil are categories of virtue and that, as such, they can be quantified. Rather, "good" and "evil" refer to the extent to which an individual is able to better express or manifest his or her divine substance or nature.

In chapter 4 of the *Ethics*, Spinoza spells out what makes a person "good." It is the ability to control the affects—passions and emotions—that keep an individual in "bondage." By being liberated from them, human beings can pursue the virtue that is knowledge of a very specific kind: the knowledge of God. This knowledge also provides practical benefits.

> The more this knowledge that things are necessary is concerned with singular things, which we imagine more distinctly and vividly, the greater is this power of the Mind over the affects, as experience itself also testifies. For we see that Sadness over some good which has perished is lessened as soon as the man who has lost it realizes that this good could not, in any way, have been kept.[22]

This knowledge is very much an intellectual love for the One immutable and eternal good. Concomitantly, this knowledge allows a person to face the vicissitudes of life with equanimity. As well, this knowledge motivates the individual to behave altruistically toward others. As Nadler describes it, "He does what he can through rational benevolence (as opposed to pity or some other passion) to insure that they, too, can achieve relief from the disturbances of the passions through understanding, and thus that they become more like him (and therefore most useful to him)."[23]

So far, Spinoza has neutralized the questions that generate theodicy by showing that what Maimonides calls natural evil is simply nature as is and what Maimonides calls moral evil is a misjudgment. Spinoza goes further. He implies that what most people would consider evil—perhaps the ultimate evil—is useful, if not actually "good." In chapter 4 of his *Ethics*, proposition 67, Spinoza writes:

A free man thinks of nothing less than of death, and his wisdom is a meditation on life, not on death.

Spinoza seems to be saying that for many individuals, death is a preoccupation—not in the sense that people think about it all the time, but rather that since it is both inevitable and final, it is the quintessential evil that must be resisted. However, in calm, thoughtful, and rational moments, people realize that death is both an inalterable aspect of life and a catalyst for living more productively. The realization that people die is not a reason to fear but a reason to strive. Knowing that we will not live forever is a call to action. Death, therefore, is a gift: stirring people to better living. Hence, the death of an innocent is not a cause for dismay, since it is foolhardy to regret what cannot be changed.

If Spinoza is right that all that happens in the world is determined by a causal mechanism that human beings can only accept, then the only available response to suffering and tragedy might appear to be passive resignation. Spinoza presents a remedy to steer away from this and craft some measure of meaning: think differently. Nothing can change what happens to us, but our response to what happens to us is entirely in our hands. Here the interpretation of Oliver Leaman is quite helpful.

Leaman explains that for Spinoza, reason enables human beings to move from passive acceptance to active engagement with what happens.[24] Consciously internalizing the external factors that affect us, human beings gain a measure of control. Job, for example, is put upon by catastrophic forces (business failure, death of loved ones, personal illness, and self-doubt), all of which he vigorously resists. But it is counterproductive for him to suffer passively, to despair over his plight, to succumb to irrational emotions, or to seek to assess blame. The last will only result in confusion and frustration. Blaming God is senseless. After all, why would God be interested in the fate of a creature such as him? It would be an assault against reason to be angry at any putative cause that cannot rationally be shown to be the source of his suffering. Job would be better served by thinking rationally and clearly about wherein his well-being lies.

Spinoza is not saying that reflecting upon his situation will make his circumstances any the less painful. Nor will it relieve Job's suffering. But had Job reacted in this way, he would have discovered that what happened to him had to happen. He would have had the realization: it is part of my nature to suffer.

Spinoza holds that everyone possesses a unique and individual nature. As such, for Job to wonder why he—as opposed to someone else—suffers is the equivalent of asking why he is Job rather than someone else. To expect that all decent people benefit on their merits is an error, since that expectation is based on the invalid general assumption that all people ought to be treated in a common way. Any urge to think this way is symptomatic of confused thinking and a fundamental misunderstanding of God.

Instead, had Job followed Spinoza's pathway and come to terms with a new understanding of his true nature, it would have put him in more control of his feelings. It would have emancipated him from frustration and depression.

How Spinoza reads another familiar biblical episode is also instructive. To attentive readers,[25] the story of Adam in the Garden of Eden raises two problems aside from the anthropomorphic depiction of God. Adam's decision to eat the forbidden fruit, according to Spinoza, is a manifestation of his nature and thus, contrary to the traditional reading of the text, cannot be a sin. Further, the understanding that Adam's decision to eat the forbidden fruit was contrary to God's will is an impossibility. To put it differently, if Adam can choose to eat the forbidden fruit in violation of God's will, it suggests that God is imperfect in the sense that God's will can be overruled. Spinoza concludes that Adam's decision is neither evil nor contrary to God's will:

> The prohibition to Adam, then, consisted only in this: God revealed to Adam that eating of the tree caused death, just as he also reveals to us through the natural intellect that poison is deadly to us. And if you asked for what purpose he revealed it to him, I answer: to make him that much more perfect in knowledge. So to ask God why he did not also give him a more perfect will is as absurd as to ask him why he did not give a circle all the properties of a sphere.[26]

God's words to Adam are not to be construed as a warning with punitive consequences but as information to advance Adam's understanding. As such, there is no worry over violating God's will or committing a sinful act. And the very question of why God did not endow Adam with a superior, more obsequious will is nonsense. Adam was created in precisely the way he needed to be created, exactly as he should be.

While Spinoza's philosophy has the advantage of rendering theodicy irrelevant, some critique of Spinoza is in order. Nineteenth-century Italian polymath Samuel David Luzzatto criticizes Spinoza on two grounds: that his ethics includes assumptions that Judaism rejects, such as considering pity and humility vices, not virtues; and that his conception of God is alien to Judaism.[27] It is obvious that Spinoza does not understand God in the traditional sense. But this is not necessarily a failing. However, arguing that all that exists in the universe must necessarily be the way it is does not explain how all that exists in the universe became what it is. In other words, Spinoza does not offer a full and compelling account of the existence of things in the world. Rather than answer this central question, he ignores it. Further, the mechanistic world devoid of will and purpose Spinoza describes is a rather bleak one. Interestingly, German philosopher Georg W. F. Hegel attacked Spinoza from an entirely different and unexpected perspective. He wrote, "The allegations of those who accuse Spinoza of atheism are the direct opposite of the truth; with him there is too much God."[28] While Luzzatto claimed that Spinoza's failing was conceptualizing an alien God, Hegel condemned Spinoza for considering any God at all. From a different angle, German philosopher Gottfried Leibniz disputed Spinoza's claim that this world is the only possible world, arguing that this world is the best of all possible worlds. God could have created things differently but opted for the one that was ideal from God's perspective.

But perhaps the most severe criticism of Spinoza comes from Spinoza himself:

> If the way I have shown to lead to these things now seems very hard, still, it can be found. And of course, what is found so rarely must be hard. For if salvation were at hand, and could be found without great effort, how could nearly everyone neglect it? But all things excellent are as difficult as they are rare.[29]

Spinoza was correct. His approach is difficult indeed.

Moses Ḥayyim Luzzatto

Italian-born Moses Ḥayyim Luzzatto (1707–47) is revered by both mystics and ethicists. Yet his influence, despite his relatively short life, is much broader. He is considered to be one of the fathers of modern Hebrew literature, a successful playwright, a logician, rhetorician, polemicist, and talmudist, though little of his writing has survived to attest to his brilliant versatility.

His connection with mysticism began at age fifteen, when he organized a mystical group in his home. At age twenty, he claims to have experienced visions of a heavenly mentor who revealed to him esoteric wisdom. He also indulged in magical practices he believed could yield supernatural powers. When word of his activities became known, the local rabbinate, still reeling from the effects of the Sabbatean debacle, forbade him to continue. Even leaving for a freer environment in Amsterdam did not avail: the rabbis there banned his writings as well. At this juncture in his career, he turned to ethics and wrote his masterpiece, *Mesillat Yesharim* (*Path of the Upright*), whose popularity persists to this day. He settled in Israel in 1743, perhaps with messianistic anticipation. Sadly, his wife and son died by plague in Safed, and he died in Acre a year later.

Unlike other thinkers considered previously, Luzzatto presents a surprisingly systematic consideration of evil and suffering. His theodicy is inferable from his description of personal providence, and in part 2 of his book *Derekh ha-Shem* (*The Way of God*) he takes up providence.

Earlier, Luzzatto distinguishes human beings from all other divine creations. Human beings alone have the capacity to commune with God and the free will necessary for achieving it.[30] Communion with God— what he calls *shelemut* (perfection)—is attainable by choosing the good despite the temptations to do otherwise. For Luzzatto, human beings "are created with both a good inclination and evil inclination and the free will to choose between them."[31] By exercising free will and choosing good over evil, each moral agent draws closer to God and thus to perfection.

In part 2, Luzzatto moves from psychology to theodicy. Good and evil are possibilities between which human beings choose "as a test for them."[32] "Evil exists," he writes, "so that human beings may overcome it."[33] In other words, the existence of evil is not a challenge to God's goodness or power. The existence of both good and evil is a necessary feature of the universe that allows each individual to attain the perfection God has intended for humanity. Wealth and poverty, for example, are tests of character:

> The wealthy man is tested to determine whether he will be cruel to the poor person who needs him or will be kind towards him; and the poor man is tested to determine if he will be satisfied with the little he has and be grateful to God or the opposite. Moreover, wealth for the wealthy is a test to determine whether or not he becomes so arrogant that he forsakes God or, despite his wealth, remains humble

and self-effacing, resisting the vanities of life and choosing instead to commit to Torah and divine service.[34]

For Luzzatto, life is a laboratory. The series of experiments that God designs are not for God to gain knowledge that God, the Supreme Intellect, does not yet possess or to test the hypothesis that God theorizes. Rather, the experiments are conducted with the aim of allowing the experimental subjects (human beings) the potential to achieve perfection. As such, the question of why the wicked prosper and why the righteous suffer is easily explained. Prosperity and suffering are not connected to merits or demerits, reward or punishment. Prosperity and suffering are testing criteria. The wealthy man is being tested. His attitude toward his accumulated wealth and how he uses it will determine whether he is approaching perfection. The wealthy man who shares his wealth with the poor merits approbation, while the wealthy man who does not deserves reprobation. The undeservedly wealthy man who sees himself as the architect of his success and thus abandons God fails the test, while the wealthy man who remains steadfastly loyal to God passes. Likewise, the poor man who is grateful for whatever he has shows his worthiness, while the poor man who complains about his condition does not.

Crucially, Luzzatto does not distinguish between the undeservedly wealthy man (the quintessentially wicked man who prospers) and the deservedly wealthy man (the righteous man who prospers) or the undeservedly poor man (the righteous man who suffers) and the deservedly poor man (the wicked man who suffers). For Luzzatto, the conditions that led to wealth or poverty are not germane; only the subject's reaction to wealth or poverty matters. The assignment of wealth or poverty is all in accord with God's divine plan, which is "impossible for us to fathom,"[35] but consistent with what God has determined "to be in each person's best interests."[36]

With the objective of facilitating each person's "perfection," God will provide or withhold assistance in order to achieve that end. The degree of divine assistance a person receives will vary not on the basis of merit, but according to that particular person's needs in attaining perfection:

It may be that strictly on the basis of past performance a person deserves little assistance and another greater assistance yet the person who deserves little or no assistance gets more and the person who deserves more gets little. It all hinges on God's calculation of how much is needed to achieve perfection.[37]

From the perspective of the untrained observer, the wicked should be punished and the righteous should be rewarded. Each person ought to get what he or she deserves: punishment for the wicked and reward for the righteous. Evidence to the contrary calls God's power or goodness into question. But Luzzatto claims that the observer who draws this conclusion is sadly mistaken, since what God allots to any given person is not contingent on that person's moral worth but on what is necessary for that person to attain perfection. Thus "it is possible that success in this world is decreed without mitigation to the good person to facilitate his divine service and perfection while it is also possible that a good person endure suffering and deprivation in this world to encourage more intense efforts on his part to achieve perfection."[38]

Specifically with regard to the wicked, Luzzatto adds that it is possible that prosperity in this world is decreed for him to show him what he stands to lose.[39] It is also possible that suffering in this world is decreed for him to prevent him from contemplating further wickedness.[40] In either case, all is intended to assist the wicked in reaching personal perfection.

Strikingly, in all of Luzzatto's consideration of good and evil, there is no attempt to reference his views with earlier biblical or Rabbinic texts. So it is entirely surprising that in section 5 he adds the observation that sometimes suffering is useful in stirring the sufferer to repentance[41]—in effect resuscitating the Rabbinic dictum that there is no suffering without sin.

Luzzatto also seems troubled by what his readers may find unacceptable. In his account so far, an entirely wicked man might live his entire life without punishment. The wicked man may simply be unwilling or unprepared to change in order to achieve personal perfection. So Luzzatto contends that there is a limit to God's tolerance of the wicked.[42]

But details on what that limit may be and what happens when the limit is reached are absent.

Sections 7 and 8 include two extraordinary ideas. The first is that God takes into consideration a person's ancestry, progeny, and contemporaries when calculating how much or how little divine assistance is given in order to facilitate a person's perfectibility. The second is that "a righteous person atones for his generation." Each will be explored in turn.

Luzzatto claims that "a person may be born into goodness on account of the fact that his father was good and also a person may sometimes gain favor due to the merits of his ancestors. Likewise, a person may gain favor on account of the children that will issue from him. And similarly, a person may benefit from his community. Or sometimes a community may be affected by the good or evil deeds of one of its members."[43] Note that one can be born into good circumstances thanks to his parents' situation or sometimes because of his parents' merits, or into bad ones for those same reasons. Since God sees the big picture—not just currently, but into the future—God takes into account a broad range of factors, and every individual is treated in accordance with those factors. This idea is not novel—at least in part. Even the Rabbis of the Talmud recognized that one's ancestors' actions can have an effect on the living.[44]

Luzzatto goes further. He claims that the wicked in this world may prosper on account of what their descendants might merit in the future yet to occur.[45] To the observer without knowledge of the future, the prosperity of the wicked in this world is cause for alarm. It looks as if God is either indifferent to evil or powerless to prevent it. Yet that is the mistaken perception of the observer. God, rather, has calculated that the good deeds to be performed by the wicked man's offspring are so laudable that the wicked man of today gains some credit through them. Since the observer will remain unaware of the future and of God's calculation, the prosperity of the wicked will seem problematic, but in reality, it is simply a manifestation of God's algorithm of justice.

Connecting with the idea that a community may be affected by the deeds of one of its members, Luzzatto claims that a righteous man (or righteous men) may also suffer as a way of atoning for his (their) generation. For

Luzzatto, this extraordinary idea is a logical inference from the Rabbinic principle that "all Israel is responsible one for the other."[46] The interdependence of all Jews implies that any Jew can also harm another Jew's spiritual standing and the opposite: any one Jew can benefit the spiritual standing of every other Jew. So the righteous person who experiences what appears to be unwarranted suffering may actually be the designated sufferer for his generation. Any person or persons in this role, says Luzzatto, must be duty-bound to accept suffering without complaint for their vicarious suffering to be efficacious. But their reward in the afterlife will be great, and their efforts will earn them special standing.[47]

While this idea offers yet another answer to the question of why the righteous suffer, it also has an incidental benefit. Vicarious suffering provides solace to anyone who believes they are suffering unjustly. No one can ever be sure that his or her suffering is not intended to atone for the entire generation. Consequently, each sufferer might rest reassured that his or her suffering is now justified and hold out the hope for special approbation in the afterlife.

Finally, Luzzatto's robust consideration of good and evil includes the application of the kabbalistic affirmation of the transmigration of souls. This is hardly unexpected of a thinker who was deeply enmeshed in the mystical tradition. For Luzzatto, the attainment of perfection is not limited to this lifetime. It may take several lifetimes for the lessons to be learned that will enable a given soul to attain perfection. Ultimately, perfection occurs after a sufficient number of *gilgulim* (recurrent lives) effectively compensate for all variants, circumstances, and conditions.[48] Returning again and again enables each individual either to rectify things in this life that were damaged in previous ones or to perfect things now that were left imperfect before. In either case, a person's current spiritual or material successes or failures may thus be a consequence of what happened in past lives. Here again, a wicked person who prospers is likely benefiting from some noble deeds performed in a previous lifetime, and a righteous person who suffers is likely suffering from some evil deeds performed in past lives. Only God, the Supreme Intellect, is aware of the conditions and circumstances that demanded such treatment.

In assessing Luzzatto, the careful reader would be compelled to question his fundamental assumption that personal perfection is attainable. Indeed, the Bible itself insists that there is no person on earth who can avoid sin.[49] If it has been and always will remain God's plan that humanity face challenges that will lead to the perfection of character, and given that there is no evidence that anyone has attained perfection, it would seem that God's plan is unworkable, raising a theological conundrum: how can any plan devised by an omniscient and omnipotent God be unworkable?

Beyond the legitimacy of Luzzatto's fundamental assumptions, there are other shortcomings to consider. First, arguing that suffering is in the victim's best interest is hardly comforting or justifiable. Second, Gersonides would challenge Luzzatto's presumption of personal providence, arguing that God does not take interest in promoting the personal perfection of every individual; God is only concerned to promote those who aim to improve themselves. Third, Judaism generally rejects the principle of vicarious atonement for suffering, since the Bible holds that everyone is held accountable for one's own sin (Ezekiel 18; Jer. 31:30; Deut. 24:16). Finally, the notion of the transmigration of souls is itself an idea in need of proof. How can anyone be assured that any transmigration occurs? Offering this notion as a solution to the problem of divine justice only dodges the question.

Moses Mendelssohn

Moses Mendelssohn (1729–86) was substantially responsible for the change in attitudes toward Jews that ushered in the Emancipation. A childhood prodigy, he left Dessau, Germany, for Berlin at age fourteen. There, he continued his Jewish studies, but after friends introduced him to secular learning, he also voraciously studied French, Latin, mathematics, science, and especially philosophy. He sought out those who could aid in his academic advancement but remained mostly an autodidact.

Mendelssohn was the first Jew to publish in German. His literary skills caught the attention of King Frederick II, who inquired after the young Jew who wrote in German. His celebrity only grew when, in 1763, the Prussian Royal Academy awarded him first prize for *Phaedon*, his philosophical treatise on God, modeled on Platonic dialogue. Among his unsuccessful competitors was Immanuel Kant. Mendelssohn became known as "the German Socrates."

At age forty, controversy compelled him to return to his Jewish roots. Resisting public pressure to convert to Christianity, Mendelssohn took the defense of Judaism, culminating with the publication of his masterpiece *Jerusalem*, in 1783, three years before his death.

In it he puts forward a vigorous and original argument for the separation of church and state. In the second part Mendelssohn distinguishes between "revealed religion" and "revealed legislation." Judaism rejects the former and accepts the latter, resulting in, to paraphrase David Rudavsky,[50] the primacy of deed over creed.

Mendelssohn's thinking on good and evil, however, appears elsewhere. An inkling of his view is discernible in two letters he wrote to a friend following personal tragedy, while a more detailed explanation appears in his Hebrew commentary on the book of Genesis. And at the end of his *Phaedon*, Mendelssohn asserts that all injustices perceived in this world will be leveled in the next world

On May 1, 1764, shortly after the death of Mendelssohn's infant daughter, he wrote a letter to his friend Thomas Abbt. (This would not be the only personal tragedy Mendelssohn and his wife Frommet would endure; later, a son would also die at age twelve.) Mendelssohn writes:

> Some recent events in my domestic life have so shattered me that I did not even feel like writing to my friends, though this is normally my favorite occupation. Death has knocked at my door, robbing me of an innocent child that lived among us for eleven months, though these, thank God, were happy and full of promise.
>
> My friend, these eleven months of innocent living were not in vain. In this short time, the little girl's mind developed amazingly. She progressed from a tiny creature that merely cried and slept into a rational being. Much in the way in which young blades of grass push through the hard soil in spring, she began to show the first signs of distinct

emotions. She indicated compassion, hatred, love, and admiration, she understood what was said to her, and tried to make herself understood.

You may well ridicule my naiveté and look upon my rationalization as a weakness—the weakness of a man seeking consolation and unable to find it anywhere except in his imagination. Perhaps a sense of self-preservation compels me (without indulging my foibles too blatantly) to adopt any doctrine conducive to my peace of mind.

Yet I cannot believe that God has put us here on earth like, say, some from upon a wave. Indeed, I must embrace the opposite view simply because it seems less absurd, and promises me more comfort.[51]

In writing candidly and poignantly of his sense of loss, Mendelssohn admits that his view of the death of an innocent baby might be a more comforting self-delusion than an adequate theodicy. Nevertheless, Mendelssohn claims that all that occurs in life is in accordance with a divine plan that human beings would be foolish to deny. To be sure, affirming some divine plan is self-serving, offering a measure of consolation to the bereaved. But to believe otherwise means asserting the randomness of all phenomena, and that would be ludicrous. The acceptance of a divine plan, albeit one that eludes human understanding, provides the mourner the assurance that the death of an innocent was not unjust, even though it might appear to be so, as well as neutralizes the question of how a good and powerful God allows the death of children.

Mendelssohn takes up the same question in another letter to Abbt:

And what about the death of infants?—No baby dies without having developed at least some rudimentary skill, if only that ability to feel [some sensations] which starts in his mother's womb. And what amazing changes, now that I think of it, take place within such a tiny seminal being until, in its next developed stage, it learns to react to hunger, warmth, or wetness! Can you doubt that these early achievements already constitute a certain actualization of whatever plan the Creator has for this child? As it undergoes a reorganization of its components, even the seed that never comes to fruition progresses from an earlier to a later stage of development; and that stage represents the seed's fulfillment of its divinely intended purpose.[52]

All life from seeds to children are part of God's plan. Some reach their final stage of development; others do not. But whatever the outcome, it is all part of God's grand plan. To be sure, the keen observer would ask: why does one seed reach fruition yet another does not, or, more pointedly, why does one baby live and another does not? While the general idea is compelling, the specifics are troubling. Here Mendelssohn injects the analogy of a watch:

> The different parts of a watch [though unlike in design and function] all serve a single purpose. This wheel turns fast, that one slowly; and a third moves almost imperceptibly. Since all of them serve a common purpose, why do they not turn at equal speed? Here you have it: a common purpose. And it is precisely because of its singleness of purpose that the plan [whether God's or the watchmaker's] requires all those multifariously functioning parts.[53]

The watch is designed to incorporate a variety of parts functioning differently but all for the common purpose of keeping accurate time. Designing all components of the watch to operate the same way will undermine the very purpose it is supposed to fulfill. If the universe is analogous to the watch and people are analogous to the components, it is reasonable to believe that God, the watchmaker, will treat people differently in order to fulfill God's ultimate purpose. It would be unreasonable to assume that all people will be endowed with the same talents, blessed with same abilities, or charged with the same functions. It would be equally unreasonable to believe that all people would be granted the same span of years. Inconsistency is not a flaw in the watch, but a necessity. The same is true in life. That some children die young and others live to adulthood is all somehow connected with God's design that humanity must accept even without a complete understanding. The innocent may suffer, and for that matter the wicked may prosper, but all in the fulfillment of God's plan.

Netivot ha-Shalom (*Paths of Peace*) was part of Mendelssohn's larger program for preparing German Jews to enter into civil society. In order to familiarize the mainly Yiddish-speaking community with the vernacular, Mendelssohn conceived of the idea of translating the Hebrew Bible into Judeo-German, that is, German written with Hebrew letters. In collaboration with others, including his disciple Simon Dubno, he completed the project in 1783. The Hebrew text was accompanied by the German translation as well as a commentary reflecting the mood of the Enlightenment. The commentary, called the *Bi'ur*, was so influential, it became the synecdoche for the entire work. Mendelssohn wrote the commentary for the first six chapters of Genesis as well as for the entire book of Exodus.

Here, his commentaries on the last verse of Genesis 1 and on the Tree of Knowledge of Good and Evil in Genesis 2 are of particular relevance.

The biblical narrative describes God's approval of what resulted from six days of Creation with the notice that all that God had made was found to be "very good" (Gen. 1:31). Mendelssohn notes that the thoughtful reader would discern the contrast with earlier days of Creation, when God declared God's handiwork merely "good."[54] But Mendelssohn's question is not what made the completion of Creation qualitatively better ("very good") than any individual day ("good"), but how a perfect deity could possibly create anything that is less than perfect. The declarations that God's creations were either "good" or "very good" imply that everything God created was less than perfect. And that, in turn, implies that incorporated into Creation were elements not absolutely good.

> The notion is that there is no complete and absolute good in the particulars that exist, but rather good and bad commingled, one included with the other.[55]

Accordingly, "many evils are to be found among the particulars of created things." As Mendelssohn explains, that is because of the very nature of created things. Created things can never be perfect, since these they are once removed from the perfect Creator. Mendelssohn avows:

It is impossible that any created thing would be perfect in its utmost perfection as it is necessarily composed of *habitus* and privation, with privation being the source of evil.[56]

Here Mendelssohn refers to a concept introduced by Aristotle[57] and expanded by Augustine.[58] *Habitus* is the possession of a certain attribute. Privation is the absence of an essential attribute. If God is incomparable and an essential attribute of God is absolute (or "utmost") perfection, every product of God's creation must be deprived of such perfection. Were this not the case and other creatures possessed absolute perfection, they would rival God, and that would be impossible. Consequently, all that God creates cannot be perfect. The absence of perfection means that, at best, the output of Creation can only be "very good." And hence privation allows for the existence of evil—"evil" being anything short of perfection.

Mendelssohn is quick to point out that it would be hasty to infer that since all Creation cannot be perfect, all of Creation must be completely evil:

For there is no existence whatsoever to absolute, complete evil; it is impossible and self-contradictory, since everything extant is good insofar it exists. And were it not that those evils were good in one respect, it would not be possible for them to have been brought into existence in a world created by a Being that is good, and does good, that loves good with the utmost love and abhors absolute evil with the utmost abhorrence.[59]

Since God is all good, all God brings into existence must be good or for the good—including evil. Were this not the case, the supremely good God would not have sanctioned its existence. Even death is good.

Death is bad in that it negates the form of a living being. However, in terms of the totality, even death is good since generation and degeneration are conjoined and interconnected, such that all degeneration is a cause for generation, and all generation is a cause for degeneration, and through them all created things change from one form to another according to God's designated purpose.[60]

Mendelssohn contends that death is beneficial when considered as part of a cyclical process rather than the end of life. Consider the nitrogen cycle as an illustration. Nitrogen is a necessary element for human life. Human beings, like all animals, lack the ability to fixate nitrogen molecules from the atmosphere. Bacteria, however, are quite successful in capturing nitrogen from the atmosphere and converting it to ammonia, necessary for generating organic molecules. The bacteria in soil pass on the ammonia to the plants that grow in the soil. The plants are eaten by animals and human beings alike. But the nitrogenous material does not remain in the body forever. While the body is alive, nitrogen is egested as waste and returned to the soil, where the cycle begins anew. When a body dies, it is entirely returned to the earth, where its component elements are broken down, only to be recycled, as it were, as nutrients for the next generation of beings. People who survive the death of a loved one see death as the ultimate evil: depriving them of association with a loved one. Yet in God's grand plan, death serves the purpose of facilitating the regeneration of life in a far broader sense.

Death, Mendelssohn notes, is not the only evil that is part of life. "Other [evils] are consequent upon the unending series of cause and effects like accidents of time and its attendant misfortunes. Still other are consequent on choice, these being the evils or moral dispositions and deeds."[61] What Maimonides terms "natural evil" is what Mendelssohn describes as evils consequent on cause and effect. Earthquakes that may result in destruction are caused by shifting tectonic plates in the earth's crust. And aging is an accident, that is, a consequence of time. Illness, incontinence, and senility are all "evils" associated with aging. All these are effects of the laws of nature. Moral evil is the result of poor choices made by people in their interpersonal relations, such as a person who chooses to steal from another person for monetary gain. Interestingly, Mendelssohn characterizes "evils due to choice" as "evil with respect to the one who chooses them."[62] That is to say, the criminal does evil to himself more than to the victim. This point is left without further elaboration.

Mendelssohn rejects the possibility that God opted to create human beings without free will. He argues to the contrary: "Desire and freedom of choice are a great benefit and good for the world in its totality, without which its perseverance would not be possible. There is no freedom of choice without the possibility of doing something or its opposite, and as such, evil choices are also good in this respect."[63] He insists that absent freedom of choice, human beings would be automatons. To be human means given the capability to choose. But with the capability to choose comes the possibility to choose to perform wicked acts. Yet, in the scheme of things, that is a small price to pay. God's plan for the world can only be effected when human beings are endowed with free will.

Mendelssohn identifies that plan when he notes that the purpose of Creation is "to correct evil and change it to good."[64] In his view, there are two ways to fulfill that plan. First, God, invoking divine "providence and compassion," can overturn the deleterious effects of wrongdoing by reversing them. And second, God can allow human beings to reconsider their choices. In this sense, even the "evil inclination" is "good"—not because it leads people astray, but in that it represents freedom of choice, a "necessity in the establishment of the world."[65]

Returning to the language of the Torah that instigated his original question, Mendelssohn remarks:

> With regard to the [six] earlier days of creation, Scripture speaks only of the particulars of creation in which there is no absolute good, but evil and good commingled. Since, however, in some respect evil too is necessary for establishing the good, God understood that it was in accord with the ultimate purpose and desired its existence, not with respect to being an evil, but in terms of its necessity for the good. . . . However, on the sixth day, when all was done in its totality . . . and with regard to the totality of the world there is no evil whatsoever, because in terms of the totality everything is good and in great accord with God's intended purpose.[66]

In Mendelssohn's view, from this narrow perspective the Torah teaches that good and evil are part of the very fabric of Creation. Given the created world in which humanity exists, it would be preposterous to even consider otherwise. As such, the very question "Why does evil exist?" is nonsense. In addition, evil is necessary for the good. In order for "good" to have any meaning, the possibility for evil to which it stands opposed must be open. From the broader perspective, anything that conforms to God's master plan is necessarily good. Hence, death, depredation, suffering, illness, even murder and the like—all part of God's plan—must be good. Ultimately, this yields the inescapable conclusion that there is no evil at all.

Mendelssohn's interpretation of the passage regarding the Tree of Knowledge of Good and Evil further develops his concept of moral evil:

> The fruit of this tree [of knowledge] gave rise to will and want, such that those who partook of it could choose between something and its converse, for good or evil. This is why it was called the tree of knowledge of good and evil, for knowledge [da'at] in our language is an expression of will.[67]

Mendelssohn, like any proficient exegete, substantiates his identification of da'at with "will" by citing passages in the Bible[68] and Rabbinic literature[69] that support his reading that human beings gained freedom of choice only after eating from the tree. An obvious question is raised by this reading: How did the first couple come to choose to violate God's instructions before eating from the fruit of the Tree of Knowledge of Good and Evil that gave them the power to choose? Anticipating the question, Mendelssohn distinguishes between acting mindfully and acting obliviously. Before eating from the fruit of the Tree of Knowledge, Adam and Eve were no different from animals, lacking a true sense of how and why they acted. "Adam and his wife did not engage in sexual intercourse as a matter of desire, but when it came to propagation, they copulated and produced offspring."[70] For Mendelssohn, "desire" means "will and want" that leads to "choose between something and its converse, for good and evil."[71] In their original state—that is, before eating the forbidden fruit—Adam and Eve were impelled by biology, not morality. Natural curiosity, not a mindful choice, drove Adam and Eve to eat the fruit. They ate it because it was available, not because it was desirable.

> But now, after their eating of the tree, man had the ability to choose; he had the will to do evil or do good, whether to himself or to others. This was, in one respect, a divine quality, but it was bad for man in that it gave him yearning and desire.[72]

Human beings were no longer to be defined as "more intelligent animals." After consuming the fruit of the Tree of Knowledge, human beings gained an element of the divine—but it came with a cost. Now imbued with desire, human beings may choose to do what is tempting but not necessarily what is right. Accordingly:

> At times, his eyes and his mind perceives the true good that brings him to felicity, but the power of the desire that overcomes proper reasoning seduced him to be drawn after bodily pleasures and to be mired in the pursuit of sensual pleasures. This is the cause of all sin and rebelliousness in man.[73]

Moral evil is the unavoidable outcome of free choice, moderated only by human rationality or what Mendelssohn calls "the faculty of apprehension." Before Adam sinned, he had free choice of the first kind, but only after his sin did he become aware of his desires that, if unchecked by apprehension, will result in evil.

While all of Mendelssohn's approach to moral evil is theoretically defensible, truth be told, human observers are mired in the nagging doubt that God's plan is sound. As Mendelssohn writes at the end of *Phaedon*, much that happens in this world is incongruent with the concept of a single good and just God:

> Occasionally one is tempted to believe man's fate is determined by a causative power delighting in evil.... The triumph of vice, perpetration

of evil deeds by crowned heads, persecution of innocence and oppression of virtue are no rare occurrences. The innocent and righteous suffer no less than the evildoers. . . . Good fortune or misfortune happen to good and evil men alike, without notable distinction. . . . If some wise, kind, and just Being were benevolently concerned with the fate of man, should not the moral universe give some evidence of the same wise order we so much admire in the physical world?[74]

Human experience calls into question the justice of God. Mendelssohn, however, argues that those willing to concede the beauty, order, and harmony that exist in the physical world despite the damage of occasional natural disasters should also be prepared to admit the justice in the moral world despite the occasional harmful acts people commit against others, especially given the existence of an afterlife:

Just as in the physical world the disorder of its parts—that is, thunderstorms, cloudbursts, earthquakes, floods, or pestilence—dissolves into the harmony of the immeasurably great whole, so do the fleeting distempers of the moral world and their effects on man's life serve merely as a transition to eternal harmony. Thus momentary suffering leads to never-ending bliss, and passing afflictions to enduring well-being.[75]

The presumption of an afterlife where any perceived injustice will be remedied goes back to the Rabbinic period, if not earlier. But positing an afterlife can be viewed as tacit admission that the world human beings experience is unjust and that God is either incapable or unwilling to change it. Mendelssohn's argument might have been far stronger had he set aside the afterlife and allowed the logic of the argument itself to do its work: If one is willing to see the beauty and order in the natural world despite the catastrophes that sometimes obtain, then one should be equally willing to see the justice in the moral world despite the occasional exceptions. When one looks at the universe as a whole, the picture may be quite different than when obsessing over particulars. It is all a matter of perspective. Looking at the whole of the universe may allow an observer to conclude the world is good. And looking at the whole of a person's life may allow an observer to conclude that God is just.

But here is where the logic fails and the afterlife becomes necessary. The whole of a person's life in this world as judged by the neutral observer may—to the contrary—seem to be undeservedly pitiable. Thus, only when accounting for the afterlife does an individual's life come into full perspective:

> To gain a proper perspective of the life of even one single individual, we would have to see it in its eternal dimension. Only then would we be able to judge the ways of Providence.[76]

Given this added dimension, Mendelssohn concludes, the problem addressed by theodicy dissolves.

Mendelssohn claims that all evils experienced are part of a divine plan. The nature of the plan, however, is unknown. Even so, this plan must be affirmed.

Here Mendelssohn appeals to faith rather than reason. He does the same in affirming the notion of an afterlife. However, faith, by definition, relies on a belief independent of logic, evidence, or rational thought. Privileging an argument on faith renders that argument immune to criticism from those who don't accept it. Demands for evidence by nonbelievers are rebuffed on the grounds that no evidence is necessary because the idea must be accepted without question as a matter of faith. Meanwhile, there is no evidence or logic that can convince a believer to believe otherwise. Accordingly, Mendelssohn's insistence on an afterlife must either be accepted or rejected but cannot be debated.

Summary

All in all, Spinoza, Luzzatto, and Mendelssohn attempt to vitiate the problem of evil in the world rather than offer solutions. Though their strategies are somewhat different, the objective is the same. In so doing, these early modern thinkers bridge rationalism and mysticism, the discursive philosophy of the medievalists and the traditional responses of the Bible and Talmud.

The Nature of Good and Evil: For Spinoza, the word "good" as it relates to a person is less a matter of judgment of morality than it is of that person's ability to control feelings and passions. For Luzzatto, evil is a failure of human will, which thereby distances humanity from the perfection that God projects for it. Evil thus exists as a test in life's laboratory, challenging human beings to overcome it and come closer to perfection. Mendelssohn resuscitates the Aristotelian concept of privation adopted by medieval thinkers such as Maimonides. Privation—that is, anything short of perfection—is what allows for the existence of evil. Evil is part of the fabric of Creation and hence, for Mendelssohn, is a necessary and inevitable component of life.

Mendelssohn would agree with Luzzatto that moral evil is the unavoidable outcome of freedom of choice. Spinoza insists that good and evil are modes of thought rather than things that exist in nature. As such, what people consider "evil" is simply the universe as it is; the question of why evil exists is meaningless, and the demand that God provide some kind of explanation for evil is exclusively a function of human confusion. For Luzzatto, evil is all part of God's plan, even though it is essentially unknowable. Mendelssohn agrees. Concomitantly, Mendelssohn agrees with Spinoza that evil is all part of life, woven into the very fabric of existence.

Questions of Justice: By equating God with natural laws, Spinoza obviates the need to defend God from charges of injustice. That the righteous sometimes suffer and the wicked sometimes prosper is just the way things are. Theodicy is symptomatic of the magical thinking of human beings. It is actually unnecessary. In essence, Spinoza consigns all questions of justice to a confusion of the mind. The perception of seeming injustices in life is rooted in the deficiencies of the human mind rather than in the deficiencies of God. The challenge human beings face is to resist magical thinking and, instead, use their reflective ability to learn from their experiences rather than passively accept them.

Luzzatto follows a strategy similar to Spinoza. But Luzzatto obviates the need to defend God from charges of injustice by arguing that all that happens is in accord with God's plan, which is to say, in every person's best interest, independent of merit and entirely dependent on bringing every person closer to perfection. Luzzatto introduces a complex set of calculations that God applies in order to effect that plan, including the mystical idea of the transmigration of souls. Mendelssohn, too, asserts that all that occurs in life is in accordance with God's plan. Even so, any perceived injustice will be remedied in the afterlife. For Mendelssohn, moral evil is the misapplication of free will. And the recompense of both the victim and the perpetrator lies in the afterlife.

CHAPTER 7

Modern Thinkers on Good and Evil

When, exactly, the modern period of history begins is debatable. Contemporary German philosopher Jürgen Habermas argues that the onset of the modern period coincides with eighteenth-century French enlightenment.[1] Jewish historian Joseph Blau intimates that modernity begins in the year 1800.[2] Philosopher Alfred North Whitehead claims that that the modern period begins with "the assertiveness of science," which he dates to the 1600s,[3] while eminent British historian Paul Johnson declares that "the modern world began on 29 May 1919" when photographs of a solar eclipse confirmed Einstein's theory of relativity.[4] But there is no disputing that by the time of Hermann Cohen, the course toward the modern period was already set.

Hermann Cohen

Mendelssohn, the Jewish genius who bested Kant, captured the imagination of the European public. But it was Hermann Cohen (1842–1918), providing his philosophical rigor, who made academia take note of Jewish intellectualism.

Cohen benefited from a traditional Jewish upbringing, learning the traditional sources from his father and expanding his skills while attending the Jewish Theological Seminary in Breslau. His contribution to Jewish philosophy would come later in his life. Cohen had achieved such a high degree of academic distinction in general philosophy, particularly in his interpretation of Kant, that he was appointed to a prestigious professorship at Marburg University when he was a mere thirty-three years old. Remaining ensconced at Marburg until his retirement, he earned a reputation as the dominant figure of a whole school of philosophic inquiry.

In his most famous and influential work, *Religion of Reason Out of the Sources of Judaism*, published in 1919, Cohen makes the shocking assertion that suffering—that is, the worldly manifestation of evil—is not an unwarranted interruption of life, but a necessary feature of it:

The suffering of man is . . . the suffering that comes from being a man.[5]

Cohen explains that human suffering is a function of human existence. Rather than think of life as a whole as pleasure interrupted by moments of unwanted suffering, life as a whole ought to be considered as suffering "only interrupted by moments of illusory pleasure."[6] To expect otherwise is a failure to understand what human life entails. Suffering enables human beings to gain perspective:

In suffering, a dazzling light suddenly makes me see the dark spots in the sun of life. Even though insight into the ground of suffering may remain forever hidden from me, it is not a theoretical interest that is aroused in me through this observation. It is the whole meaning of ethics, as the teaching of man and his worth, of which I have to despair, if this, man's worth, is primarily expressed in suffering. The whole meaning of humanity in that case would become untenable to me, to say nothing of whether I could still take any interest at all in my own existence.[7]

While the causes of suffering are mysterious, the experience of suffering is beneficial. Cohen hastens to add that it is not suffering per se that is desirable, but what suffering motivates. Observing the suffering of others, according to Cohen, should activate an empathic concern for others, since "it is only narrow-mindedness that could make me indifferent to suffering."[8] The observer should therefore be motivated to try to relieve that other person's suffering. As Cohen puts it, the suffering of others should make it "a question mark for my whole orientation in the moral world."[9] And the only acceptable resolution to the question of suffering is compassion.

Just as suffering arouses the individual's compassion for others, suffering also transforms the individual who suffers. Cohen pivots toward consideration of the individual's suffering by stating, "Suffering may be the common lot of men. Nevertheless, it must first of all become the *watchword* for the I."[10] Suffering liberates the individual "from the shadow of selfishness."[11] It encourages each individual to alleviate his or her own suffering rather than accept it "with plain indifference."[12] Most of all, the permanency of suffering "gives my existence its correct meaning,"[13] which is the pursuit of redemption, not the pursuit of pleasure. In sum:

> Suffering is not a defect, no dysteleology, but an independent link in the moral system and thus, full of purpose.[14]

One purpose, for Cohen, is to gain a deeper connection with God. With regard to Job, Cohen writes that "he is in need of suffering and deserves to pass through it, though not so much as a single individual but as a self in correlation with God."[15] In Cohen's terms, striving for moral improvement establishes a "correlation" between the individual and God. And suffering is what impels the individual to aspire to moral improvement.

Cohen further emphasizes that "suffering is the punishment that man demands inexorably of himself for himself."[16] That is to say, suffering is not only relentless and unavoidable; it is self-imposed. Individuals make themselves suffer as the penalty for moral failings, which guides them to virtue. As such, and in opposition to the Talmud, Cohen disallows interpreting suffering as God's punishment for sin.

In Cohen's view, all humanity is bound to suffer. But within humanity, one group suffers most of all. "The suffering within the human race," writes Cohen, "has been primarily the suffering of *Israel*."[17] What is more, the Jewish people has an "obligation to suffer"[18] as a precondition for redemption[19]—and not just for Jews, but for all of humanity. Suffering is

Israel's "vital force"[20] and, as such, "has no tragic connotation."[21] In fact, the very suffering of the Jewish people over the centuries has earned the Jewish people special status. "The historical suffering of Israel," Cohen writes in his chapter "The Messianic References in the Prophetic Writings," "gives it its historical dignity,"[22] what he later calls Israel's "privileged position."[23] Not only does suffering merit Israel its elevated status; Israel's vicarious suffering for humanity acquires for it the "right to convert"[24] the nations of the world.

Cohen contrasts the Jewish perspective on suffering with that of other systems of faith. All religions grapple with the problem of suffering and evil to a greater or lesser extent. But what distinguishes Judaism from them, Cohen contends, is Judaism's view of suffering as a means to an end, while other systems of faith mistakenly believe that suffering is an end in itself. For Cohen, in Judaism "only the correlation of God and man can be an end in itself,"[25] that is, a profoundly personal relationship. So Judaism develops a unique approach.

> It became possible to represent the divine itself as suffering, as human suffering. Although in this idea the end of the redemption of men is seen along with and beyond suffering, yet the redeemer himself [i.e., the Messiah] must take this suffering upon himself. And through this idea, suffering becomes and is the end.[26]

Jews suffer for humanity, and the Messiah suffers for Israel. Redemption, which brings the end of suffering, can only occur when Jews practice penitence, show compassion, engage in "self-sanctification,"[27] and follow the mitzvot, "turning into the correlation with God."[28]

Perhaps more than any other modern philosopher, Cohen's philosophy of suffering and evil offers a robust account for the existence and the persistence of antisemitism. Jews remain persecuted because Jews are the world's designated sufferers. But if Jewish peoplehood requires suffering and even martyrdom, who would welcome such misery? Without a more deeply convincing rationale for enduring the world's animus,

Jews themselves would appear to find his thinking less a justification for remaining Jewish and more an invitation to abandon Judaism altogether.

Another troublesome aspect of Cohen's philosophy is his identification of suffering with the economic depredation of the poor. His categorical statement "The bearers of human suffering are the poor"[29] is only somewhat moderated by the subsequent statement that the suffering of men is "mainly . . . the social suffering of the poor."[30] Yet surely there are other, and arguably more serious, manifestations of suffering than economic ones—physical maladies and natural disasters among them. And, of course, there is the challenge of what Kant called "radical evil." Cohen's theory of suffering and evil seems ill-equipped to address the profound issues raised by the Holocaust.

Moreover, Cohen does not offer a theodicy. God, to Cohen, is not an agent who interferes with nature, despite the fact that many biblical passages dispute this contention. And since all that makes up God's character is beyond human comprehension, there is little use in trying to account for evil in the world. Instead, as the educator and author Rabbi Simon Noveck notes concerning Cohen's view, "what is important for man is not the preoccupation with God's nature but rather the imitation of His values."[31] Yet, according to Cohen, God would want to foster human suffering because that suffering makes humans more compassionate. Imitating God would thus mean adding to human suffering, a position a neutral observer would find odd. Thus, redirecting humanity away from theology and toward ethics may well serve Cohen's emphasis on the ethical component of "ethical monotheism," but begs the question of whether the One God's values are in fact worthy of imitation.

Even more critically, Cohen assumes that by observing the suffering of others one is necessarily led to compassion and motivated to ease their suffering. But one can rightly question his assumption. Many notice the suffering of others but fail to experience compassion, let alone act to relieve the pain of the victim.

Lastly, some critics of Cohen have claimed that Cohen conceives God as more an idea than a transcendental being. In this case, Fackenheim writes, "Jews today can put far less trust in Cohen's God Idea than the ancient God of Israel."[32]

Samuel Alexander

In his day Samuel Alexander (1859–1938) was considered one of the premiere metaphysicians in the world, but his fame has faded over time, his name has been relegated to virtual obscurity, and his system has been woefully neglected. Nevertheless, his original thinking on God merits some attention.

Alexander was born to Jewish parents in Sydney, Australia, his father dying just before his birth. Migrating to England in 1877, he was acclaimed as one of the top students at Oxford, bridging mathematics and the classics. A prize-winning essay on moral philosophy served as the basis of his 1899 book *Moral Order and Progress*, and then his interests turned to psychology. In 1893 he won a professorship in philosophy at the University of Manchester, where he remained until his death. Never married, he left a substantial part of his estate to the Hebrew University in Jerusalem, having taken up the cause of European Jewry's resettlement in Palestine.

Alexander represented what was then called "emergentism," best described as seeing human consciousness as more than the neurochemical processes of the brain. Instead, he argued, human consciousness emerges from and is not limited to these processes. In his *Space Time and Deity*, he puts it this way:

> We are forced . . . to go beyond the mere correlation of the mental with these neural processes and to identify them. There is but one process which, being of a specific complexity, has the quality of consciousness.[33]

The result is that

> the [emergent] quality and the constellation to which it belongs are at once new and expressible without residue in terms of the processes proper to the level from which they emerge.[34]

In other words, what emerges is qualitatively different from the sources from which the quality emerged. Human consciousness, for example, differs from any of the components that give rise to it and thus cannot be reduced to any of its component parts. To put it simply, the mind is not the same as the brain, although a brain is a necessary precursor for the mind. Emergent qualities evolve until they reach their ultimate and final form.

Applied to God, Alexander writes:

As existents within Space-Time, minds enter into various relations of a perfectly general character with other things and with one another. These account for the familiar features of mental life: knowing, freedom, values and the like. In the hierarchy of qualities the next higher quality to the highest attained is deity. God is the whole universe engaged in process towards the emergence of this new quality, and religion is the sentiment in us that we are drawn towards him, and caught in the movement of the world to a higher level of existence.[35]

Just as consciousness begins with brain and culminates with the mind, the universe begins with space-time, progresses with matter that leads to mind, and culminates with God. Alexander calls the impetus for this evolving process a "nisus"—that is, a striving force. Accordingly, "as an actual existent, God is the infinite world with its nisus towards deity,"[36] by which he means that God is the whole world progressing toward the quality of deity, the highest level of virtue imaginable.

The progression is not yet complete. Nonetheless, in answer to the question "Does God exist?" Alexander would say that even though the progression toward deity has not yet reached its ultimate form, God does exist in the sense that the evolving world itself (a necessary component of God) exists.

In conceptualizing God in this way, Alexander believed he had solved the problem of evil. God is not caught up in the machinery of the world. God is not the designer of a world that includes natural evils or an indifferent actor that tolerates moral evil. As Alexander conceives it, God does not precede the world as its creator but, instead, is the world's product.

"God . . . is in the strictest sense not a creator but a creature."[37] Accordingly, "God is not responsible for the miseries endured in working out his providence, but rather we are responsible for our acts."[38] Consequently, the human exercise of free will for noble purposes becomes an imperative.

Alexander's conception of God is unique, though startling in that it contradicts the basic Jewish understanding of God as perfect and indivisible as recorded in both biblical and Rabbinic sources. And although Alexander's directive for humanity is laudable, he assumes that the God-in-the-making is progressing toward a higher state of being. While this evolution may be demonstrable biologically, it is not necessarily true theologically. And besides, human observation and experience would challenge the presumption that the world is progressing toward godliness.

Martin Buber

Martin Buber (1878–1965) is arguably the most influential Jewish philosopher of the twentieth century.[39] His career spanned three continents and many interests. Born in Vienna and raised by his grandfather, a distinguished rabbinic scholar, Buber went on to study and teach philosophy in Germany, the United States, and Israel. He championed the Zionist cause, founded one of the most influential journals of Jewish thought in central Europe (*Der Jude* [The Jew]), published extensively on Hasidism, worked cooperatively with Franz Rosenzweig on a new German translation of the Bible, promoted adult education, participated in Jewish-Christian dialogue, advocated Arab-Jewish reconciliation, and supported a binational state in Palestine.

Buber is generally considered a religious existentialist, but this label fails to adequately describe his philosophy. Buber's basic insight, which, as contemporary theologian Michael Wyschograd notes,[40] runs through all of his work, is that people relate to other people or to objects in one of two ways: as a means to an end or as an end in itself. Tools, for example, are designed to perform certain tasks. People use tools for completing the assigned task, and this seems as it should. Sometimes people treat other people like tools, using them for a particular purpose. Treating people this way is not intrinsically bad. In fact, in certain contexts, treating people this way is both necessary and appropriate. Consider the case of the checkout clerk at the local supermarket. When it is time to scan one's merchandise, the clerk is there to process the purchase. The purchaser has little interest in the clerk as a person (even when there is a summary greeting exchanged), only in getting out of the store as expeditiously as possible. From the purchaser's perspective, the clerk is there to serve the purchaser's particular needs. Buber appreciates that much of life is like this.

In contrast, when a person is fully attentive to another, fully present, and fully engaged, the relationship between the two becomes mutual. Buber likens this relationship to a dialogue with each person listening and responding deeply and directly to the other. He calls this standing "with the whole of one's being over against another being" and characterizes its result as stepping "into an essential relation with him."[41] Remarkably, Buber contends that such a relationship is even possible with inanimate objects. An art lover, for example, can enter into a deep and direct relation with a work of art. A music lover might enter into such a relation with a symphony. A nature lover can enter into such a relation with certain natural phenomena. Viewing the *Mona Lisa*, listening to Mozart's *Requiem*, beholding a sunrise over the Grand Canyon—each can have a powerful effect on the attentive viewer or listener.

The vocabulary Buber develops to represent his insight is featured in his 1922 masterpiece *Ich und Du*, translated into English by Ronald Gregor Smith in 1958 as *I and Thou*. An I-It relationship is generated any time one person or object is viewed by another as a "thing" to be observed, assessed, or judged. This is not a genuine relationship, since it is one-sided. By contrast, in an I-Thou relation both the observer and the observed come together, each "I" subsumed under the merged relationship. The I-Thou relationship is, as one could imagine, the hardest to achieve and the hardest to maintain. And yet, it is by far the richer.

Lurking over the entirety of Buber's enterprise is God as the ultimate (or "primary") Thou with whom to relate.

In the relation to God, unconditional exclusiveness and unconditional inclusiveness are one. For those who enter into the absolute relationship, nothing particular retains any importance—neither things nor beings—but everything is included in the relationship. For entering into the pure relationship does not involve ignoring everything but seeing everything in Thou, not renouncing the world but placing it upon its proper ground. Looking away from the world is no help toward God; staring at the world is no help either; but whoever beholds the world in him stands in his presence. "World here, God there"—that is It-talk; and "God in the world"—that, too, is It-talk; but leaving out nothing, leaving nothing behind, to comprehend all—all the world—in comprehending the Thou, giving the world its due and truth, to have nothing besides God but to grasp everything in him, that is the perfect relationship.[42]

An encounter with God, for Buber, differs from any other relationship. It is a total relationship. It requires a readiness to enter into a genuine and authentic dialogue. And when such a relationship is secured, the "I" feels fully suffused with God's presence. In fact, at this point for Buber, God and God's presence are one and the same. As Buber puts it:

The deepest basis of the Jewish idea of God can be achieved only by plunging into that word by which God revealed Himself to Moses, "I shall be there." It gives exact expression to the personal "existence" of God (not to His abstract being).[43]

Buber refers to Exodus 3:14, where God describes God's self with the Hebrew word *ehyeh*, often rendered as "I am" but translated by Buber as "I shall be there." Rather than defining God's self in philosophical terms or listing God's powers, God chooses to inform Moses that God is just there with him and will be there for the people Israel. In other words, God is a presence to be encountered, not an idea to be analyzed or a metaphysical concept to parse.

To Buber, suffering and evil take root when the human sense of God's presence has been compromised. As Buber describes in his *Eclipse of God*, encountering God is the possibility of experiencing human life in relation to a great and transcendent reality, and the "eclipse of God" is the foreclosing of this possibility:

> Eclipse of the light of heaven, eclipse of God—such indeed is the character of the historic hour through which the world is passing.... An eclipse of the sun is something that occurs between the sun and our eyes, not the sun itself.... But... one misses everything when one insists on discovering within earthly thought the power that unveils the mystery. He who refuses to submit himself to the effective reality of transcendence as such... contributes to the human responsibility for the eclipse.[44]

Buber is driving at what he holds to be the relatively modern phenomenon of indifference—if not outright resistance and hostility—to God. Importantly, Buber insists that the inability of moderns to behold God does not mean that God does not exist no more than the blockage of the sun by the moon during an eclipse means the sun does not exist. In his view, jaded materialism and self-indulgence have driven people from a sense of reciprocal interconnectedness to mere individualism where others are valued only for their usefulness to us.

> Man has become incapable of apprehending a reality absolutely independent of himself.... Man's capacity to apprehend the divine images is lamed in the same measure as is his capacity to experience a reality absolutely independent of himself.[45]

To Buber, the modern age is characterized by the predominance of I-It relationships that block access to the primary Thou. And those I-It relationships have been promoted by the modern scientific obsession with cognition, rationality, and proof. As contemporary philosopher Leora Batnitzky diagnoses the situation according to Buber, "If people do not have faith in God, it is because they have not experienced God."[46] And to those who insist on some philosophical proof for the existence of God as a prerequisite for belief, Buber retorts, "It is not necessary to know something about God in order to really believe in Him: many true believers know how to talk *to* God but not *about* Him."[47]

Buber is not arguing that the problem of evil is a recent one. The first half of his book *Good and Evil* analyzes five psalms that shed light on doing right versus wrong, the difference between the righteous and the wrongdoers of the world, and "so of the world struggle between good and evil"[48] that has persisted since primordial time. Instead, Buber is contending that the problem of evil has intensified in the modern period, when the reality of God's presence is widely doubted.

As such, for Buber, the solution to the persistent problem of evil does not lie in God's attributes, but in the human soul. More concerned with human psychology than with theodicy, Buber writes, "The struggle must begin within one's own soul—all else will follow upon this."[49] He goes on to say, "A man only knows factually what 'evil' is insofar as he knows about himself."[50]

One dimension of evil located internally is indecision.[51] Another, more critical dimension is aimlessness—a loss of direction. As Buber puts it:

> Good and evil, then, cannot be a pair of opposites like right and left or above and beneath. "Good" is the movement in the direction of home, "evil" is the aimless whirl of human potentialities without which nothing can be achieved and by which, if they take no direction but remain trapped in themselves, everything goes awry.[52]

"Home," for Buber, means within God's presence. "Good" is the process of turning to God (or re-turning to God): a discovery (or re-discovery) of direction. As Oliver Leaman notes, it is entirely consistent of Buber to connect good and evil with direction, since Buber's philosophical machinery is based upon dialogue, itself a relational notion.[53] Dialogical relations are bidirectional. Where there is no dialogue or there is ineffective dialogue with the primary Thou, that is, a failure to connect with God, there is an ineluctable loss of direction resulting in evil. Or, to put it another way, when I-It relationships dominate human life, evil flourishes. Good can replace evil when the primary I-Thou relationship is restored. The purpose of man, Buber contends, is "to overcome the chaotic state of his soul, the state of undirected surging passion,"[54] "achieving direction," which is "good."[55]

Those who are within God's presence will interpret "evil" quite differently from those who are not. Life, as unpredictable as it is, will pose challenges to every individual. These unexpected challenges can be energizing or deflating. Sudden illness or economic failure could be causes for despair. Yet Buber writes:

> He who is aware of this Presence acts in the changing situations of life differently from him who does not perceive this Presence.[56]

For those who have turned away from God, these situations are manifestations of evil. But for those who have turned to God, the situation is not at all bleak.

> For the "oppressed" man death was only the mouth towards which the sluggish stream of suffering and trouble flows. But now it has become the event in which God—the continually Present One, the One who grasps man's hand, the Good One—"takes" a man.[57]

Individuals outside of God's presence interpret the events that befall them as "evils." They view themselves as oppressed, suffering victims heading toward the ultimate evil: death. In contrast, individuals who have embraced God's presence see all these events as part of the journey on which God takes them. As such,

> however cruel and contrary this destiny might appear when viewed apart from intercourse with God, when it is irradiated by His "knowing" it is "success," just as every action of this man, his disappointments

and even his failures, are success. O the happiness of the man who goes the way which is shown and "known" by God![58]

The aimless person sees life as filled with evils. In contrast, those who are in dialogue with God see each happening as evidence of God's presence. Hence, even suffering itself gives meaning to life[59] and serves a "positive function."[60] Further, suffering may have a positive role. Job, for example, learns that all apparent sufferings come to an end when he establishes an authentic I-Thou relationship with God.[61] Suffering, Buber claims without evidence, led Job to this realization.

Given the fact that to Buber "good and evil" are psychological attitudes, Buber is constrained to explain the various biblical passages that treat good and evil as moral judgments. According to Buber's understanding of the original Hebrew, "knowing good and evil" has nothing to do with judging but everything to do with sensing a presence. "The decisive event for 'knowing' in biblical Hebrew," Buber explains, "is not that one looks at an object, but that one comes in touch with it."[62] Likewise, the "knowledge of good and evil" linked to eating the forbidden fruit "means nothing else than cognizance of . . . opposites,"[63] which the commentators "have not understood at all."[64]

By cognizance Buber means awareness. Just as a person has an awareness of good and evil, a person has an awareness of his or her own true self, "what in his unique and non-repeatable created existence he is intended to be."[65] A person who is fully aware of the ideal can then compare his or her own conduct against it. After measuring the difference, each individual ought to act in the way that would lead to the fulfillment of his or her ideal self. Sometimes a person may fall short and act contrary to his or her individual ideal. To Buber, that person, by religious definition, is a sinner.[66] Sinners, according to Buber, "miss God's way."[67] In contrast, those who persistently stray and develop a disposition toward waywardness are wicked. In short, "the sinner does evil, the wicked man is evil."[68]

Broadly speaking, Buber claims the modern world is characterized by a suspension of the ethical, often as a consequence of following "false absolutes [that] rule over the soul."[69] But all is not lost. "The eclipse of the light of God is no extinction; even to-morrow that which has stepped in between may give way."[70]

While Buber's emphasis on relationships is attractive, the fundamental flaw of Buber's thinking about good and evil, as contemporary philosopher Steven T. Katz points out,[71] is his failure to offers a coherent theory for making moral judgments and determining moral actions. Here, Katz is intimating that Buber bases the entirety of his approach on interpersonal relationships rather than on ethical norms. For Buber, the main categories of ethical thought and action are based on what one person is in relation to another person rather than on objective standards. This approach can lead to horrific yet entirely foreseeable results. For instance, sociopaths may be entirely convinced that, contra Buber, in brutalizing others they are following God's way as well as fulfilling their own judgment of who they were meant to become. Without some objective standard against which to measure all conduct, such perversions are possible.[72] This is what philosopher Charles Kegley calls Buber's "problem of norms."[73] Christian ethicist Roy Branson points out that Buber's weak concept of evil prevents him from more clearly seeing the need for definite standards to curb the despotic actions of which human beings are capable.[74] With the problem of evil located internally, Buber has nothing to say about natural evil and little to say about the evil resulting from the depredation of human beings at the hands of other human beings. Moreover, it seems ridiculous, and abhorrent, to characterize the evil of genocide as merely a loss of direction.

Mordecai Kaplan

At age eight, Mordecai (born, Mottel) Kaplan (1881–1983) arrived in New York. His father, Rabbi Israel Kaplan, was recruited by Rabbi Jacob Joseph, the city's first (and only) chief rabbi, to serve on his newly established *beit din*. Israel Kaplan had received rabbinic ordination from no fewer than three of the leading European rabbis of the day: Rabbi Yitzḥak Elḥanan Spektor of Kovno, Rabbi Naftali Tzvi Yehudah Berlin, and Rabbi Yitzḥak Ya'akov Reines. Reines would later confer an Orthodox *semikhah* on the younger Kaplan while he was in Europe on his honeymoon.

Mordecai Kaplan was also ordained by the Jewish Theological Seminary of America in 1902, just as Solomon Schechter arrived as its president, and he became the first graduate to serve a large Orthodox congregation, Kehilat Jeshurun in New York City. Unhappy as a pulpit rabbi, he accepted Schechter's invitation to serve as principal of the newly created Teacher's Institute in 1909. He also taught in the rabbinical school from 1910 until his retirement in 1963. Over the course of his long career Kaplan influenced at least two generations of Conservative rabbis. His controversial views incited some Orthodox rabbis to ban him and burn his books. His radical ideas also alienated him from other JTS faculty members—and became the impetus for his founding of the Reconstructionist movement.

As early as 1914, Kaplan, having accepted the assumptions of biblical criticism, wrote that one need not accept the veracity of the Torah in order to affirm its supremacy: "Having rendered Israel the instrument of divine revelation is no less effective in maintaining its pre-eminence."[75] The supremacy of the Torah, Kaplan argued, is not contingent on its godly authorship, but on its acceptance by the Jewish people. And the supremacy of the Torah does not entail its inviolability. In the realm of human conduct, the Torah has a vote, but not a veto.

> Inasmuch as no man can know, merely on the basis of personal experience, what is right and wrong in every situation, the traditional standards of right and wrong cherished by our people and sanctioned by the Torah as aids to spiritual discipline can and should be regarded with reverence, and should be observed, wherever experience has not challenged their validity. But we must not cling to the standards of the past, if they work mischief in the present.[76]

Kaplan's approach to good and evil is directly related to his approach to God. For Kaplan, God is "the Power both in and beyond nature which moves men to seek value and meaning in life,"[77] or the "cosmic process that makes for man's life abundant for salvation."[78] Simply put, God is the sum of all the creative forces in the universe. God is at once in nature but also above nature. Were God merely identical with nature, there would be no room for finding meaning in life, since natural forces are devoid of meaning. So God is a force that induces humanity to act in ways that ennoble it. However, defining God as a "process" is Kaplan's way of warning against construing God as an eternal, immutable, transcendental being who creates and rules over the universe. Thus the traditional view of God has no place in Kaplan's theology.

Kaplan contended that understanding God as a process was entirely consistent with Maimonides (whose genuine piety, unlike his own, was unquestioned) as well as with modern scientific and philosophic thought. Maimonides, for example, had written that God "does not receive impressions and affections so that there might pertain to Him a quality belonging to the affections. Nor does He have dispositions so that there might be faculties and similar things pertaining to Him. Nor is He, may He be exalted, endowed with a soul, so that He might have a habitus pertaining to Him — such as clemency, modesty, and similar things ... no attribute ... may ... subsist in Him."[79] Applying Maimonides, Kaplan wrote, when "we are told that God is living, we should not take that to mean that God is a being who possesses the attributes of life, which he shares with other living beings, but that God is life itself. Likewise, when we are told that God is good, we should realize that God and goodness are one and the same."[80] Life, knowledge, and goodness are not beings or entities. They are processes. And, "since God is life, knowledge, goodness, what else can He be but Process?"[81]

Yet, Kaplan noted with exasperation, "the conception of God as a cosmic Process has been subjected to considerable misunderstanding and misplaced resentment, as though it constituted a complete break with the traditional, or conventional, idea of God."[82]

However, some semantic revisions are in order. Terms once attributed to God representing the highest degree of human aspirations must be understood differently. Since God, according to Kaplan, can no longer be thought of as a being — albeit a transcendental one — with attributes that would include fairness and justice and goodness, the problem that theodicy attempts to resolve does not at all arise. The existence of humans with attributes such as partiality, inequity, and wickedness cannot be blamed on God, since God is no longer conceived as a being presumably possessing the opposite characteristics.

Given Kaplan's approach to understanding God, he interprets Genesis 3:6 as teaching that eating the fruit from the Tree of Knowledge of Good and Evil is the archetypal sin from which all human suffering springs. According to Kaplan, the narrative intimates that "the attempt of man to *play the part of a god*, to set himself up as a deity, to usurp God's role as law-giver and to become a law unto himself, to make his own desires the standard of his action, to *taste* for himself the good and the evil without reference to divine sanctions or to any laws"[83] (emphasis Kaplan's) explains human beings' downfall. Read symbolically,[84] the Eden story should not provoke questions about the nature or meaning of "good" and "evil," but encourage thoughtful consideration of how people abuse human freedom when "they make their own interests and passions the sole determinants of their behavior."[85]

As for other biblical passages, such as Psalms 73 and 92, where the Psalmist reaffirms that the wicked will ultimately be punished and the righteous vindicated, Kaplan comments that this "brave affirmation" was belied by observable events and the history of the Jewish experience. "Men saw the triumph of those who were manifestly evil. All too often, the wicked ended their days in peace and left behind them numerous progeny who showed not the least tendency to come to terms with those whom their fathers had persecuted."[86] As a result, the idea of the afterlife was invented—an idea that "saved the Jewish religion."[87] According to Kaplan, the Jewish view of the afterlife was a calculated but mistaken strategy to resolve the problem of good and evil. The conceived problem itself resulted from the tradition's inability to respond to reality—and thus, to Kaplan, was testament to the fact that creative and novel solutions are sometimes needed to perpetuate Judaism in desperate times. In making these points, Kaplan reads the psalms as socio-historical evidence rather than as religious literature. As such, the psalms add nothing to understanding the nature of good and evil. With his notion of God, Kaplan has no need to address the underlying question "How does an all-good and all-powerful God allow the wicked to prosper?" In essence, denying the existence of a personal, supernatural God obviates questions of theodicy. "Why did God do this to me?" is meaningless when there is no such God who does anything to anyone.

Yet in his copious writings Kaplan does take up the subject of good and evil. He considers two questions: the very existence of good and evil in the world and how to cope with evil in the world.

In a 1926 diary, Kaplan assigned a naturalistic explanation for the existence of evil, writing that "evil in the world is due to chance."[88] Absent any qualification, it would seem that Kaplan includes both moral and natural evil in this generalization. One of Kaplan's principal interpreters, Mel Scult, explains that someone can just be in the wrong place at the wrong time.[89] Whether victimized by storm or by stormtrooper, all victimization is random. And neither comes as a consequence of "the will of God."[90] Death, to Kaplan, is not evil. Death is simply inexorable; it is a feature of nature.

As such, most of Kaplan's efforts are pragmatically devoted to coping with evil. In 1927 Kaplan officiated at the funeral of a drowned child. Reflecting in writing on what he had spoken publicly, Kaplan writes:

> I am chiefly interested in having a conception of God which can give me courage to go on fighting against the terrible odds of unwarranted suffering and meaningless death.[91]

Cancer and earthquakes are entirely random. These and other catastrophes are not acts of God. However, in working toward their elimination and in giving comfort to the afflicted, we find godliness, what Kaplan called "the functioning of godhood through man."[92] In response to the British White Paper of 1939, Kaplan identifies the greatest evil as "meaningless suffering."[93] Kaplan writes that there can be no greater goal than "to redeem this suffering of its meaninglessness."[94] In order to do so, people must rise above the "herd" and courageously assert "individuality."[95] And, with regard to the human effort to overcome meaningless suffering, Kaplan contends:

There is equally little doubt that with the appropriate application of intelligence there is no natural catastrophe against which he cannot protect himself.[96]

Even so, Kaplan concedes that certain evils (which he does not identify) can never be eradicated. Humanity must face this reality with perseverance, hope, and optimism. "Man, to be fully human," Kaplan writes, "must never make peace with evil."[97]

Despite the considerable efforts of Kaplan's disciples to explain and defend their mentor, Steven T. Katz judges Kaplan's approach to the reconstruction of Judaism "a near total failure as a philosophy of Judaism."[98] When it comes to the problem of good and evil, Kaplan, Katz contends, is inconsistent. For example, in *The Meaning of God in Modern Jewish Religion*, Kaplan, like Maimonides, describes evil as a privation.[99] It is not something itself but an absence of something. Darkness, for example, does not exist independently; darkness is merely the absence of light. Yet in *Judaism as a Civilization*, Kaplan states that evil cannot be a privation.[100]

Katz further claims that Kaplan's approach is incoherent. Take, for example, what Kaplan says about natural evil. In *The Meaning of God*, Kaplan writes:

The modern man cannot possibly view earthquakes and volcanic eruptions, devastating storms and floods, famines and plagues, noxious plants and animals, as "necessary" to any preconceived plan or purpose. They are simply that phase of the universe which has not yet been completely penetrated by godhood.[101]

The traditional Jewish view of natural disasters would ascribe them to God, who includes them as part of God's cosmic plan (regardless of whether we humans understand it). But Kaplan rejects the traditional view that sees God as "an absolute being who has planned and decreed every twinge of pain, every act of cruelty."[102] Instead, Kaplan redefines God as "the animating, organizing forces and relationships which are forever making order out of chaos."[103] But clearly, earthquakes and the like are not subject to "organizing forces and relationships." Earthquakes and the like are utterly outside the purview of "relationships" and are unaffected by them. They cannot be conquered by will and intelligence. Thus, Katz says, Kaplan ought to have distinguished between natural evils (which are outside human control) and moral evils (which are subject to human control). His conflating of the two renders his approach to evil incoherent.

Further, in his quest to replace supernaturalism with naturalism, Kaplan imputes values to nature. He writes that "elements of helpfulness, kindness, and fair play is [sic] not limited to man alone but is [sic] diffused throughout the natural order."[104] But any authentic naturalism, Katz notes, divides facts from values. All the true naturalist can say is "Nature exists, the end."[105]

Then there is the problem the Holocaust presents to Kaplan's theology. Notably, Kaplan wrote almost nothing about the Holocaust, though he published much during that time period.[106] And in his initial writings about the subject, Kaplan seems more concerned with understanding the ideology of nationalism rather than condemning the suffering nationalism produced. More to the point, the philosophical problem for Kaplan is that if he is correct and evil is "the chance invasion of sheer purposelessness"[107] or "chaos uninvolved by . . . creative energy . . . will and intelligence,"[108] the Holocaust—which we now know was the intended product of a carefully executed program preceded by vigorous preparation, organization, and planning—could, astonishingly, *not* be defined as evil. Yet it would be hard to imagine any accounting of the Holocaust that would not characterize it as "evil." The Holocaust thereby renders Kaplan's definition of evil farcical.

Though Kaplan's persistent and heartfelt call to improve the world is laudable, it leaves the problem of evil untouched.

Hannah Arendt

While not strictly a philosopher of religion or a theologian, the political theorist Hannah Arendt (1906–75) nonetheless made a significant contribution to the understanding of evil. Born Johanna Cohn Arendt, she was raised in an assimilated Jewish family in Hanover and Konigsberg. In a

1964 interview, Arendt describes her marginal connection with Judaism as follows:

> As a child I did not know that I was Jewish. . . . The word "Jew" was never mentioned at home when I was a child. As a child, now a slightly older one, I knew that I looked Jewish. That is, I looked different from all the others.[109]

Her father died when she was seven, and her mother and grandfather were responsible for her early upbringing. While a student at the University of Marburg, she had an affair with the philosopher Martin Heidegger. Her liaison with him persisted intermittently over many years despite the fact that Heidegger remained an unrepentant Nazi.[110]

Arendt earned her doctorate in philosophy under Karl Jaspers in 1929, but the changing political climate forced her out of Germany and ultimately to the United States, where she became an influential writer and public intellectual. Her *Origins of Totalitarianism* (1951), *The Human Condition* (1958), and *On Revolution* (1963) established her reputation.

In her most popular and most controversial work, *Eichmann in Jerusalem* (1963), she coined the phrase that has resulted in a different understanding of evil. When the trial of Adolf Eichmann, one of the architects of Hitler's Final Solution, had begun in Jerusalem in 1961, she offered to cover the trial. She had personal motivations: having been briefly imprisoned by the Nazi regime, she was delighted to witness how its agents might be held accountable. She was also interested in seeing how her political theories on totalitarian regimes comported with reality. Her five-part series on what she observed at the trial was published in 1963 and expanded into book form one year later.

What struck Arendt about Eichmann was his ordinariness. Here was an average student who could only find work as a traveling salesman through a family connection. He joined the Nazi Party out of the hope for career advancement rather than out of conviction. He thought more highly of himself than his accomplishments would attest. He had a certain boastfulness about him. He had a faulty memory. Examined by a team of six psychiatrists prior to his trial, they certified him as "normal" (a diagnosis later to be repudiated). Eichmann lacked any overtly identifiable "wickedness." He gave the impression of a law-abiding, low-level bureaucrat who had an office job performed with some degree of competence for which he was too quick to take credit. Arendt noted that to her and to the other observers at the trial, Eichmann was more a clown than a monster. It was only at his execution that Arendt came to realize that if there were a lesson to be learned from Eichmann, it was "the lesson of the fearsome, word-and-thought-defying *banality of evil*."[111] As she explains:

> It would have been very comforting indeed to believe that Eichman was a monster. . . . The trouble with Eichmann was precisely that there were so many like him, and that the many were neither perverted nor sadistic, that they were, and still are, terribly and terrifyingly normal.[112]

She adds:

> Eichmann was not Iago and not Macbeth, and nothing would have been further from his mind than to determine with Richard III "to prove a villain." Except for an extraordinary diligence in looking out for his personal advancement, he had no motives at all. And this diligence in itself was in no way criminal; he certainly would never have murdered his superior in order to inherit his post. He *merely*, to put the matter colloquially, *never realized what he was doing*.[113]

Moral evil, Arendt contends, is not necessarily the intentional harm committed by one human being against another or others. As she writes in her final and unfinished book, *The Life of the Mind*, "The sad truth is that most evil is done by people who never make up their minds to be good or evil." In her view, moral evil can also ensue from being oblivious to the suffering one human being causes another.

While Arendt helps better define the characteristics of evil, she does nothing to explain its origins or its theological implications.

Eugene Borowitz

For fifty-four years, the prolific writer, renowned educator, and scholar of distinction Rabbi Eugene Borowitz (1924–2016) served on the faculty of the Reform seminary Hebrew Union College–Jewish Institute of Religion in New York. Yet Borowitz refused to tolerate the notions rife in liberal Judaism that religion was secondary to national identity and Jewish autonomy was reducible to freedom of choice. He writes:

> I believe that we modern Jews properly exercise our autonomy only when we do so in terms of our relationship with God as part of the people of Israel and as the latest expression of its long Covenant tradition.[114]

To Borowitz, Jews are not granted license to do whatever they please. Autonomy, properly understood, means electing to act in ways that reflect authentic Jewish living, measured by acceptance of and adherence to the covenant that links Jews to God. Borowitz calls this approach "faithful biblical autonomy"[115] or "open traditionalism."[116]

He was painfully aware of the horrors of the Holocaust. In *The Masks Jews Wear* (1973), he writes:

> Any God who could permit the Holocaust, who could remain silent during it, who could "hide His face" while it dragged on, was not worth believing in. There might well be a limit to how much we could understand about Him, but Auschwitz demanded an unreasonable suspension of understanding.[117]

Borowitz goes on to state that the traditional explanation for suffering as the consequence of sin and punishment was faulty, since "the social suffering was too great to be seen as any sort of Divine punishment or instruction."[118] The magnitude of the Holocaust was incongruent with any attempt to see it as punishment for some unstated sin.

Yet, to Borowitz, God's failure to protect God's people during the Holocaust did not prove that God does not intervene in human history. The

State of Israel's subsequent success in the Six-Day War disputed that possible conclusion.

To some extent, Borowitz's argument is grounded in his reluctance to elevate the Holocaust to the position of the central event of our time. In *How Can a Jew Speak of Faith Today?* (1969), he explains:

> I only know that for me, and I believe for the Jewish people as a whole, the Holocaust was shattering, but not determinative. It was not the Sinai of our time.[119]

Accordingly, the Holocaust should not become "our paradigm for future history."[120]

A closer look at his writings about God and the Holocaust reveals Borowitz's assertion that Auschwitz demanded an "unreasonable suspension of understanding." The implication here is that sometimes God's activity or inactivity conflicts with human presumptions. For example, it may seem that God does not comport with the standards of fairness or justice ascribed to God. Innocents suffer. Yet God is presumed to wield the power to prevent that suffering and endowed with the will to want to prevent suffering. Lacking a compelling account of why suffering persists requires a suspension of those presumptions. In ordinary circumstances, suspending those presumptions is reasonable, given all the limitations of human understanding.

To illustrate, in his memoir *Once More We Saw Stars* dealing with the death of his young daughter Greta, author Jayson Greene tells how he is "the living reminder of the most unwelcome message in human history: Children—yours, mine—they don't necessarily live."[121] Yet most children do. For the exceptional instances when they don't, we are reasonably willing to give God a pass, although we still cannot explain the tragedy.[122]

The Holocaust, however, is so egregious an event and one of such unspeakable horrors that it would be unreasonable to give God a pass. It seems that Borowitz does not deny the theological uniqueness of the Holocaust. He is, however, unprepared to reformulate an entire theology based upon it.

A better appreciation of Borowitz's views on suffering and evil can be found in one of his lesser known books, *A New Jewish Theology in the Making* (1968). Rather than examining how the living God ought to be understood—likely an insurmountable challenge—he argues that the real focus ought to be on humanity:

> To rebuild his life, to be true to his sense of history, postwar man needed to understand not only his limitations but also his profound capacity for evil even in the guise of doing good.[123]

Borowitz identifies the capacity for evil as a component of human nature. Given the disillusionment of the postwar period, it behooves humanity to concentrate not on theodicy but on anthropodicy, the justification of human nature in light of suffering and evil. And, emerging from this *analysis* are the heroic efforts of the Jewish people, who put "faith in the Good Deed" and did what needed to be done:[124]

> Without ever having to think about it, the masses of American Jewry emerged from World War II not with a sense of man's helplessness before the evil consequences of his well-intentioned behavior or the powerlessness of his will before his own evil inclinations, but rather with what can legitimately be called an irreplaceable faith in man's capacity to know the righteous act and accomplish it successfully.[125]

Confronted by moral evil, the Jewish people have come to realize that all people have the ability to transcend it by committing to pursuing the good. Borowitz writes of the modern American Jew:

> Centuries of Jewish devotion and observance have conditioned his psyche so thoroughly that virtually no amount of rebellion, flight, and camouflage has been able to purge him of the conviction that a man is both capable of knowing and doing the good.[126]

As a whole, Borowitz speaks of replacing the old theology—framed by questions of God's power and goodness in the face of evil and suffering—with a new theology, one he calls "a theology of *mitzvah*, a rationale of the Jewish way of life and belief."[127] For Borowitz, it would seem that given the human power to know the good and the conviction to pursue it, any failure in confronting the existence of evil is no longer a matter of asking "Where is God?" but "Where is humanity?"

But his "new theology," Borowitz confesses, is really no classical theology at all. Jews have historically responded to crises by generating systems of thought that remedied their confusion. For Jews who were firmly rooted in their tradition, those responses grew convincingly out of these roots.

Still, tradition has demanded certain assumptions that can no longer be facilely accepted:

> We can say that most people in other ages were reasonably secure in their faith. When spiritual problems or possibilities arose among them, or when new ways of thinking about their belief came to them, they created intellectual systems which reflected their situation. Theologies of certainty thus arose and became traditional among us. Not sharing that sort of stability, religiously or culturally, I cannot properly carry on that enterprise. For myself and the many like me who find large measures of doubt and vacillation included in their faith, I work at what I have come to call the theology of comparative uncertainty—if it may be called theology at all.[128]

The "theology" of mitzvah is, better, an *ideology* of mitzvah. To Borowitz, in the aftermath of the spiritual malaise that is postwar Judaism, Jews have responded to evil and suffering by attending to living Jewish lives rather than reconstructing theological concepts that doubt has called into question. Rather than analyzing the consequences of faith in God, Jews put faith in themselves. Questions about God thereby retreat into the background.

This newfound confidence clearly fits with the autonomy that Borowitz would endow modern Jews. And the result is a new covenant:

Under such a covenant, man can in rare instances stand on his rights as partner and question even God. . . . Even against God, man has a certain autonomy.[129]

Borowitz first gained notoriety in 1961 for originating what he termed "covenant theology." The principles that inhered in that doctrine were developed and explored in much of his writing thereafter, particularly in his comprehensive work on theology, *Renewing the Covenant* (1991). He relentlessly promoted and defended the view that autonomy and tradition were not irreconcilable; in fact, the two were complementary. The task he took on, Alan Mittleman explains, "is to ground a theory of Jewish duty that is stronger than that supported by modern liberal Judaism, yet weaker than the stark heteronomy of Orthodoxy has demanded."[130]

The new covenant would generally require Jews "to accept God's sovereignty,"[131] but reserves the right of respectful dissent. Consequently, Jews can legitimately conclude that none of the historical defenses of God in the face of evil are adequate (and perhaps none are possible) and yet remain fully committed to living Jewish lives. In this Borowitz differs from the Jobian response of applying a "veil of ignorance" over God's actions. Borowitz holds that Jews can truly believe that God acts unjustly—the only plausible circumstance in which human beings as rightful partners can exercise their autonomy and question God. Yet, at the end of the day, human actions matter more.

By intimating that God acts unjustly, Borowitz solves the problem of theodicy by sacrificing the premise that God is omnibenevolent. The inescapable consequence of this concession is the troublesome question "Why then give allegiance to an unjust God?"

Neil Gillman

Rabbi Neil Gillman (1933–2017), chair of the Philosophy Department and dean of the Rabbinical School of the Jewish Theological Seminary of America, served with distinction as a faculty member for forty-six years, earning a reputation for making theology accessible to a modern audience.

In *Sacred Fragments* (1990), Gillman asserts that the "massive trauma" of the Holocaust renders "inadequate" the explanation that moral evil is the price to be paid for human free will.[132] Likewise unsatisfactory is the outcome of the book of Job, namely that "suffering is simply part of God's complex plan; it has no further explanation."[133] Moralistic explanations fail to address the scope and magnitude of the Holocaust. Naturalistic explanations may explain the causes of suffering but fail to explain the reasons:

> We want to know, for example, why nature itself is so constructed that it can produce the AIDS virus—not how, but why? Why does a seven-year-old child suddenly develop cancer of the brain? Why are some babies born with congenital heart defects? Why are people killed in hurricanes, tidal waves, and tornadoes?[134]

For Gillman, the theological problem has proved intractable to date. "There simply are no totally adequate explanations for the death of an innocent child from leukemia, or the lightning bolt that kills an innocent young man." Arguing that a baby suffers and dies for its sins is rabbinically unsupportable and morally unconscionable. Explaining that nature operates only in accordance with physical laws and thus is indifferent to the age or virtue of its victims tells only a limited story—how a child may contract leukemia—and does not help in justifying why this particular child was so afflicted. Furthermore, the problem of theodicy "has become the core issue, the issue that threatens to upset the entire system" of Judaism.[135] So Gillman sets to the task of trying to develop an approach that will be both theologically sound and personally comforting.

He looks to the understanding of religion proposed by the American anthropologist Clifford Geertz.[136] For Geertz, the focus of any religion is how to cope with the tension between order and chaos, "a tumult of events which lack not just interpretations but *interpretability*."[137] The events erupting in human life that baffle believers, challenging the very idea of orderliness and the comprehensibility of all that happens, constitute the ultimate religious challenge. Geertz divides the challenge into three component parts: the analytical challenge, the challenge of human endurance, and the challenge of moral insight.

For his part, Gillman reframes the three divisions as, respectively, the intellectual challenge, the emotional challenge, and the moral challenge. He concentrates on the last.

More generally, Gillman sees Judaism as an ordering device conveyed through its particular system of symbols that he calls "myth." Myth, here, should not be taken as a fanciful story, but as "a pattern of meaning imposed on a complex set of data."[138] As such, the moral challenge compels believing Jews to wrestle with the moral intuition that life ought to be fundamentally fair and that notions of good and evil are both sensible and congruent, given that human experience often suggests the opposite. At stake is whether the myth of Judaism coheres.

Gillman suggests that the biblical and Rabbinic approaches to theodicy coalesce—an unjustifiably reductionist and overly narrow position. But (granting him this liberty for the purpose of his analysis) following the biblical and Rabbinic doctrines that assign suffering to sin and reward to obedience requires accepting the doctrines of divine providence, the veracity of revelation, and the entire system of law built upon it—all of which, Gillman implies, will not do for a significant number of Jews today. Besides, he argues, the book of Job itself, which he characterizes as "the most antireligious book in the Bible,"[139] repudiates the biblical and Rabbinic approach. In the world according to Job, chaos triumphs over order, though God tries to convince him otherwise. And therein lies the problem:

It is precisely we humans who need to understand it, who must have a way of coping with the chaos—not God.[140]

Job is bereft of any explanation. God may be in control of a complex world, but Job is left only to accept, not understand. Any solution to the problem of theodicy, to use philosopher Shubert Spero's felicitous phrase, "must ultimately be relegated to the impenetrable mystery of God's unique and unitary nature."[141]

Given this state of affairs, Gillman posits four possible options.

First, Jews today may conclude that suffering is an inexplicable mystery. This may very well be true but, if so, provides no comfort for the victim of suffering.

Second, some—but not all—instances of suffering are the inevitable results of human freedom. This leaves the kinds of suffering caused by nature unexplained.

Third, by positing an afterlife where all the inequities of life can be remedied, humanity can be assured of the ultimate righteousness of God. However, this possibility is a hope, not a guarantee.

Finally, Jews today might be compelled to live with the option that chaos is an irremediable dimension of God's Creation.

This last option particularly intrigues Gillman. More comfortable with biblical scholar Jon D. Levenson's idea that God's mastery of the chaotic forces of life remains fragile[142] than with Conservative rabbi Harold Kushner's idea that God's power is limited, Gillman concludes that chaos seems to be an intrinsic dimension of God's Creation.

In doing so, Gillman concedes that a part of the Jewish religious myth has unraveled. But, he, argues, the fact that one part of the Jewish religious myth is exposed as inadequate "does not forecast the undoing of the myth as a whole." Judaism is still intellectually and emotionally satisfying. The Jewish pattern of imposing meaning into the complexity of the world's injustices undergoes transformation over time, reflecting what Gillman terms "plasticity." As a result, Judaism's inability to formulate a convincing explanation for the suffering of the innocent is a failing, but not a fatal flaw:

> To this believing Jew, then, the substance of the classic Jewish religious myth, however broken, remains palpably alive, despite the death of the doctrine of suffering as punishment, and maybe even because of Job.[143]

Gillman's conclusion is a personal one—one that he is wont to impose on others. No doubt, however, he represents the thinking of other Jews today who would agree that the traditional association of suffering as punishment for sin is unacceptable. And with no other suitable explanation available, all Jews can do is soldier on with an irreparably damaged but still serviceable myth.

Harold Kushner

Gillman calls Rabbi Harold Kushner's 1981 book *When Bad Things Happen to Good People* "arguably the most widely read book written by a rabbi in centuries."[144] Not a formally trained philosopher,[145] Kushner (b. 1935) seems to have struck a responsive chord with a general readership who have by and large found his words helpful. Why this is the case requires examination.

Kushner writes from a personal perspective. Like Mendelssohn, he endured the death of a child. His son Aaron Zev died at age fourteen from a rare aging disease called progeria. Aaron's sickness and death caused Kushner to "rethink everything that he had been taught about God and God's ways."[146] He came to see that

> the misfortunes of good people are not only a problem to the people who suffer and to their families. They are a problem to everyone who wants to believe in a just and fair and livable world.[147]

One's individual beliefs in justice and fairness are contingent upon belief in a God who is just and fair and who lovingly imposes justice and fairness in the world. Yet, experience teaches otherwise:

> Like every reader of this book, I pick up the daily paper and fresh challenges to the idea of the world's goodness assault my eyes: sense-less murders, fatal practical jokes, young people killed in automobile accidents on the way to their wedding or coming home from their high school prom. I add these stories to the personal tragedies I have known, and I have to ask myself: Can I, in good faith, continue to teach people that the world is good, and that a kind and loving God is responsible for what happens in it?[148]

Kushner is faced with a dilemma. On the one hand, he wants to offer solace to the afflicted, independent of theological considerations. Yet on the other hand, he feels compelled to offer some theological explanation for the existence of suffering and evil. He is far more successful in the former than he is in the latter.

In a symposium titled "Why Is There Evil under God?" held at New York City's 92nd Street Y in December 1982, Kushner revealed his dilemma. As reported in the *New York Times*, Kushner denied that his project was theological at all, claiming that his intent was to "confront the problem of evil not theologically but very practically." Likening theology to a form of "insanity," he warned that a purely theological approach, one aimed at explaining evil instead of doing something about it, led to "the trap of trying to defend God rather than trying to comfort people," a trap he exposes in his book.[149] And yet, more than two chapters of his book are devoted to exposing the inadequacy of earlier theodicies. Given Kushner's engagement with theology despite his criticism of the enterprise, some analysis of his conclusions is in order.

Of the biblical and Rabbinic attempts to justify an omnipotent and omnibenevolent God despite the presumed existence of evil, Kushner lists seven rationales and their respective failings. First, he acknowledges, the talmudic idea that "we deserve what we get, that somehow our misfortunes come as punishment for our sins"[150] is not without some appeal. This idea, in fact, has three distinct benefits: it makes the world orderly and understandable; it provides the best possible reason for good conduct; and it preserves the idea of an all-powerful and all-loving God who is control of the world and all the events that transpire in it. But to Kushner, these benefits pale in comparison to the harm the idea inflicts. It offers no comfort to a parent who has lost a child. It generates guilt. "It makes people hate God."[151] And, from Kushner's perspective, most disturbing of all, it does not fit the facts. Sometimes innocents die, and sometimes the wicked prosper. On the contrary, if people always received what they deserve, we would have to say that a righteous person was anyone who lived long and well, whether or not he was honest and charitable, and a wicked person was anyone who suffered, even if that person's life was otherwise commendable.[152]

Second is the Psalmist's view that what seems to be unfair now will be redressed in time. The wicked may prosper now, but in due course they will be punished. The righteous may suffer now, but in due course they will be rewarded. Kushner dismisses this idea:

> God does not always give the righteous man the time to catch up. . . .
> The world, alas, is not so neat a place as the psalmist would have us believe. . . .
> Besides, what should the righteous man do in the meantime?[153]

Third, some people look for consolation by presuming that there is a good reason for suffering to which they are not privy. Kushner dismisses the Jobian solution as wishful thinking.

Fourth, some people consider suffering as "educational" — not in the didactic sense of gaining knowledge but in the sense of personal growth and self-improvement. In other words, as Philo and Baḥya argued, suffering is in the sufferer's best interests. Kushner rejects this idea as well:

> The problem with a line of reasoning like this one is that it isn't really meant to help the sufferer or to explain his suffering. It is meant primarily to defend God, to use words and ideas to transform bad into good and pain into privilege.[154]

Worse still, considering a case in which the educational justification applies leads to the inalterable conclusion that the lesson is insignificant and comes at too high a cost:

> We have all read stories of little children who were left unwatched for just a moment and fell from a window or into a swimming pool and

died. Why does God permit such a thing to happen to an innocent child? It can't be to teach a child a lesson about exploring new areas. By the time the lesson is over, the child is dead. Is it to teach the parents and baby-sitters to be more careful? That is too trivial a lesson to be purchased at the price of a child's life. Is it to make the parents more sensitive, more compassionate people, more appreciative of life and health because of their experience? Is it to move them to work for better safety standards, and in that way save a hundred future lives? The price is still too high, and the reasoning shows too little regard for the value of an individual life.[155]

Further, Kushner is offended by the prospect, advanced by the Besht and Hermann Cohen, that God hurts some people so that others can learn from their troubles. In his view it is implausible for God to distort one life to enhance another person's spiritual sensitivity.

Fifth, Kushner condemns the possibility, broached by the Psalmist and affirmed by the midrash, Sa'adiah, Rabbi Yosef Ya'avetz, and the Kotzker Rebbe, that God designs tests for people that allow them to discover how strong they are and allows God to reward their faithfulness. Kushner lambasts these as "sadistic games."[156] When these "tests" are said to be administered under the notion that God never sends more of a burden than a person can bear, Kushner cites the response of a woman whose son died: "If only I was a weaker person, Robbie would still be alive."[157] The greater good would seem to be failing the test rather than passing it.

Sixth, Kushner weighs the positing of a glorious afterlife when all injustices will be remedied: "Sometimes, because our souls yearn for justice, because we so desperately want to believe that God will be fair to us, we fasten our hopes on the idea that life in this world is not the only reality."[158] Ultimately, though, he deems the injection of a postmortem remediation as affirmed by the Rabbis a last-gasp effort to resuscitate a failed theology. It has a modest advantage but a substantial disadvantage:

Belief in a world to come where the innocent are compensated for their suffering can help people endure the unfairness of life in this world without losing faith. But it can also be an excuse for not being troubled or outraged by injustice around us, and not using our God-given intelligence to try to do something about it.[159]

Moreover, the concept of an afterlife remains unsubstantiated.

Finally, Kushner glosses over the strain of thought proffered by ibn Daud, Maimonides, and Gersonides that suggests that "evil" is unreal and exists only as a contrast with "good." It is a fine example of scholastic semantics, but it doesn't make the death of loved ones any less painful. "Their deaths and injuries are no less real because of our verbal cleverness."[160]

After disposing of what Kushner considers ineffective and even hurtful theodicies, he comes to the conclusion that "maybe God does not cause our suffering. Maybe it happens for some reason other than the will of God."[161] Kushner presents his conclusion as a mere possibility, but he is dissembling. Stylistically he may ask the question "Could it be that God does not cause the bad things that happen to us?"[162] but for him there is no question at all. All that happens in this world happens according to natural laws:

> Innocent people do suffer misfortunes in this life. Things happen to them far worse than they deserve—they lose their jobs, they get sick, their children suffer or make them suffer. But when it happens, it does not represent God punishing them for something they did wrong. The misfortunes do not come from God at all.[163]

Rather, the process that began at Creation—replacing chaos with order—is still underway. As a result, "the events of the universe follow firm natural laws."[164] The results are sometimes distressing, since nature is amoral:

> Gravity makes objects fall. Sometimes they fall on people and hurt them. Sometimes gravity makes people fall off mountains and out of windows. Sometimes gravity makes people slip on ice or sink under

water. We could not live without gravity, but that means we have to live with the dangers it causes.[165]

The regularity of the laws of nature makes science possible and certain life experiences predictable. But there is a price to be paid:

Laws of nature treat everyone alike. They do not make exceptions for good people or for useful people. . . . Laws of nature do not make exceptions for nice people. A bullet has no conscience; neither does a malignant tumor or an automobile gone out of control. That is why good people get sick and get hurt as much as anyone.[166]

Though this is not a happy truth, it is a necessary one:

A world in which good people suffer from the same natural dangers that others do causes problems. But a world in which good people were immune to those laws would cause even more problems.[167]

For example, such a world would allow the righteous to put themselves in peril without fear of consequences, since they are under God's protection.

In the final analysis, while Kushner has no answer to what he perceives is the only question that really matters, he assumes that everything operates according to natural laws:

I don't know why one person gets sick, and another does not, but I can only assume that some natural laws which we don't understand are at work. I cannot believe that God "sends" illness to a specific person for a specific reason. I don't believe in a God who has a weekly quota of malignant tumors to distribute, and consults His computer to find out who deserves one most or who could handle it best.[168]

Consequently, Kushner is left with a good and loving God, but one of limited powers:

God wants justice and fairness but cannot always arrange for them.[169]

And:

God does not cause our misfortunes. Some are caused by bad luck, some are caused by bad people, and some are simply an inevitable consequence of our being human and being mortal, living in a world of inflexible natural laws. The painful things that happen to us are not punishments for our misbehavior, nor are they in any way part of some grand design on God's part. Because the tragedy is not God's will, we need not feel hurt or betrayed by God when tragedy strikes. We can turn to Him for help in overcoming it, precisely because we can tell ourselves that God is as outraged by it as we are.[170]

In sum, "pain is the price we pay for being alive,"[171] and while pain is unavoidable, God—"who neither causes nor prevents tragedies"[172]—can provide the inspiration, perseverance, and strength to overcome them.

To be sure, Kushner's approach resonated with the public. But popularity is no equivalent to scholarly rigor. In assessing Kushner's approach, at least four failings emerge.

Kushner was not the first to invoke natural law as a way of explaining evil in the world. Spinoza, as readers might recall, attributed all that happens in this world to natural laws. But Kushner is not Spinoza's epigone. Kushner distinguishes between God the creator and God the judge of the world, affirming the former but denying the latter. Spinoza makes no such distinction. Kushner's distinction thus raises a question that does not apply to Spinoza: How is it possible for God to create a universe over which God has no control? Kushner does not explain.

Further, Kushner posits that some events in the world happen randomly, meaning neither by God's will nor by natural law. Sometimes Kushner refers to this circumstance as "bad luck."[173] Yet how this possibility comes to be goes unexplained. Indeed, the very idea of a world created by a designing God would appear to refute the notion of randomness.

Kushner is troubled by the invocation of an unproven afterlife as a solution to the problem of theodicy. An afterlife is an unwarranted assumption. Yet Kushner is not averse to making an equally unsubstantiated assumption: that "everything happens according to natural laws."[174]

Finally, while Kushner is sensitive to how the concept of suffering as a consequence of sin can do psychological harm, so can the belief that sometimes bad things happen without explanation. In his book *If God Is So Good Why Is the World So Bad?* Rabbi Benjamin Blech opens with an anecdote of a woman who, after reading Kushner's book, said, "I now have two healthy children. We are so happy. But any minute now I expect something terrible to happen. If God doesn't run the world like this book says . . ."[175] Blaming tragedy on sin may be discomfiting and disturbing, but so can making tragedy inexplicable and potentially imminent.

Martha Nussbaum

Martha Nussbaum (née Craven) was born in New York City in 1947. Her early interest in the classics suffuses her philosophical writing. At Harvard she became the first woman to hold the Junior Fellowship and then went on at Harvard to earn both master's and doctorate degrees. Denied tenure in the classics department, she left Harvard for Brown University and Oxford before coming to the University of Chicago, where she holds the position of Ernst Freund Distinguished Service Professor of Law and Ethics. She has received sixty-two honorary degrees from institutions around the world. Among her notable books are *The Fragility of Goodness: Luck and Ethics in Greek Tragedy and Philosophy*, *Cultivating Humanity*, *Anger and Forgiveness*, and *Monarchy of Fear*.

She converted to Judaism in 1969 and celebrated an adult bat mitzvah in 2008. She remains proudly affiliated with the Reform movement.

When Bill Moyers, in a 2008 interview, asked Nussbaum what goes through her mind when she, as a Jew, uses the word "God," she replied:

> Well, I am kind of agnostic about what that really means. And I guess what I do think is that there's some moral basis to life that makes us dignified beings, not mere bundles of matter. And that's why we

deserve respect for one another. We are not just bundles of atoms being pushed around. But, there's something spiritual about us whether we give that a religious interpretation or not. And so, it's that sense of there being dignity to life that I associate with the word "God." I mean, that's probably a pretty radical and agnostic way of interpreting it. But, that's what I think.[176]

For Nussbaum, what happens to people in the world is neither random nor predetermined. Neither is God a transcendental being. God is the scaffold supporting the moral basis of life that allows humans to become dignified beings.

Nussbaum explains why God cannot be a transcendental being in *The Fragility of Goodness*. In examining the works of the ancient Greek poets and philosophers, Nussbaum tries to reconcile philosophical and literary ideas about moral thinking on the age-old question "How should one live?" The answer on which she settles is aptly described by philosopher Charles Pinchess:

> We seek a way of life that is stable enough such that we can live it purposefully and with some degree of control but that yet remains open to the intrusions of the world, to luck. This is the life neither of gods nor of animals, but of humans; a life which controls what it can in the world, yet recognizes that it should not control all, not merely because it *cannot*, but because so to control would be to lose the world, itself beautiful and mysterious in its separateness from and frequent hostility to our purposes, and, as well, to lose ourselves, that is, ourselves whose uniqueness resides in our passionate interaction with, adjustment to, and sometimes tragic defeat at the hands of this world which we can ultimately only partially understand or control. This is the life, the essentially human life, lived out in what must always be a fragile goodness.[177]

A world manipulated by a transcendental deity would lack the perils and challenges necessary to make the world beautiful and mysterious.

Of course this allows for not only the possibility of evil but its victory. But it is in reaction to the victory of evil that humanity gains a fuller understanding of life and its vulnerability.

In her essay "Love's Knowledge," Nussbaum notes that Ulysses rightly rejects the advances of the goddess Calypso, who offers him safety and serenity on her island of perfect bliss. Ulysses chooses instead to brave the dangerous seas to return to his beloved Penelope. To Nussbaum, there is something marvelous about facing danger: human beings can demonstrate love through taking risks for others and through self-sacrifice. The ancient Greeks, therefore, often had the gods fall in love with humans, but not the reverse. That is because mortals can do the things that immortals cannot: suffer and die. Evil earns the envy of the gods. Rather than judging suffering and death to be evils, Nussbaum sees them as assets.[178]

In this she is influenced by the late British philosopher Bernard Williams, who regarded suffering as a corrective for an overly optimistic view of life. She explains his view:

> The news that the suffering we witness is the result of distant, unapproachable, implacable, unintelligent necessity would in a sense be bad news: for it would mean that it had to happen, and that similar things will go on happening no matter what we do. That is what Williams means by saying that such news is a corrective to overly optimistic offers of "good news."

Building upon his analysis, Nussbaum comments:

> But I think that there is another sense in which that kind of news is good: it means that there is nobody to blame and nothing more to do. We can sit back and resign ourselves to the world as it is, knowing that its horrors lie outside our control.[179]

Contemporary thinker Martin Kavka interprets Nussbaum to mean that while evil lies outside of human control, it can nevertheless be abated by human action. And through moral action, humanity can experience transcendence.[180]

Nussbaum's approach seems remarkably similar to that of Hermann Cohen, who viewed evil in the world as both inevitable and integral to bettering human character. But Nussbaum offers a far less robust account of the nature of good and evil. More pointedly, Nussbaum wants to think that there is some spiritual component of life rather than randomness yet at the same time include the element of luck, which is entirely random. Likewise, Nussbaum maintains that in a world of "unintelligent necessity" no human action can make a difference, and yet she advocates for action to overcome evil. The inconsistency demands explanation, and none is forthcoming.

Judith Plaskow

Judith Plaskow is an eminent American feminist theologian. Earning a doctorate in theology from the Yale University Divinity School in 1975, she embarked on an academic career that eventually led her to Manhattan College, where she taught for thirty-two years until her retirement. She also served as president of the Association of Jewish Studies as well as the American Academy of Religion. In 1985 she helped create the *Journal for Feminist Studies in Religion*, which she also edited for its first ten years of publication. Her book *Standing Again at Sinai: Judaism from a Feminist Perspective* (1990) greatly influenced the course of the academic discussion of the role of women in Judaism. While others argued that roles previously foreclosed to Jewish women (like the rabbinate) ought to be opened, Plaskow argued that such gestures were insufficient. What was really required was a total reinterpretation of Judaism informed by female perspectives.

By her own admission, it was only later in life that Plaskow came to be interested in the nature of God and the correlative problem of evil in the world. Her views are incorporated in the book *Goddess and God in the World: Conversations in Embodied Theology* (2016), coauthored with Carol P. Christ. Plaskow explains her initial thinking:

In my chapter on God in *Standing Again at Sinai* the issue of imagery continued to take precedence over my experiences of God and the elaboration of my own theology. The chapter criticized the inadequacy of traditional images for God and suggested new metaphors that might expand the Jewish religious imagination in ways that cohere with feminist understandings of Torah and Israel. It only hinted at the concept of God that lay behind these metaphors because, at the time, I was less interested in who God *is* than how Jews speak to and about God.[181]

Consistent with her grand project of the reinterpretation of Judaism, Plaskow's focus was more on changing how Jews describe God and, consequently, how Jews relate to God, than about the nature of God, the subject of theology. Accordingly, Plaskow had no context for explicitly considering the problem of evil—something which, she would later admit, was a "failure":[182]

God's responsibility for evil had simply ceased to be a problem for me in that I no longer thought of God as an omnipotent being with the power and responsibility to intervene in creation. God(dess), the ground and wellspring of life, could only act through the world, not upon it from the outside. The enterprise of theodicy—the effort to justify God's goodness and power given the existence of evil—had become much less interesting than the ways in which our language about God supports social, political, and religious inequalities of power.[183]

Later life experiences, including sensing God's presence in nature and in artistic beauty, recovered for Plaskow a prominence of place for serious consideration of the nature of God.[184] Her theological reawakening also dredged up an old tension between her "understanding of God as a nonpersonal, sustaining presence and the personal images of the liturgy"[185] familiar to her from her youth. Resolving the tension led Plaskow to fashioning what she calls her "credo" that offers "an alternative to the omnipotent father of classical theism":[186]

I see God as the creative energy that underlies, animates, and sustains all existence; God is the Ground of Being, the source of all that is; the power of life, death, and regeneration in the universe. God's presence fills all of creation, and creation simultaneously dwells in God. In technical theological language, I am a panentheist: I believe in a God who is present in everything and yet at the same time is not identical with all that is.[187]

As Plaskow notes, her credo is "very simply" stated, but not so simple to grasp. The Rabbis long ago introduced the concept of panentheism by simultaneously asserting that "there is no place free of the *Shekhinah* [God's presence]" and "God is the place of the universe but the universe is not God's place."[188] God is both immanent—that is, present in the world as human beings experience it—as well as transcendent—that is, above and beyond the world. This sentiment is also a core principle of Hasidism, appearing in the teachings of the Ba'al Shem Tov and his disciples, like Rabbi Eliezer of Lizensk.[189] Yet noting that Plaskow's credo is not a novel one does not make it any more clear or comprehensible.

The word "panentheism" derives from the Greek, meaning "all within God." (Panentheism should not be confused with pantheism, which asserts that God is identical with nature.) A good way to understand panentheism in comparison with traditional theism is through a mental image. Traditional theists picture the universe as one circle, with God in another circle above it. From above, God rules over the universe and occasionally intervenes in the universe below—but God remains separate from the universe. Panentheists picture two concentric circles with God in the outer circle and the world in the inner circle. The idea is that all things are contained within the essence of God, yet God is more than the sum total of all things.

Plaskow sees a great Oneness in this picture, subsuming all things good and evil. There is great beauty in nature but also great cruelty. There is nobility in human conduct but also barbarity. And even the best of intentions may lead to actions with unforeseen harm. "To deny God's presence in all this," she says, "to see God only in the good, seems to me to leave huge aspects of reality outside of God."[190] God, then, is just as much responsible for the evil in the world as God is for the good. Preserving the idea of Oneness, which Plaskow also calls "wholeness" and "inclusiveness," is more important theologically, she claims, than defending God's goodness.[191] Plaskow situates within this Oneness all of the human family, "bound to each other in the continued unfolding of the adventure of creation,"[192] making human beings more alike than unalike and forever interconnected. However, in this Oneness there is "no commander who issues orders from outside the web of creation."[193]

In the absence of a heteronymous (authority outside of the individual) moral code, Plaskow takes on the problem of explaining human account-ability. If there is no supreme God who imposes a moral code, there is no basis by which to prejudice good over evil, since good and evil are equal components in the Oneness of the world. Yet, Plaskow posits, the very Oneness of the world has "built into it an ethical imperative."[194] Knowing the world as God's "unifying ongoing creation" necessarily means knowing that humanity is required to "tend and care for that creation."[195] Hence, Plaskow understands Judaism's concern for "commandedness" that undergirds specific injunctions as well as the sanctification of daily life to cohere with her notion of Oneness. Humanity derives its notion of moral obligations from its perception of the nature of the world.

Plaskow's argument could be stated as follows: If everything in the world is filled with God, human beings have a vested interest in preserving the world and all that is in it, including other human beings. To preserve humanity requires seeking what is best for it. What is best for humanity is what is right and good. Hence, the imperative to act ethically is embedded in the notion of the Oneness of the world.

Plaskow also contends that the book of Job supports her view that God's presence is as much associated with evil as it is with good. In con-trast to those interpreters who hold that God's answer to Job teaches that God's perspective is broader than humanity's and without access to the big picture, human beings, like Job, will only interpret Job's suffering as unfair, Plaskow reads the text as an affirmation that fairness is not a divine concern. God's natural world is filled with good and evil. It is, at the same time, turbulent and unrestrained, joyous and beautiful.

The fundamental flaw with panentheism is that it flies in the face of the biblical text. The Bible portrays God as separate and apart from the world: God brings the world into being and holds humanity accountable to a code of conduct that God, as the supreme authority, imposes upon people. The Bible also presumes that God will ultimately defeat evil. But that cannot be possible if God has no power over it. In addition, panentheism maintains that its fundamentally naturalistic assumptions (that God is in nature) must be supplemented by a metaphysical claim (that God transcends nature) without explaining why that additional claim is necessary. According to American philosopher Robert Corrington, a thoroughgoing naturalism is all that is needed,[196] making panentheism unnecessary. Plaskow's renewed consideration of God was born in part by her reacquaintance with the power of nature as she experienced it: in a magnificent waterfall in South America and in the biblical verses that speak of God in the rushing waters (Amos 5:24) and the rocky crags (Job 39:28). Readers can certainly appreciate why these natural phenomena—and all she includes in the "glory of nature"[197]—are inspiring to Plaskow. However, she does not explain in her conceptualization of God why she needs to go beyond a naturalistic account and propose a panentheistic one, a kind of account that is, according to British philosopher R. T. Mullins, "woefully vague."[198]

Further, panentheism cannot compellingly explain why God is worthy of worship when God does not rule over nature but is merely a part of nature that includes evil.

Readers may also question Plaskow's justification for "commandedness" within the Oneness of the universe. For example, people may all agree that helping people in distress would be a good thing to do yet still refrain from doing so. Without the impetus of a commanding power that insists upon it, helping people in distress could be viewed as an empty bromide to be ignored at will.

Summary

Modern Jewish thinkers have tended to advance the rational approaches that originated with the medieval philosophers and were developed by Spinoza and Mendelssohn.

The Nature of Good and Evil: For Cohen, the existence of evil in the world is a given, not a question. The real question is, given the existence of evil in the world, how may a human being best respond to it? Borowitz shares Cohen's view. For Buber, evil exists when a sense of God's presence is absent. The persistence of evil is not attributable to a deficiency in God, but to deficiencies in the human soul. Alexander argues that evil is a consequence of the emergent God who has not yet reached ultimate perfection. Kaplan argues that evil is merely an unavoidable part of merciless nature, described by the English poet Tennyson as "red in tooth and claw." Plaskow agrees, as does Kushner, the latter arguing that evil is the price to be paid for the comfort and regularity of natural laws. Arendt points out that evil is not necessarily discovered in some dramatic contravention of morality, but may surface in a person's simple routine.

Questions of Justice: Cohen denies that suffering is an unwarranted interruption of life. Instead, suffering is a necessary feature of it. As such, suffering motivates an empathic concern for others. Concomitantly, suffering elevates the victim by liberating the victim from selfishness and thus gaining a deeper connection with God. Suffering is also the métier of the Jewish people that earns Jews special status. Alexander holds that evil is incompatible with God. Evil exists only as an indication that God has not yet fully emerged. For Buber, suffering is entirely subjective. Those who have an abiding relationship with God will not judge their difficult circumstances as suffering. Kaplan offers a different and controversial way out of the problem theodicy attempts to solve. Since God is not a supernatural, transcendental being possessing the power to affect events, God cannot be responsible for evil and suffering. Nussbaum echoes Kaplan's view. Plaskow agrees with Kaplan and Nussbaum that God is not at all an omnipotent father but comes to an entirely different conclusion. Good and evil are both part of nature, and nature is part of God; as such, God cannot be held up to standards of justice and fairness any more than nature can. Borowitz argues that humanity has less a need for theodicy than for anthropodicy. Gillman wants humanity to live with the unsatisfying reality that the inexplicability of evil is an irresolvable feature of Creation, while Kushner wants Jews to admit that God is powerless to prevent evil. For Nussbaum, God's powerlessness is a blessing because it allows humans to strive to become more dignified beings on their own.

CHAPTER 8

The Special Problem of the Shoah

The Shoah has profoundly affected the Jewish understanding of the nature of evil. Likewise, the Shoah presents the problem of reconciling that revised understanding of the nature of evil with the traditional conception of God.

Holocaust, Shoah, Ḥurban?

Before an analysis of how the Shoah has altered the Jewish understanding of evil, some consideration of the relevant vocabulary is in order. Words often reflect the theological approach of those who employ them—a phenomenon some scholars call "the psychology of labels."[1] And the three words most commonly used to describe the effects of Hitler's "Final Solution"—namely, Holocaust, Shoah, and ḥurban—mirror how the associated events ought to be implicitly interpreted.

The word "holocaust" derives from the ancient Greek *holos kaustos*, meaning "burnt whole." The term appears in the Christian Gospels as the rendering of the type of sacrifice (*ʿolah*) offered to God but not shared with either the propitiant or the officiant. In other words, it is entirely consumed by the fire on the altar, with none of the flesh eaten by the one who brought the animal to the Temple or priest who made the offering.[2] Sixteenth- and seventeenth-century English translations of the Christian Bible render the word *ʿolah* as "holocaust."

Gradually, the English usage of the word "holocaust" expanded beyond its biblical origins and came to mean any wide-scale devastation, usually, but not exclusively, by fire. In a letter to American rabbi Israel Goldstein dated December 24, 1942, Dr. Chaim Weizmann, later to become the first president of the nascent State of Israel, bemoaned witnessing the destruction of European Jewry in what he called "this holocaust." A few weeks earlier, the United Kingdom's *News Chronicle* used the word "holocaust" in the same way. Before the Second World War and continuing into the 1950s, this initial description of the fate of European Jewry as "a holocaust" did not mean more than a synonym for catastrophe or destruction. Neither Weizmann nor the members of the British House of Lords who debated the horrors of "this holocaust" in 1943 considered the term to be more than that.

Elie Wiesel is generally credited with introducing the word "Holocaust" in the way it is used today.[3] In his first book, *And the World Was Silent*, written in Yiddish and published in Buenos Aires in 1956, he refers to "the Holocaust." Wiesel would later regret his neologism, claiming that any word is inadequate to describe the unspeakable and that the word "Holocaust" itself has been overused and trivialized beyond meaning.[4]

Yet there are far more substantial theological reasons for unhappiness with the word. On the biblical understanding of the word, to suggest that the fate of the Jewish people was a "Holocaust" would necessarily mean that the entirety of the Jewish people was destroyed (by immolation). This is factually untrue. And were it true, it would shatter the concept of the election of Israel. That is to say, the idea of a chosen people is meaningless if the chosen people were extinct. Further, in accord with the original biblical understanding, the word "holocaust" suggests that the victims were "sacrifices"—which ineluctably leads to questioning the nature of the God who would require the "sacrifice" of six million people (including one and a half million children) and what purpose those sacrifices have served. Hence, the very word "Holocaust" as the essential descriptor of the outcome of Nazi genocide comes with the theological affirmation that the people Israel are no longer chosen (except for destruction) and that the God of Israel inexplicably requires the shedding of the blood of innocents.[5] This outcome caters to the worst impulses of Christian antisemites and virulent atheists.

If the word "Holocaust" is inappropriate for linguistic and theological reasons, the word "Shoah" is inadequate for similar reasons. The biblical root of the word sometimes connotes calamity, disaster, devastation, or destruction (Isa. 10:3, 47:11; Ps. 63:10; Prov. 1:27, 3:25), and used together with its variant (*sho'ah u-teshu'ah*), the resultant phrase signifies a "desolate wasteland" (Zeph. 1:15; Job 30:3, 38:27). Meanwhile, the same root from which the word *sho'ah* derives may also mean nothing more than "a great noise" that has no adverse associations whatsoever. Accordingly, the prophet Zechariah (4:7) predicts that the mountains standing as an obstacle to the return from exile will become a source of such fine-looking stones for the Temple's reconstruction that those who see them will offer shouts (*teshu'ot*) of "Beautiful! Beautiful!" More importantly, the Hebrew word *sho'ah* is just as likely to convey natural catastrophes like floods or earthquakes—phenomena devoid of any moral judgment. On this reason alone the celebrated Hebrew poet Uri Tzvi Greenberg refused to use the word *sho'ah* to describe the outcome of Hitler's Final Solution and condemned all those who did.[6]

The word *ḥurban* (destruction) derives from the biblical root for "desolation." The Rabbis specifically apply the term to the destruction of the Temple and the associated depredations.[7] The use of a familiar Rabbinic term to describe Nazi genocide, with only a minor modification (*Der letster ḥurban*, i.e., "the latest Destruction"[8]), immediately resonated with many of those who were religiously committed. Thus, Rabbi Isaac Hutner, one of the most revered Orthodox authorities of the twentieth century, championed its usage particularly because of its religious overtones.[9]

The "minor modification" refers to the fact that some distinction had to be made between the original *ḥurban* and any subsequent *ḥurban*. Using the term *ḥurban* without qualification would equate the historical significance of the Nazi genocide with that of the destruction of the Temples. The result of this equation would elevate the gravity of the attempted destruction of European Jewry—what historian Steven T. Katz calls "the near apocalyptic character of the catastrophe"[10]—to the equivalent of the loss of the Temples. Especially problematic here is the fact that the Rabbis connect the destruction of both Temples with the failings of Jews rather than the power of the Jews' enemies. As such, equating Nazi genocide with the destruction of the Temples assumes that the "latest ḥurban" was a result of similar failings. It integrates the ḥurban into the traditional Jewish theology that affirms, "There is no death without sin."[11]

Beyond this, equating the first destruction (ershter ḥurban) with the latest destruction (letster ḥurban) is dubious. The Babylonians and, later, the Romans were intent on the domination and pacification of Jews. The Nazis were intent on the elimination of Jews. The distinction is of existential importance. And as such, ironically, the latest destruction would seem to be the more ominous, a conclusion that those who hold to the traditional ascription of the loss of the Temples as the greatest tragedy that Jews have suffered would be reluctant to draw.

Given the fact that none of the three words used to identify the events connected with the imposition of Hitler's Final Solution is without flaw, some have searched for alternatives. Historian William Styron, for example, prefers to use "Auschwitz" as a generic description.[12] Similarly, theologian Richard Rubenstein[13] applies "Auschwitz" metonymically to the larger program of the mass murder of Jews under the Nazi regime. While this word has gained some traction, its focus solely on the final element of the Final Solution does not capture the vastness of the Nazi enterprise. Israeli writer Amos Oz's terminology, "the murder of the Jews of Europe,"[14] is both wordy and lacks historical specificity. And philosopher Arthur Cohen's introduction of the word "tremendum" (awe, in Latin)[15] was too arcane to ever catch on.

That each of the three commonly used words for the intended destruction of Jews under the Nazi regime comes with theological baggage does not necessarily disqualify any of these terms from proper usage. Indeed, many reputable Jewish scholars use the word "Holocaust" as a matter of convention. Yet the fact that no consensus exists on an appropriate term signals in this sphere, too, the unsettling nature of the events connected with the intended Nazi genocide.

Exceptionality

That said, the special problem of the Shoah lies in its exceptionality. And its uniqueness lies in its scope rather than its magnitude. The numbers of Jews murdered by "Hitler's willing executioners,"[16] to use controversial scholar Daniel Goldhagen's evocative expression, are not proportionately larger than other mass murders in Jewish history or quantitatively larger than other mass murders in general history.

The Nazis murdered six million European Jews out of a world Jewish population of approximately fifteen to seventeen million as of 1939. This figure represents close to 40 percent of world Jewry. Analyzing the estimates of deaths during other cataclysmic events in Jewish history, Katz concludes that the Assyrian conquest of Northern Israel resulted in the loss (but not death) of more than 51 percent of the Jewish population.[17] Yet, he argues that this first major catastrophe in Jewish history was "nearly as demographically repercussive in percentage terms as the Shoah, though far less costly in human lives."[18] While the precise casualties of the Babylonian conquest are unknown, it could be as much as 40 percent of the population, or about the same as the Shoah.[19] If Josephus's calculations are correct, the number of Jews killed by the Romans during the Great Revolt of 66–70 CE may be as high as three million, or 36 percent of the population.[20] During the Bar Kokhba revolt (132–35 CE) an estimated 30 percent of the Jewish population of Palestine were killed.[21] (The numbers of deaths during the period of Crusader violence, the Spanish Inquisition, or the 1648 Cossack uprising under Chmielnicki do not come close to these earlier catastrophes.)[22] Thus, Katz asserts, while quantitatively more Jews were murdered by the Nazis than at any other time in Jewish history, "the disparity between the proportions involved is not such that it would provide a sufficient criterion, in any but a strictly mathematical form, for establishing a strong . . . claim as to the incommensurability of the Shoah."[23]

So, too, analyses of apposite cases of mass murder in world history reveal that several were quantitatively larger than the Nazis' murder of six million Jews. As many as 112 million aboriginals lost their lives during the European conquest of the Western Hemisphere—a staggering 96 percent of the native population.[24] As many as twenty million Russians were killed in one decade alone during Stalin's reign of terror, and sixty-six million thereafter.[25] The Turks destroyed an estimated 35–60 percent of the Armenian population between 1915 and 1917; and thirty to sixty million lives were claimed in the Chinese Civil War of the 1930s and 1940s.[26]

The exceptionality of the Shoah is its scope, what Katz calls its "phenomenological uniqueness."[27] Never before had a state set out in principle and by policy to physically annihilate an entire people. Historian Jacob Talmon expatiates:

> Never since the dawn of history had the world witnessed such a campaign of extermination. . . . An entire nation was handed over by a "legitimate" government to murderers organized by the authorities and trained to hunt and kill, with one single provision, that everyone, *the entire nation*, be murdered—man, women, old and young. . . . For the condemned there was no judge to whom to appeal for a redress of injustice; no government from which to ask protection and punishment for the murderers. . . . The Holocaust visited on Jews is different from all these earlier massacres in its conscious and explicit planning, in its systematic execution, in the absence of any emotional element in the remorselessly applied decision to exterminate *everyone*, but *everyone*; in the exclusion of any possibility that someone, when his turn came to be liquidated, might escape his fate by surrendering, by joining the victors and collaborating with them, by converting to the victors' faith, or by selling himself into slavery in order to save his life.[28]

In other words, what makes the Shoah incommensurable with any prior and subsequent episode of human slaughter is the Nazis' ideologically driven program to annihilate an entire people—the Jewish people. The total resources of the state were marshaled to achieve this supreme national goal; military manpower and matériel were even diverted for this purpose. The goal was comprehensively planned, and the methods of execution were systematically applied. The planned elimination of the

Jews was not justified as a defensive reaction by a nation at risk. It was not designed to gain territory or to enrich the national treasure (although that subsequently became an ancillary benefit). It was not a matter of religious coercion. Neither defection nor conversion could ensure the potential victims of a reprieve from their fate.

Theological Responses to Exceptionality

Theologically, the historical exceptionality of the Shoah tends to elicit three responses.

The first is to accept the historical uniqueness of the event but deny that any theological adjustment is necessary. The problem of theodicy—that is, the justification of God's goodness in the face of the existence of evil—is the same no matter the number of victims or the determination of the persecutors.

The second is to admit that the same answers that applied in the past will not serve any longer. While the dilemma remains unchanged, the same answers will no longer do. The scope of the Shoah will not permit it. Radical responses are necessary when addressing a radical evil.

The third is to avoid the dilemma altogether by reframing the problem. Rather than look at the Shoah as a problem for theodicy, one can look at the Shoah as a problem for Jewish continuity.

Those who follow the first way I call theological traditionalists; the second way, radical revisionists; and the third way, deflectors.

Theological Traditionalists

Theological traditionalists aim to uphold the traditional view of God as all-good and all-powerful and apply earlier biblical precedents and Rabbinic tools in addressing the question of where was God in the midst of such extensive evil. That God rewards the righteous and punishes the wicked is emphasized in Leviticus 26:3–39. Among the rewards for keeping God's commandments are material plenty, political peace, inner tranquility, military victory, human fertility, and divine protection. Disobedience will incur punishment ranging from sickness and psychological terror to national destruction and exile. The prophet Ezekiel professes:

The person who sins, he alone shall die. A child shall not share the burden of a parent's guilt, nor shall a parent share the burden of a child's guilt; the righteousness of the righteous shall be accounted to him alone, and the wickedness of the wicked shall be accounted to him alone. (Ezek. 18:20)

The Psalmist (Ps. 89:31), too, declares that punishment applies only to those who violate God's laws. Based on these passages, the Talmud concludes that there is no death without sin or suffering without cause.[29] Consequently, traditionalists must identify the sin that resulted in the Shoah and its associated suffering.

Theological traditionalist thinkers—represented in this chapter by Kalonymus Kalman Shapira, Shlomo Zalman Ehrenreich, Ḥayyim Yisrael Tsimerman, and Eliezer Berkovits—all explain the evils of the Shoah either by connecting the iniquities with some identified sin of the people or by otherwise employing a traditional Jewish explication.

Kalonymus Kalman Shapira

Why should an individual be affected by these current sufferings more than by all the sufferings which have swept over Israel in the past? Why is it that while learning in Scripture, Talmud, or midrash about the sufferings of Israel from former times to the present, one's faith was not weakened, but now it is weakened? For those people who say that Israel has never experienced sufferings such as these are mistaken. At the time of the destruction of the Temple, and at the fall of Betar, etc., there were [sufferings] such as these. . . .

Every individual among us must repent and not rely on the community as a whole, claiming that the goodness of the many in the community will save him.[30]

Rabbi Kalonymus Kalman (or Kalmish) Shapira (1889–1943), known as the Piazesner Rebbe, descended from a line of great Hasidic masters originating with Rabbi Elimelekh of Lizensk and continuing through the Maggid of Koznitz and the Seer of Lublin. He established his court in a small community south of Warsaw, where he also founded the Da'at Moshe yeshiva to help revitalize Polish Hasidism. No doubt his views on good and evil were affected by his personal trauma: his only son, his daughter-in-law, and his mother were killed in a German bombing attack of Warsaw in the fall of 1939, and his daughter was taken to Treblinka in 1942.[31] Waffen SS soldiers shot the rebbe to death in 1943.

Despite his own losses, or perhaps because of them, he gave spiritual succor to his many disciples and refugees, principally through the sermons he preached on Shabbat and holidays. Anticipating the worst, he collected his handwritten sermons during the winter of 1942–43 and buried them in a milk can. During some construction after the war, the pages he buried were discovered and sent to his surviving brother in Tel Aviv, who brought them to publication, first in Hebrew and then in English.

Rabbi Shapira offers at least five explanations for suffering and evil.

First, he argues for a revised taxonomy. He does not deny the reality of evil, but its classification as such. He argues that since God is just, and God is the author of all that is, whatever emanates from God must be just.[32] This does not mean that suffering and depredation must be accepted with equanimity. Even Moses, imagined by the Talmud to have been transported forward in time, questioned the fate of Rabbi Akiva.[33] Jews can question God and even rail against God so long as any allowable dramatic outburst does not transmogrify into a theological challenge. In a sermon preached on Hanukkah 1941, Rabbi Shapira notes how Nazi persecution had even damaged the faith of the "wholehearted," compelling them to ask of God, "Why have You forsaken us?" He tells his congregation, "If a Jew utters these words in a form of prayer or supplication, as an outpouring of his heart before God, it is a good thing. But if, God forbid, he really is questioning—even if not God directly but his internal faith—then May God protect us!"[34]

Rabbi Shapira insists that God's justice is inscrutable. While human beings may be able to probe the souls of fellow human beings, Shapira is reputed to have said to Aharon Rapoport, a disciple of the Ostrowzer Rebbe, that he may not probe the ways of God.[35] Even so, it was not beyond the Piazesner Rebbe to make an appeal to God to treat God's people like a lost object that needs to be restored ("God—the owner—will return to find us and restore to us all good things and redeem us"),[36] or to challenge God ("Why then do You keep silent at our suffering? How long will You keep silent? . . . We no longer have the strength to endure nor the spirit to be strong!"),[37] or to hold God accountable to God's very commandment requiring the saving of human life ("Even for the sake of one soul in peril must the laws of Shabbat be suspended").[38]

Second, Shapira holds that when Jews acknowledge God to be the source of suffering, God becomes a partner in suffering. Accordingly, suffering leads to a state of joy.[39] Failure to acknowledge God as the source of all suffering, however, results only in despair.[40]

Third, Shapira counterbalances suffering as the route that leads to a true appreciation of the absence of suffering.[41] In fact, it is through such adversity that Jews are called back to Torah and mitzvot and the way is prepared for the Messianic Era.[42] In a sermon delivered on August 16, 1941, Shapira elucidates:

> When Jews contemplate their physical and spiritual destruction, and the annihilation of the Torah and the Law that will result from all of this, God forbid, obviously their pain is great. But, through our longing for Torah and worship, we can sweeten all judgments and bring about a connection that constitutes a spiritual and physical salvation and a total redemption for all Israel.

Fourth, Shapira differentiates between what he terms *ḥesed nistar* (God's hidden kindness) and *ḥesed nigleh* (God's revealed, overt kindness). He categorizes suffering as a form of *ḥesed nistar*[43]—that is, an instance of God's kindness that cannot be readily seen as such. However, it presents the sufferer with an opportunity to draw near to God. Since suffering encourages the sufferer to pray and study, which, in turn, effects God's favor (*ḥesed nigleh*), suffering is thus a vehicle for transforming *ḥesed nistar* into *ḥesed nigleh*.

Shapira's fifth explanation is perhaps the most remarkable. He suggests that suffering is a form of sacrifice to God and one that God lovingly accepts,[44] just as God accepted Abraham's intended sacrifice of Isaac. Furthermore, according to Hebrew University professor Pesach Schindler, Shapira holds that God needs this form of sacrifice, since God, too, is in need of redemption![45] On the portion that begins the book of Leviticus, Shapira offered this homily:

> They each receive one from the other: God receives their broken-heartedness and penitence, and they receive God's compassion. . . . Prayer below effects [redemption] above.[46]

By making the sacrifice of suffering, humanity assists God in achieving redemption.[47]

All things considered, Rabbi Shapira came to recognize that rational analysis cannot explain the problem of suffering. Despite the sad condition of Jews in Poland, "the fact that He is our God and that we believe in Him has nothing to do with reason or logic."[48]

While suffering cannot be explained, however, he held that it can be overcome: through trust (bitaḥon) in God and God's justice: "The most important things to learn from suffering is faith in God, the deep trust that God will save us."[49]

In one way, Shapira clearly understood the distinctive nature of the Nazi threat as well as the limitations of the traditional connection between sin and punishment. He acknowledged in his Hanukkah sermon of 1941:

> If only people would bear in mind that it is not because we robbed or did anything wrong to anyone that we are being persecuted, but because we are Jews—Children of Israel bound to God and to His holy Torah. . . . It would explain why our enemies are not satisfied with just killing us or extinguishing the divine spark inside us but feel they have to annihilate simultaneously both [the] body and soul of the Jew.[50]

He disavows any substantive difference between the current wave of persecution and previous ones:

What excuse does a person have to question God and have his faith damaged by this prevailing suffering more than all the Jews who went through suffering in bygone times?[51]

Accordingly, he urges his disciples to hold fast in their faith (*emunah*) and trust in the ultimate divine redemption.

Notably, Shapira offers multiple explanations for interpreting suffering and evil during the Shoah—itself an indication of dissatisfaction with any one of them. All the more so, that he would even suggest the radical idea that God is need of redemption through Jewish suffering is an indication of the lengths to which he was willing to go in justifying God's conduct.

We do not know, had Shapira survived and was compelled to grapple with the enormity of the event, whether he might have responded differently. We can only say that to the end of his life, he upheld the standard declamation that all God's ways are just and Jews must live by the eternal affirmation of that theological truth.

Shlomo Zalman Ehrenreich

[Our] sins and iniquities should pain us more than our troubles.[52]

Rabbi Shlomo Zalman Ehrenreich (1863–1944), a student of the Satmar Rebbe, Rabbi Moshe Teitelbaum, is more adamantine in his defense of traditional theodicy.[53]

Ehrenreich was transported to his death in Auschwitz in May 1944 from the Hungarian ghetto to which he was confined. A local gentile family preserved some of the manuscripts he left behind, in which he reveals his thoughts.

Ehrenreich applies Jeremiah's call to weep more for the exiled than for the dead (Jer. 22:10) to the "thousands of Jews [who] have been expelled from Germany and Austria. Everything has been taken from them and they suffer immeasurable troubles. They have nowhere to turn." He specifically mentions the Jews transported from Grosswardein (Oradea) who had swastikas branded into their faces and flesh. Some, he adds, had no fingers; the evil ones bit them off. Ehrenreich offers a theological justification:

> It is the hand of God, on account of the sins that were done in Germany. [The Jews in Germany] assimilated among the Gentiles. For several generations they married non-Jewish wives. . . . Rabbis sat in their houses on the third floor while their daughters, wives, and granddaughters went to the theater.[54]

In short, he affirms the traditional approach: there is no death without sin and no suffering without transgression. Assimilation, persistent intermarriage, and unscolded cultural engagement are the sins; Nazi persecution is the punishment.

Ehrenreich does realize that many of the Jewish victims were innocent, and "it is difficult to understand why He would punish the innocent." So he qualifies his remarks in two ways. First, he cites the statement in the Talmud that rules that the good are punished along with the bad[55]—a statement that finds a predecessor in the biblical narrative that has God hold all Israel accountable for the sin committed by Sabbath violators alone.[56] Second, he asserts, "One cannot question this. It is God's judgment."

To Ehrenreich, God uses the Nazis to punish the Jews for their sins just as God used the Assyrians to punish the Israelites for theirs.[57] There is no mystery here. "In order that we should have a broken heart, He [i.e., God] sends us troubles and poverty." What is required of European Jews in the moment is "penitent return":

> If we take it upon ourselves to observe the holy Sabbath, the laws of family purity, and not to eat non-kosher meat or other forbidden foods and to strengthen the holy Torah, then God will certainly hear our voices and will have mercy.[58]

The remedy is simple. The formula is time-honored. The outcome is assured.

All of the cruel and violent deaths were according to measure and balance. There is no accident, heaven forbid. Everything is according to a just and precise calculation and everything is for the good of the sinner to cleanse his sin.[59]

Rabbi Ḥayyim Yisrael Tsimerman (1901–67?) straddled two streams of thought: Hasidism and Musar. Though he was under the influence of earlier Hasidic teachers, his advanced training was in the Novogrodok Musar yeshiva in Warsaw and, later, in the Musar-oriented Ateret Yosef Kollel in Palestine. Even so, he served as the rabbi of the Sokolover Hasidim in Tel Aviv.

Fortuitously, he had emigrated from Poland to Palestine in the late 1920s, thus avoiding the horrors suffered by Polish Jewry under the Nazi regime. Unlike Shapira and Ehrenreich, Tsimerman lived through the Shoah and its aftermath, enabling him to consider the exceptionality of the event. Yet neither distance nor time impelled Tsimerman to budge from his traditional theological response to the Shoah as elucidated in his 1947 publication *Tamim Pa'alo* (His works are perfect).

He certainly understands the nature of the question posed by the Shoah, as he writes at the outset:

The question about the six million Jews who were killed in the sanctification of God's name throughout Europe and all other places, dying every sort of death in the world, is the principle question of the day. It is a painful and agonizing question, one which penetrates into the inner depths of the heart. It upsets the entire nation of Israel, from the small to the great, from regular folk to the pious. Everyone, without exception, is posing this quandary: Why did God do this to the nation? It is a *hurban* unlike anything since the world came into existence, a disaster of six million Jews of our nation.[60]

Tsimerman more than acknowledges the uniqueness of the Shoah. He sees it as a profound challenge to the traditional connection of death with sin and suffering with transgression, since many of the victims were innocents or saints. That sinners deserve punishment is undeniable—but the pious should have been spared.

Yet the Shoah

included those who feared God, who were perfect; geniuses; scholars; pious ones; pure pietists. It included people of good deeds engaged in [the study of the] holy Torah day and night, [and those] who never stopped for a moment to speak of Torah. It included the center of religious Judaism, the yeshivas with their rabbis, deans, and yeshiva heads. It included the students, great and small, who studied in them, their instructors and tutors, and schoolchildren who studied in their schools.[61]

The question of "why" is profound, pervasive, and persistent:

When you meet with your neighbors, in the synagogue, in the street, on the bus, in your home and in your neighbor's home. Anywhere you speak with someone, you are immediately asked the question: Why? . . . Even today, two years after the world has turned to peace, the question does not stop.[62]

The inability of others to formulate an answer compels Tsimerman to break the silence and "probe the ways of God and His conduct."[63] By looking into the traditional literature (holy books) exclusively and intently, Tsimerman is convinced he has found the material to formulate multiple answers designed to satisfy different cohorts from the pious to the secular.

Since the traditional theological explanation for suffering, as consequence of sin, fails when there is no recognizable sin that satisfactorily explains the suffering of innocents, Tsimerman relies on a talmudic text to assert that the pious were not innocent: "Whoever can forbid his household from sinning but does not, is liable for the sins of the household; if he can forbid his fellow citizens [but does not], he is liable for the sins of his fellow citizens."[64] They were culpable because they failed to protest against the trespasses of others, such as the publication of newspapers on Shabbat, the opening of Jewish businesses on Shabbat, and Jews intermingling with non-Jews, all of which had happened without the rigorous condemnation of religious leaders. Furthermore, Maimonides had ruled that a pious person was liable if he allowed an evil person to do as he pleased.[65] Hence, the suffering and deaths of the saintly rabbis and great scholars of Europe were not a challenge to traditional theodicy but a corollary of it.

His last answer offers a novel twist on the traditional understanding of repentance as the precursor to redemption. According to one talmudic authority, "If all Israel repents, the Messiah will come. If not, he will not come."[66] Rabbi Shmuel Edels (1555–1631) comments, "When the time for redemption comes, the Holy One, blessed be God, will establish a king as harsh as Haman for the people and this will return them to the right path so that they repent."[67] Tsimerman implies that in order to bring about messianic redemption, God appointed Hitler as his tool for effecting national repentance. This tool is a bludgeon, not a scalpel. That is to say, the damage was broad and severe — precisely as described by the mystic Rabbi Isaac Luria,[68] who goes on to explain that souls refined by torment and violent death will transmigrate into purer forms and live in anticipation of the imminent Messianic Era. Tsimerman presumes that the Shoah was thus part of God's ultimate plan. God coordinated the almost unimaginable suffering "according to a just and precise calculation" where "everything is for the good of the sinner in order to cleanse his sin."[69] This leads him to conclude, "As the million terrible troubles and the birth pangs of the Messiah have been fulfilled, similarly all the promises of the prophets concerning the end of days will be completely fulfilled."[70] He assures his readers: the apocalyptic vision of the prophets can and will end with "everlasting salvation."[71]

Assurances aside, Tsimerman could justifiably be accused of preaching to the choir. Only those who already accept the idea of the transmigration of souls and only those who unquestionably accept the theological opinions of individual talmudic scholars as exigent rather than speculative would likely be convinced by his explanations. And his former explanation justifying the deaths of the pious does nothing to justify the murder of a million and a half children who had no responsibility to protest.

Eliezer Berkovits

The pious believer who was not there but meekly submits, not to his own destruction, but to that of six million of his brethren, insults with his faith the faith of the concentration camps. . . . In the presence of the holy faith of the crematoria, the ready faith of those who were not there, is vulgarity. But the disbelief of the sophisticated intellectual in the midst of an affluent society—in the light of the holy disbelief of the crematoria—is obscenity.[72]

Transylvanian-born Rabbi Eliezer Berkovits (1908–92) earned a doctorate in philosophy from the University of Berlin after he received rabbinical ordination from the Hildesheimer Rabbinical Seminary. He served as a pulpit rabbi in congregations in Berlin, in Leeds, England, in Sydney, Australia, and finally in Boston before devoting the rest of his career to academics, chairing the Department of Jewish Philosophy at the Hebrew Theological College in Skokie, Illinois. He published widely on a variety of themes, including three books on the Shoah. In *Faith after the Holocaust*, published in 1973, Berkovits makes his initial and most sustained defense of a modified version of traditional Jewish theodicy.[73]

Berkovits is troubled by the implications of traditional Jewish theodicy. If someone is observed to be suffering, it is impossible to determine absolutely whether this person is a victim suffering from the sinner's wrongful act or a sinner suffering from divine punishment for committing the wrongful act. In stressing the latter, traditional Jewish theodicy has practically ignored the former (except largely to say that God permits evil to exist so that people may be tested by it and, through the experience, become more sensitive, caring, and sympathetic). Furthermore, when suffering is associated exclusively with sin, it requires making sinners out of martyrs, and "the idea that all this has befallen us because of our sins is an utterly unwarranted exaggeration. There is suffering because of sins; but that all suffering is due to it is simply not true."[74] Further, "the idea that Jewish martyrology through the ages can be explained as divine judgment is obscene."[75] To believe that Auschwitz was a punishment for Israel's sins "would be a desecration of the Divine name."[76]

The modification Berkovits offers is couched in philosophical language that bears unwrapping. Despite popular usage that presumes God to be "good," Berkovits says God can do neither good nor bad.[77] For God, goodness is neither an ideal or a value: it is existence. In Berkovits's words, "With man the good is axiology; with God, ontology."[78] Berkovits is saying that human beings alone assign value to what is good and strive and struggle to attain it; that is the meaning of axiology. God, however, does not assign value to what is good. God *is* good, that is, goodness is the very nature of God's being: God's ontology. The difference between human beings and God when it comes to value is simple: "Man alone can create value," says Berkovits. "God is Value."[79] With this distinction comes a consequence:

> But if man alone is the creator of values, one who strives for the realization of ideals, then he must have freedom of choice and freedom of decision. And this freedom must be respected by God Himself. God cannot as a rule intervene whenever man's use of freedom displeases Him. . . . For freedom and responsibility are of the very essence of man. Without them man is not human. If there is to be man, he must be allowed to make his choices in freedom.[80]

So God withdraws in order to maximize human freedom. The biblical expression for God's withdrawal is *hester panim*, "the hiding of the face," as it appears at the end of Psalm 44 in the context of ostensible divine indifference to the suffering some human beings inflict upon other human beings. God, as it were, averts the divine eyes from the misuse of the freedom with which God has endowed humanity. Given such freedom, human beings "will often use it wrongly," and as they do, "there will be suffering for the innocent."[81] God's withdrawal may be explained just as plausibly as a testament to God's patience with humanity and the infinitude of divine mercy than as a failure to intervene on behalf of the victims.

As to the question of the exceptionality of the Shoah, Berkovits asserts that "the Sho'ah does not stand by itself."[82] The Shoah "stands out as unique in the annals of man for the magnitude of the disaster, for unimaginable cruelty and unbridled inhumanity."[83] But from the point of view of the problem the Shoah poses to faith, it is not unique. Considering the totality of Jewish history, Berkovits concludes that "we have had innumerable Auschwitzes,"[84] from the destructions of the Temples to the Crusades to the Chmielnicki massacres. And each catastrophe was perceived by those who lived through it as "not different from the problem which confronts us in our days."[85]

That, Berkovits explains, is because "the problem of God's providential presence is always raised in relationship to man's subjective experience of His presence."[86] For this reason, "while the Holocaust is unique in the objective magnitude of its inhumanity, it is not unique as a problem of faith resulting from Jewish historical experience."[87] Survivors of all previous catastrophes were equally confounded by God's withdrawal.

For a Jew who lacks faith, God will be "forever absent."[88] For a Jew who lives by faith, God's absence is never absolute. The faithful Jew "does not doubt God's presence, though he is unable to set limits to the duration and intensity of his absence."[89] So, after the Holocaust, the proper question to Berkovits is not why God absented the divine self from Auschwitz, seemingly tolerating so much evil, but, rather: can the Jewish people still remain faithful witnesses to God's elusive presence?[90]

Berkovits maintains that Jews can and must do so. "There must be a dimension beyond history in which all suffering finds its redemption through God."[91] And while this is an article of faith and not a reasoned argument, he holds that no reasoned argument can suffice. Cementing his traditionalist response, Berkovits concedes that he cannot provide a "justification for the ways of providence."[92] He can only advocate their acceptance.

Evaluation of the Theological Traditionalists

Any evaluation of the theological traditionalists must begin with a kind of begrudging admiration for their effort. They refuse to allow an event as monstrous in its intent and as catastrophic in its outcome to sway them from upholding the beliefs they hold as sacred.

Once this admiration subsides, however, the neutral reader must ask whether traditional theology can apply to the unique phenomenon of the Shoah. Rabbi and scholar Robert Gordis would argue not so much:

> The mountain of human misery created by the Nazi holocaust poses a major problem for traditional Biblical faith that God works in history, and for its corollary that His righteousness is manifest in human affairs.[93]

The Holocaust fundamentally challenges these basic Jewish theological assumptions. All attempts to try to bypass these assumptions seem puny and ill-conceived.

In addition, the theological traditionalists discussed in this chapter (except Berkovits) attribute the Shoah to sin. Shapira assigns the death of his family to his own sins. Ehrenreich assigns the depredations of the Shoah to the sins of assimilation and intermarriage. Tsimerman blames the failed moral leadership of the rabbis and scholars who did not do enough to keep European Jewry committed to Jewish observance. While the identifiable sin varies, the intent is the same. The formula that states, "There is no death without sin," is fastidiously affirmed.

Yet to many Jews, such attempts to locate the Shoah within the ambit of thinking that ascribes death and suffering to sin seem desperate and offensive. Rabbi Irving Greenberg speaks for them when he writes:

> Now that [the victims of the Holocaust] have been cruelly tortured and killed, boiled into soap, their hair made into pillows, and their bones into fertilizer, their unknown graves and the very fact of their death denied to them [by Holocaust deniers], the theologian would inflict on them the only indignity left: that is, insistence that it was done because of their sins.[94]

Further, Israel Prize winner and Holocaust survivor David Weiss Halivni argues that the effort to associate the Shoah with sin is not only morally outrageous, since it falsely and maliciously accuses innocents of wrongdoing; it is also unwarranted on a strict reading of the Bible. Halivni insists that the "Shoah was not the consequence of sin."[95] In fact, Halivni really argues that the Shoah *could not be* a consequence of sin. The operative verse is Leviticus 26:44, "Yet, even then, when they are in the land of their enemies, I will not reject them or spurn them so as to destroy them, annulling My covenant with them: for I the Lord am their God." On Halivni's reading, at the conclusion of a series of warnings against violating God's covenant and the dire consequences of violation, the Torah reassures the Israelites that despite their sins, God will not "utterly destroy" them. The covenant God swore to the Patriarchs can never be abrogated.

The fundamental question for Halivni is how to understand the meaning of "utterly destroy." For traditionalists, Halivni claims, the intent must be total annihilation, because Jews would never conceive of God as a power who would break a promise. Since Leviticus 26:44 states that God promises never to utterly destroy the people Israel, there will always be survivors. The fact that there are Shoah survivors means that the promise was kept, even after sin.

But, argues Halivni on philological grounds, this is not what "utter destruction" means. Utter destruction means the "irremediable destruction of a people's institutional infrastructure,"[96] as the medieval commentator and grammarian Rabbi David Kimhi comments on Jeremiah 30:11 and 46:28. And this is precisely what happened during the Shoah:

> Institutional Jewish life in Eastern Europe was uprooted and almost totally erased; the only survivors were as brands snatched from the fire.[97]

Consequently, Leviticus 26:44 does not apply, and the Shoah cannot be attributable to sin.

Even setting aside Halivni's analysis and letting stand Ehrenreich's contention that the Shoah is the consequence of the sin of assimilation, the assimilation of European Jewry did not begin in 1939. That process began more than 150 years earlier, following the emancipation of German

Jewry. Hence, Ehrenreich would have to explain why the punishment for that sin was delayed; and if the punishment could be delayed for that long a time, it could very well have been delayed longer.

Timing is also a problem for Tsimerman. If the sin for which the Shoah is punishment was the failed religious leadership of Europe's Jews, the punishment could have been exacted one hundred years earlier when, following the tsarist draft decree of 1827, Jewish leaders colluded with Russian authorities in determining which Jewish children would be sent off for twenty-five years of military service. Contemporary scholar David Roskies cites a popular Russian Jewish folk song that included this indictment:

> Little children are torn from their lessons
> And pressed into coats that have soldiers' buttons.
> Our rabbis, our bigshots are in cahoots,
> Teaching our kids to be recruits.[98]

Additionally, the theological traditionalists in this chapter go further in explaining the suffering in the Shoah. Both Ehrenreich and Tsimerman see the lesson of the Shoah as Israel's need for repentance. For Ehrenreich, repentance is the condition for God's mercy after the Shoah; for Tsimerman and Shapira, repentance is a prerequisite for messianic redemption. Repentance, however, is traditionally conceived as a commitment to personal transformation following the realization of sin. It is an individualized response and not connected to any catastrophe. And as far as messianic redemption is concerned, opinions vary. While some say that it is contingent on reforming character, others say that it is independent of any such reform. For example, one Rabbinic tradition states that messianic redemption would ensue if all Jews kept just one Sabbath properly.[99]

Shapira additionally posits that suffering makes the victims ever more appreciative of their blessings, and suffering also draws the victim closer to God. But even if this were the case, the need for a catastrophe as vast and as profound as the Shoah goes unexplained.

As for Berkovits, contemporary writer and critic Dr. David Hazony notes that saying "the Holocaust's theological challenge is not a new one," as

Berkovits does, "is not the same as offering theological answers."[100] And the theological answers Berkovits does offer are not entirely persuasive. For instance, to the question "Could God allow the Holocaust to happen to the Jewish people?" Berkovits's answer is a qualified yes. Endowing humanity with free will requires that God make a substantive withdrawal from human affairs. And God's withdrawal necessarily, though unfortunately, allows for radical evil. Yet philosopher Steven T. Katz no doubt speaks for many objectors when he writes:

> It increasingly seems to me that it would have been preferable, morally preferable, to have a world in which "evil" did not exist, at least not in the magnitude witnessed during the Shoah, even if this meant doing without certain heroic moral attributes or accomplishments. . . . The price is just too high. This is true even for the much exalted value of freedom itself. . . . Better to introduce limits, even limits on that freedom of the will requisite to moral choice, than to allow Auschwitz.[101]

In conclusion, on theological grounds, moral grounds, logical grounds, and strictly textual grounds, the traditionalist position seems to fail.

Radical Revisionists

Radical revisionists conclude that the standard responses to the problem of evil cannot stand up to the intensity of the evil observed or experienced during the Shoah. The traditional view that there is no death without sin and no suffering without iniquity fails to explain the experience of the Shoah. The traditional view that God will preserve the innocent and punish the wicked is repudiated by the facts of the Shoah. As a result, profound changes are necessary in the way Jews must think of God.

The radical revisionists Richard Rubenstein, Alexander Donat, Arthur Cohen, and Hans Jonas are among those advocating these changes.

Richard Rubenstein

I believe the greatest single challenge to modern Judaism arises out of the question of God and the death camps. I am amazed at the silence of contemporary Jewish theologians on this most crucial and agonizing of all Jewish issues. How can Jews believe in an omnipotent, beneficent God after Auschwitz? Traditional Jewish theology maintains that God is the ultimate, omnipotent actor in historical drama. It has interpreted every major catastrophe in Jewish history as God's punishment of a sinful Israel. I fail to see how this position can be maintained without regarding Hitler and the SS as instruments of God's will. The agony of European Jewry cannot be likened to the testing of Job. To see any purpose in the death camps, the traditional believer is forced to regard the most demonic, anti-human explosion of all history as a meaningful expression of God's purposes. The idea is simply too obscene for me to accept.[102]

Richard Rubenstein (b. 1924) remains one of the most polarizing voices for rethinking God in the aftermath of the Shoah since the 1966 publication of his provocative collection of articles and essays *After Auschwitz: Radical Theology and Contemporary Judaism.*

During most of the World War II years Rubenstein studied at both the University of Cincinnati and the Hebrew Union College–Jewish Institute of Religion (the Reform movement's rabbinical school) in the same city. After a hiatus, he completed his rabbinical studies at the Conservative movement's Jewish Theological Seminary in New York and was ordained in 1952. In 1960 Harvard awarded him a doctoral degree in theology.

During the ensuing decade he engaged in vigorous debate with Christian theologians struggling with the implications of those who argued for the "death of God." The publication of his controversial views was, in an important way, the product of interfaith theological dialogue.

Rubenstein recalls how he was invited to meet a series of religious and cultural leaders in Germany during the late summer of 1961, just before the building of the Berlin Wall. One interview was particularly influential in shaping his religious outlook. After meeting with Heinrich Grüber, dean of the Evangelical Church of East and West Berlin, Rubenstein confesses that he "reached a theological point of no return. . . . If I believed in God as the omnipotent author of the historical drama and Israel as His Chosen

People, I had to accept Dean Grüber's opinion that it was God's will that Hitler committed six million Jews to slaughter. I could not possibly believe in such a God nor could I believe in Israel as the chosen people of God after Auschwitz."[103]

Grüber was a devout Christian, ardent participant in interfaith dialogue, witness against Eichmann at his Jerusalem trial, and rescuer of Jews. But rather than see Nazi atrocities as an assault against God's goodness, he saw them as a fulfillment of God's will. "For some reason," Rubenstein recounts Grüber's view, "it was part of God's plan that the Jews died." What is more, if sin is the prerequisite for death, the nature of the "sin" for which the Jews were condemned to death had gone unmentioned.

Rubenstein might have been able to discount Grüber's assertion as the residue of centuries of Christian antisemitism beginning with the charge that Jews were "Christ-killers." But the Bible asserts that both the Assyrians and the Babylonians were "the rod of God's anger." The Talmud asserts that there is no death without sin. And both the Bible and the Talmud assert that Israel is the chosen people. Grüber was merely affirming what *Judaism* holds to be true.

To Rubenstein this led to an inevitable and unconscionable conclusion: "As long as we continue to hold to the doctrine of the election of Israel, we will leave ourselves open to the theology expressed by Dean Grüber, that because the Jews are God's Chosen People, God wanted Hitler to punish them."[104]

The same could be argued for the doctrine of theodicy. Judaism was a grand theological experiment: a radical shift from ancient religions. But as a theological experiment it failed. Judaism had failed as a theology not because of any ontological weakness, but because empirical evidence had proved its doctrines incapable of explaining reality.

After the deaths of six million Jews, Rubenstein wrote in his introduction, "We cannot restore the religious world that preceded their demise."[105] He questioned the claim of traditional Jewish theology "that God is the ultimate, omnipotent actor in historical drama. It has interpreted every major catastrophe in Jewish history as God's punishment of sinful Israel.

I fail to see how this position can be maintained without regarding Hitler and the SS as instruments of God's will."[106]

The challenge posed by the Shoah requires a radically new understanding of God. As early as 1955 Rubenstein came to the conclusion that the idea of a traditional God who is the all-powerful creator, "the transcendent theistic God of Jewish patriarchal monotheism,"[107] the God worshiped by Jews as a royal father, is no longer tenable. This idea of God suffered the same fate as the Jewish victims in the gas chambers and crematoria, and no wishful thinking can restore it. As Rubenstein puts it, "The Father-God is a dead God. Even the existentialist leap of faith cannot resurrect this dead God after Auschwitz."[108] What remains is only the notion of God as "the primal ground of being out of which we arise and to which we return."[109]

And yet, "the death of God," Rubenstein emphasizes, "does not mean the end of all gods. It means the demise of the God who was the ultimate actor in history"[110]—that is, the intervening God, the God who should have saved the six million.

Rubenstein argues for replacing the idea of an intervening God with the idea of an antiseptic, distant, and unknowable God, what Rubenstein calls "the Holy Nothingness."[111] At best, God may be understood in a more vague and more philosophically defensible way as "the focus of ultimate concern."[112]

Even without a theistic God, Rubenstein believes Jewish religious life can still function and even flourish. "In a world devoid of God," as understood in the traditional way, "we need Torah, tradition, and the religious community far more than in a world where God's presence was meaningfully experienced."[113] Jewish traditions are, on Rubenstein's account, "the way in which we share the decisive times and crises of life."[114] The need for this kind of sharing remains—and even deepens—in the aftermath of the Shoah. The most successful recipe for Judaism after the Holocaust would include "a mystical paganism which utilizes the historic forms of Jewish religion."[115]

Rubenstein's radical theological revisionism is breathtaking in its boldness and reflects the seriousness of the challenge the Shoah presents to traditional Jewish theology. His abandonment of tradition has generated both visceral condemnation and more thoughtful analysis.[116] Meanwhile, Rubenstein's take on the Shoah has become the irresistible force in all subsequent theological discussion.[117]

Alexander Donat

> From morning to night we cried out for a sign that God was with us. From the depths of our disaster, amid the hangings, the gas chambers, and the incomprehensible manifestations of evil, we shouted: "Omnipotent God, merciful and compassionate One, where are You?" We searched for Him, but we did not find him.[118]

By 1939 Alexander Donat (1906–83) graduated from writing as a journalist to becoming publisher of a Polish daily. Surviving the liquidation of the Warsaw Ghetto in 1943, Donat was deported to Maidanek and then to Dachau. After the war, Donat, along with his wife and son, immigrated to New York, where he wrote and published on Shoah themes.

In a 1975 English lecture entitled "Voices from the Ashes,"[119] later transcribed and published as a Hebrew article,[120] Donat admits that he is not a trained philosopher making tightly argued, logically valid statements about the Shoah. He identifies as a searcher for truth. That search has led him everywhere:

> I looked for answers in every possible source and attempted to evaluate them. In trying to understand these explanations, I examined them with the test I thought conclusive: How do they look from the top of the smokestack? This is extreme and harsh but infallible, incorruptible, and lucid.[121]

Donat, as a survivor, claims a privileged position. He is not asserting that only survivors can "know" the truth because they experienced the horrors of the death camps and witnessed the smoke rising from the crematoria. Rather, he is making the more modest claim that the litmus test of any theological explanation of the Shoah is how it resonates with survivors like him. Any scholarly disquisitions must be validated by experience.

Donat comes to the conclusion that "the total evil that was done to us . . . cannot be justified with any excuse."[122] He proceeds to reject all the extant explanations. That God's ways are inscrutable is unsatisfyingly evasive. To accept on faith all God's actions as good or part of some grander unknown plan is intellectually cowardly. Aside from being "an exercise in evasion,"[123] to explain the Shoah as an abuse of free will makes God a partner with evil. Buber's notion of an eclipse of God is juvenile. Even children know that an eclipse can be observed indirectly; an all-knowing God should be able to do the same. And, as he claims Fackenheim does, making belief in God a kind of "protest" against Hitler's Final Solution is not an answer at all. It is unfounded loyalty to a God who disappoints.

Exposing the inadequacy of all the "excuses," Donat proclaims:

I cannot understand how it is possible to believe in a God who allowed 1.5 million children to die in gas chambers and mass graves. No sophistry, no rhetoric, or casuistry, no flood of description or poetry, no mysterious or flowery prose can answer this question. The answer is unique and as simple and final as an order to the right or to the left.[124] There is no other option. Either this is the God of Treblinka—or else there is nothing. My choice is clear: There is nothing.[125]

Like Rubenstein, Donat rejects a traditional God outright.[126] But unlike Rubenstein, Donat does not try to reconstruct a new way of imagining God. To Donat, the only passable and possible conclusion to his search is atheism.

In Donat's view, while a belief in any God is necessarily a casualty of the Shoah, Judaism itself is indispensable. But it is a Judaism without God. Like Urbach, Donat sees the inherent value in Jewish peoplehood. For Donat, this includes strong support for the State of Israel. And the concept of social justice is ennobling. As an "affirmation of life, love, justice, freedom, and truth," Judaism needs to be preserved.

But whether a godless version of Judaism can sustain these ideals remains an open question.

The most penetrating of post-*tremendum* assaults upon God has been the attack upon divine silence. Silence is surely in such a usage as metaphor for inaction: passivity, affectlessness, indeed at its worst and most extreme, indifference and ultimate malignity. Only a malign God would be silent.[127]

Arthur A. Cohen (1928–87) was born and raised in New York City. After earning both his bachelor of arts degree and master's degree from the University of Chicago, he returned to New York, enrolling as a postgraduate student in philosophy at the Jewish Theological Seminar of America, but he abandoned his academic career in favor of the publishing business. His interest in philosophy and theology continued, however, leading to his 1981 book *The Tremendum: A Theological Interpretation of the Holocaust.*

To Cohen, the Shoah is no less than the defining event in Jewish history that has inverted all that has preceded it. He terms this theological abyss "the *tremendum*." Philosophically speaking, the *tremendum* is an "ontological immensity," meaning that while we "can and do continue to perform old routines . . . we know that all has changed."[128] As such, "the God who emerges as possible to thought beyond the *tremendum* is no longer the God of traditional theology."[129] The Shoah has erased all memory and historical reflection of God. The Shoah has annihilated all past hopes and expectations of God. Simply put, the Shoah cannot fit into the matrix of traditional Jewish theology.

In disallowing traditional ideas about God, the Shoah obliges Jews to "regard all settled doctrines anew."[130] Jewish belief and practice must be reorganized—in Cohen's words, "constellated"—so as to "enable them to endure meaningfully in a universe that endures the *tremendum* and withstands it and a God who creates a universe in which such destructiveness occurs."[131] This requires building a bridge across the abyss.

For Cohen, the superstructure for this bridge necessitates three specific theological components. First, "the God who is affirmed must abide in a universe whose human history is scarred by genuine evil without making evil empty or illusory." In other words, all so-called theological explanations of the Shoah that rescue God by diminishing the gravity of the Shoah and its indelible wickedness are unsatisfactory. The same is true for any purported explanation that "disallows the real presence of God before, even if not within, history." Second, evil is part of the structural integrity of the universe God has created and, as such, is imbued with value and meaning even as human beings aim to defeat it. And third, God cannot be held to be aloof from "the life of his creation"[132]—that is, uninvolved in history—an implied repudiation of Rubenstein. For Cohen, God must be "dipolar": an entity of "absolute being," but also a deity of active "involvement with the created."[133] Should any of these three components be denied or disproved, God "ceases to be more than a metaphor for the inexplicable."[134]

While Cohen's project is bridge building, the image he constructs is that of a balance. On the one side is the conception of God as remote and impervious, endowed by human beings with their ideals and aspirations. On the other side is the conception of God who intervenes in human affairs, more often than not to the delight of God's beneficiaries, but sometimes to their distress. The *tremendum* invites human beings to tip the balance in favor of the former conception in order to win "a sense of God whom we may love and honor, but whom we no longer fear and from whom we no longer demand."[135]

Hans Jonas

Only a completely unintelligible God can be said to be absolutely good and absolutely powerful yet tolerate the world as it is. . . .

Auschwitz calls . . . the whole traditional concept of God into question.[136]

German-born Hans Jonas (1903–93) studied philosophy and theology under Martin Heidegger at the University of Freiberg. In 1933, five years after the University of Marburg awarded him a doctorate and the same year Hitler rose to power, Jonas immigrated to Palestine. With the onset of the Second World War, Jonas enlisted in the British army and fought in

North Africa. He returned to Palestine and served as an officer in Israel's War of Independence. In 1949 he resumed his academic career in Canada and then in New York, where he chaired the philosophy department of the New School for Social Research.

Jonas's 1984 address on the occasion of receiving the University of Tübingen's Leopold Lucas Prize was later published as an article entitled "The Concept of God after Auschwitz: A Jewish Voice." Like Rubenstein and Cohen, Jonas urges a revision in the way God ought to be conceived.

"After Auschwitz," Jonas insists, "the Jew can no longer hold onto the time-honored theology of his faith that has been shattered by it."[137] "Auschwitz," he adds, "marks a divide between a 'before' and an 'after,' where the latter will be forever different from the former."[138] Referring to the traditional responses to the problem of evil, Jonas states, "Nothing of this will still serve us in dealing with the event for which 'Auschwitz' has become the symbol."[139] The Jewish victims did not die for the sake of their faith or because of their faith. The Jewish victims did not die for their "belief or unbelief," not for punishment or trial or witness or messianic hope. Jews were murdered under the fiction that they had been selected for wholesale annihilation. While the emergent and unavoidable question is "Why did God let this happen?" the more trenchant question is "What God could let it happen?" To this second question Jonas reverts to what he calls his initial "groping answer."[140]

His initial answer took the form of a conjecture: a Platonic myth. For some mysterious reason, God, the infinite One, risks entering into space and time. God renounces the divine being to allow the universe to come into existence. Eons later, life emerges from the void. Life is "the world accident for which the becoming deity had waited."[141] But with life comes death. "Mortality," says Jonas, "is the price which the new possibility of being called 'life' had to pay for itself."[142] Evolving from this life is humanity. With humanity comes a critical change. "The advent of man means the advent of knowledge and freedom."[143] With freedom comes unlimited possibility. And while God hoped that humans would choose the best, they often chose the worst.

After the Shoah, Jonas added to this tentative answer by scrutinizing the existence of (moral) evil as a function of human free will. Jonas intimates that the assertion of free will is unsatisfactory in the face of Auschwitz, despite Berkovits's insistence of adequacy. "After Auschwitz," writes Jonas, "the Jew can no longer simply hold onto the time-honored theology of his faith that has been shattered by it."[144] Citing the traditional Jewish concept of human free will as an explanation for Nazi excesses will not do. Here Jonas seems to side with Donat, who asserted that the notion of free will is an evasion rather than an explanation. An omnipotent and omnibenevolent God could very well have placed limits on free will, thus ensuring human responsibility but preventing excessive suffering.

But, Jonas adds three theological qualifiers. First, he argues against what he calls the biblical idea of "divine majesty," whereby God is inure to human feelings. Rather, the re-envisioned, post-Auschwitz God is a suffering God. God suffers from disappointment in human conduct, and God suffers empathetically with the victims. Second, Jonas argues for a becoming God—that is to say, a God who changes and learns, a God who is affected by what occurs. Third, bound up with the idea of a suffering and a becoming God is a caring God "who has left something for other agents to do."[145] Most critically, from Jonas's perspective, this newly engineered concept of God no longer construes God as omnipotent.

Here Jonas argues that the very concept of omnipotence is logically implausible.

Absolute, total power means power not limited by anything, not even by the mere existence of something other than the possessor of that power; for the very existence of such another would already constitute a limitation, and the one would have to annihilate it so as to save its absoluteness. Absolute power then in its solitude has no object on which to act. But as objectless power it is a powerless power, canceling itself out: "All" equals "zero" here. . . . The existence of another object limits the power of the most powerful agent at the same time that it allows it to be an agent.[146]

Power consists in the capacity to overcome some resistance, some opposing force. Therefore, that on which power acts must have some power of its own. And if that something is independently powerful, then the power upon which it acts is not all-powerful.

Jonas goes further in showing that aside from its logical deficiency, divine omnipotence cannot be simultaneously affirmed along with divine goodness. As he argues, "We can have divine omnipotence together with divine goodness only at the price of complete divine inscrutability." That is, "Only a completely unintelligible God can be said to be absolutely good and absolutely powerful, yet tolerate the world as it is."[147] For Jonas, the post-Auschwitz God cannot be the God traditionally conceived.

Evaluation of the Radical Revisionists

To their credit, revisionists are brutally honest. Post-Holocaust theological revisionists reject outright either the traditional ascription of omnipotence, omnibenevolence, and omniscience to God or any belief in God altogether. They readily admit that the scope and magnitude of the Shoah have entirely compromised traditional views of God *and* compel a fundamental reevaluation of the nature of God. Furthermore, that reevaluation necessarily results in a repudiation of God as traditionally imagined.

While the revisionists' honesty is laudable, the result is discomfiting. Rubenstein, for example, advocates a new Judaism in which God is disassociated from providence. Yet how Jews would pray to Rubenstein's "Holy Nothingness" is unimaginable. And if God were no longer conceived as an actor in history, as Rubenstein insists, the celebration of Passover as evidence of God's incursion into human affairs is rendered void, and any commemoration of plagues, the Exodus, and the rescue at the Reed Sea as traditionally understood seems meaningless. Moreover, the Torah that Rubenstein wants to retain loses its significance if it is removed from its historical context.

Donat rejects God altogether. But without the commanding, authoritative, all-powerful presence of God, all Jewish practice would seem to be reduced to optional activity. Without a commander, there can be no commandments, and without commandments, there is no unity in purpose or observance. Instead of Judaism, Donat's theological revisionism would seem to lead to Judaisms.

Moreover, for some Jewish thinkers, Jewish life is inconceivable without a belief in the One God. Maimonides, for instance, makes the acceptance of the belief in the One God a prerequisite for conversion to Judaism.[148] That said, the real issue is not whether an individual Jew must believe in God (on this there is some dispute[149]), but whether Judaism is conceivable without God, and here the answer is unmistakably no. Judaism and the Torah (as the foundational text of Judaism) are predicated on the existence of God. Hence, Donat's revisionist approach is contrary to the very understanding of what Judaism is.

Furthermore, without God, Donat would be hard-pressed to show how justice, freedom, and truth—all values he wishes to retain—are validated. Scientist David Gelernter conceives of a thought experiment that may apply here.[150] Suppose only reasonable people inhabited the world. Being reasonable, all would agree that committing murder is wrong, even if the intended victim is someone hated. The wrongfulness of murder might be attributable to rational and psychological grounds—an inner prompting—with no need for invoking God. But suppose someone was about to commit a brutal murder. Presumably, a reasonable person would feel obliged to intervene, again because of an inner prompting to compel any would-be murderer to desist. Yet any reasonable person must admit that the would-be murderer is also motivated by inner promptings. To prejudice one's own inner promptings over another's appears unjustifiable unless one is prepared to declare oneself the supreme and absolute moral authority. And that is unreasonable. The only other justification is to assert that there exists a supreme God who validates universal moral laws. Justice, a value that Donat wants to uphold, ceases to be subjective only when there is a God.

As to Cohen, simultaneously conceiving of God as both remote and personal, aloof and immanent, unknowable and accessible, is neither a bridge nor a balance but a contradiction. What's more, Cohen's reconfiguring of God as an observer rather than an interferer makes God a mere bystander in human history. As such, God would no longer be the entity to which Jews could direct their aspirations or their appeals. And if, as Cohen claims, to accommodate the Holocaust one must conclude that evil is built into the very fabric of the universe, the solution to the question of why so much evil is necessary can only be that God alone knows. In other words, the answer is inexplicable. Hence, in Cohen's view, one inexplicable question (why did God allow the Holocaust to happen?) is replaced by an inexplicable answer (only God knows), hardly a superior situation.

A useful place to concentrate in evaluation of Jonas is his denial of divine omnipotence. Traditionally, Jews conceive of God as all-good and all-powerful (omnipotent). What tradition affirms logics confirms. A supreme being such as God must be supremely powerful. A god who is not all-powerful is unfit to qualify as God. And a god who is not all-good is unworthy to be worshiped as God. By disputing God's omnipotence, Jonas accounts for the evil of the Shoah (God was powerless to prevent it) but renders God unfit to qualify as God.

In sum, their honesty aside, the radical revisionists' attempts to settle the problem of the Shoah are questionable in part and unsettling as a whole.

Deflectors

This third group of thinkers may share some common ideas with the theological traditionalists, but they differ from the latter in wishing to shift the focus from speculation about God to discussion about humanity in general and the Jewish people in particular. In the eyes of Abraham Joshua Heschel, Joseph Soloveitchik, Emil Fackenheim, Robert Gordis, Emmanuel Levinas, Jonathan Sacks, and Elie Wiesel, among others, rather than remain preoccupied over the question of "Wherein lies the blame?" Jews would be wiser to consider "Wherewith lies salvation?"

Abraham Joshua Heschel

What should have been our answer to Auschwitz? . . . Our people's faith in God at this moment in history did not falter. At this moment in history Isaac was indeed sacrificed, his blood shed. We all died in

Auschwitz, but our faith survived. We knew that to repudiate God would be to continue the holocaust.[151]

The first philosopher to grapple with the theological challenge of the Shoah was Rabbi Abraham Joshua Heschel (1907–72). Though rooted in the Hasidic universe as a descendant of a venerable and celebrated Hasidic dynasty, he was also an autodidact of considerable achievement, and his academic path took him elsewhere. He earned a doctoral degree from the University of Berlin in 1933 and began a regime of scholarly publication. His deportation from Germany to Poland in 1938 made him vulnerable to further depredation, and his acceptance of a 1939 invitation to teach at the Hebrew Union College in Cincinnati saved him from the worst of the Shoah. In 1945 he moved on to the Jewish Theological Seminary of America (JTS), where he was appointed professor of Jewish ethics and mysticism. He remained on the JTS faculty for the remainder of his life.

In one of his earliest and most popular works, *Man Is Not Alone*, published in 1951, Heschel characterizes the Shoah as "history's most terrible horrors. . . . There has never been so much distress, agony and terror. . . . At no time has the earth been so soaked with blood."[152] While both contemporaries and survivors are led to conclude that either God was responsible for this great evil or indifferent to it, Heschel argues that either conclusion is folly, since it wrongfully shifts blame from the perpetrators to God. To Heschel, this is not a new or an unexpected development. "For generations," he says, "God was thought a watchman hired to prevent us from using our loaded guns. Having failed us in this, He is now thought of as the ultimate Scapegoat."[153] Since Adam ate the forbidden fruit, human beings have persistently failed to live up to their ethical imperatives. Since Adam hid afterwards, human beings have tried to evade accountability. But human failure to act well should not be mistaken for God's failure to intervene. Moral evil is a function of human conduct. Choosing good over evil or the reverse is entirely a human choice. As Heschel puts it, "The divine does not interfere with their actions nor intervene in their conscience."[154] Given free will, human beings can heap "wickedness upon cruelty and malice upon evil."[155]

Heschel argues, at least initially, that the question "Where was God during the Shoah?" misplaces the blame. Just posing the question removes moral responsibility from where this responsibility actually lies: in Hitler and his henchmen.

But denying the efficacy of the question is not the same as responding to the dilemma it poses. To resolve the dilemma, Heschel goes on to draw a distinction between the "hidden God" and the "hiding God." It was always God's intention to be "manifest and near,"[156] says Heschel. But when God's will is defied, God reluctantly withdraws. Effectively, man in his wickedness has put God into exile. God chooses to temporarily hide "when the people forsake Him, breaking the Covenant which he has made with them." But though God is in hiding, God is still present and never hidden, "waiting to be disclosed, to be admitted into our lives."[157]

Oddly, Heschel appears to blur the distinction between the perpetrators and the victims of the Shoah. What Heschel wants to say, so it seems, is that Nazi evil forced God into exile. In disgust with Nazi abominations, God had no choice but to "leave man to himself."[158] What appears to survivors and contemporaries as God's indifference or worse is an understandable divine reaction to the human betrayal of God's moral imperatives. Thus the Nazis were guilty on two levels. They were guilty of committing unspeakable evils, and they were guilty of exiling God, preventing God from redressing those evils.

However, Heschel connects the temporary hiding of God with violations of the covenant by the Jewish people: "His will [was] defied."[159] "God did not depart of His own volition, He was expelled."[160] That being the case, readers are left to wonder what violations would warrant enduring such horrors. Furthermore, Heschel fails to explain why, if God's hiding is only temporary, God would not choose to intervene on behalf of a people desperately wanting to admit God into their lives.

Heschel appears to retreat from offering a theodicy and instead offers a call to faith. "There are times when defeat is all we face," he says, "when horror is all that faith can bear. And yet, in spite of anguish, in spite of terror, we are never overcome with ultimate dismay."[161] In the end, the best we can do is live with faith despite our inability to find answers to ultimate questions.

"Man cannot afford to be noncommittal about a reality upon which the meaning and manner of his existence depend. . . . In whatever decision he makes, he implicitly accepts either the presence of God or the absurdity of denying it. The nonsense of denial is too monstrous to be conceivable."[162]

In the end, there is no convincing explanation to the question of God's response to the Shoah. But "it is better to be defeated with Him than be victorious without Him."[163]

Joseph Soloveitchik

Judaism, with its realistic approach to man and his place in the world, understood that evil cannot be blurred or camouflaged and that any attempt to downplay the extent of the contradiction and fragmentation to be found in reality will neither endow man with tranquility nor enable him to grasp the existential mystery. Whoever wishes to delude himself by diverting himself from the deep fissure in reality . . . is nought but a fool and a fantast. It is impossible to overcome the hideousness of evil through philosophic-speculative thought.[164]

Rabbi Joseph B. Soloveitchik's "Kol Dodi Dofek" ("Listen, My Beloved Knocks") was first given as an address at Yeshiva University on Israel Independence Day six years after Heschel's *Man Is Not Alone* (1956) and first published as an essay in Hebrew in the 1961 anthology *Torah u-Melukhah: Al Makom Hamedinah B'yahadut* (*Torah and dominion: On the place of the state in Judaism*).

Soloveitchik (1903–93) descended from an illustrious rabbinical family in Poland. In 1925 he entered the University of Berlin, where six years later he was awarded a doctorate in philosophy. That same year—1931—he married and immigrated to the United States. While residing in Boston, he frequently commuted to New York, where he taught Talmud at Yeshiva University. Outsiders recognized him as the dean of Orthodox rabbis in America during the second half of the twentieth century. His students revered him as "the Rav."

Soloveitchik's address was not an attempt to explain the Shoah theologically, but to affirm God's abiding presence in the establishment of the modern

State of Israel despite God's seeming absence during the Shoah. Within his address Soloveitchik grapples with the problem of suffering and evil.

For Soloveitchik, suffering and evil are real and inevitable. "Evil is an undeniable fact."[165] Pain and suffering are unavoidable consequences of human existence. In its ongoing struggle to offer some kind of explanation for suffering, Judaism needs to draw a distinction between fate and destiny. Fate leads each individual to ask, "Why are these terrible things happening to me?" Destiny, by contrast, leads each individual to ask, "How may I rise above the terrible things that happen to me?" In Soloveitchik's account of Judaism, "man's task in the world is to transform fate into destiny."[166] Jews must resourcefully and imaginatively transcend evil; they must move from being the objects of suffering to the subjects who overcome it. To achieve this goal, Jews must turn to *halakhah*. Specifically, *halakhah*, or Jewish law, requires that Jews abandon the path of "inquiry into the hidden ways of the Almighty" and, instead, determine "the path whereon man shall walk when suffering strikes. We ask neither about the cause of evil nor about its purpose, but, rather, about how it might be mended and elevated."[167] Metaphysical speculation is useless. Jewish religious law mandates the path of repentance: self-renewal and redemption in the face of affliction. It requires asking, "What is the obligation incumbent upon the sufferer deriving from the suffering itself?"[168]

The kind of repentance Soloveitchik envisions is not as traditionally understood as a remedy for sin. Rather, it is the repentance necessary to rectify suffering. It is the process of emerging out of the depths of suffering with a renewal of faith and hope. Toward this end, Soloveitchik points to the reaction of the Shulamite maiden to the anticipated arrival of her lover as implied in Song of Songs (5:2). Rather than open the door and let him in, she hesitates. Despite his persistent pleading, she does not answer. When, finally, she comes to her senses, the moment of union had passed: he has vanished, and her search for him is for naught.

Soloveitchik is contending that rather than proof of God's indifference, the Shoah and its aftermath are proof of God's presence. God is here and knocking, but the Jewish people, like the Shulamite maiden, have resisted letting God in.

That God is present is evident from the "almost supernatural" establishment of the State of Israel,[169] the victory of the nascent State of Israel in its War of Independence, the consequent refutation of the long-held Christian myth of the eternal servility of the Jewish people, the renewal of Jewish identity especially among the youth, the realization now that Jewish blood cannot be spilled so easily, and the existence of the State of Israel as a safe haven for Jews anywhere in jeopardy. These phenomena do not and cannot explain the seeming self-concealment of God during the Shoah. Rather, they enable Jews to "rise from the depths of the Holocaust possessed of a heightened spiritual stature."[170]

Note that Soloveitchik is not arguing that the Shoah was the necessary precursor for the establishment of Israel or that statehood has ended what he calls "this era of suffering, this dark chapter of our history."[171] So long as the State of Israel remains at risk, he writes, that era "did not come to an end."[172] To make Israel's establishment contingent on the Shoah would demand accepting that the death of six million was the requirement. The calculation is too grim to accept.

Emil Fackenheim

> The evil of the Holocaust world . . . is philosophically intelligible after Auschwitz only in the exact sense in which it was already understood in Auschwitz—and Buchenwald, Lublin, and the Warsaw Ghetto—by the resisting victims themselves. . . . No deeper or more ultimate grasp is possible for philosophical thought that comes, or ever will come, after the event. This grasp—theirs no less than ours—is epistemologically ultimate. . . . Resistance in that extremity was a way of being. For our thought now, it is an ontological category.[173]

Rabbi Emil Fackenheim (1916–2003) is less concerned with justifying God's conduct during the Shoah than in inspiring Jewish commitment in its aftermath.[174]

For him, the Holocaust changed everything.

The Holocaust changed the Jewish *raison d'être* from the fulfillment of a divine mission to putative resistance to Hitler's objective. The divine imperative is no longer to be a light unto the nations, but to endure as a people. After the Shoah, Jews have no option but to identify as Jews.

The Holocaust also changed the ways Jews and Christians read the Bible and how members of both faiths engage with one another. For Jews, biblical insights into justice and goodness no longer apply. For Christians, it changed the way they must look at themselves. The fact that too few chose to save Jews exposes the weakness of Christian love. The Holocaust has changed the way Christians must look at Jews and how Jews will judge Christians.

Born and raised in Germany during the turbulent prewar period, Fackenheim was ordained as a rabbi in 1939. Following a three-month internment in a Nazi concentration camp, he was able to leave for Scotland and then on to Canada, where he earned a doctorate in philosophy from the University of Toronto in 1945. After a distinguished academic career, he immigrated to Israel, where he spent the last years of his life.

His initial contribution to theological discussion of the Shoah was in an article, "Jewish Faith and the Holocaust," published in *Commentary* magazine in 1967. *God's Presence in History*, a small volume expanding on some of his ideas, was published three years later. In the latter work Fackenheim refers to "the commanding voice of Auschwitz," although the earlier article included what others would later identify as "the 614th commandment," namely that "Jews are forbidden to hand Hitler posthumous victories."

Fackenheim argues that after the Shoah, a secular Jew will come no closer to believing in God and a religious Jew will come no closer to understanding God. But both the secular Jew and the religious Jew must commit to living as Jews, despite misgivings or hesitations, because to do otherwise would be responding "to Hitler by doing his work."[175] Since Hitler's ultimate goal was the elimination of all Jews, any Jew who voluntarily opts out of Judaism today is fulfilling Hitler's objective. Hitler and his evil minions "denied, mocked, murdered the God of Israel six million times,"[176] and concomitantly repudiated four thousand years of Judaism. To give up living a Jewish life today is tantamount to "siding with the murderers" and "doing what they left undone."[177]

This commanding voice of Auschwitz entails specific actions. Each Jew has "a duty to remember"[178] even in the face of world opinion that counsels Jews to forget the past rather than remain obsessed with the Holocaust. Each Jew has a duty to survive not merely as a human being, but *as a Jew*. For Fackenheim, the affirmation of Jewishness is essential: "The murderers of Auschwitz cut off Jews from humanity and denied them the right of existence; yet in being denied that right, Jews represented all humanity. Jews after Auschwitz represent all humanity when they affirm their Jewishness and deny the Nazi denial."[179] Hence, survival by Jews as Jews is "a commandment that brooks no compromise."[180] Each Jew has a duty to protest "any evil resembling Auschwitz." Without such a commitment to fight against evil, survivors — and presumably their contemporaries and descendants — lose their right to survive. As Fackenheim puts it, "The Jewish survivors of Auschwitz have no right to survive unless they engage in such protests."[181] Each Jew also has a duty to reject Christian secessionism, the claim that Jewish life is an anachronism after its replacement by Christianity. Furthermore, each Jew has a duty to affirm hope and deny despair. And each Jew has a duty to band together with other Jews in common purpose and unity.

For Fackenheim, the commanding voice of Auschwitz offers a stirring prescription for life but no justification of death. In fact, all that Jews, both secular and religious, are left with is, in his view, "madness." Auschwitz has left Jews with a theological conundrum that threatens to tear them apart. If one can say anything conceptually coherent about God, it is that all God explains is inexplicability itself.[182]

Thus Fackenheim absolves himself and others from finding an answer to the question of God's role in the Shoah. But with this absolution comes the prescription to resist succumbing to Hitler's ultimate objective.

Robert Gordis

In a world where Hitler held sway for half a decade, and his poisonous legacy has survived for half a century, untold numbers of men and women have discarded the faith by which they lived, and now echo Macbeth's view of life as "a tale told by an idiot, full of sound and fury, signifying nothing." But ethical nihilism can lead only to catastrophe. By exploring the implications of the Holocaust, we may discover, not a solution, but an approach to the Holocaust, which can enable men and women to face it and rise above it.[183]

The shadow cast by the Holocaust on contemporary religious thinking is a recurrent theme in the writing of Conservative rabbi and scholar Robert Gordis (1908–92). It undergirds his 1960 book *A Faith for Moderns* and prominently appears in every one of his subsequent philosophical monographs.

Gordis considers the Shoah "the great watershed in contemporary Jewish thought."[184] It "poses a major problem for traditional biblical faith"[185] as well as its corollary, that God's righteousness is manifest in human affairs.

Gordis repudiates Richard Rubenstein's attempt to solve the problem by rejecting belief in God as the "Lord of history" as "a peculiar form of moral blindness."[186] At what point, asks Gordis, does the absence of God's intervention against evil become monstrous? Even the loss of a single innocent life should demand justification. The problem of theodicy does not suddenly arise in the twentieth century; it has a long and complex history. This fact compels Jews to look at the ways Judaism has grappled with evil historically and thus learn how to react to evil today.

In rejecting Rubenstein, Gordis identifies five biblical ideas he considers useful in "constructing a view of human life and destiny capable of sustaining [modern human beings] in the face of the evils of existence."[187] This view of human life is not intended to explain the presence or absence of God in the Shoah. Rather, these five biblical ideas can provide a way of persevering despite the presence or absence of God in the Shoah. Together, they become, in his words, "a manifesto calling men to life, to hope, and to action."[188]

First, to avoid despair, moderns must affirm the glory of life and the goodness of God even in the face of death. Second, people must confront evil in the world and act to defeat it. Third, the existence of evil is essentially inexplicable. It is beyond human understanding. However, the fact that evil remains a mystery does not mean that people are paralyzed, unable to confront it and even overcome it. Fourth, the major ills that afflict human life are not the will of God but the acts of human beings. Human free will is a great blessing but, when misused, a terrible curse. Moderns must admit to the "perilous nature of human freedom."[189] Finally, the interdependence of humanity—by which Gordis means the simultaneous affirmation of the dignity of each human being and the unity of all humanity descendant from a single ancestor—becomes even more important in the aftermath of the Shoah. The interplay of these two sides of a single coin can spawn universal cooperation in defeating suffering and evil as the most fitting response to the Shoah.

Like Fackenheim, Gordis sees any effort to justify the goodness of God in the aftermath of the Shoah as a fool's errand. Finding an effective pragmatic response to the Shoah is considerably better than becoming embroiled in a hopeless theological argument.

Emmanuel Levinas

The unburied dead in wars and extermination camps . . . render tragic-comic the concern for oneself and illusory the pretension of the rational animal to have a privileged place in the cosmos.[190]

Born in Kovno, Lithuania, Emmanuel Levinas (1906–96) received a traditional education before enrolling in the University of Strasbourg, where he earned his first degree in philosophy in 1927. He went on to study with Edmund Husserl and Martin Heidegger at the University of Freiburg before returning to Strasbourg to complete his doctorate. Drafted into the French army in 1939, he was taken prisoner by the Germans and reunited with his wife and daughter after the war's end. He published widely and ultimately received an appointment to the Sorbonne. An academic of the highest level, he persisted in teaching Talmud and Bible throughout his career.

Levinas claims that theodicy is a "grand idea necessary to the inner peace of the soul in our distressed world."[191] Human beings want and need to believe in a "metaphysical order" that affirms "the absolute goodness" of God as a way of making suffering comprehensible. But this enterprise is doomed from the start, since suffering "is essentially gratuitous and absurd and apparently arbitrary."[192] As proof, Levinas points to "the disproportion between suffering and every theodicy" evidenced with supreme clarity at Auschwitz.[193] Moreover, the very attempt to justify human suffering is itself scandalous. So Levinas turns to Fackenheim.

In Levinas's view, there is something paradoxical in Fackenheim. The same God who remained silent at Auschwitz nevertheless issues a command of faithfulness after Auschwitz. But despite the paradox, in Levinas's view Fackenheim offers the best response to useless suffering, provided it is "given a universal signification."[194] That is to say, all humanity must take responsibility for protecting each other, for caring for each other, for preventing the suffering of the Other. Since the Shoah is more an indictment of human indifference than of God's impotence, hence what is required now is not any of the metaphysical attempts to justify God's (in)actions, but a universal resolve to prevent useless suffering. This in turn requires what American culture critic R. Clifton Spargo calls "vigilant memory."[195]

Levinas universalizes the Shoah. While Jews were targeted for suffering, the Shoah is a lesson for all. Humanity must make a choice: in its indifference abandon the world to useless suffering, or, inspired by the suffering of others and with a "faith without theodicy,"[196] rise to a level of compassion that proves the victims of the Shoah did not suffer for nothing.

Jonathan Sacks

> The Holocaust is a mystery wrapped in silence.... Yet the Holocaust still asks this question of us: If Jews were condemned to die together, shall we not struggle to find a way to live together?[197]

Fackenheim's response to the Shoah also frames the thinking of Rabbi Jonathan Sacks (1949–2020), Orthodox trained and Cambridge educated, who served as a congregational rabbi and principal of Jews' College, London, until his appointment as chief rabbi of the United Hebrew Congregations of the British Commonwealth in 1991. As of this writing, he has authored twenty-seven books, several of which have won international awards. In a 1992 book entitled *Crisis and Covenant: Jewish Thought after the Holocaust*,[198]

Sacks first stresses the uniqueness of the Shoah and its impact on religious belief and then sketches a course of action.

Sacks contends that while the question "Where was man at Auschwitz?"—a question Heschel puts forward as critical—is indeed important, the question of "Where, too, was God?" may not be ignored. But asking the second question creates a theological antinomy: either God was present or God was absent. No matter the answer, the consequence is horrifying. "That He was present seemed a blasphemy; that He was absent, even more so."[199]

Sacks also asserts that the uniqueness of the Shoah lies in the fact that during all previous attempts at annihilation the Jewish people could rely on redemption or refuge, but in the Shoah, neither was available. More profoundly, Sacks further contends that the Shoah "did not simply raise six million times over the traditional question of theodicy: Why do the innocent suffer? It raised the ultimate question of Jewish existence."[200] While even the death of one innocent challenges the notion that God is just, the death of six million innocents does more than multiply the problem six million times. The death of six million challenges the very nature of the eternality of the Jewish people and the promise of God's protection.

Accordingly, the Shoah left the "faith of Israel inextricably tied to the fate of Israel." There is no satisfactory explanation for the Shoah, but there is a necessary reaction to it. In this context, he argues, Fackenheim's urging of collective commitment to group survival is momentous. It is an act of faith to combat both abandonment of Judaism on the one side and total despair on the other. Every act that demonstrates trust in the future, including a rise in the Jewish birth rate, is a statement of religious courage in the face of a religious crisis.

According to Sacks's account, contemporary Jews lack a shared set of Jewish meanings as the Holocaust is integrated into collective Jewish memory. For religious believers, faith is confirmed; for many others, faith is lost. Such divergent views seem unlikely to converge over time. The abiding message, however, is also a clarion call for Jewish amity, if not unity:

Though they might not share a common language, they shared a common fate. . . . They might not see themselves, but they were seen by others, as members of the same people.[201]

Elie Wiesel

It seemed as impossible to conceive of Auschwitz with God as to conceive of Auschwitz without God. Therefore, everything had to be reassessed because everything had changed. . . .

After the Holocaust it is difficult to live with God, but it is impossible to live without him.[202]

Elie Wiesel (1928–2016) has been the preeminent voice in Holocaust literature. Born into a Hasidic family in Sighet, Romania, he received a traditional Jewish education. When he was fifteen, the Wiesel family was deported to Auschwitz; he was the sole survivor. After the war, he settled in Paris and began a career in journalism, eventually becoming a novelist of considerable repute. Relocating to the United States in the 1960s, he entered academics, with appointments at the City College of New York and Boston University. He published widely on a full range of Jewish topics, from the Holocaust to biblical literature to Hasidism. His humanitarian work for many causes earned him the Nobel Peace Prize in 1986.

In his 1964 essay entitled "A Plea for the Dead,"[203] Wiesel reports of his chance encounter with one of the presiding judges at the Eichmann trial in Jerusalem. Wiesel asked him whether after having read the documents and heard the witnesses, he had come any closer to understanding the Shoah. The judge said he had not, since the Shoah is "inaccessible to reason." And, the judge added, perhaps that is best—it is a gift from God—since it saves us from madness or suicide.

For Wiesel, the Shoah signifies the failure of civilization and the defeat of reason. Accordingly, it is beyond understanding. Thus Wiesel approaches scholars who claim to offer viable explanations with a mixture of both envy and disbelief. "I myself," he says, "have not yet succeeded in explaining the tragedy of a single [victim]."[204]

To Wiesel, the inexplicability of the Shoah and God's place in it is not only a gift, but also a tribute and an apology: "Not to understand the dead is a way of paying them an ancient debt; it is the only way to ask their pardon."[205] Since there is no reasonable explanation for the Shoah and God's place in it, any attempt to explain the Shoah does a disservice to the victims. In fact, it insults the victims. The only way to honor the victims is to remain silent. Silence elevates the victims and admits the indifference of the bystanders. Silence asserts that the victims' worthy lives and unconscionable deaths cannot be reduced to "word play" or "intellectual acrobatics."[206]

In his 1995 autobiography, *All Rivers Run to the Sea: Memoirs*, Wiesel writes that "nothing justifies Auschwitz" and "were the Lord Himself to offer me a justification, I think I would reject it."[207]

In the end Wiesel contends that an explanation of the Shoah is neither elusive nor erroneous. Rather, any explanation of the Shoah is to be denied, period. There can be no theological justification of the Shoah.

Thus, Wiesel leaves us in an odd place wherein no theological justification is ever appropriate.

Evaluation of the Deflectors

Collectively, deflectors are intellectually disingenuous. This should not imply a deficiency in character. The deflectors are all sincere and honorable. Rather, the collective disingenuousness of deflectors reflects the profundity of the problem of the Shoah. Deflection is essentially a strategy of misdirection, generally employed because of the tacit recognition that one's position is untenable or indefensible or because one plainly has no answer to the question at stake. In this case, deflection diverts attention away from addressing one seemingly insoluble argument and toward a different argument that is doubtlessly important but certainly more easily addressed.

To wit, Heschel warns against misplacing blame from the Nazis to God. He advocates a call to faith rather than a call to question. Soloveitchik argues that the emergence of the modern State of Israel shows that God is present in Jewish history regardless of whether the Shoah might appear to show that God is absent. For Fackenheim, Gordis, and Sacks, the Shoah demands Jewish perseverance. For Levinas, what matters is not whether God is just, but whether humanity learns to be more compassionate and responsible for one another. Finally, Wiesel punctuates the entire discussion with a question mark and an exclamation point. How to explain the Shoah is unanswerable, and any attempt to do so is itself practically sinful.

These and other deflectors argue that the evils of the Shoah are not God's fault, but the Nazis' fault for perpetrating them as well as the world's fault for failing to intervene. Indeed, it is true that God did not put a single victim into a gas chamber. But the crucial question is not whether God committed any atrocity, but how could an all-powerful and all-good God tolerate atrocities? For this question the deflectors have no answer.

Deflection, at root, is an unwillingness to come to terms with an unpleasant reality. In the case of the Shoah, the unpleasant reality is that the traditional views of good and evil are inadequate to explain the exceptionality of the catastrophe.

Summary

The special case of the Shoah stands as a formidable challenge to traditional Jewish theology on evil and suffering.

The Nature of Good and Evil: Post-Holocaust thinkers as a whole pay scant attention to the nature of good and evil. Shapira invokes the Lurianic concept of *tzimtzum*—God's contraction or withdrawal—from the world to account for evil. Berkovits similarly invokes the notion of *hester panim*—the hiding of God's face. Cohen sees evil as a phenomenon woven into the fabric of the universe. But these thinkers are exceptions in this regard. The sheer scope of the Shoah impels most post-Holocaust thinkers to concentrate on how to account for the depravity and unfathomable cruelty of the Nazi regime and the seeming absence of divine intervention.

Questions of Justice: Unsurprisingly, the answers of each of the three categories of respondents—theological traditionalists, radical revisionists, and deflectors—reflect their respective worldviews.

The theological traditionalists discussed assign the evils of the Shoah to the sins of the people, from personal sins to the sins of intermarriage and assimilation to the failed moral leadership of the rabbis and scholars who did not do enough to keep the people committed to upholding God's law,

For the radical revisionists, the questions of (in)justice raised by the Shoah are insurmountable. There is simply no tool in the traditional toolbox that can defend God. Hence they advance new definitions of God or reject God altogether.

For the deflectors, questions of justice are too insoluble to resolve, and therefore these questions must be set aside. In their place, lessons are substituted.

To date, if or how the challenge of the Shoah will result in changes to traditional Jewish theology remains unresolved.

Conclusion

Throughout this book we have tackled a fundamental challenge: how Judaism can account for the existence of an all-powerful, all-knowing, and all-good God and the simultaneous existence of evil in the world. Abraham insisted that God, the judge of all earth, cannot act unjustly—and yet the injustices of the world have been noted from the days of the Bible to the aftermath of the Holocaust. Shakespeare, no less than Job, was perplexed by the death of innocents. When Macduff learns of the murder of his wife and children, he rages against God, saying, "Did Heaven look on and would not take their part?" (*Macbeth*, 4.3.223). Today, like the Rabbis of the Talmud, Job, and Shakespeare, we want to know why the righteous suffer and why the wicked prosper.

God is expected to protect the innocent, punish the wicked, uphold the good, and vanquish evil. Out of the disappointment of these expectations gone unmet emerge theodicies—attempts to justify the goodness of God in the face of unvanquished evil. Yet despite the ardor and the acuity Jewish thinkers apply to the task, theodicies flounder and the problem of how to account for a just good in a merciless world persists. Jewish sources have grappled with problems of good and evil for more than three thousand years without coming to a consensus. This does not bode well for resolution.

Still, we should neither be surprised nor disheartened. Philosophers have identified a number of problems that evade solutions. Among them is the so-called qualia problem that relates to whether objects in the universe have any inherent properties or whether what people perceive as physical reality is merely a representation of what is impressed upon their senses. Another major problem is the existence of the universe itself. Unlike earlier thinkers who wondered why the universe is the way it is, Gottfried Wilhelm Leibniz (1646–1716) wondered why there is a universe at all, or, as some thinkers frame the question, why is there something rather than nothing? In Leibniz's view, it is entirely plausible to conjecture that there could have been nothing whatsoever. In today's terms, those who accept the big bang theory presume that there is a beginning point to the universe. But that must also assume that there was a state of nothingness before the big bang. That state could have persisted eternally—a far simpler and easier supposition than trying to explain the reason for the big bang. Since Leibniz raised the question, no philosopher has been able to solve it to the satisfaction of other philosophers.

The problems of why evil exists and why humans suffer may be among these insoluble questions. To review, here are the salient Jewish answers to these questions raised in the preceding chapters.

Thirty-Five Jewish Answers to Why There Is Evil in the World

1. Evil is a result of poor human choices (Deut. 4:1, 11:26–27, 30:15–16, 19; Mic. 3:2; 2 Esdras), but the wicked will be punished (Pss. 37:7–10,13, 73:19–20; Prov. 1:26, 2:21–22, 11:21, 11:31, 13:21, 14:22; 1 Enoch).
2. Evil is created by God (Isa. 45:5–7; Zohar).
3. Evil exists to improve the character of the victim (Ps. 94:12; Baḥya; Shapira).
4. There is no effective or convincing way to account for it (Job; 2 Esdras; *Eikhah Rabbah* 3:40; Gillman).
5. Evil is the product of fallen angels (1 Enoch), the Sons of Darkness (Dead Sea Scrolls), demonic forces (Dead Sea Scrolls; Songs of the Sage), or Satan (*Bahir*).
6. Evil conduct is a consequence of astral influences (Babylonian Talmud, *Shabbat* 156a–b; Dead Sea Scrolls; Crescas).

7. The justice that characterized the past is no longer in force (*Midrash Tehillim* 71).

8. Evil is part of the fabric of the universe (*Mekhilta de-Rabbi Yishmael*, Bo, section 11; Babylonian Talmud, *Bava Kamma* 60a; *Bahir*; Zohar; Hermann Cohen). It is entirely natural (Spinoza; Kaplan).

9. Evil is a manifestation of God's wrath (Ps. 7:12; Babylonian Talmud, *Berakhot* 7a).

10. Evil is inevitable (*Tosefta Sotah* 10:3).

11. Evil is the result of the human inclination to act wickedly (Deut. 30:15; Josh. 24:15: Jer. 21:8–14; *Pesikta Rabbati* 32b; *Bereshit Rabbah* 22:6; *Testament of Amram*; *Bahir*; Borowitz).

12. Evil arises from the deficiency or defect in matter (Philo; ibn Daud).

13. Evil is a misperception (Sa'adiah; Maimonides), and what is perceived as evil dissolves when considered within its eternal dimension (Mendelssohn).

14. Evil is not real; it is merely the absence of good (ibn Daud; Maimonides; Gersonides).

15. Evil exists only insofar as it is an idea to be nullified (Rabbi Menaḥem Mendl of Vitebsk; Maggid of Koznitz).

16. Evil is illusory (Rabbi Ya'akov Yitzḥak of Lublin; Rabbi Meshullam Zusya).

17. Evil exists as a result of the end product of divine emanations (*Sefer Yetzirah*; Rabbi Yitzḥak ben Ya'akov ha-Kohen).

18. Evil was a consequence of the sin of Adam and Eve (Rabbi Yitzḥak ben Ya'akov ha-Kohen).

19. The existence of evil allows human beings the opportunity to overcome it (Zohar; Luzzatto; Nussbaum).

20. Evil is a result of God's withdrawal from the primeval universe (Isaac Luria; Berkovits).

21. Good can be neither known nor appreciated without evil (Maimonides; Rabbi Pinḥas of Koretz).

22. There is good in evil (Ba'al Shem Tov; Rabbi Levi Yitzḥak of Berditchev; Rabbi Barukh of Medzhybyzh; Rabbi Naḥman of Breslov).

23. Evil leads human beings to rejoice in their goodness (Ba'al Shem Tov; Shapira).

24. Evil exists in order to be converted to good (Rabbi Shne'ur Zalman of Liady).

25. Evil allows for the attainment of good (Rabbi Elimelekh of Lizensk).

26. Evil people serve as a good example (Belzer Rebbe).

27. Evil is a necessary outcome for a greater good (Rabbi Menachem Mendel Schneerson).

28. Evil is an incomplete good—a perfection not yet fully realized (Rabbi Avraham Yitzḥak Kook).

29. Evil serves to elevate the good (Rabbi Avraham Yitzḥak Kook).

30. Evil exists because God has not yet become fully evolved (Samuel Alexander).

31. Evil is a consequence of human indecisiveness and aimlessness (Buber).

32. Evil is the result of human beings setting themselves up as gods (Kaplan).

33. Evil is entirely a consequence of chance (Kaplan).

34. God is not powerful enough to defeat evil (Kushner; Jonas).

35. Evil exists because there is no God to prevent it (Donat).

Twenty-Two Reasons Why You Are Suffering

1. You deserve it because you have violated God's laws (Lev. 26:14–38; Deut. 28:15–68; Jer. 9:12,14–15; Babylonian Talmud, *Shabbat* 55a–b).

2. You are being punished for the sins of your ancestors (Exod. 34:7; Babylonian Talmud, *Berakhot* 7a; Gersonides; Zohar).

3. You are not wholly righteous (Babylonian Talmud, *Rosh Hashanah* 16b; Philo; Sa'adiah; Albo).

4. Your suffering is inexplicable (Babylonian Talmud, *Menaḥot* 25b) but will be redressed in the afterlife (*Tanḥuma* B, Va-yiggash 104b; *Sifrei Devarim* 377; Sa'adiah).

5. You are suffering because God loves you (Babylonian Talmud, *Berakhot* 5a).

6. Your suffering is a test or trial administered by God (Pss. 94:12, 119:71; *Bereshit Rabbah* 31:2; Sa'adiah; Ya'avetz; Rabbi Menaḥem Mendl of Kotzk).

7. Your early death is actually a benefit to you (*Kohelet Rabbah* 7, 15, 1)

8. You are suffering for others (Babylonian Talmud, *Berakhot* 62b; Babylonian Talmud, *Shabbat* 33b; Zohar).

9. You are suffering for your moral improvement (Philo; Baḥya).

10. You are suffering to encourage you to repent of your misdeeds (Philo).

11. You suffer now in order to secure a greater reward later (Baḥya).

12. You suffer because you are a human being subject to the frailties of your physical existence (Maimonides; Gersonides).

13. You suffer because of your reluctance to pursue your own perfection (Gersonides).

14. You suffer for sins committed in a previous life (*Bahir*).

15. Your suffering is part of God's plan (Zohar), and to deny this would be foolish (Mendelssohn; Rabbi Moshe Leib Erblich of Sassov; Maggid of Mezerich; Rabbi Avraham Yitzḥak Kook).

16. That you or any human beings suffer is simply the way things are. This is not an indictment of God but a fact of nature (Spinoza; Kushner).

17. Your suffering, like all suffering, is a necessary feature of life (Hermann Cohen).

18. Your suffering generates empathy and compassion in others. (Ba'al Shem Tov; Hermann Cohen)

19. Your suffering will lead you to God (Rabbi Naḥman of Breslov; Shapira).

20. Your suffering hastens the arrival of redemption (Rabbi Avraham Yitzhak of Sadagorda; Tsimerman).

21. Your suffering is the result of a divine injustice, which you have every right to resent (Borowitz).

22. There is no satisfactory answer (Gillman).

Jewish Matters of *Teiku* (Unresolved)

In his comprehensive study of talmudic disputes, scholar and rabbi Louis Jacobs lists more than three hundred questions for which no definitive answer is offered between two alternatives. Instead, the matter is left as *teiku,* "unresolved" in Aramaic. The problem of good and evil is far more severe in that it requires choosing between dozens of alternatives, not just two. If the sages of the Talmud could not choose between two plausible alternatives, it would be absurd to think that choosing from among dozens of alternatives would be feasible. Unresolved questions have been an acceptable outcome since the time of the Talmud. The problem of good and evil may very well be one more.

The Virtues of Uncertainty

Leaving the question of good and evil unresolved may even be a virtue. Discussing why the important issues of Jewish interpretation and practice were not settled during the earliest periods of Jewish history, the Talmud concludes, "Our ancestors left us room in order to distinguish ourselves."[1] Perhaps here, too, questions regarding good and evil have been left unsettled so that Jews continue to search for answers and distinguish themselves. Indeed, the search for answers is a duty. As Hans Jonas, in considering post-Holocaust thinking, put it:

> We owe it to the fast receding shadows of the victims that their long-gone cry to a silent God be not left with some sort of an answer if we can find one for them and for us. So must we try.[2]

Wherein a Possible Solution May Lie

Recall that the problem of good and evil in Judaism is rooted in the simultaneous affirmation of four propositions: that evil exists, that God is all-powerful, that God is wholly good, and that God is all-knowing. In order to account for evil and suffering in the world, one of these four propositions must be false. Let's examine each in turn and consider the consequences.

Asserting that evil is a mere illusion, as some thinkers claim, will not do. First, it flies in the face of biblical texts that speak to the reality of evil and the suffering that humanity endures. Second, as Louis Jacobs argues, if evil is a mere delusion, that delusion itself is an evil: it is a corruption of the truth, which is an evil.[3] Moreover, as early twentieth-century metaphysician John M. E. McTaggart writes:

> A delusion . . . is as real as anything else. A savage's erroneous belief that the earth is stationary is just as real a fact as an astronomer's correct belief that it moves. The delusion that evil exists, then, is real.

And thus:

> A delusion or an error which hid from us the goodness of the universe would itself be evil. And so there would be evil after all.[4]

To deny that God is wholly good renders God indifferent to pain and suffering and oblivious to moral turpitude. This denial contradicts the biblical conception of God who feels for the suffering of the stranger, widows, and orphans; rails against wickedness and violence; and demands justice and righteousness of both gentiles and Jews. Besides, there would be no convincing reason for any Jew to give allegiance or pray to a God who is cruelly apathetic to the pain of God's chosen people specifically or any other people generally. Finally, as Jacobs asks, why would God create such a world that requires the creatures that inhabit it to suffer?[5] Lacking any adequate answer to this question makes God seem sadistic. And a sadistic God would hardly be worthy of adulation.

Hence, Jacobs believes:

> Any adequate solution, from the Jewish point of view, must, then, if not deny at least qualify the . . . proposition—that God is omnipotent.[6]

Indeed, some modern Jewish thinkers deny God's omnipotence. Yet the denial that God is omnipotent would render God no more than a benevolent monarch: a good and decent ruler who sees to the needs of all the realm's subjects but is not necessarily able to fulfill them. But the biblical and Rabbinic conception of God is not as an ordinary king, but the Supreme King. That status is contingent on the possession of certain unique powers, such as the ability to create something out of nothing and to bring the dead back to life. If conceptualizing God as not wholly good renders God unworthy to be worshiped as God, then conceptualizing God with limited powers renders God unsuited to be worshiped as God.

However, to some thinkers, an absolute denial of God's omnipotence is not necessary. The proposition that God is omnipotent only needs to be qualified, not rejected entirely. One way to qualify God's omnipotence is to suggest that God has no choice but to allow for the existence of evil, since without it some good or goods would be unrealizable. Compassion would be impossible without suffering. Charitableness would be impossible without want. And free will is understandable only when human beings have the opportunity to choose between good *and* evil, implying that the universe must include evil as well as good. It would be meaningless to hold that God endows humanity with free will, that is, to choose between good and evil, if there is no evil to reject.

Even so, all that can be demonstrated by this line of reasoning is that *some* evil is necessary, not how much of it.[7] And to argue that God alone knows what measure of evil is necessary appeals to ignorance: only God's infinite wisdom can make that calculation and human beings can never know or understand on what basis such a calculation is made. Indeed, this is the outcome of the book of Job, yet, nevertheless, an unsatisfying response.

On these very grounds the "morally sufficient reason" defense is also called into question. The morally sufficient reason defense asserts that a wholly good, all-powerful, and all-knowing God would certainly intervene to vanquish evil unless there was a compelling reason not to intervene. But since God alone can judge what constitutes a morally sufficient reason, humanity is no closer to gaining an understanding of God's inaction in the face of evil.

Furthermore, those who argue that evil is woven into the fabric of the universe must contend with the scriptural declaration that the universe God created is "very good" (Gen. 1:31), even if this declaration does not entirely preclude the existence of evil inherent in the universe.

Note that, logically, even a partial qualification of God's omnipotence is a total denial of God's omnipotence. Omnipotence is the claim that there is no limitation to God's power whatsoever. Anything less than this claim effectively renders God praecipotent—that is, substantially powerful—more powerful than any other agent—but not omnipotent.

The only fertile avenue seemingly left to explore is one that Jacobs did not consider at all: the claim that God is omniscient. Here, the argument would be that because God is wholly good and wholly powerful, God would certainly intervene to vanquish evil, but God is not aware of all the evil that exists. If God is not aware of an evil, there are no grounds for blaming even a wholly good and all-powerful God for not intervening. This argument differs from the claim made by some Jewish thinkers that God withdraws or "hides" from evil. To withdraw from an evil implies an awareness that the evil exists. In other words, God knows of the evil but chooses to allow it to persist. The argument that God is unaware of all evil asserts that God had no knowledge that a particular evil exists. Indeed, there are some textual grounds to support this argument. For instance, with regard to the wickedness of the residents of Sodom, God is reputed to say, "I will go down to see whether they have acted altogether according to the outcry that has reached Me; if not, I will take note" (Gen. 18:21). Rabbinic interpretation notwithstanding, the Torah suggests that God lacks the awareness of the extent of Sodomite wickedness and must investigate further. Similarly, after Adam and Eve violate the order not to eat from the Tree of Knowledge, God seems to be unaware of Adam's whereabouts; God asks, "Where are you?" (Gen. 3:9). From antiquity to modernity, no major Jewish thinker has tried to address the problem of good and evil from this perspective.

Given the perspicacity of Jewish thinkers, we are compelled to ask why not. Perhaps no Jewish thinker has explored such a solution because limiting God's omniscience on the basis of biblical theology ignores Rabbinic theology that affirms God's omniscience. Judaism is a postbiblical religion. Any proposal that reverts to biblical assumptions denies Rabbinic Judaism. Yet conceivably a distinction could be made between biblical religion and biblical theology such that one could recognize the evolution of biblical religion into Jewish practice as mediated by the Rabbis while simultaneously affirming biblical theology.

Assuming this distinction could be defended, still left to consider is how a God with limited knowledge is worthy of reverence. Here the retort would be to distinguish between knowledge and awareness. Possessing information differs from awareness of circumstances. For instance, knowing that murder is a crime that requires capital punishment is different from the awareness that a given murder has been committed. Knowing that violence is evil is not the same as being aware of any particular instance of violence. God, it might be argued, has the former but lacks the latter.

The possibility remains that one day a definitive answer might be offered based on any of the four propositions considered, despite the fact that no such answer has been forthcoming. But there is also the possibility that the problem of good and evil addressed by theodicy will remain eternally intractable.

Even so, the journey through the sources remains valuable and instructive. The plethora of theodicies demonstrate that thinkers past and present fixate on two quintessential Jewish values: justice and goodness. These are archetypical values that emerged from the earliest sources. So crucial are these values in Judaism that even God is expected to act in accordance with them. And by holding God accountable for upholding justice and goodness, all Jews are expected to be similarly bound. Hence, in thinking about good and evil, Judaism necessarily advocates the pursuit of good and the conquering of evil as a fundamental responsibility. As the prophet Micah put it, God "has told you . . . what is good, and what the Lord requires of you: only to do justice, and to love goodness, and to walk modestly with your God" (Mic. 6:8).

NOTES

INTRODUCTION

1. Goldstein's self-definition has evolved. In 2018 at the University of Toronto she identified herself as a *naturalist*: "I'm a naturalist. I don't think anything supernatural exists. By supernatural I mean a transcendent God, immaterial souls and an afterlife. I think humans are just part of nature."

2. Kathryn Reed, "15 Questions with Rebecca N. Goldstein," *Harvard Crimson*, February 11, 2010, www.thecrimson.com/article/2010/2/11/very-fm-think/.

3. Hick, *Philosophy of Religion*, 40.

4. Husik, *History of Medieval Jewish Philosophy*, 432.

5. Frank, "What Is Jewish Philosophy?" in Frank and Leaman, *History of Philosophy*, 6.

6. See Seeskin, "Problem of Jewish Philosophy," 2.

7. Seeskin, "Problem of Jewish Philosophy," 2.

8. Alfasi, *Torat ha-Hassidut*.

9. Isa. 45:7.

10. Maimonides, *Mishneh Torah*, Laws of Repentance 5:4.

11. Blackburn, *Being Good*, 45.

12. Neiman, *Evil in Modern Thought*, 1. She notes as well that in the eighteenth century the word *Lisbon* was used much as we use the word *Auschwitz* today.

13. Arendt, "Nightmare and Flight," in *Hannah Arendt*, 134.

1. THE BIBLE AND APOCRYPHA

1. Or "distressed." See Num. 11:10.

2. The argument would be that the content of the Torah is not the utterance of an omniscient and commanding God, but the literary borrowing of ancient authors.

3. See Heidel, *Babylonian Genesis*, 129.

4. Speiser, *Genesis*, 28.

5. Sarna, *Understanding Genesis*, 9.

6. Sarna, *Understanding Genesis*, 8.

7. Berlin and Brettler, *Jewish Study Bible*, 13.

8. *Commentary on the Torah*, Gen. 1:4, trans. Chavel, 30.

9. Naḥmanides, *Commentary on the Torah*, trans. Chavel, 59.

10. Maimonides, *Guide of the Perplexed*, book 3, chap. 13.

11. Compare Exod. 32:15–25 with Deut. 9:15–20. Notably, the text of the Passover Haggadah welcomes additional interpolations to the story of the Exodus.

12. Pritchard, *Ancient Near East*, 37–41.

13. See *Targum Yonatan* on Gen. 3:22; Rashi; Rabbi Shabbetai Bass, *Siftei Hakhamim*; and Rabbi Jacob Zvi Mecklenberg, *K'tav ve-Kabbalah*, who explains that by eating the fruit of the tree, human beings gained "the ability to independently distinguish between good and evil and choose good and avoid evil."

14. Ibn Ezra, *Commentary on the Torah*, Gen. 3:5.

15. Naḥmanides, *Commentary on the Torah*, Gen. 3:22.

16. Kimḥi, *Commentary on the Torah*, Gen. 2:17.

17. R. Friedman, *Commentary on the Torah*, 17.

18. *Ḥizkuni* on Gen. 7:21.

19. *Kuzari* 2:48. See also Rabbi Nissim Gaon's introduction to the Talmud, printed on the first page of the Vilna edition. See also Novak, *Natural Law in Judaism*, 39–50.

20. Gordis, "Knowledge of Good and Evil," 123–38.

21. Though not very convincingly, see Speiser, *Genesis*, 31. Speiser contends that the verb *yd'* is sometimes used for sexual relations other than the connubial kind. This is true (e.g., Gen. 19:5) but misses Gordis's point. Gordis does not argue that *yd'* applies exclusively to heterosexual relations between man and wife.

22. Pritchard, *Ancient Near East*, 75.

23. Speiser, *Genesis*, 16, calls it a conscious awareness, being in full possession of one's mental and physical powers.

24. This seems to be the view of Seforno, *Commentary on the Torah*, Gen. 3:4. By eating from the fruit of the Tree of Knowledge of Good and Evil, they, like God, would have complete knowledge.

25. While the law of primogeniture is included in the Torah (Deut. 21:17), examples abound where the later born are privileged over the firstborn: Isaac over Yishmael, Jacob over Esau, Joseph over his brothers, among others.

26. Though shepherding was not an honorable occupation for ancient Egyptians. See Gen. 46:34.

27. Speiser, *Genesis*, 33.

28. This translation is less clumsy than the word "uplift" for the Hebrew *s'et*.

29. The attempt by the inhabitants of Sodom to be intimate with the two men—really angels—who take up residence with Lot (Gen. 19:5) confirms this judgment.

30. Don Isaac Abarbanel prefers to explain the Hebrew word *nissa'* as "elevated" rather than "tested." God wanted to beatify Abraham for his unquestioned obedience. Yet Abraham already proved his loyalty by his willingness to blindly relocate (Gen. 12:4).

31. Seforno, *Commentary on the Torah*, Deut. 30:15.

32. Naḥmanides, *Commentary on the Torah*, Deut. 30:15.

33. Hirsch, *Commentary on the Torah*, Deut. 30:15.

34. R. Friedman, *Commentary on the Torah*, Deut. 30:19, 660.

35. The Jewish Publication Society 1917 translation renders the opening Hebrew word *hoy* as a more evocative "Woe!"

36. Cf. Malbim's commentary on this verse. He describes three distinctions that human beings have the power to make: intellectual, comparative, and aesthetic.

37. It is well known because it is recited, in part, each morning as a blessing that precedes the recital of *Shema*.

38. Compare Ps. 121:1.

39. See, for example, Exod. 20:4–6; Lev. 17, 19:26; Lev. 19:4.

40. Most modern scholars consider this psalm an "entrance liturgy" for the Temple. Cf. Brettler and Berlin, *Jewish Study Bible*, 1297.

41. The Hebrew uses the same verb the Torah uses to describe Abraham in Gen. 17:1.

42. In contrast, see Ps. 112:1.

43. The subsequent vindication of the victim is a common theme in the book of Psalms. See, for example, Psalms 14 and 34. The temporary prosperity of the wicked is also featured in Ps. 92:7–8.

44. Choosing good over evil is also advised in Ps. 34:15.

45. Another common theme in the book of Psalms is the sense of feeling forsaken, literally or perceptually. See Psalms 22 and 31.

46. See Psalm 27.

47. See, for example, Ps. 112:1–6.

48. See also Prov. 10:16, where the Hebrew parallelism suggests that the product of evil actions is sin (*hatat*, in Hebrew), which stands in opposition to life, that is, death.

49. Gruber, in Berlin and Brettler, *Jewish Study Bible*, 1499.

50. For Maimonides, *Guide of the Perplexed*, part 3, chap. 22, especially telling in this verse is that Job is described as morally proficient but not philosophically advanced ("wise"). Lacking this knowledge, he falls into an error that he comes to correct only later.

51. And not "He crushes me for a hair" as the JPS translation has it, following the *Targum* and the Peshita.

52. M. Greenberg, "Job," 289.

53. M. Greenberg, "Job," 297.

54. M. Greenberg, "Job," 299.

55. Maimonides, *Guide of the Perplexed*, part 3, chap. 23.

56. Maimonides, *Guide of the Perplexed*, part 3, chap. 23, end.

57. Altschuler, *Metzudat David* on Job 40:4.

58. Jerusalem Talmud, *Sotah* 5:6.

59. Jerusalem Talmud, *Sotah* 5:6.

60. *Yalkut Reuveni*, Va-yelekh.

61. Jerusalem Talmud, *Sotah* 5:6.

62. Jerusalem Talmud, *Sotah* 5:6; Babylonian Talmud, *Bava Batra* 15a; *Yalkut Reuveni*, Va-yelekh.

63. Jerusalem Talmud, *Sotah* 5:6; *Yalkut Reuveni*, Va-yelekh.

64. Jerusalem Talmud, *Sotah* 5:6; *Yalkut Reuveni*, Va-yelekh.

65. Jerusalem Talmud, *Sotah* 5:6.

66. Jerusalem Talmud, *Sotah* 5:6.

67. Babylonian Talmud, *Bava Batra* 15a.

68. Babylonian Talmud, *Bava Batra* 15b.

69. See also Job 31:29.

70. Job 2:10.

71. Scheindlin, *Book of Job*, 26.

72. Ariel, *What Do Jews Believe?*, 105.

73. Mitchell, *Book of Job*, xvi.

74. Bickerman, *Four Strange Books*, 165.

75. Garfinkel, "Qoheleth," 54.

76. Michael Fox, *Time to Tear Down*, 14.

77. Michael Fox, *Time to Tear Down*, 14.

78. Cf. Psalm 94.

79. Gordis, *Koheleth*, 292.

80. Some scholars consider this verse to be parenthetical (A. Cohen and Reichert "Ecclesiastes," in *Five Megilloth*, 122), and others consider it the extraneous gloss of a pious commentator. See Gordis, *Koheleth*, 227.

81. Gillman, *Death of Death*, 77.

82. Gillman, *Death of Death*, 84–85.

83. Gillman, *Death of Death*, 87.

84. Goodspeed, *The Apocrypha*, 47–48.

85. The canon of biblical text was still dynamic in the second century of the Common Era, with mishnaic authorities still arguing over which books ought to be included. See *Mishnah Yadayim* 3:5; *Mishnah Eduyot* 5:3; *Tosefta Yadayim* 2:13. See also Babylonian Talmud, *Shabbat* 30b.

86. 2 Esdras 7:102–4.

87. As Fishbane, *Text and Texture*, 21, notes, "The fruit of the knowledge of good and evil is pain, enmity, shame, and death. . . . The knowledge of good and evil, no matter how life-building and 'eye-opening,' also includes the consciousness of death."

88. 2 Esdras 3:20–22. Goodspeed, *The Apocrypha*, 48.

89. Jerusalem Talmud, *Sanhedrin* 28a.

90. See, for example, Babylonian Talmud, *Ḥagigah* 12a; Babylonian Talmud, *Niddah* 16b; Jerusalem Talmud, *Berakhot* 11c.

91. Goodspeed, trans., *The Wisdom of Sirach*, in *The Apocrypha*, 15:11–12, 251.

92. Goodspeed, trans., *The Wisdom of Sirach*, in *The Apocrypha*, 15:17–20, 251–52.

93. The Syriac Apocalypse of Baruch 54:15–19 similarly argues that although Adam's sin resulted in human mortality, all human descendants of Adam are freely choosing beings who must take personal responsibility: "Each of us has been the Adam of his own soul." See also Urbach, *The Sages*, 423.

94. Stone, *Scripture, Sects, and Visions*, 31.

95. Sarna, *Understanding Genesis*, 4–6. Brandon, *Judgment of the Dead*, 57, suggests that the word *she'ol* itself is the Hebrew equivalent of the Mesopotamian *kur-nu-gi-a*, the "land of no return."

96. Raphael, *Jewish Views*, 60.

97. D. Russell, *Method and Message*, 42.

2. RABBINIC APPROACHES

1. Babylonian Talmud, *Berakhot* 7a.

2. The inadequacy of the principle of ancestral merit is exposed by the fact that the Talmud "retires" the principle. According to Babylonian Talmud, *Shabbat* 55a, ancestral merit ceased during the period of the monarchy. From then on it ceased to function.

3. *Mishnah Avot* 4:19.

4. *Eikhah Rabbah* 3:40.

5. Jerusalem Talmud, *Ḥagigah* 2:1. Another version there, and in Babylonian Talmud, *Kiddushin* 39b, says that Elisha lost his faith when he witnessed the martyrdom of great teachers of Torah. He could not accept that a just God would allow his servants to suffer so greatly.

6. *Vayikra Rabbah* 28:1.

7. Babylonian Talmud, *Rosh Hashanah* 16b.

8. Babylonian Talmud, *Bava Metzi'a* 87b.

9. Babylonian Talmud, *Berakhot* 61b.

10. Babylonian Talmud, *Kiddushin* 40a.

11. Interestingly, Rava does not even conceive of a person who is evil toward people and yet remains God-fearing.

12. Babylonian Talmud, *Berakhot* 7a.

13. Babylonian Talmud, *Shabbat* 55a.

14. Babylonian Talmud, *Shabbat* 55a–b.

15. Babylonian Talmud, *Shabbat* 55a.

16. See also Meiri, *Beit ha-Behirah*, *Berakhot* 7a, s.v. "a man must," and *Avot* 1, where Meiri writes that the ways of God are simply unknown to human beings.

17. Literally, "turn around."

18. Students arranged their seats in concentric semicircles, with the teacher sitting at the open end. The best students sat in the first row. Moses sits in the back, indicating how little he understands Rabbinic hermeneutics.

19. Literally, "this is what came into My mind."

20. The Romans tortured Rabbi Akiva to death by flaying him alive. His martyrdom is dated to 135 CE, the end of the Bar Kokhba revolt.

21. Babylonian Talmud, *Menahot* 25b.

22. Babylonian Talmud, *Berakhot* 5a.

23. Like the one cited, Prov. 3:12 and Deut. 8:5.

24. *Tanhuma*, Recension B, Mikkets 101a–b.

25. *Shir ha-Shirim Rabbah* 2:16, 2.

26. Babylonian Talmud, *Berakhot* 5b.

27. That is, Rabbi Yehoshua ben Levi.

28. Babylonian Talmud, *Shabbat* 156a–b.

29. Babylonian Talmud, *Mo'ed Katan* 28a.

30. Babylonian Talmud, *Tosefta Sukkot* 2:6.

31. Babylonian Talmud, *Pesahim* 113a.

32. Urbach, *The Sages*, 284.

33. See also Abarbanel on Deuteronomy 4, s.v. *ukhvar dibarti*.

34. Babylonian Talmud, *Horayot* 10b.

35. *Tanhuma*, Recension B, Va-yiggash 104b; *Kohelet Rabbah* 1:4.

36. *Midrash Tehillim* 73:1.

37. That is, in the afterlife. The anachronistic assumption here is that Moses and the people were aware of the concept, though short on details.

38. *Sifre*, trans. Hammer, 377.

39. Urbach, *The Sages*, 4.

40. Babylonian Talmud, *Berakhot* 17a.
41. Babylonian Talmud, *Avodah Zarah* 2a.
42. Babylonian Talmud, *Ta'anit* 11a.
43. Babylonian Talmud, *Berakhot* 10a and parallels.
44. Bremmer, *Rise and Fall*, 2001.
45. Pereira et al., "Immortality of the Soul," 101–27.
46. Gillman, *Death of Death*, 106.
47. See Weinberg, *Short History*, 9–14; Urbach, *The Sages*, 34.
48. In particular, *Phaedo*.
49. Heraclitus, for instance, held that the world is in flux. He is reputed to have said, "You cannot step into the same river twice." See Robinson, *Introduction*, 89–91. And Xenophanes held that the process of dilation and compression was cyclical (Robinson, *Introduction*, 50–51).
50. The Greeks held that the body was a prison for the soul, *soma sema*, from which the soul sought escape (cf. Plato, *Phaedo* 61e–62c), a view adopted by Christians (see Romans 8:13) and the Dead Sea sectarians (see Dead Sea Scrolls, 1QS, xi 9, xi 12; 1QHa vii 2) but rejected by the Rabbis (see Babylonian Talmud, *Sanhedrin* 91b).
51. *Bereshit Rabbah* 34:2 and, with minor variations, *Bereshit Rabbah* 31:3 and *Midrash Tehillim* 11, 4.
52. *Mishnah Avot* 5:4. See *Avot de-Rabbi Natan* 33 for the listing of all ten trials.
53. Schatz, *Ethics of the Fathers*, 207.
54. See Abarbanel on Gen. 22:1, who interprets the word "test" (*nissa'*) exactly this way.
55. Babylonian Talmud, *Berakhot* 5a.
56. Jerusalem Talmud, *Shekalim* 5:4.
57. *Sifrei Devarim* 32; Babylonian Talmud, *Sanhedrin* 101a.
58. According to Babylonian Talmud, *Berakhot* 5a, by enduring suffering, the righteous are rewarded by God with the privilege of seeing their descendants grow old.
59. *Midrash ha-Gadol*, Va-yera'.
60. *Midrash ha-Gadol* is, according to scholarly consensus, a fourteenth-century compilation of earlier material.
61. See Jubilees 12, which serves as the source of the well-known legend of Abraham's smashing his father's idols.
62. *Kohelet Rabbah* 7, 15, 1.
63. Cf. Eccles. 7:20.
64. Elman, "Suffering of the Righteous," 330.
65. This reading follows the manuscript. See *Midrash Psalms*, ed. Buber, 119 n. 3.
66. Elman, "Suffering of the Righteous," 330.
67. Babylonian Talmud, *Shabbat* 33b.
68. *Mekhilta de-Rabbi Yishmael*, Bo, sec. 11, ed. Horowitz, 38.

69. Babylonian Talmud, *Bava Kamma* 60a.

70. Babylonian Talmud, *Berakhot* 7a. What is translated here as "wrath" appears in Hebrew as *hemah, za'am,* and *haron* and in Aramaic as *rit-ha.*

71. Babylonian Talmud, *Avodah Zarah* 4a.

72. Elman, "Suffering of the Righteous," 333.

73. Babylonian Talmud, *Rosh Hashanah* 32b.

74. *Tosefta Sotah* 10:3, ed. Lieberman, 214.

75. Babylonian Talmud, *Sanhedrin* 113b.

76. *Bereshit Rabbah* 39:6.

77. It is expressed by way of a rhetorical question: "Can God be suspected of injustice?" (Babylonian Talmud, *Berakhot* 5b).

78. Developed in Persia between the third and seventh centuries, Manichaeism taught of an ongoing struggle between the spiritual world of light and the material world of darkness.

79. Jerome's fourth-century Latin vulgate translation of the Bible renders *bli'ya'al* (Deut. 13:13–14) as a proper noun, meaning "the evil power." And the Christian Gospels describe Jesus's encounter with Satan.

80. J. Russell, *The Devil,* 179.

81. J. Russell, *The Devil,* 183.

82. J. Russell, *The Devil,* 183.

83. The Babylonian Rabbis were notoriously superstitious and believed that humanity was at war with demons. See Trachtenberg, *Jewish Magic and Superstition,* 25–43 However, these demons, while causing mischief and even harm, could not compel a person to commit a wrongful act.

84. See J. Russell, *The Devil,* 188 and n. 17, for a list of the names of the evil masters and their origins.

85. Urbach, *The Sages,* 472.

86. *Pesikta Rabbati* 32b.

87. *Bereshit Rabbah* 9:7.

88. Boyarin, *Carnal Israel,* 63. The only reason the evil inclination is called "evil" is because the Rabbis inherited the term and chose to retain it.

89. Jerusalem Talmud, *Nedarim* 9:1.

90. Babylonian Talmud, *Kiddushin* 30b.

91. Babylonian Talmud, *Ḥagigah* 16a.

92. *Tanḥuma,* Recension B, Metsora'.

93. *Tanḥuma,* Recension B, Noach 15b.

94. Babylonian Talmud, *Sukkah* 52b.

95. Babylonian Talmud, *Kiddushin* 30b.

96. Babylonian Talmud, *Kiddushin* 30b. See also Babylonian Talmud, *Avodah Zarah* 17a.
97. Babylonian Talmud, *Kiddushin* 81b.
98. Babylonian Talmud, *Berakhot* 5a.
99. See Babylonian Talmud, *Kiddushin* 81a. "Rabbi Meir and his Torah" frighten Satan away.
100. Literally, "three parsangs"—about ten miles in the ancient Persian calculation of distance.
101. Babylonian Talmud, *Sukkah* 52a.
102. If the evil inclination corresponds to passion, it makes sense that those who have a passion for study have other passions as well. See Boyarin, *Carnal Israel*, 134–66.
103. His exact identity and dates are unknown. See Hyman, *Toldoth Tannaim, ve-Amoraim*, vol. 1, 143.
104. Babylonian Talmud, *Kiddushin* 40a.
105. This also explains why the Rabbis spend little time trying to explain natural evils like earthquakes and birth defects.
106. The Josephian view that the Essenes wrote and preserved the Dead Sea Scrolls was championed by archaeologist Roland de Vaux in the 1950s but soon challenged by other scholars. See, e.g., Ginzberg, *Unknown Jewish Sect*, 396–97; and cf. Wise et al., *Dead Sea Scrolls*, 16–20.
107. Dead Sea Scrolls, 1QM, in Wise et al., *Dead Sea Scrolls*, 151. All translations are taken from Wise et al. The first digit in each Dead Sea Scroll reference identifies the cave number in which the scroll was found. The Q refers to Qumran, the site of the initial discovery of the scrolls.
108. Dead Sea Scrolls, 1QM, in Wise et al., *Dead Sea Scrolls*, 151.
109. Dead Sea Scrolls, 1QM, in Wise et al., *Dead Sea Scrolls*, 152.
110. Dead Sea Scrolls, 1QM, in Wise et al., *Dead Sea Scrolls*, 152.
111. Dead Sea Scrolls, 4Q491–96, in Wise et al., *Dead Sea Scrolls*, 162.
112. Dead Sea Scrolls, 4Q177, in Wise et al., *Dead Sea Scrolls*, 234.
113. That is, the forces of evil. See Wise et al., *Dead Sea Scrolls*, 234.
114. Dead Sea Scrolls, 4Q177, in Wise et al., *Dead Sea Scrolls*, 234.
115. Dead Sea Scrolls, 4Q177, in Wise et al., *Dead Sea Scrolls*, 234.
116. Dead Sea Scrolls, 4Q177, in Wise et al., *Dead Sea Scrolls*, 234.
117. Dead Sea Scrolls, 4Q177, in Wise et al., *Dead Sea Scrolls*, 235.
118. Dead Sea Scrolls, 4Q186, Fragment 1, Column 1, in Wise et al., *Dead Sea Scrolls*, 245.
119. Dead Sea Scrolls, 4Q417, 2.12; CD 2:16.
120. Wise et al., *Dead Sea Scrolls*, 381.

121. According to the Rabbis, Lilith, Adam's first partner and equal, transforms into a demon who seeks to injure newborn baby boys. See Babylonian Talmud, *Eruvin* 18b; *Tanḥuma B*, 1:20; *Bereshit Rabbah* 20:11.

122. Dead Sea Scrolls, 4Q510, Fragment 1, in Wise et al., *Dead Sea Scrolls*, 415.

123. Compare Matt. 3:6 with Dead Sea Scrolls, 1QS iii, in Wise et al., *Dead Sea Scrolls*, 4–9.

124. See Acts 26:18; Romans 5:12–21, 8:22.

125. *Tanḥuma*, Recension A, Tazria' 9.

126. Urbach, *The Sages*, 274–75.

127. Schenck, *Brief Guide to Philo*, 57.

128. Sandmel, *Philo of Alexandria*, 134.

129. Weinberg, *Short History*, 14.

130. Philo, *De Somniis* (On Jacob's Dream) 1.67; Schenck, *Brief Guide to Philo*, 52.

131. Philo, *De Opificio Mundi* (On the Creation of the World) 8.

132. Philo, *De Specialibus Legibus* (On the Special Laws) 1.329; Philo, *De Opificio Mundi* (On the Creation of the World) 75.

133. Philo, *Legum Allegoriae* (Allegorical Commentaries) 3.96; Philo, *De Scarificiis Abelis et Caini* (The Sacrifices of Abel and Cain) 8.

134. See Sandmel, *Philo of Alexandria*, 134.

135. Plato considered the Forms eternal ideas that have a higher reality than any physical counterpart.

136. Philo, *De Specialibus Legibus* (On the Special Laws) 1.329. See also Philo, *Quis Rerur Divinarum Heres* (Who Is the Heir?) 206.

137. Philo, *De Providentia* 2.1. In his *Republic*, book 2, 364a–b, Plato expresses the problem this way: "Injustice pays better than justice, for the most part."

138. See Wolfson, *Philo*, vol. 2, 279–303.

139. Philo, *De Providentia* (Of Providence) 2.54.

140. Philo, *De Providentia* 2.7.

141. This position is adopted by Rabbi Ḥayyim ben Attar, *Or ha-Ḥayyim*, Deut. 4:39, s.v. "and you should know."

142. Philo, *De Præmiis et Pœnis* (Of Reward and Punishment) 20.119.

143. Philo, *De Providentia* (Of Providence) 2.4–6.

144. Philo, *De Specialibus Legibus* (On Special Laws) 4.34, 181.

145. See Cicero, *Disputations*, 4.9, 22.

146. Philo, *De Specialibus Legibus* (On Special Laws) 4.16, 95.

147. Philo, *De Specialibus Legibus* 4.16, 95.

148. Philo, *De Specialibus Legibus* 5.15, 84.

149. Philo, *De Specialibus Legibus* 4.16, 95.

150. Philo, *De Decalogo* (On the Decalogue) 28.142.

151. Philo, *De Praemiis et Poenis* (On Reward and Punishment) regarding Isaac's twins. Wolfson, *Philo*, vol. 2, 275ff., sees Philo's conception of the struggle between the rational soul (*De Opific.* 46.134) and the irrational soul (*De Spec.* 4.23, 123–24, 125), parallel to the two inclinations, as an example of Philo's combining Greek philosophy with Jewish tradition.

152. Philo, *De Specialibus Legibus* (On Special Laws) 4.4, 4.

153. Philo, *De Vita Moses* (On the Life of Moses) 2.9; Philo, *De Specialibus Legibus* (On Special Laws) 1.9, 55.

154. See Wolfson, *Philo*, vol. 2, 275.

155. Sandmel, *Philo*, 133–34.

3. MEDIEVAL PHILOSOPHY

1. See Weinberg, *Short History*, 143.

2. Weinberg, *Short History*, 143.

3. Weinberg, *Short History*, 147.

4. Sa'adiah, *Prolegomena to Doctrines and Opinions*, in Lewy, Heinemann, and Altmann, *Three Jewish Philosophers*, 25.

5. Sa'adiah, *Doctrines and Opinions*, treatise 9, chap. 1, in Lewy, Heinemann, and Altmann, *Three Jewish Philosophers*, 183.

6. Saadia Gaon, *Book of Beliefs*, treatise 5, chap. 1, trans. Rosenblatt, 208.

7. Eccles. 3:17, "I mused: 'God will doom both righteous and wicked for there is a time for every experience and every happening"; and Eccles. 12:14, "that God will call every creature to account for everything unknown, be it good or bad."

8. Saadia Gaon, *Book of Beliefs*, treatise 5, chap. 2, trans. Rosenblatt, 210.

9. Saadia Gaon, *Book of Beliefs*, treatise 5, chap. 2, trans. Rosenblatt, 210. This is also the opinion of Rabbi Samuel Edels, *Hiddushei Maharsha* on *Berakhot* 7a.

10. See 2 Chron. 32:25; 2 Chron. 16:2.

11. See Ps. 31:20, "How abundant is the good that You have in store for those who fear You"; and Deut. 32:34, "Lo, I have it all put away; sealed up in My storehouses, to be My vengeance and recompense at the time that their foot falters."

12. Sa'adiah, *Book of Doctrines and Beliefs*, treatise 5, in Lewy, Heinemann, and Altmann, *Three Jewish Philosophers*, 35.

13. Sa'adiah, *Book of Doctrines and Beliefs*, in Lewy, Heinemann, and Altmann, *Three Jewish Philosophers*, 136.

14. Lewy, Altmann, and Heinemann, *Three Jewish Philosophers*, 135, n. 2.

15. Sa'adiah, *Book of Doctrines and Beliefs*, in Lewy, Heinemann, and Altmann, *Three Jewish Philosophers*, 136. See Babylonian Talmud, *Kiddushin* 40b: a person who sins at the end of life loses all earlier merit.

16. Sa'adiah, *Book of Doctrines and Beliefs*, in Lewy, Heinemann, and Altman, *Three Jewish Philosophers*, 136.

17. Sa'adiah, *Book of Doctrines and Beliefs*, in Lewy, Heinemann, and Altmann, *Three Jewish Philosophers*, 137.

18. Sa'adiah, *Book of Doctrines and Beliefs*, in Lewy, Heinemann, and Altmann, *Three Jewish Philosophers*, 137.

19. Sa'adiah, *Book of Doctrines and Beliefs*, in Lewy, Heinemann, and Altmann, *Three Jewish Philosophers*, 137.

20. Saadia Gaon, *Book of Beliefs*, treatise 5, chap. 3, trans. Rosenblatt, 213.

21. Saadia Gaon, *Book of Beliefs*, treatise 5, chap. 3, trans. Rosenblatt, 213.

22. Saadia Gaon, *Book of Beliefs*, treatise 5, chap. 3, trans. Rosenblatt, 216.

23. As Sa'adiah learns from Jer. 5:19, "And when they ask, 'Because of what did the Lord our God do all these things?' you shall answer them, 'Because you forsook Me and served alien gods on your own land, you will have to serve foreigners in a land not your own.'"

24. Sa'adiah, *Book of Doctrines and Beliefs*, in Lewy, Heinemann, and Altmann, *Three Jewish Philosophers*, 138.

25. Sa'adiah does not explain why people might think suffering is easy. Perhaps his intention is that people might think suffering is easy to endure when you know the reason for it.

26. Lewy, Altmann, and Heinemann, *Three Jewish Philosophers*, 139.

27. Baḥya, *Duties of the Heart*, Gate 5, trans. Feldman, 279.

28. Baḥya, *Duties of the Heart*, Gate 2, trans. Feldman, 97–98.

29. Baḥya, *Duties of the Heart*, Gate 8, trans. Feldman, 417.

30. See also Baḥya, *Duties of the Heart*, Gate 5, trans. Feldman, 279.

31. Baḥya, *Duties of the Heart*, Gate 5, trans. Feldman, 270.

32. Baḥya, *Duties of the Heart*, Gate 8, in Schweid, *Classic Jewish Philosophers*, 56.

33. Baḥya, *Duties of the Heart*, Gate 3, chap. 5, trans. Hyamson, vol. 2, 55.

34. Husik, *History of Medieval Jewish Philosophy*, 198–99.

35. Aristotle, *Physics*, book 1.

36. Aristotle rejected the idea that something could exist that had matter and no form even though he refers to this entity as "prime matter." What exactly Aristotle meant by the term "God" is complex and eludes easy definition. He did not, however, mean "God" as Jews understand.

37. Heschel, *Maimonides*, 145.

38. Maimonides, *Guide of the Perplexed*, "Introduction to the First Part," ed. Pines, vol. 1, 6.

39. Halbertal, *Maimonides*, 3.

40. Husik, *History of Medieval Jewish Philosophy*, 236.

41. Husik, *History of Medieval Jewish Philosophy*, 237.

42. Strauss, "Literary Character." See also Strauss, "How to Begin."

43. That is, a special attribute shared by all members of the species.

44. A common thread in medieval philosophy is the distinction between the supernal world of the spheres and the sublunar or netherworld that is the domain of human beings and animals.

45. Maimonides, *Guide*, book 1, chap. 1, ed. Pines, vol. 1, 23.

46. Maimonides, *Guide*, book 1, chap. 2, ed. Pines, vol. 1, 24.

47. Marvin Fox, *Interpreting Maimonides*, 181–82, presumes that without mentioning the point, Maimonides draws this conclusion from the declaration in Gen. 1:31 that God found all that God created "very good," meaning perfect after its kind.

48. Maimonides, *Guide*, book 1, chap. 2, ed. Pines, vol. 1, 24.

49. Maimonides, *Guide*, book 1, chap. 2, ed. Pines, vol. 1, 25.

50. Maimonides, *Guide*, book 1, chap. 2, ed. Pines, vol. 1, 24.

51. Human beings are allowed to choose to eat fruit from whichever tree they desire—except one.

52. Maimonides, *Guide*, book 1, chap. 2, ed. Pines, vol. 1, 25.

53. Maimonides, *Guide*, book 1, chap. 2, ed. Pines, vol. 1, 25.

54. Maimonides, *Guide*, book 1, chap. 2, ed. Pines, vol. 1, 25.

55. Maimonides, *Guide*, book 1, chap. 2, ed. Pines, vol. 1, 25.

56. Marvin Fox, *Interpreting Maimonides*, 189.

57. Maimonides, *Guide*, book 1, chap. 2, Pines, vol. 1, 24.

58. Maimonides, *Mishneh Torah*, Laws of Repentance 5:1. The present author follows, with minor variation, the translation of Philip Birnbaum, 41–42.

59. Maimonides, *Guide*, book 3, chap. 13, Pines, vol. 2, 453.

60. Maimonides, *Guide*, book 3, chap. 13, Pines, vol. 2, 453.

61. Maimonides, *Guide*, book 2, chap. 30, Pines, vol. 2, 354.

62. Marvin Fox, *Interpreting Maimonides*, 195.

63. To argue that God is responsible for moral evil—at least indirectly, since God could have created human beings who would never choose to do evil—is impossible. Free will is precisely what defines human beings. To deprive human beings of the possibility of choosing to do evil would make them angels, not human.

64. Aaron ben Elijah offers two other criticisms as well. See Husik, *History of Medieval Jewish Philosophy*, 374.

65. Halbertal, *Maimonides*, 332.

66. Halbertal, *Maimonides*, 332.

67. Maimonides, *Guide*, book 3, chap. 12, Pines, vol. 2, 443.

68. Maimonides, *Guide*, book 3, chap. 12, Pines, vol. 2, 443.

69. Halbertal, *Maimonides*, 332.

70. Maimonides notes that this category of evil is likely in the course of great wars but is otherwise rare.

71. Maimonides, *Guide*, book 3, chap. 12, ed. Pines, vol. 2, 443.

72. Maimonides, *Guide*, book 3, chap. 12, ed. Pines, vol. 2, 445.

73. Maimonides, *Guide*, book 3, chap. 12, ed. Pines, vol. 2, 442.

74. Halbertal, *Maimonides*, 334.

75. Maimonides, *Guide*, book 3, chap. 17, ed. Pines, vol. 2, 469.

76. Maimonides, *Guide*, book 3, chap. 17, ed. Pines, vol. 2, 469.

77. Maimonides, *Guide*, book 3, chap. 17, ed. Pines, vol. 2, 470.

78. Babylonian Talmud, *Berakhot* 5a.

79. Maimonides, *Guide*, book 3, chap. 17, ed. Pines, vol. 2, 471. This is particularly the case with the subject of trials wherein God "sends down calamities upon an individual, without their having been preceded by a sin, in order that his reward be increased" (book 3, chap. 24, ed. Pines, vol. 2, 497).

80. Maimonides, *Guide*, book 3, chap. 23. Instead, Job comes to understand that "true happiness, which is the knowledge of the deity, is guaranteed to all who know Him and that a human being cannot be troubled in it by any of all the misfortunes in question."

81. Maimonides, *Mishneh Torah*, Laws of Repentance 8:2, trans. Hyamson.

82. Maimonides, *Mishneh Torah*, Laws of Repentance 8:2, trans. Hyamson.

83. Maimonides, *Mishneh Torah*, Laws of Repentance 8:1, trans. Hyamson.

84. Maimonides, *Mishneh Torah*, Laws of Repentance 8:2, trans. Hyamson. See also *Guide*, book 3, chap. 23, ed. Pines, vol. 2, 492.

85. Maimonides, *Mishneh Torah*, Laws of Repentance 8:2, trans. Hyamson.

86. Maimonides, *Mishneh Torah*, Laws of Repentance 8:4, trans. Hyamson.

87. Maimonides, *Guide*, book 3, chap. 23, ed. Pines, vol. 2, 492–93.

88. The observer, however, may have a different perspective.

89. Maimonides, *Guide*, book 3, chap. 18, ed. Pines, vol. 2, 471.

90. Maimonides, *Guide*, book 3, chap. 18, ed. Pines, vol. 2, 475.

91. Maimonides, *Guide*, book 3, chap. 18, ed. Pines, vol. 2, 475.

92. Maimonides, *Mishneh Torah*, Laws of Repentance 3:2.

93. Maimonides, *Guide*, book 3, chap. 24, ed. Pines, vol. 2, 497–98.

94. Maimonides, *Guide*, book 3, chap. 24, ed. Pines, vol. 2, 498.

95. See Deut. 12:2ff.

96. Gersonides, *Wars of the Lord*, introduction, trans. Feldman, 97–98.

97. Gersonides, *Wars of the Lord*, book 2, trans. Feldman, 147.

98. Gersonides, *Wars of the Lord*, book 4, chap. 6, trans. Feldman, 181.

99. Gersonides, *Wars of the Lord*, book 4, chap. 4, trans. Feldman, 174.

100. Gersonides, *Wars of the Lord*, book 4, chap. 6, trans. Feldman, 186.

101. Gersonides, *Wars of the Lord*, book 4, chap. 6, trans. Feldman, 186.

102. Gersonides, *Wars of the Lord*, book 4, chap. 6, trans. Feldman, 184.

103. Gersonides, *Wars of the Lord*, book 4, chap. 5, trans. Feldman, 178, 179.

104. Gersonides, *Wars of the Lord*, book 4, chap. 6, trans. Feldman, 184.

105. Gersonides, *Wars of the Lord*, book 4, chap. 6, trans. Feldman, 186.

106. Gersonides, *Wars of the Lord*, book 4, chap. 6, trans. Feldman 186.

107. Gersonides, *Wars of the Lord*, book 4, chap. 6, trans. Feldman 186.

108. Gersonides, *Wars of the Lord*, book 4, chap. 6, trans. Feldman, 187.

109. Gersonides, *Wars of the Lord*, book 4, chap. 6, trans. Feldman, 188.

110. Gersonides, *Wars of the Lord*, book 4, chap. 6, trans. Feldman, 188.

111. Gersonides, *Wars of the Lord*, book 4, chap. 6, trans. Feldman, 185.

112. Feldman, in Gersonides, *Wars of the Lord*, trans. Feldman, 148–49.

113. Gersonides, *Wars of the Lord*, book 4, chap. 5, trans. Feldman, 178.

114. Hume, *Dialogues*, ed. Popkin, 71.

115. Hume, *Dialogues*, ed. Popkin, 71.

116. Feldman, in Gersonides, *Wars of the Lord*, trans. Feldman, 141. Husik, *History of Medieval Jewish Philosophy*, 342 agrees.

117. Gersonides, *Wars of the Lord*, book 4, chap. 7, trans. Feldman, 209.

118. Maimonides, *Guide*, book 3, chap. 20, ed. Pines, vol. 2, 481.

119. Husik, *History of Medieval Jewish Philosophy*, 345.

120. Feldman, in Gersonides, *Wars of the Lord*, trans. Feldman, 141.

121. Albo, Joseph, *Sefer ha-Ikkarim*, sec. 4, chap. 7.

122. Husik, *History of Medieval Jewish Philosophy*, 406.

123. Albo, *Sefer ha-Ikkarim*, sec. 4, chap. 7. See Eccles. 7:20.

124. Though Albo does not specify, sins of covetousness (Exod. 20:14) and enmity (Lev. 19:17) would fall into this category.

125. This approach is also adopted by Rabbi David Kimḥi, *Commentary on Hosea* 14:10; Rabbi Isaac Luria, *Yam Shel Shlomo*, *Bava Kamma* 5.23; and Rabbi Meir Malbim, *Commentary on the Bible*, Jeremiah 12:1.

126. Albo, *Sefer ha-Ikkarim*, sec. 4, chap. 12.

127. Angel, *Voices in Exile*, 10, identifies two such flaws: (1) the pivot away from Torah and toward secular studies and (2) the study of Torah as a prideful intellectual exercise intended to show off intellectual prowess.

128. Ya'avetz, *Ḥasdei ha-Shem*, 37.

4. KABBALAH

1. See Jacobs, "Mysticism," in *Jewish Religion*, 359; Elliot R. Wolfson, "Mysticism, Judaism and," in Neusner, Avery-Peck, and Green, *Encyclopedia of Judaism*, 1799.

2. Dan, *Early Kabbalah*, 166.

3. Scholem, *Major Trends*, 37.

4. The word "mysticism" derives from *muo*, the Greek word for what is concealed. Mysticism purports to offer insight into hidden information.

5. Dan, *Gershom Scholem*, 65.

6. *Mishnah Ḥagigah* 2:1.

7. Babylonian Talmud, *Ḥagigah* 14b.

8. See Halevi, *Kuzari*, part 4; introduction to first printed edition of *Sefer Yetzirah*, Amsterdam, 1713.

9. Scholem, *Major Trends*, 84.

10. Babylonian Talmud, *Sanhedrin* 65b reports how two disciples of Rabbi Yehudah the Patriarch, Rabbis Ḥanina and Hoshaya, used the information in *Sefer Yetzirah* to create a delicious tasting calf each Friday that they could enjoy on Shabbat. Rabbis Ḥanina and Hoshaya were reputed to be very much interested in cosmogony.

11. In Hebrew, "numbers" is *misparim*, a play on the word *m'saprim*, as if to say the glory of God is revealed through numbers. The idea that the existing world is dependent on basic numbers dates back to the Greeks and Pythagoras (sixth century BCE).

12. Westcott, trans., *Sefer Yetzirah*, chap. 1, sec. 1.

13. Westcott, trans., *Sefer Yetzirah*, chap. 1, sec. 5.

14. Westcott, trans., *Sefer Yetzirah*, chap. 1, sec. 9.

15. Westcott, trans., *Sefer Yetzirah*, chap. 1, sec. 12.

16. Scholem, *Kabbalah*, 385–89, discusses the evolution of the character of Samael from his original association in the book of Enoch as a fallen angel to the talmudic description of him as the archangel in charge of Rome to a satanic figure.

17. As translated by Dan, "Samael, Lillith," 18–19.

18. As translated by Dan, "Samael, Lillith," 38–39.

19. *Sefer ha-Bahir* is traditionally ascribed to the first-century teacher Rabbi Nehunya ben Ha-Kaneh. However, scholars who find no reference to this work earlier than the thirteenth century dispute this view.

20. The Zohar is traditionally ascribed to the first-century Rabbi Shimon bar Yoḥai. However, on the basis of the pioneering work of Gershom Scholem, scholars have universally acknowledged it to be a pseudepigraphic work of thirteenth-century Spain, most likely authored by Moses de Leon.

21. Aryeh Kaplan's translation divides the book into two hundred sections.

22. Identical to the Gnostic *nurea*.

23. *Sefer ha-Bahir*, sec. 11–12.

24. Dan, *Gershom Scholem*, 140.

25. Dan, *Gershom Scholem*, 140.

26. Green, introduction to *The Zohar*, trans. Matt, vol. 1, xxxi.

27. Green, introduction to *The Zohar*, trans. Matt, vol. 1, xxxi.

28. Green, introduction to *The Zohar*, trans. Matt, vol. 1, xxxi.

29. Green, introduction to *The Zohar*, trans. Matt, vol. 1, lv, describes this attribution to "a grand literary fiction" innocently intended to elevate the profound truths contained in it to a position of greater acceptance.

30. Green, introduction to *The Zohar*, trans. Matt, vol. 1, xxxi. Scholem gives a comprehensive list of proofs for dating the text to the thirteenth century, including its language and style. See Scholem, *Major Trends*, 156–204.

31. Scholem, *Major Trends*, 238.

32. *The Zohar*, trans. Sperling, Simon, and Levertoff, Emor 88b, vol. 5, 144. The Soncino text, translated by Sperling and Simon, follows the Mantua version and pagination.

33. *The Zohar*, trans. Sperling, Simon, and Levertoff, vol. 3, 214.

34. *The Zohar*, trans. Sperling, Simon and Levertoff, Tetsavveh 184a, vol. 4, 125.

35. *The Zohar*, trans. Sperling, Simon and Levertoff, Tetsavveh 184a, vol. 4, 125.

36. *The Zohar*, trans. Sperling, Simon, and Levertoff, Terumah 163a, vol. 4, 62.

37. Scholem, *Major Trends*, 239.

38. See, for example, *The Zohar*, trans. Sperling, Simon, and Levertoff, Va-ethannan 267b, vol. 5, 359–60; Mikkets, 201b–202a, vol. 2, 266.

39. *The Zohar*, trans. Sperling, Simon, and Levertoff, Mishpatim 113a, vol. 3, 336.

40. *The Zohar*, trans. Sperling, Simon, and Levertoff, Mishpatim 113a, vol. 3, 336.

41. Babylonian Talmud, *Makkot* 24a.

42. See Sarna, *JPS Torah Commentary: Exodus*, 110.

43. That is, a grave sin punishable by death.

44. *The Zohar*, trans. Sperling, Simon, and Levertoff, Mishpatim 113b, vol. 3, 337.

45. *The Zohar*, trans. Sperling, Simon, and Levertoff, Mishpatim 113b, vol. 3, 337.

46. *The Zohar*, trans. Sperling, Simon, and Levertoff, Mishpatim 113b, vol. 3, 337.

47. *The Zohar*, trans. Sperling, Simon, and Levertoff, Pinhas 218a, vol. 5, 326.

48. *The Zohar*, trans. Sperling, Simon, and Levertoff, Pinhas 218b, vol. 5, 326.

49. *The Zohar*, trans. Sperling, Simon, and Levertoff, Pinhas 218b, vol. 5, 326.

50. *The Zohar*, trans. Sperling, Simon, and Levertoff, Pinhas 218b, vol. 5, 326.

51. *The Zohar*, trans. Sperling, Simon, and Levertoff, Emor 101a, vol. 5, 128.

52. *The Zohar*, trans. Sperling, Simon, and Levertoff, Bereshit, 17b, vol. 1, 74.

53. Magid, "From Theosophy to Midrash," 45.

54. Scholem, *Major Trends*, 238. See also Scholem, "Tradition and New Creation," 127.

55. Scholem, *Major Trends*, 238.

56. Berman, *"Other Side" of Kabbalah*, 61.

57. The term *kelipah* itself migrated into the Zohar from the writings of Rabbi Eleazar of Worms. Berman, *"Other Side" of Kabbalah*, 61, notes that sometimes *kelipah* is used synonymously with "the Other Side."

58. Magid, "From Theosophy to Midrash," 60.

59. See *Zohar* II, 163b, 173b; and Berman, *"Other Side" of Kabbalah*, 60.

60. See Laenen, *Jewish Mysticism*, 168.

61. Scholem, *Major Trends*, 273.

5. HASIDIC MASTERS

1. See Rudavsky, *Modern Jewish Religious Movements*, 116–21, who describes in detail the events that engendered the gloom and despondency of this period. While this appraisal of Hasidism is eminently sound from a historical perspective, it has not prevented scholars from suggesting alternative explanations for the origins of Hasidism. Idel, *Hasidism*, 4, for example, describes Hasidism as a reaction to Sabbateanism through its neutralization of the messianic elements without combatting Kabbalah as such. Piekarz, *Ideological Trends of Hasidism*, describes Hasidism as the dissemination of the moralistic and ethical teaching of the Safed mystics. However, Sabbateanism was itself a response to the despair resultant from persecution and suffering. Likewise, the Safed mystics were largely responding to the depredations suffered during and after the expulsion from Spain. Dubnow, *History of Hasidism*, 3, argues that Hasidism filled the spiritual void created by an aloof rabbinate. And Dinur, "Origins of Hasidism," attributes the origins of Hasidism to a reaction to the exploitation of Polish Jewry by a clique of wealthy Jewish leaders. These two explanations can also be subsumed under Rudavsky's.

2. In the introduction to his *Tales of the Hasidim*, 2–3, Martin Buber identifies the core of Hasidic teaching as a life of "exalted joy" necessary as an aid in surviving sorrow and despair.

3. See Rashi on Gen. 41:45.

4. See Nigal, "New Light."

5. Joseph, *Tzafenat Pane'ah*, 18d in Nigal, "New Light," 346.

6. Joseph, *Tzafenat Pane'ah* 18d in Nigal, "New Light," 346.

7. Vitebsk, *Pri Ha'aretz* on Mattot and Mas'ei.

8. Lamm, *Religious Thought of Hasidism*, 453, claims that a more precise statement of the problem is that Hasidism formulates a conflict between God's immanence and God's goodness, with immanence understood as the idea that God is within all that exists.

9. Sassover, *Hemdah Genuzah*, 4.

10. Heschel, *Passion for Truth*, 40.

11. Shem Tov, *Keter Shem Tov*, part 1, 84, 88, 127. Though a basis for good, evil is still ranked below good. Shem Tov, *BESHT al ha-Torah*, vol. 1, 70, s.v. *vayar hashem . . . v'hineh tov m'od*, "Evil is a little less than actual good."
12. Berger, *Esser Orot*, 63.
13. Rabbi Barukh of Medziboz, *Butzina D'nehora*, 20, in Newman, *Hasidic Anthology*, 97.
14. Breslov, *Kitzur Likutey Moharan*, 5.
15. See Babylonian Talmud, *Ta'anit* 21a, where the statement "This, too, is for the best" is ascribed to Naḥum Ish Gamzu (with *gamzu* interpreted to mean a composite of two Hebrew words: "this too"); and Babylonian Talmud, *Berakhot* 60b, where the same attitude is ascribed to Rabbi Akiva, a student of Naḥum.
16. See *Mishnah Berakhot* 9:5. The actual wording is: "Just as a man is obligated to recite a blessing over the good, a man is obligated to recite a blessing over the bad."
17. Babylonian Talmud, *Berakhot* 60b.
18. Buber, *Tales of the Hasidim*, vol. 1, 318.
19. See Jacobs, *Hasidic Thought*, 9.
20. Heschel remarks that the Besht "taught that evil was a temporary manifestation of the as-yet-hidden good." Heschel, *Passion for Truth*, 40.
21. "Weal and woe" prosaically mean good and evil. In other words, everything that happens is in accordance with God's will.
22. Bloch, *Priester der Liebe*, 21.
23. Breslov, *Likutei Moharan*, 1, 65, 3, cited by Lamm, *Religious Thought of Hasidism*, 466–67.
24. Vitebsk, *Likutei Amarim*, letter 4, 7a.
25. Vitebsk, *Pri Ha'aretz*, Sabbath during Passover and Aḥarei Mot.
26. See Hallamish, "Teachings of Rabbi Menaḥem Mendl," 286–87.
27. Maggid of Koznitz, *Avodat Yisrael*, Mikkets, 19b–20a.
28. In Jacobs, *Hasidic Thought*, 135–38.
29. Hallamish, "Teachings of Rabbi Menahem Mendel," 287.
30. See Lamm, *Religious Thought of Hasidism*, 457.
31. In Dubnow, *Toldot ha-Hasidut*, 54.
32. Shapiro, *Nofet Tzufim*, 52.
33. Lizensk, *No'am Elimelekh*, 16; Newman, *Hasidic Anthology*, 95–96.
34. Rokeah, *Dover Shalom*, 80.
35. Babylonian Talmud, *Eruvin* 100b.
36. Buber, *Tales of the Hasidim*, vol. 2, 86.
37. Buber, *Tales of the Hasidim*, vol. 2, 151.
38. The text should be emended to read "wrong" unless the statement is to be understood sarcastically.
39. Buber, *Tales of the Hasidim*, vol. 1, 237–38.

40. Bloch, *Priester der Liebe*, 23; Newman, *Hasidic Anthology*, 484.

41. Bloch, *Priester der Liebe*, vol. 2, 60.

42. Heschel, *Passion for Truth*, 251.

43. Kobrin, *Or Yesharim*, 57.

44. *Likutei Moharan Tinyata*, no. 13, 144a, cited by Jacobs, *Hasidic Thought*, 62.

45. See Ps. 44:21, "He knows the secret of the heart." And when the Psalmist (26:2) invites God to "test my heart and mind," it is not intended to be an invitation to suffer but an examination of intentions.

46. Buber, *Tales of the Hasidim*, vol. 2, 72.

47. Schneerson, *Mada ve-Emunah*.

48. Schneerson, *Mada ve-Emunah*.

49. Yehudah Bauer, "God as Surgeon," *Haaretz*, June 1, 2007. Bauer goes on to claim that he has evidence that the Rebbe said that Hitler, like Nebuchadrezzar in Jer. 25:9, was a messenger sent by God to carry out God's divine plan. See also Bauer, *Rethinking the Holocaust*. Rabbi Schneerson's defenders reject this comparison, pointing to his published letters, such as one printed in *Sefer ha-Sichot* 5751 (1991), vol. 1, 233, in which Rabbi Schneerson writes, "The destruction of six million Jews in such a horrific manner that surpassed the cruelty of all previous generations, could not possibly be because of a punishment for sins. Even the Satan himself could not possibly find a sufficient number of sins that would warrant such genocide! There is absolutely no rationalistic explanation for the Holocaust except for the fact that it was a Divine decree . . . why it happened is above human comprehension — but it is definitely not because of punishment for sin."

50. Gelman, *Essays*, 82.

51. Kook, *Orot ha-Kodesh*, vol. 3, 478.

52. Kook, *Orot ha-Kodesh*, vol. 3, 478.

53. Kook, *Orot ha-Tehiyah*, 45.

54. Kook, *Orot ha-Kodesh*, vol. 2, 454.

55. Kook, *Mo'adei Hara'ayah*, 258.

56. Kook, *Arpilei Tohar* (1914), 2.

57. Lamm, *Religious Thought of Hasidim*, 453.

6. EARLY MODERN THINKERS

1. Leaman, *Evil and Suffering*, 121.

2. Spinoza, in Elwes, *Chief Works of Spinoza*, xxxi.

3. Spinoza, in Elwes, *Chief Works of Spinoza*, 44.

4. Spinoza, in Elwes, *Chief Works of Spinoza*, 45.

5. Nadler, "Baruch Spinoza."

6. Spinoza, *Ethics*, chapter 1, proposition 15, scholium VI, in Curley, *Collected Works*, vol. 1. See also Spinoza, *Tractatus Theologico*, in Elwes, *Chief Works of Spinoza*, 83.

7. Spinoza, *Letters*, in Curley, *Collected Works*, vol. 1, 166.

8. Spinoza, *Letters*, in Curley, *Collected Works*, vol. 1, 277.

9. Spinoza, *Ethics* I, appendix, in Curley, *Collected Works*, vol. 1, 440–41.

10. Nadler, *Best of All*, 228.

11. Spinoza, *Tractatus Theologico*, in Elwes, *Chief Works of Spinoza*, 246.

12. Spinoza, *Ethics* I, appendix, in Curley, *Collected Works*, vol. 1, 443.

13. Nadler, *Best of All*, 231.

14. Leaman, *Evil and Suffering*, 128.

15. Runes, *Spinoza Dictionary*, 21–22. Also Wolf, *Spinoza's Short Treatise*, 59–60.

16. Wolf, *Spinoza's Short Treatise*, 59.

17. Wolf, *Spinoza's Short Treatise*, 59.

18. Wolf, *Spinoza's Short Treatise*, 60. In Spinoza, *Ethics* II, in Curley, *Collected Works*, vol. 1, 545, Spinoza writes, "As far as good and evil are concerned, they also indicate nothing positive in things, considered in themselves, nor are they anything other than modes of thinking, or notions we form because we compare things to one another."

19. Wolf, *Spinoza's Short Treatise*, 59.

20. Wolf, *Spinoza's Short Treatise*, 59.

21. Wolf, *Spinoza's Short Treatise*, 60.

22. Spinoza, *Ethics* V, proposition 6, in Curley, *Collected Works*, vol. 1, 590.

23. Nadler, "Baruch Spinoza."

24. Leaman, *Evil and Suffering*, 122–29.

25. See, for example, Spinoza, *Letters* 18, in Curley, *Collected Works*, vol. 1, 354.

26. Spinoza, *Letters* 19, in Curley, *Collected Works*, vol. 1, 359. Spinoza, *Ethics* IV, 94 in Curley, *Collected Works*, vol. 1, 575.

27. Frank and Leaman, *History of Philosophy*, 560.

28. Hegel, *Lectures*, ed. Haldane, vol. 3, 281–82.

29. Spinoza, *Ethics* V, proposition 42s, in Curley, *Collected Works*, vol. 1, 600.

30. Luzzatto, *Derekh ha-Shem*, part 1, "On Humankind," sec. 1, trans. Kaplan, 93.

31. Luzzatto, *Derekh ha-Shem*, part 1, "On Humankind," sec. 1, trans. Kaplan, 95.

32. Luzzatto, *Derekh ha-Shem*, part 2, sec. 1, trans. Kaplan, 109.

33. Luzzatto, *Derekh ha-Shem*, part 2, sec. 1, trans. Kaplan, 109.

34. Luzzatto, *Derekh ha-Shem*, part 2, sec. 1, trans. Kaplan, 111.

35. Luzzatto, *Derekh ha-Shem*, part 2, sec. 3, trans. Kaplan, 113.

36. Luzzatto, *Derekh ha-Shem*, part 2, sec. 3, trans. Kaplan, 111, 113.

37. Luzzatto, *Derekh ha-Shem*, part 2, sec. 4, trans. Kaplan, 115.

38. Luzzatto, *Derekh ha-Shem*, part 2, sec. 4, trans. Kaplan, 115.

39. Luzzatto, *Derekh ha-Shem*, part 2, sec. 4, trans. Kaplan, 115.

40. Luzzatto, *Derekh ha-Shem*, part 2, sec. 4, trans. Kaplan, 115.

41. Luzzatto, *Derekh ha-Shem*, part 2, sec. 5, trans. Kaplan, 117.

42. Luzzatto, *Derekh ha-Shem*, part 2, sec. 6, trans. Kaplan, 117.

43. Luzzatto, *Derekh ha-Shem*, part 2, sec. 7, trans. Kaplan, 119.

44. See Babylonian Talmud, *Eduyot* 2:9.

45. Luzzatto hastens to add that in the afterlife a person is judged solely on personal actions, good or bad, in this life.

46. Babylonian Talmud, *Shevuot* 39a.

47. Here, too, the christological similarities go unchallenged.

48. Luzzatto, *Derekh ha-Shem*, part 2, sec. 8, trans. Kaplan, 121.

49. See Eccles. 7:20.

50. Rudavsky, *Modern Jewish Religious Movements*, 61.

51. Jospe, *Moses Mendelssohn*, 159. Also cited by Hensel, *Mendelssohn Family (1729-1847)*, 23–24.

52. Jospe, *Moses Mendelssohn*, 158.

53. Jospe, *Moses Mendelssohn*, 158.

54. See, for example, Gen. 1:4,13,18.

55. Breuer and Sorkin, *Moses Mendelssohn's Hebrew Writings*, 303.

56. Breuer and Sorkin, *Moses Mendelssohn's Hebrew Writings*, 303.

57. Aristotle, *Physics* 192a.

58. See Augustine, *City of God*, XI, 9. "Evil has no positive nature; but the loss of good has received the name 'evil.'" Augustine argues that evil has no real existence; it is merely the absence of good. Since evil does not exist in and of itself, God cannot be held responsible for it.

59. Breuer and Sorkin, *Moses Mendelssohn's Hebrew Writings*, 303–4.

60. Breuer and Sorkin, *Moses Mendelssohn's Hebrew Writings*, 304.

61. Breuer and Sorkin, *Moses Mendelssohn's Hebrew Writings*, 303.

62. Breuer and Sorkin, *Moses Mendelssohn's Hebrew Writings*, 304.

63. Breuer and Sorkin, *Moses Mendelssohn's Hebrew Writings*, 304.

64. Breuer and Sorkin, *Moses Mendelssohn's Hebrew Writings*, 304.

65. Breuer and Sorkin, *Moses Mendelssohn's Hebrew Writings*, 304.

66. Breuer and Sorkin, *Moses Mendelssohn's Hebrew Writings*, 304.

67. Breuer and Sorkin, *Moses Mendelssohn's Hebrew Writings*, 312.

68. See Ps. 144:3; Exod. 33:12; 2 Sam. 19:36.

69. See Babylonian Talmud, *Shabbat* 38b.

70. Breuer and Sorkin, *Moses Mendelssohn's Hebrew Writings*, 312.

71. Breuer and Sorkin, *Moses Mendelssohn's Hebrew Writings*, 312.

72. Breuer and Sorkin, *Moses Mendelssohn's Hebrew Writings*, 312.

73. Breuer and Sorkin, *Moses Mendelssohn's Hebrew Writings*, 314.

74. Jospe, *Moses Mendelssohn*, 202–3.

75. Jospe, *Moses Mendelssohn*, 203.

76. Jospe, *Moses Mendelssohn*, 203.

7. MODERN THINKERS

1. Habermas, "Modernity," 4.

2. Blau, *Modern Varieties of Judaism*, 23.

3. Whitehead, *Science*.

4. Johnson, *Modern Times*, 1.

5. H. Cohen, *Religion of Reason*, 225.

6. H. Cohen, *Religion of Reason*, 225.

7. H. Cohen, *Religion of Reason*, 19.

8. H. Cohen, *Religion of Reason*, 18–19.

9. H. Cohen, *Religion of Reason*, 18.

10. H. Cohen, *Religion of Reason*, 228.

11. H. Cohen, *Religion of Reason*, 19.

12. H. Cohen, *Religion of Reason*, 19.

13. H. Cohen, *Religion of Reason*, 228.

14. H. Cohen, *Religion of Reason*, 227.

15. H. Cohen, *Religion of Reason*, 227.

16. H. Cohen, *Religion of Reason*, 226.

17. H. Cohen, *Religion of Reason*, 229.

18. H. Cohen, *Religion of Reason*, 229.

19. H. Cohen, *Religion of Reason*, 235.

20. H. Cohen, *Religion of Reason*, 234.

21. H. Cohen, *Religion of Reason*, 224.

22. H. Cohen. *Religion of Reason*, 283.

23. H. Cohen, *Religion of Reason*, 434.

24. H. Cohen, *Religion of Reason*, 283.

25. H. Cohen, *Religion of Reason*, 230.

26. H. Cohen, *Religion of Reason*, 230.

27. H. Cohen, *Religion of Reason*, 104.

28. H. Cohen, *Religion of Reason*, 224.

29. H. Cohen, *Religion of Reason*, 433.

30. H. Cohen, *Religion of Reason*, 433.

31. Noveck, *Great Jewish Thinkers*, 123.

32. Fackenheim, *To Mend the World*, 273.

33. Alexander, *Space, Time, and Deity*, vol. 2, 5.

34. Alexander, *Space, Time, and Deity*, vol. 2, 45.

35. Alexander, *Space, Time, and Deity*, vol. 2, 428.

36. Alexander, *Space, Time, and Deity*, vol. 2, 353.

37. Alexander, *Space, Time, and Deity*, vol. 2, 398.

38. Alexander, *Space, Time, and Deity*, vol. 2, 400.

39. Certainly this was the case among Protestant thinkers.

40. Edwards, *Encyclopedia of Philosophy*, vol. 1, s.v. "Buber," 410. This observation is disputed by Walter Kaufmann, in his edition of Buber, *I and Thou*, 16.

41. Buber, *Eclipse of God*, 110.

42. Buber, *I and Thou*, 127.

43. Buber, *Eclipse of God*, 50.

44. Buber, *I and Thou*, 17.

45. Buber, *Eclipse of God*, 9.

46. Buber, *I and Thou*, xiii.

47. Buber, *Eclipse of God*, 20.

48. Buber, *Good and Evil*, 3.

49. Buber, *Good and Evil*, 64.

50. Buber, *Good and Evil*, 88.

51. Buber, *Good and Evil*, 134.

52. Buber, *Between Man and Man*, 78.

53. Leaman, *Evil and Suffering*, 168.

54. Buber, *Good and Evil*, 139.

55. Buber, *Good and Evil*, 140.

56. Buber, *Good and Evil*, 43.

57. Buber, *Good and Evil*, 44.

58. Buber, *Good and Evil*, 57.

59. Buber, *Eclipse of God*, 27.

60. Buber, *Eclipse of God*, 74.

61. See Buber, *Good and Evil*, 42.

62. Buber, *Good and Evil*, 56.

63. Buber, *Good and Evil*, 73.

64. Buber, *Good and Evil*, 70, 83.

65. Buber, *Eclipse of God*, 84.

66. Buber, *Good and Evil*, 59.

67. Buber, *Good and Evil*, 59.

68. Buber, *Good and Evil*, 59.

69. Buber, *Eclipse of God*, 103.

70. Buber, *Eclipse of God*, 111.

71. Katz, "Mordecai Kaplan's Theology," 125.

72. In his 1995 book *Not in God's Name*, Rabbi Jonathan Sacks coined the term "altruistic evil" to describe the phenomenon of committing evil in the name of some good.
73. Kegley, "Martin Buber's Ethics," 181.
74. Branson, "Individual and the Commune," 93.
75. Kaplan, "Supremacy of the Torah," 186.
76. Kaplan, *Future of the American Jew*, 382.
77. Kaplan, *Sabbath Prayer Book*, xix.
78. Kaplan, *Sabbath Prayer Book*, xx. Also, God is "the source of our will-to-salvation" (xx). God gives humanity the power to cope. For further reading, see Schulweis, "A Critical Assessment of Kaplan's Ideas of Salvation," 257–70.
79. Maimonides, *Guide of the Perplexed*, book 1, chap. 52, ed. Pines, 116.
80. Kaplan, *Questions Jews Ask*, 102.
81. Kaplan, *Questions Jews Ask*, 102.
82. Kaplan, *Questions Jews Ask*, 102.
83. Kaplan, *Future of the American Jew*, 274.
84. The symbolic reading of Scripture is a regular technique in Kaplan. See Scult, "Kaplan's Re-interpretation," 294–318.
85. Kaplan, *Future of the American Jew*, 275.
86. Kaplan, *Judaism as a Civilization*, 368.
87. Kaplan, *Judaism as a Civilization*, 368.
88. Cited by Scult, *Radical American Judaism*, 251.
89. Scult, *Radical American Judaism*, 251.
90. Scult, *Radical American Judaism*, 251.
91. Scult, *Radical American Judaism*, 254.
92. Scult, *Radical American Judaism*, 252.
93. Scult, *Radical American Judaism*, 262.
94. Scult, *Radical American Judaism*, 262.
95. Scult, *Radical American Judaism*, 262.
96. Scult, *Radical American Judaism*, 258.
97. Scult, *Radical American Judaism*, 259.
98. Katz, "Mordecai Kaplan's Theology," 116.
99. Kaplan, *Meaning of God*, 63–64.
100. Kaplan, *Judaism as a Civilization*, 115–16.
101. Kaplan, *Meaning of God*, 76.
102. Kaplan, *Meaning of God*, 76.
103. Kaplan, *Meaning of God*, 133. These relationships are human relationships.
104. Kaplan, *Meaning of God*, 75.
105. Katz, "Mordecai Kaplan's Theology," 120.

106. Scult, *Radical American Judaism*, 249.

107. Kaplan, *Meaning of God*, 75–76.

108. Kaplan, *Meaning of God*, 72.

109. Cited by Ettinger, *Hannah Arendt, Martin Heidegger*, 4.

110. Ettinger well chronicles their lengthy relationship.

111. Arendt, *Eichmann in Jerusalem*, 252. Italics hers.

112. Arendt, *Eichmann in Jerusalem*, 276.

113. Arendt, *Eichmann in Jerusalem*, 287.

114. Borowitz, "Autonomous Self," 52.

115. Borowitz "Autonomous Self," 54.

116. Borowitz, *New Jewish Theology*, 207.

117. Borowitz, *Masks Jews Wear*, 99.

118. Borowitz, *How Can a Jew Speak?*, 52.

119. Borowitz, *How Can a Jew Speak?*, 52.

120. Borowitz, *How Can a Jew Speak?*, 52.

121. Greene, *Once More*, 77.

122. In *A New Jewish Theology in the Making*, 43, Borowitz calls God's providence in human history "inscrutable."

123. Borowitz, *New Jewish Theology*, 58.

124. Borowitz, *New Jewish Theology*, 59.

125. Borowitz, *New Jewish Theology*, 59–60.

126. Borowitz, *New Jewish Theology*, 60.

127. Borowitz, *New Jewish Theology*, 60.

128. Borowitz, "Autonomous Self," 55–56.

129. Borowitz, *New Jewish Theology*, 211.

130. Mittleman, "Judaism and Postmodernity."

131. Borowitz, *New Jewish Theology*, 211.

132. Gillman, *Sacred Fragments*, 201.

133. Gillman, *Sacred Fragments*, 193.

134. Gillman, *Sacred Fragments*, 187–88.

135. Gillman, *Doing Jewish Theology*, 224.

136. Geertz, "Religion as a Cultural System," 90: "A religion is a system of symbols which acts to establish powerful, pervasive, and long-lasting moods and motivations in men by formulating conceptions of a general order of existence and clothing these conceptions with such an aura of factuality that the moods and motivations seem uniquely realistic."

137. Geertz, "Religion as a Cultural System," 100.

138. Gillman, *Doing Jewish Theology*, 226.

139. Gillman, *Doing Jewish Theology*, 230.

140. Gillman, *Doing Jewish Theology*, 230.

141. Spero, *Morality*, 118.

142. See Levenson, *Creation*, 15–25, 49–50.

143. Gillman, *Doing Jewish Theology*, 235.

144. Gillman, *Doing Jewish Theology*, 232.

145. Kushner, *When Bad Things Happen*, 14.

146. Kushner, *When Bad Things Happen*, 1.

147. Kushner, *When Bad Things Happen*, 15.

148. Kushner, *When Bad Things Happen*, 16.

149. Kushner, *When Bad Things Happen*, 13.

150. Kushner, *When Bad Things Happen*, 18.

151. Kushner, *When Bad Things Happen*, 20.

152. Kushner, *When Bad Things Happen*, 20.

153. Kushner, *When Bad Things Happen*, 20.

154. Kushner, *When Bad Things Happen*, 33.

155. Kushner, *When Bad Things Happen*, 34.

156. Kushner, *When Bad Things Happen*, 35.

157. Kushner, *When Bad Things Happen*, 36.

158. Kushner, *When Bad Things Happen*, 38.

159. Kushner, *When Bad Things Happen*, 39.

160. Kushner, *When Bad Things Happen*, 38.

161. Kushner, *When Bad Things Happen*, 40.

162. Kushner, *When Bad Things Happen*, 41.

163. Kushner, *When Bad Things Happen*, 55–56.

164. Kushner, *When Bad Things Happen*, 64.

165. Kushner, *When Bad Things Happen*, 64.

166. Kushner, *When Bad Things Happen*, 70.

167. Kushner, *When Bad Things Happen*, 71.

168. Kushner, *When Bad Things Happen*, 72.

169. Kushner, *When Bad Things Happen*, 129.

170. Kushner, *When Bad Things Happen*, 150.

171. Kushner, *When Bad Things Happen*, 76.

172. Kushner, *When Bad Things Happen*, 156.

173. Kushner, *When Bad Things Happen*, 150.

174. Kushner, *When Bad Things Happen*, 72.

175. Blech, *If God Is So Good*, x.

176. Nussbaum, "Martha Nussbaum."

177. Pinches, "Friendship and Tragedy."

178. Nussbaum, "Love's Knowledge," 275.

179. Martha Nussbaum, "Tragedy and Justice."

180. Kavka, "Judaism and Theology," 357.

181. Christ and Plaskow, *Goddess and God*, 126.

182. Christ and Plaskow, *Goddess and God*, 128.

183. Christ and Plaskow, *Goddess and God*, 128.

184. Christ and Plaskow, *Goddess and God*, 176, 177.

185. Christ and Plaskow, *Goddess and God*, 181.

186. Christ and Plaskow, *Goddess and God*, 184.

187. Christ and Plaskow, *Goddess and God*, 184.

188. *Ba-midbar Rabbah* 12:4; *Bereshit Rabbah* 68:9.

189. Rudavsky, *Modern Jewish Religious Movements*, 126.

190. Christ and Plaskow, *Goddess and God*, 185.

191. Christ and Plaskow, *Goddess and God*, 184.

192. Christ and Plaskow, *Goddess and God*, 186.

193. Christ and Plaskow, *Goddess and God*, 187.

194. Christ and Plaskow, *Goddess and God*, 187.

195. Christ and Plaskow, *Goddess and God*, 187.

196. See Corrington, "My Passage," 132.

197. Christ and Plaskow, *Goddess and God*, 176.

198. Mullins, "Difficulty with Demarcating Panentheism," 325–26.

8. THE PROBLEM OF THE SHOAH

1. Korman, "Holocaust in Historical Writing," 259–62; Garber and Zuckerman, "Why Do We Call," 197–211.

2. Lev. 1:3ff.

3. See Young, *Writing and Rewriting*, 85–86; Katz, Biderman, and Greenberg, *Wrestling with God*, 5.

4. Wiesel, "Some Questions," 13.

5. Because of the theological connotations associated with the term "Holocaust," Walter Lacquer argues that the word is "singularly inappropriate." See Lacquer, *Terrible Secret*, 7.

6. See also Tal, "Excursus on the Term *Shoah*," 10–11; and Oz, "The Meaning of Homeland," 19: "A holocaust is a natural event, an outbreak of forces beyond human control. The murder of European Jews by German Nazis was no Holocaust."

7. Babylonian Talmud, *Yoma* 39b; *Mo'ed Katan* 26a; *Ḥagigah* 5b; *Avodah Zarah* 9b.

8. According to Roskies, the proper Yiddish term should be *der driter hurban*, meaning "the third catastrophe," with the destruction of the First and Second Temples respectively the first two. Roskies, *Against the Apocalypse*, 261.

9. Hutner, "Is the Term Shoah Acceptable in Describing the Destruction of European Jewry during World War II?," lecture given at Mesivta Chaim Berlin and published in the *Jewish Observer* under the same title, October 1977, 3–9. But to secular Jews in general and to Labor Zionists in Palestine in particular, the term *ḥurban* was too religiously loaded. So the term "Shoah," no matter how problematic, emerged as the preferred choice.

10. Katz, *Holocaust in Historical Context*, vols. 1–2.

11. Babylonian Talmud, *Shabbat* 55a.

12. Styron and West, *Conversations with William Styron*, 34; Styron, "Auschwitz," 336.

13. Rubenstein, *After Auschwitz*, x–xi.

14. Cited by L. Russell, *Teaching the Holocaust*, 49.

15. A. Cohen, *The Tremendum*, 1.

16. Goldhagen, *Hitler's Willing Executioners*, 14.

17. Katz, *Holocaust in Historical Context*, vol. 1, 72.

18. Katz, *Holocaust in Historical Context*, vol. 1, 73.

19. Katz, *Holocaust in Historical Context*, vol. 1, 76.

20. Katz, *Holocaust in Historical Context*, vol. 1, 78.

21. Katz, *Holocaust in Historical Context*, vol. 1, 81.

22. Katz, *Holocaust in Historical Context*, vol. 1, 82, puts the Jewish death count during the Crusades to 3,000 at most, or fewer than 2 percent of the population. He also cites Monter, *Frontiers of Heresy*, 53, who calculates the total number of Jewish deaths during the Inquisition at 1,865. Shmuel Ettinger, cited by Katz, *Holocaust in Historical Context*, vol. 1, 164, estimates that the Cossacks killed 10,000 Jews, fewer than 10 percent of the population.

23. Katz, *Holocaust in Historical Context*, vol. 1, 84.

24. Katz, *Holocaust in Historical Context*, vol. 1, 88.

25. Katz, *Holocaust in Historical Context*, vol. 1, 66.

26. Katz, *Holocaust in Historical Context*, vol. 1, 67.

27. Katz, *Holocaust in Historical Context*, vol. 1, 28.

28. Talmon, "Seedbed of the Holocaust and of the Revival," *Jerusalem Post*, April 20, 1978, cited in Gutman et al., *Holocaust and Its Significance*, 236–37.

29. Babylonian Talmud, *Shabbat* 55a.

30. Shapira, *Esh Kodesh*, 139, Shabbat Shuvah sermon, 1942.

31. Schindler notes that in a letter to his brother Yeshiah in Palestine dated Winter 1943, Shapiro blames their deaths on his own sins. See Schindler, "Suffering and Evil," 20.

32. Shapira, *Esh Kodesh*, 114. See also Babylonian Talmud, *Berakhot* 60b.

33. Babylonian Talmud, *Menaḥot* 29b. Rabbi Akiva's students did so as well (see Babylonian Talmud, *Berakhot* 61b).

34. Shapira, *Esh Kodesh*, 139.

35. See Friedensohn, "Harab Reb Yehezkel Halevi Halstuk," 55.

36. Shapira, *Esh Kodesh*, 11.

37. Shapira, *Tzav ve-Zeruz*, 23–24.

38. Shapira, *Esh Kodesh*, 126–27.

39. Shapira, *Esh Kodesh*, 21–22, 114.

40. Shapira, *Esh Kodesh*, 157–58.

41. Shapira, *Esh Kodesh*, 147.

42. See Teikhtal, *Em ha-Banim Semehah*, 78–79.

43. Shapira, *Esh Kodesh*, 137.

44. Shapira, *Esh Kodesh*, 27.

45. Shapira, *Esh Kodesh*, 70–71.

46. Shapira, *Esh Kodesh*, 27–28.

47. Schindler, "Suffering and Evil," 27.

48. Shapira, *Esh Kodesh*, 139.

49. Shapira, *Esh Kodesh*, 100. See also Shapira, *Esh Kodesh*, 56–58.

50. Shapira, *Esh Kodesh*, 139.

51. Shapira, *Esh Kodesh*, 139.

52. Ehrenreich, sermon, February 26, 1939, cited in Katz, Biderman, and Greenberg, *Wrestling with God*, 63.

53. Rabbi Moshe Teitelbaum's uncle Rabbi Yoel Teitelbaum authors a traditional theological response to the Holocaust in his 1958 book *Va-Yo'el Moshe*, a vitriolic condemnation of Zionism, which he identifies as the sin that was punished by God through the Nazis.

54. Ehrenreich, "Mah She-darashti B'yom Alef Parshat Tetzaveh 7 Adar 5699," in *Derashot Lehem Shelomoh*, cited in Katz, Biderman, and Greenberg, *Wrestling with God*, 63.

55. Babylonian Talmud, *Bava Kamma* 92a.

56. Exod. 16:28 tells how, contrary to God's command, some Israelites went out to collect manna on Shabbat, but Exod. 16:28 records that God castigates the entire people, not just the sinners.

57. See Isa. 10:5.

58. Ehrenreich, "Mah She-darashti B'yom Alef Parshat Tetzaveh 7 Adar 5699," in *Derashot Lehem Shelomoh*, cited in Katz, Biderman, and Greenberg, *Wrestling with God*, 65.

59. Tsimerman, *Tamim Pa'alo*, end, cited in Katz, Biderman, and Greenberg, *Wrestling with God*, 166.

60. Tsimerman, *Tamim Pa'alo*, cited in Katz, Biderman, and Greenberg, *Wrestling with God*, 158.

61. Tsimerman, *Tamim Pa'alo*, cited in Katz, Biderman, and Greenberg, *Wrestling with God*, 158.

62. Tsimerman, *Tamim Pa'alo*, cited in Katz, Biderman, and Greenberg, *Wrestling with God*, 158.

63. Tsimerman, *Tamim Pa'alo*, cited in Katz, Biderman, and Greenberg, *Wrestling with God*, 158.

64. Babylonian Talmud, *Shabbat* 54b.

65. Maimonides, *Mishneh Torah*, Laws of Opinions 6:7.

66. This is the opinion of Abba Arekha, known as Rav, in Babylonian Talmud, *Sanhedrin* 97b.

67. Edels, *Hiddushei Maharsha*, commentary on *Sanhedrin* 97b.

68. See Vital, *Sha'ar Hakavanot*, 1.

69. Tsimerman, *Tamim Pa'alo*, cited in Katz, Biderman, and Greenberg, *Wrestling with God*, 166.

70. Tsimerman, *Tamim Pa'alo*, cited in Katz, Biderman, and Greenberg, *Wrestling with God*, 166.

71. Tsimerman, *Tamim Pa'alo*, cited in Katz, Biderman, and Greenberg, *Wrestling with God*, 167.

72. Berkovits, *Faith after the Holocaust*, 3–6.

73. Berkovits, *Faith after the Holocaust*, 94.

74. Berkovits, *Faith after the Holocaust*, 94.

75. Berkovits, *Faith after the Holocaust*, 94.

76. Berkovits, *Faith after the Holocaust*, 135.

77. Berkovits, *Faith after the Holocaust*, 104.

78. Berkovits, *Faith after the Holocaust*, 105.

79. Berkovits, *Faith after the Holocaust*, 105.

80. Berkovits, *Faith after the Holocaust*, 105.

81. Berkovits, *Faith after the Holocaust*, 105.

82. Berkovits, *Faith after the Holocaust*, 135.

83. Berkovits, *Faith after the Holocaust*, 89.

84. Berkovts, *Faith after the Holocaust*, 90.

85. Berkovits, *Faith after the Holocaust*, 90.

86. Berkovits, *Faith after the Holocaust*, 90.

87. Berkovits, *Faith after the Holocaust*, 90.

88. Berkovits, *Faith after the Holocaust*, 135.

89. Berkovits, *Faith after the Holocaust*, 136.

90. Berkovits, *Faith after the Holocaust*, 131.

91. Berkovits, *Faith after the Holocaust*, 136.

92. Berkovits, *Faith after the Holocaust*, 136.

93. Gordis, "Cruel God or None," 277.

94. I. Greenberg, "Cloud of Smoke," 25.

95. Halivni and Ochs, *Breaking the Tablets*, 17.

96. Halivni and Ochs, *Breaking the Tablets*, 18.

97. Halivni and Ochs, *Breaking the Tablets*, 18.

98. Roskies, *Against the Apocalypse*, 59.

99. *Shemot Rabbah* 25:12; Jerusalem Talmud, *Ta'anit* 1:1.

100. Hazony, *Human Responsibility*, 186–87.

101. Katz, *Post-Holocaust Dialogues*, 274–75.

102. Rubenstein, *After Auschwitz*, 153.

103. Rubenstein, *After Auschwitz*, 46.

104. Rubenstein, *After Auschwitz*, 58.

105. Rubenstein, *After Auschwitz*, x.

106. Rubenstein, *After Auschwitz*, 153.

107. Rubenstein, *After Auschwitz*, 237.

108. Rubenstein, *After Auschwitz*, 237–38.

109. Rubenstein, *After Auschwitz*, 237.

110. Rubenstein, *After Auschwitz*, 154. Here Berkovits would challenge the categorical nature of Rubenstein's claim. Berkovits, *Faith after the Holocaust*, states (136), "God is responsible for having created a world in which man is free to make history." But God's withdrawal is the result of God's benevolence, not God's impotence. Berkovits's God can always choose to intervene.

111. Rubenstein, *After Auschwitz*, 237.

112. Rubenstein, *After Auschwitz*, 238.

113. Rubenstein, *After Auschwitz*, 152–53.

114. Rubenstein, *After Auschwitz*, 153.

115. Rubenstein, *After Auschwitz*, 240.

116. See, for example, Katz, "Richard Rubenstein," 313–50. Katz identifies nine weaknesses in Rubenstein and soberly dissects Rubenstein's argument, but he does not dismiss Rubenstein out of hand.

117. There have even been attempts to rehabilitate Rubenstein's views and claim his critics have mischaracterized him. See Braiterman, "Hitler's Accomplice?," 75–89.

118. Donat, *Voices from the Ashes*, 1, cited in Katz, Biderman, and Greenberg, *Wrestling with God*, 275.

119. Delivered in New York City during the 1975 conference "The Sho'ah: One Generation Later."

120. Alexander Donat, "A Voice from the Ashes: Wandering in Search of God," *Yalkut Moreshet* 21 (June 1976), and in an abbreviated form in *Mahashavot* 46 (1977).

121. Cited by Katz, Biderman, and Greenberg, *Wrestling with God*, 276.

122. Katz, Biderman, and Greenberg, *Wrestling with God*, 276.

123. Katz, Biderman, and Greenberg, *Wrestling with God*, 281.

124. A reference to the selection process, especially in the death camps.

125. Katz, Biderman, and Greenberg, *Wrestling with God*, 285.

126. And Donat says so: "I reject the God of Treblinka and Auschwitz and all the attempts to avoid the problem." Katz, Biderman, and Greenberg, *Wrestling with God*, 286.

127. A. Cohen, *The Tremendum: A Theological Interpretation of the Holocaust*, cited in Katz, Biderman, and Greenberg, *Wrestling with God*, 579.

128. A. Cohen, *The Tremendum*, cited in Katz, Biderman, and Greenberg, *Wrestling with God*, 572.

129. A. Cohen, *The Tremendum*, cited in Katz, Biderman, and Greenberg, *Wrestling with God*, 568.

130. A. Cohen, *The Tremendum*, cited in Katz, Biderman, and Greenberg, *Wrestling with God*, 573.

131. A. Cohen, *The Tremendum*, cited in Katz, Biderman, and Greenberg, *Wrestling with God*, 573.

132. A. Cohen, *The Tremendum*, cited in Katz, Biderman, and Greenberg, *Wrestling with God*, 575.

133. A. Cohen, *The Tremendum*, cited in Katz, Biderman, and Greenberg, *Wrestling with God*, 577.

134. A. Cohen, *The Tremendum*, cited in Katz, Biderman, and Greenberg, *Wrestling with God*, 575.

135. A. Cohen, *The Tremendum*, cited in Katz, Biderman, and Greenberg, *Wrestling with God*, 580. The image of scales is conveyed by Cohen's implicit language, namely, "If we can begin to see God *less* [emphasis mine] as the interferer. . . ." "Less" suggests an emphasis without denying the value of that which it is measured against. In other words, Cohen allows for the possibility of God to intervene in human affairs. Consequently, Katz, Biderman, and Greenberg, *Wrestling with God*, 565, mischaracterizes Cohen by claiming that Cohen denies that God intervenes in human affairs.

136. Jonas, "Concept of God," 3.

137. Jonas, "Concept of God," 3; Katz, Biderman, and Greenberg, *Wrestling with God*, 628.

138. Katz, Biderman, and Greenberg, *Wrestling with God*, 628.

139. Katz, Biderman, and Greenberg, *Wrestling with God*, 629.

140. Jonas, "Concept of God," 3.

141. Jonas, "The Concept of God after Auschwitz," cited in Katz, Biderman, and Greenberg, *Wrestling with God*, 630.

142. Jonas, "Concept of God," 4; also cited in Katz, Biderman, and Greenberg, *Wrestling with God*, 630.

143. Jonas, "The Concept of God after Auschwitz," cited in Katz, Biderman, and Greenberg, *Wrestling with God*, 631.

144. Jonas, "The Concept of God after Auschwitz," cited in Katz, Biderman, and Greenberg, *Wrestling with God*, 628.

145. Jonas, "The Concept of God after Auschwitz," cited in Katz, Biderman, and Greenberg, *Wrestling with God*, 632.

146. Jonas, "The Concept of God after Auschwitz," cited in Katz, Biderman, and Greenberg, *Wrestling with God*, 633.

147. Jonas, "The Concept of God after Auschwitz," cited in Katz, Biderman, and Greenberg, *Wrestling with God*, 633.

148. Maimonides, *Mishneh Torah*, Laws of Forbidden Intercourse 14:1–2.

149. See Kellner, *Must a Jew Believe?*

150. Gelernter, *Judaism*, 193–95.

151. Heschel, *Israel*, 112.

152. Heschel, *Man Is Not Alone*, 151.

153. Heschel, *Man Is Not Alone*, 151–52.

154. Heschel, *Man Is Not Alone*, 153.

155. Heschel, *Man Is Not Alone*, 153.

156. Heschel, *Man Is Not Alone*, 153.

157. Heschel, *Man Is Not Alone*, 154.

158. Heschel, *Man Is Not Alone*, 154.

159. Heschel, *Man Is Not Alone*, 153.

160. Heschel, *Man Is Not Alone*, 153.

161. Heschel, *Man Is Not Alone*, 154–55.

162. Heschel, *Man Is Not Alone*, 81–82.

163. Heschel, *Man Is Not Alone*, 92.

164. Soloveitchik, in Braiterman, *God after Auschwitz*, 72.

165. Soloveitchik, "Kol Dodi Dofek," in Katz, Biderman, and Greenberg, *Wrestling with God*, 383.

166. Soloveitchik, "Kol Dodi Dofek," in Katz, Biderman, and Greenberg, *Wrestling with God*, 384.

167. Soloveitchik, "Kol Dodi Dofek," in Katz, Biderman, and Greenberg, *Wrestling with God*, 385.

168. Soloveitchik, "Kol Dodi Dofek," in Katz, Biderman, and Greenberg, *Wrestling with God*, 388.

169. Soloveitchik, "Kol Dodi Dofek," in Katz, Biderman, and Greenberg, *Wrestling with God*, 390. Near the end of his essay he refers to the birth of the State of Israel

as a "miracle," but a miracle that "came just a bit late." Soloveitchik, "Kol Dodi Dofek," in Katz, Biderman, and Greenberg, *Wrestling with God*, 393.

170. Soloveitchik, "Kol Dodi Dofek," in Katz, Biderman, and Greenberg, *Wrestling with God*, 388.

171. Soloveitchik, "Kol Dodi Dofek," in Katz, Biderman, and Greenberg, *Wrestling with God*, 388.

172. Soloveitchik, "Kol Dodi Dofek," in Katz, Biderman, and Greenberg, *Wrestling with God*, 388.

173. Fackenheim, *To Mend the World*, 248, italics in the original.

174. Hence, and in contrast to Katz, *Holocaust in Historical Context*, vol. 1, 29, who lists Fackenheim as a theological radical, he is listed here as a deflector.

175. Fackenheim, *God's Presence in History*, 84.

176. Fackenheim, *God's Presence in History*, 89.

177. Fackenheim, *God's Presence in History*, 89.

178. Fackenheim, *God's Presence in History*, 85.

179. Fackenheim, *God's Presence in History*, 86.

180. Fackenheim, *God's Presence in History*, 86.

181. Fackenhein, *God's Presence in History*, 86.

182. Fackenheim, *God's Presence in History*, 39.

183. Gordis, *Judaic Ethics*, 80.

184. Gordis, "Cruel God or None," 277.

185. Gordis, "Cruel God or None," 277.

186. Gordis, "Cruel God or None," 279.

187. Gordis, "Cruel God or None," 279.

188. Gordis, "Cruel God or None," 284.

189. Gordis, "Cruel God or None," 283.

190. Levinas, *Collected Philosophical Papers*, 127.

191. Levinas, "Useless Suffering," in Katz, Biderman, and Greenberg, *Wrestling with God*, 452. The original French essay was written in 1982. The English translation is that of Richard Cohen in Bernasconi and Wood, *Provocation of Levinas*, 156–67.

192. Levinas, "Useless Suffering," in Katz, Biderman, and Greenberg, *Wrestling with God*, 452.

193. Levinas, "Useless Suffering," in Katz, Biderman, and Greenberg, *Wrestling with God*, 453.

194. Levinas, "Useless Suffering," in Katz, Biderman, and Greenberg, *Wrestling with God*, 454.

195. Spargo, *Vigilant Memory*, 46.

196. Levinas, "Useless Suffering," in Katz, Biderman, and Greenberg, *Wrestling with God*, 454.

197. The beginning and end of Sacks's revised draft lecture at Yad Vashem, 1986.

198. Reproduced as "The Valley of the Shadow" in Katz, Biderman, and Greenberg, *Wrestling with God*, 674–80.

199. Sacks, "The Valley of the Shadow," in Katz, Biderman, and Greenberg, *Wrestling with God*, 674.

200. Sacks, "The Valley of the Shadow," in Katz, Biderman, and Greenberg, *Wrestling with God*, 676.

201. Sacks, "The Valley of the Shadow," in Katz, Biderman, and Greenberg, *Wrestling with God*, 679–80.

202. Wiesel's Nobel Peace Prize acceptance speech, 1986, and Toronto speech, 1987.

203. Reprinted in Morgan, *Holocaust Reader*, 67–77.

204. Wiesel, "A Plea for the Dead," in Morgan, *Holocaust Reader*, 70.

205. Wiesel, "A Plea for the Dead," in Morgan, *Holocaust Reader*, 75.

206. Morgan, *Holocaust Reader*, 77.

207. Wiesel, "A Plea for the Dead," in Katz, Biderman, and Greenberg, *Wrestling with God*, 683.

CONCLUSION

1. Babylonian Talmud, *Ḥullin* 7a.

2. Jonas, "The Concept of God after Auschwitz," in Katz, Biderman, and Greenberg, *Wrestling with God*, 628.

3. Jacobs, *Principles of the Jewish Faith*, 90.

4. McTaggart, *Some Dogmas of Religion*, 209–10.

5. Jacobs, *Principles of the Jewish Faith*, 91.

6. Jacobs, *Principles of the Jewish Faith*, 92.

7. See Mackie, "Evil and Omnipotence," 209.

BIBLIOGRAPHY

Abarbanel, Isaac. *Commentary on the Torah*. B'nei Arbel: Jerusalem, 1964.

Albo, Joseph. *Sefer ha-Ikkarim* [Book of essential principles]. Warsaw: n.p., 1877.

Alexander, Samuel. *Space, Time, and Deity*. Vol. 2. New York: Dover, 1966.

Alfasi, Isaac. *Torat ha-Hassidut* [The teaching of Hasidism]. Vol. 3. Jerusalem: Mosad Harav Kook, 2006.

Altschuler, David. *Metzudat David* [David's fortress]. Livorno: n.p., 1753.

Angel, Mark. *Voices in Exile: A Study in Sephardic Intellectual History*. Hoboken NJ: Ktav, 1991.

Arendt, Hannah. *Eichmann in Jerusalem: A Report on the Banality of Evil*. New York: Penguin, 1964.

———. *Hannah Arendt: Essays in Understanding, 1930–1954*. New York: Schocken, 2005.

Ariel, David S. *What Do Jews Believe?* New York: Schocken, 1995.

Aristotle. *Physics*. Oxford: Clarendon, 1960.

Augustine. *City of God*. Translated by Marcus Dods. New York: Modern Library, 1950.

Baḥya ibn Pakuda. *Duties of the Heart*. Translated by Moses Hyamson. New York: Feldheim, 1978.

———. *Duties of the Heart*. Translated by Yaakov Feldman. Northvale NJ: Jason Aronson, 1996.

Bauer, Yehudah. *Rethinking the Holocaust*. New Haven: Yale University Press, 2001.

Berger, I. *Esser Orot* [Ten lights]. Warsaw: n.p., 1913.

Berkovits, Eliezer. *Faith after the Holocaust*. New York: Ktav, 1973.

Berlin, Adele, and Marc Zvi Brettler, eds. *The Jewish Study Bible*. New York: Oxford University Press, 1999.

Berman, Nathaniel. *The "Other Side" of Kabbalah: Divine and Demonic in the Zohar and Kabbalistic Tradition*. Leiden: Brill, 2018.

Bernasconi, Robert, and David Wood, eds. *The Provocation of Levinas: Rethinking the Other*. London: Routledge, 1988.

Bickerman, Elias. *Four Strange Books of the Bible*. New York: Schocken, 1984.

Blackburn, Simon. *Being Good*. Oxford: Oxford Paperbacks, 2002.

Blau, Joseph. *Modern Varieties of Judaism*. New York: Columbia University Press, 1966.

Blech, Benjamin. *If God Is Good Why Is the World So Bad?* Deerfield Beach FL: Simcha Press, 2003.

Bloch, Chaim. *Priester der Liebe* [The priest of love]. Vienna: n.p., 1930.

Borowitz, Eugene B. "The Autonomous Self and the Commanding Community." *Theological Studies* 45 (1984): 34–56.

———. *How Can a Jew Speak of Faith Today?* Philadelphia: Westminster Press, 1969.

———. *The Masks Jews Wear*. New York: Simon and Schuster, 1973.

———. *A New Jewish Theology in the Making*. Philadelphia: Westminster Press, 1968.

Boyarin, Daniel. *Carnal Israel*. Berkeley: University of California Press, 1993.

Braiterman, Zachary. *God after Auschwitz: Tradition and Change in Post-Holocaust Thought*. Princeton NJ: Princeton University Press, 1999.

———. "Hitler's Accomplice? The Tragic Theology of Richard Rubenstein." *Modern Judaism* 17, no. 1 (February 1997): 75–89.

Brandon, Samuel George Frederick. *Man and His Destiny in the Great Religions*. Manchester: Manchester University Press, 1963.

———. *The Judgment of the Dead: An Historical and Comparative Study of the Idea of Post-Mortem Judgment in the Major Religions*. London: Weidenfeld and Nicolson, 1967.

Branson, Roy. "The Individual and the Commune: A Critique of Martin Buber's Social Philosophy." *Judaism* 24, no. 1 (Winter 1975): 82–96.

Bremmer, Jan N. *The Early Greek Concept of the Soul*. Princeton NJ: Princeton University Press, 1983.

———. *The Rise and Fall of the Afterlife*. London: Routledge, 2009.

Breslov, Naḥman. *Kitzur Likutey Moharan*. Edited by Yakov Gabel. Jerusalem: Breslov Research Institute, 2009.

———. *Likutei Moharan*. Edited and collected by Rabbi Natan of Nemirov. Ostroh: n.p., 1808.

Breuer, Edward, and David Sorkin, trans. *Moses Mendelssohn's Hebrew Writings*. New Haven: Yale University Press, 2018.

Buber, Martin. *Between Man and Man*. Translated by Ronald Gregor Smith. New York: Macmillan, 1967.

———. *Eclipse of God: Studies in the Relation Between Religion and Philosophy*. New York: Harper and Row, 1957.

———. *Good and Evil*. New York: Charles Scribner's Sons, 1953.

———. *I and Thou*. Translated and edited by Walter Kaufmann. New York: Charles Scribner's Sons, 1970.

———. *Tales of the Hasidim*. Vol. 2. New York: Schocken, 1947.

Carmy, Shalom, and David Shatz. "The Bible as a Source of Philosophical Reflection." In *History of Jewish Philosophy*, edited by Daniel Frank and Oliver Leaman, 13–25. London: Routledge, 1977.

Christ, Carol P., and Judith Plaskow. *Goddess and God in the World*. Minneapolis: Fortress Press, 2016.

Cohen, Abraham, and V. Reichert. "Ecclesiastes." In *The Five Megilloth*. London: Soncino Press, 1984.

Cohen, Arthur. *The Tremendum: A Theological Interpretation of the Holocaust*. New York: Continuum, 1981.

Cohen, Hermann. *Religion of Reason Out of the Sources of Judaism*. Translated by Simon Kaplan. Oxford: Oxford University Press, 1972.

Corrington, Robert S. "My Passage from Panentheism to Pantheism." *American Journal of Philosophy and Theology* 23, no. 2 (May 2002): 129–53.

Dan, Joseph. *The Early Kabbalah*. Mahwah NJ: Paulist Press, 1986.

———. *Gershom Scholem and the Mystical Dimension of Jewish History*. New York: New York University Press, 1988.

———. "Samael, Lilith, and the Concept of Evil in Early Kabbalah." *AJS Review* 5 (1980): 17–40.

Dinur, Benzion. "The Origins of Hasidism and Its Social and Messianic Foundations." In *Essential Papers on Hasidism*, edited by Gershon David Hundert, 86–277. New York: New York University Press, 1991.

Donat, Alexander. *Voices from the Ashes*. N.p., n.d.

Dubnow, Simon. *Toldot ha-Hasidut* [*History of Hasidism*]. Tel Aviv: n.p., 1930. Reprinted in English as *History of Hasidism*. Tel Aviv: n.p., 1960.

Edels, Samuel. *Hiddushei Maharsha*. Lublin: n.p., 1672.

Edwards, Paul. *The Encyclopedia of Philosophy*. 8 vols. New York: Macmillan and Free Press, 1967.

Ehrenreich, Shlomo Zalman. *Derashot Leḥem Shelomoh*. Brooklyn: n.p., 1976.

Elman, Yaakov. "The Suffering of the Righteous in Palestinian and Babylonian Sources." *Jewish Quarterly Review* 80, no. 3/4 (January–April 1990): 315–39.

Elwes, R. H. M. *The Chief Works of Spinoza*. New York: Dover, 1951.

Ettinger, Elzbieta. *Hannah Arendt, Martin Heidegger*. New Haven: Yale University Press, 1995.

Fackenheim, Emil. *God's Presence in History*. New York: New York University Press, 1970.

———. *The Jewish Bible after the Holocaust: A Re-reading*. Bloomington: Indiana University Press, 1990.

————. *To Mend the World: Foundations of Post-Holocaust Jewish Thought*. Bloomington: Indiana University Press, 1994.

Fishbane, Michael. *Text and Texture*. New York: Schocken, 1979.

Formstecher, Salomon. *Religion of the Spirit*. Frankfort am Main: n.p., 1841.

Fox, Marvin. *Interpreting Maimonides*. Chicago: University of Chicago Press, 1990.

Fox, Michael V. *A Time to Tear Down and a Time to Build Up: A Rereading of Ecclesiastes*. Eugene OR: Wipf and Stock, 2010.

Frank, Daniel H., and Oliver Leaman, eds. *History of Jewish Philosophy*. 2 vols. New York: Routledge, 1997.

————. *History of Philosophy*. New York: Routledge, 1997.

Friedensohn, Moshe. "Harab Reb Yehezkel Halevi Halstuk, Ha'admor Me'ostrowze." In *Eleh Ezkerah* (These I remember), vol. 4, edited by Isaac Levin. New York: Institute for Research of Orthodox Jewry, 1961.

Friedman, Maurice S. "The Nature of Evil." In *Martin Buber: The Life of Dialogue*, edited by Maurice Friedman, 101–12. Chicago: University of Chicago Press, 1976.

Friedman, Richard E. *Commentary on the Torah*. San Francisco: HarperSanFrancisco, 2001.

Garber, Zev, and Bruce Zuckerman. "Why Do We Call the Holocaust 'The Holocaust'? An Inquiry into the Psychology of Labels." *Modern Judaism* 9, no. 2 (1989): 197–211.

Garfinkel, Stephen. "Qoheleth: The Philosopher Means Business." In *Bringing the Hidden to Light: The Process of Interpretation; Studies in Honor of Stephen Geller*, edited by Kathryn Frakes Kravitz and Diane M. Sharon, 51–62. Winona Lake IN: Eisenbrauns, 2007.

Geertz, Clifford. "Religion as a Cultural System." In *The Interpretation of Cultures*, 87–125. New York: Basic Books, 2017.

Gelernter, David Hillel. *Judaism: A Way of Being*. New Haven: Yale University Press, 2009.

Gelman, Ezra. *Essays on the Thought and Philosophy of Rav Kook*. Teaneck NJ: Farleigh Dickinson University Press, 1991.

Gersonides. *The Wars of The Lord*. Translated by Seymour Feldman. Vol. 2. New York: The Jewish Publication Society, 1987.

Gillman, Neil. *The Death of Death*. Woodstock VT: Jewish Lights, 1996.

————. *Doing Jewish Theology*. Woodstock VT: Jewish Lights, 2010.

————. *Sacred Fragments: Recovering Theology for the Modern Jew*. Philadelphia: The Jewish Publication Society, 1990.

Ginzberg, Louis. *An Unknown Jewish Sect*. New York: Jewish Theological Seminary of America, 1976.

Glatzer, Nahum N. *The Essential Philo*. New York: Schocken, 1971.

Goldhagen, Daniel. *Hitler's Willing Executioners: Ordinary Germans and the Holocaust*. New York: Knopf Doubleday, 1996.

Goldsmith, Emanuel S., and Mel Scult. *The American Judaism of Mordecai Kaplan*. New York: New York University Press, 1990.

Goodspeed, Edgar J., trans. *The Apocrypha: An American Translation*. New York: Vintage, 1959.

Gordis, Robert. "A Cruel God or None—Is There No Other Choice?" *Judaism* 21, no. 3 (Summer 1972): 277–84.

———. *Judaic Ethics for a Lawless World*. New York: Ktav, 1986.

———. "The Knowledge of Good and Evil in the Old Testament and the Qumran Scrolls." *Journal of Biblical Literature* 76 (1957): 123–38.

———. *Koheleth—The Man and His World: A Study of Ecclesiastes*. New York: Schocken, 1971.

Green, Arthur. Introduction to *The Zohar*, edited by Daniel Matt, vol. 1, xxxi–lxxxi. Stanford CA: Stanford University Press, 2004.

Greenberg, Irving. "Cloud of Smoke, Pillar of Fire: Judaism, Christianity and Modernity after the Holocaust." In *Auschwitz: Beginning of a New Era? Reflections on the Holocaust: Papers on the Holocaust, Held at the Cathedral of Saint John the Divine, New York City, June 3 to 6, 1974*, edited by Eva Fleischner, 7–55. New York: Ktav, 1977.

Greenberg, Moshe. "Job." In *The Literary Guide to the Bible*, edited by Robert Alter and Frank Kermode, 283–304. New York: Modern Language Studies, 1989.

Greene, Jayson. *Once More We Saw Stars*. New York: Knopf, 2019.

Gutman, Israel, Chaim Schatzker, Yitzchak Mais, and Irit Sivan. *The Holocaust and Its Significance*. Jerusalem: Zalman Shazar Center, 1984.

Habermas, Jürgen. "Modernity—An Incomplete Project." In *Postmodern Culture*, edited by Hal Foster, 3–15. London: Pluto Press, 1985.

Halbertal, Moshe. *Maimonides: Life and Thought*. Translated by Joel Linsider. Princeton NJ: Princeton University Press, 2014.

Halevi, Yehudah. *Kuzari*. New York: Schocken, 1964.

Halivni, David Weiss, and Peter Ochs. *Breaking the Tablets*. Lanham MD: Rowman and Littlefield, 2007.

Hallamish, Moshe. "The Teachings of Rabbi Menahem Mendel of Vitebsk." In *Hasidism Reappraised*, edited by Ada Rapoport-Albert, 268–87. London: Littman Library of Jewish Civilization, 1997.

Hammer, Reuven, trans. *Sifre: A Tannaitic Commentary on the Book of Deuteronomy*. New Haven: Yale University Press, 1986.

Hazony, David. *Human Responsibility in the Thought of Eliezer Berkovits*. PhD diss., Hebrew University of Jerusalem, 2011.

Hegel, George Friedrich Wilhelm. *Lectures on the History of Philosophy*. Vol. 3, edited by E. S. Haldane. London: Routledge and Keegan, 1955.

Heidel, Alexander. *The Babylonian Genesis: The Story of Creation*. Chicago: University of Chicago Press, 1963.

Hensel, Sebastian. *The Mendelssohn Family (1729–1847)*. New York: Greenwood Press, 1968.

Herschenhorn and Strassberg. *Or Zaddikim* [The light of the righteous]. Lublin: n.p., 1927.

Heschel, Abraham Joshua. *Israel: An Echo of Eternity*. New York: Farrar, Straus, and Giroux, 1969.

———. *Maimonides: A Biography*. New York: Farrar Straus Giroux, 1982.

———. *Man Is Not Alone*. New York: Octagon, 1972.

———. *A Passion for Truth*. New York: Farrar, Straus, Giroux, 1973.

Hick, John. *Philosophy of Religion*. Englewood Cliffs NJ: Prentice-Hall, 1963.

Hirsch, Samson Raphael. *Commentary on the Torah*. 7 vols. New York: Judaica Press, 1989.

Hume, David. *Dialogues concerning Natural Religion*. Edited by Richard H. Popkin. Indianapolis: Hackett, 1987.

Husik, Isaac. *A History of Medieval Jewish Philosophy*. New York: Atheneum, 1969.

Hyman, Aaron. *Toldoth Tannaim, ve-Amoraim* [History of the *tannaim* and *amoraim*]. 3 vols. Jerusalem: Boys Town, 1964.

Idel, Moshe. *Hasidism: Between Ecstasy and Magic*. New York: SUNY Press, 1995.

Jacobs, Louis. *Hasidic Thought*. New York: Behrman House, 1976.

———. *The Jewish Religion*. Oxford: Oxford University Press, 1995.

———. *Principles of the Jewish Faith*. New York: Basic Books, 1964.

Johnson, Paul. *Modern Times*. New York: Harper and Row, 1983.

Jonas, Hans. "The Concept of God after Auschwitz: A Jewish Voice." *Journal of Religion* 67, no. 1 (January 1987): 1–13.

Jospe, Eva. *Moses Mendelssohn: Selections from His Writings*. New York: Viking, 1975.

Jospe, Raphael, and Dov Schwartz, eds. *Encounters in Modern Jewish Thought: The Works of Eva Jospe*. Vol. 2. Brighton MA: Academic Press, 2013.

Kaplan, Mordecai M. *The Future of the American Jew*. New York: Reconstructionist Press, 1981.

———. *Judaism as a Civilization*. New York: Schocken, 1967.

———. *The Meaning of God in Modern Jewish Religion*. New York: Reconstructionist Press, 1962.

———. *The Meaning of God in Modern Jewish Religion*. Detroit: Wayne State University Press, 1995.

———. *Questions Jews Ask: Reconstructionist Answers*. New York: Reconstructionist Press, 1966.

———, ed. and trans. *The Sabbath Prayer Book*. New York: Reconstructionist Foundation, 1945.

————. "The Supremacy of the Torah." *Students' Annual of the Jewish Theological Seminary*, New York, 1914, 180–92.

————. "What Judaism Is Not." *The Menorah Journal* 1, no. 4 (October 1915): 208–15.

Katz, Steven T. *The Holocaust in Historical Context: The Holocaust and Mass Death before the Modern Age*. Vol. 2. New York: Oxford University Press, 1994.

————. "Mordecai Kaplan's Theology and the Problem of Evil." *Jewish Social Studies*, n.s., 12, no. 2 (Winter 2006): 115–26.

————. *Post-Holocaust Dialogues: Critical Studies in Modern Jewish Thought*. New York: New York University Press, 1983.

————. "Richard Rubenstein, the God of History, and the Logic of Judaism." *Journal of the American Academy of Religion* 46, no. 3 (1978): 313–50.

Katz, Steven T., Shlomo Biderman, and Gershon Greenberg, eds. *Wrestling with God*. New York: Oxford University Press, 2007.

Kavka, Martin. "Judaism and Theology in Martha Nussbaum's Ethics." *Journal of Religion and Ethics* 31, no. 2 (Summer 2003): 343–59.

Kegley, Charles. "Martin Buber's Ethics and the Problem of Norms." *Religious Studies* 5, no. 2 (December 1969): 181–94.

Kellner, Menachem. *Must a Jew Believe Anything?* Oxford: Littman Library of Jewish Civilization, 2006.

Kimḥi, David. *Commentary on the Torah*. Pressburg: n.p., 1842.

Kobrin, Moshe. *Or Yesharim*. Brest-Litovsk: n.p., n.d.

Kook, Abraham Isaac. *Arpilei Tohar*. Jaffa: A. Ittin, 1914.

————. *Mo'adei Hara'ayah*. Jerusalem: n.p., n.d.

————. *Orot ha-Kodesh* [Holy lights]. Edited by David Cohen. 4 vols. Jerusalem: Mosad Harav Kook, 1964.

————. *Orot ha-Tehiyah* [The lights of renaissance]. In *Orot*, edited by Naor Bezalel. Jerusalem: Koren, 2014.

Korman, Gerd. "The Holocaust in Historical Writing," *Societas* 2, no. 3 (1972): 251–70.

Kushner, Harold. *When Bad Things Happen to Good People*. New York: Schocken, 1981.

Lacquer, Walter. *The Terrible Secret: Suppression of the Truth about Hitler's Final Solution*. Boston: Little, Brown, 1980.

Laenen, J. H. *Jewish Mysticism: An Introduction*. Louisville: Westminster John Knox Press, 2001.

Lamm, Norman. *The Religious Thought of Hasidism*. New York: Yeshiva University Press, 1999.

Leaman, Oliver. *Evil and Suffering in Jewish Philosophy*. Cambridge: Cambridge University Press, 1995.

Levinas, Emmanuel. *Collected Philosophical Papers*. Pittsburgh: Duquesne University Press, 1998.

———. "Useless Suffering." In *Entre Nous: Thinking-of-the-Other*, translated by Michael B. Smith and Barbara Harshav, 91–102. New York: Columbia University Press, 1998.

Levenson, Jon D. *Creation and the Persistence of Evil*. San Francisco: Harper and Row, 1988.

Lewy, Hans, Alexander Altmann, and Isaak Heinemann, eds. *Three Jewish Philosophers*. New York: Atheneum, 1969.

Lieberman, Saul. *Tosefta Kifshuta*. 15 vols. New York: Jewish Theological Seminary of America, 1967–93.

Lizensk, Elimelekh. *No'am Elimelekh* [The pleasantries of Elimelekh]. Warsaw: n.p., 1881.

Luzzatto, Moses Hayyim. *Derekh ha-Shem: The Way of God*. Translated by Aryeh Kaplan. Jerusalem and New York: Feldheim, 1997.

Mackie, John L. "Evil and Omnipotence." *Mind* 64, no. 254 (April 1955): 200–210.

Magid, Shaul. "From Theosophy to Midrash: Lurianic Exegesis and the Garden of Eden." *AJS Review* 22, no. 1 (1997): 37–75.

Maimonides, Moses. *The Guide of the Perplexed*. Edited by Shlomo Pines. 2 vols. Chicago: University of Chicago Press, 1963.

———. *Mishneh Torah*. Vol. 16. Jerusalem: S. Frankel, 2001.

———. *Mishneh Torah*. Edited by Philip Birnbaum. New York: Hebrew Publishing, 1967.

———. *Mishneh Torah*. Translated by Moses Hyamson. New York: Feldheim, 1971.

Malbim, Meir Leibush. *Commentary on the Bible*. Vol. 15. New York: M. P. Press, 1974.

Manoah, Hezekiah. *Sefer Hizkuni*. Cremona: n.p., 1559.

McTaggart, John McTaggart Ellis. *Some Dogmas of Religion*. London: E. Arnold, 1906.

Meiri, Menahem. *Beit ha-Behirah*. Vol. 14. Jerusalem: Shevi'it, 1974.

Mitchell, Stephen. *The Book of Job*. New York: Harper Perennial, 1987.

Mittleman, Alan. "Judaism and Postmodernity." *First Things*, February 1993. www.firstthings.com/article/1993/02/001-judaism-and-postmodernity.

Monter, E. William. *Frontiers of Heresy*. Cambridge: Cambridge University Press, 1990.

Morgan, Michael L. *A Holocaust Reader: Responses to the Nazi Extermination*. New York: Oxford University Press, 2001.

Mullins, R. T. "The Difficulty with Demarcating Panentheism." *Sophia* 55 (2016): 325–46.

Nadler, Steven. "Baruch Spinoza." Stanford Encyclopedia of Philosophy, edited by Edward N. Zalta, Spring 2019. https://plato.stanford.edu/archives/spr2019/entries/c/.

———. *The Best of All Possible Worlds*. New York: Farrar Straus Giroux, 2008.

Nahmanides. *Biur* [Commentary] on the Torah. Lisbon: n.p., 1489.

———. *Commentary on the Torah*. Translated by Charles B. Chavel. Vol. 5. New York: Shilo, 1971.

Neiman, Susan. *Evil in Modern Thought*. Princeton NJ: Princeton University Press, 2015.

Neusner, Jacob, Alan Avery-Peck, and William Scott Green, eds. *Encyclopedia of Juda-ism*. Vol. 3. Leiden: Brill, 2005.

Newman, Louis I. *The Hasidic Anthology*. New York: Bloch, 1944.

Nigal, Gedaliah. "New Light on the Hasidic Tale and Its Sources." In *Hasidism Reap-praised*, edited by Ada Rapoport-Albert, 345–53. London: Littman, 1997.

Novak, David. *Natural Law in Judaism*. Cambridge: Cambridge University Press, 2008.

Noveck, Simon. *Great Jewish Thinkers of the Twentieth Century*. Washington: Bnai Brith Department of Adult Jewish Education, 1969.

Nussbaum, Martha. "Love's Knowledge." In *Love's Knowledge: Essay on Philosophy and Literature*, 261–85. Oxford: Oxford University Press, 1992.

———. "Martha Nussbaum on Separating Church and State: Interview with Bill Moyers." *Bill Moyers*, April 18, 2008. http://billmoyers.com/content/ Martha-nussbaum-on-separating-church-and-state/.

———. "Tragedy and Justice," *Boston Review* 28, no. 5 (October 1, 2003). http://bos-tonreview.net/books-ideas/martha-c-nussbaum-tragedy-and-justice.

Oz, Amos. "The Meaning of Homeland." *New Outlook* 31, no. 1, (1988): 19–25. Reprinted in Nitza Ben-Dov, ed. *The Amos Oz Reader*, 235–52. New York: Houghton Mifflin Harcourt, 2009.

Pereira, Vera, Luís Faísca, and Rodrigo de Sá-saraiva . "Immortality of the Soul as an Intuitive Idea: Towards a Psychological Explanation of the Origins of Afterlife Beliefs." In *Journal of Cognition and Culture* 12, no. 1–2 (2012): 101–27.

Piekarz, Medel. *Ideological of Trends of Hasidism in Poland during the Interwar Years and the Holocaust*. Jerusalem: Bialik Institute, 1990.

Pinches, Charles. "Friendship and Tragedy: The Fragilities of Goodness." *First Things*, May 1990. https://www.firstthings.com/article/1990/05/ friendship-and-tragedy-the-fragilities-of-goodness.

Plato. *Complete Works*. Edited by John M. Cooper. Indianapolis: Hackett, 1997.

Polnoye, Jacob Joseph. *Tsafenat Pane'ah* [Revealer of secrets]. Koretz: n.p., 1782.

Pritchard, James, ed. *The Ancient Near East: An Anthology of Texts and Pictures*. Princeton NJ: Princeton University Press, 1958.

Raphael, Simcha Paull. *Jewish Views of the Afterlife*. Northvale NJ: Jason Aronson, 1996.

Reed, Kathryn, "15 Questions with Rebecca N. Goldstein." *Harvard Crimson*, February 11, 2010. www.thecrimson.com/article/2010/2/11/very-fm-think/.

Robinson, John M. *An Introduction to Early Greek Philosophy*. Boston: Houghton Mif-flin, 1968.

Rokeah, Shalom. *Dover Shalom* [Speaker of peace]. Pshemishl: n.p., 1910.

———. *Or Shalom* [Light of peace]. B'nei Brak: n.p., n.d.

Roskies, David. *Against the Apocalypse*. Cambridge MA: Harvard University Press, 1984.

Rubenstein, Richard. *After Auschwitz: Radical Theology and Contemporary Judaism*. New York: Bobbs-Merrill, 1966.

Rudavsky, David. *Modern Jewish Religious Movements*. New York: Behrman House, 1979.

Runes, Dagobert, D., ed. *Dictionary of Philosophy*. New York: Philosophical Library, 1950.

———. *Spinoza Dictionary*. New York: Philosophical Library, 1951.

Russell, David Syme. *The Method and Message of Jewish Apocalyptic: 200 BC–AD 100*. London: SCM Press, 1964.

Russell, Jeffrey B. *The Devil: Perceptions of Evil from Antiquity to Primitive Christianity*. Ithaca: Cornell University Press, 1977.

Russell, Lucy. *Teaching the Holocaust in School History: Teachers or Preachers?* New York: Continuum, 2006.

Saadia Gaon. *The Book of Beliefs and Opinions*. Translated by Samuel Rosenblatt. New Haven: Yale University Press, 1942.

Sacks, Jonathan. *Not in God's Name*. New York: Schocken, 2017.

Safran, Bezalel, ed. *Hasidism: Continuity or Innovation?* Cambridge MA: Harvard University Press, 1988.

Sandmel, Samuel. *Philo of Alexandria*. Oxford: Oxford University Press, 1979.

Sarna, Nahum M. *The JPS Torah Commentary: Genesis*. Philadelphia: The Jewish Publication Society, 1989.

———. *The JPS Torah Commentary: Exodus*. Philadelphia: The Jewish Publication Society, 1991.

———. *Understanding Genesis*. New York: Schocken, 1972.

Sassover, Moshe Leib. *Hemdah Genuzah*. Beigeleisen, n.d.

Schatz, Morris. *Ethics of the Fathers in the Light of Jewish History*. New York: Bloch, 1970.

Scheindlin, Raymond P. *The Book of Job*. New York: W. W. Norton, 1998.

Schenck, Kenneth. *A Brief Guide to Philo*. Louisville KY: Westminster John Knox Press, 2005.

Schindler, Pesach. "Suffering and Evil." In *Hasidic Responses to the Holocaust in the Light of Hasidic Thought*, 19–28. Northvale NJ: Ktav, 1990.

Schneerson, Menachem M. *Mada ve-Emunah* [Science and faith]. Kfar Chabad: Machon Lubavitch, 1980.

Scholem, Gershom. *Kabbalah*. New York: Quadrangle, 1974.

———. *Major Trends in Jewish Mysticism*. New York: Schocken, 1954.

———. "Tradition and New Creation in the Ritual of the Kabbalists." In *On the Kabbalah and Its Symbolism*, 118–57. New York: Schocken, 1996.

Schulweis, Harold. "A Critical Assessment of Kaplan's Ideas of Salvation." In *The American Judaism of Mordecai M. Kaplan*, edited by Emanuel S. Goldsmith, Mel Scult, and Robert M. Seltzer, 257–70. New York: New York University Press, 1992.

Schweid, Eliezer. *The Classic Jewish Philosophers*. Leiden: Brill, 2008.

Scult, Mel. "Kaplan's Re-interpretation of the Bible." In *The American Judaism of Mordecai M. Kaplan*, edited by Emanuel S. Goldsmith, Mel Scult, and Robert M. Seltzer, 294–318. New York: New York University Press, 1992.

———. *The Radical American Judaism of Mordecai Kaplan*. Indianapolis: University of Indiana Press, 2015.

Seeskin, Kenneth. "The Problem of Jewish Philosophy." In *Jewish Philosophy in a Secular Age*. New York: State University of New York Press, 1987.

Seforno, Ovadiah. *Commentary on the Torah*. Venice: Giovanni Gryphia, 1567.

Shapira, Kalonymus Kalman. *Esh Kodesh* [Holy fire]. Jerusalem: n.p., 1960.

———. *Tzav ve-Zeruz*. Jerusalem: Va'ad Hasidei Piasetzna, 1961/62.

Shapiro, Pinhas. *Nofet Tzufim*. Warsaw: n.p., 1929.

Shem Tov, Israel. *BESHT al ha-Torah*. Jerusalem: Machon Nofet Tzufim, 2012.

———. *Keter Shem Tov*. Brooklyn: Kehot, 2016.

Sherwin, Byron. *Kabbalah: An Introduction to Jewish Mysticism*. Lanham MD: Rowman and Littlefield, 2006.

Spargo, R. Clifton. *Vigilant Memory: Emmanuel Levinas, the Holocaust, and the Unjust Death*. Baltimore: John Hopkins University Press, 2006.

Speiser, Ephraim A. *Genesis*. New York: Doubleday, 1964.

Sperling, Harry, Maurice Simon, and Paul Philip Levertoff, trans. *The Zohar*. London: Soncino Press, 1970.

Spero, Shubert. *Morality, Halakhah and the Jewish Tradition*. New York: Ktav, 1983.

Spinoza, Benedict. *The Chief Works of Benedict de Spinoza: A Theologico-Political Treatise*. Translated by R. H. M. Elwes. New York: Dover Publications, 1951.

———. *The Collected Works of Spinoza*. Edited and translated by Edwin Curley. Princeton NJ: Princeton University Press, 1985.

Stone, M. E. *Scripture, Sects, and Visions: A Profile of Judaism from Ezra to the Jewish Revolts*. Eugene OR: Wipf and Stock, 2005.

Strauss, Leo. "How to Begin to Study *The Guide of the Perplexed*." In Maimonides, *The Guide of the Perplexed*, edited by Shlomo Pines, xi–lvi. Chicago: University of Chicago Press, 1963.

———. "The Literary Character of *The Guide of the Perplexed*." In *Essays on Maimonides*, edited by Salo Baron, 37–91. New York: Columbia University Press, 1941.

Styron, William. "Auschwitz." In *This Quiet Dust and Other Writings*, 336–39. New York: Vintage, 1982.

Styron, William, and James L. West. *Conversations with William Styron*. Jackson: University Press of Mississippi, 1985.

Tal, Uriel. "Excursus on the Term *Shoah*." *Shoah: A Review of Holocaust Studies and Commemorations* 1, no. 4 (1979): 10–11.

Teikhtal. *Em ha-Banim Semehah* [The mother of sons rejoices]. Edited and translated by Pesach Schindler as *Restoration of Zion as a Response during the Holocaust*. Hoboken NJ: Ktav, 1999.

Teitelbaum, Yoel. *Va-Yo'el Moshe*. New York: n.p., 1961.

Trachtenberg, Joshua. *Jewish Magic and Superstition: A Study in Folk Religion*. New York: Behrman House, 1939.

Tsimerman, Hayyim Yisrael. *Tamim Pa'alo* (His work is perfect: Responsa concerning the terrible destruction of six million Jews, may God avenge their blood). Jerusalem: n.p., 1947.

Urbach, Ephraim E. *The Sages*. Cambridge MA: Harvard University Press, 1979.

Vital, Hayyim. *Sha'ar Hakavanot*. Venice: n.p., 1624.

Vitebsk, Menahem Mendl. *Likutei Amarim* [Collected sayings]. Lemberg: n.p., 1911.

———. *Pri Ha'aretz*. Kapust: n.p., 1814.

Weinberg, Julius R. *A Short History of Medieval Philosophy*. Princeton NJ: Princeton University Press, 1964.

Westcott, William Wynn, trans. *Sefer Yetzirah: The Book of Creation*. Calgary: Theophania Publishing, 1991.

Whitehead, Alfred North. *Science and the Modern World*. New York: New American Library, 1962.

Wiesel, Elie. "Some Questions That Remain Open." In *Comprehending the Holocaust: Historical and Literary Research*, edited by Asher Cohen, Yoav Gelber, and Charlotte Wardi. Frankfurt am Main: Peter Lang, 1988.

Wise, Michael, Martin Abegg Jr., and Edward Cook. *The Dead Sea Scrolls: A New Translation*. San Francisco: HarperCollins, 1996.

Wolf, A., ed. and trans. *Spinoza's Short Treatise on God, Man, and His Well-Being*. New York: Russell and Russell, 1963.

Wolfson, Harry A. *Philo: Foundations of Religious Philosophy in Judaism, Christianity, and Islam*. Cambridge MA: Harvard University Press, 1947.

Ya'avetz, Yosef. *Ḥasdei ha-Shem*, 30–37. In *Kol Sifrei Rav Yosef Ya'avetz*, vol. 2. Jerusalem: n.p., 1934.

Young, James. *Writing and Rewriting the Holocaust: Narrative Consequences of Interpretation*. Indianapolis: Indiana University Press, 1988.

GENERAL INDEX

Aaron of Nicomedia, 123

Abarbanel, Isaac, 335n30, 338n33, 339n54

Abel, 2, 10, 11, 12, 13, 342

Abraham, 2, 4, 11, 13–15, 43, 50, 52, 57, 64, 79, 80, 81, 88, 141, 148, 283, 323, 335n30, 335n41, 339n61

Abraham Yitzhak of Sadagorda, 188, 327

Adam, 8, 50, 52, 120, 127, 151, 167, 169, 182–84, 203, 204, 219–20, 308, 325, 331, 337, 342

Adam Kadmon, 168

afterlife, 62, 104, 143, 163, 221, 326, 333(intro)n1; biblical hints of, 77; Gillman on, 255; Kaplan on, 242; Kushner on, 259, 260, 263; Luzzatto on, 210, 354n45; Maimonides on, 126–27, 144; Mendelssohn on, 221–22, 224; origins of concept, 76, 90; Rabbinic views, 62, 74–77, 338n37; reward and punishment, 75, 90, 126–27, 139, 143, 144, 163, 165, 170, 210; Sa'adiah on, 107–9, 144; Zohar on, 163, 165, 170

Akkadian, 6, 12

Albo, Joseph, xx, 139–42, 144, 326, 347n124

Alexander, Samuel, xix, xxi, 230–32, 271

Alfasi, Isaac, xix

Alpafonias, 151–52

Altschuler, David, 42

Angel, Marc, 347n127

angels, 7, 51, 91, 96–98, 119, 138, 147, 150, 160, 324, 335n29, 345n63

antisemitism, 228, 297

apocrypha, xvii, xx, 1, 2, 50–56, 57, 58

Arendt, Hannah, xviii, xxi, xxv, 245–47

Ariel, David S., 44

Aristotle, 115, 123, 216, 344n36

Asmodeus, 151–52

assimilation, 285, 292, 293, 322

astral influence, 72–74, 104, 324

atzilut, 149

Augustine, 216, 354n58

Auschwitz, 284, 308, 333n12, 365n126; as a generic description of the Holocaust, 276, 290, 291, 295, 296, 297, 298, 302–5, 307, 312–14, 317, 318; as a theological problem, 248, 249, 319–20 autonomy, 248, 251–52

Ba'al Shem Tov, Israel, xx, 172, 268, 325, 326, 327

Baḥya, xx, 111–14, 143, 144, 258, 324, 327

banality of evil, 247

Barukh of Medzhybyzh, 175, 325

baseball, 10

Batnitzky, Leora, 235

Bauer, Yehudah, 190, 352n49

Berditchev, Levi Isaac, 174–75, 325

Berkovits, Eliezer, 280, 289–91, 292, 294, 295, 304, 321, 325, 364n110

Berlin, Adele, 335n40

Berlin, Naftali Tzvi Yehudah, 239

Berman, Nathaniel, 350n57

Bickerman, Elias, 47

binding of Isaac, 2, 13–15

Birnbaum, Philip, 345n58

Blackburn, Simon, xxiv

Blau, Joseph, 225

Borowitz, Eugene, 248–52, 271, 272, 325, 327, 358n122

Boyarin, Daniel, 92, 340n88, 341n102

Braiterman, Zachary, 364n117

Brandwein, Yehudah Tzvi, 185

Branson, Roy, 239

breaking of the vessels, 168

Bremmer, Jan N., 76

Brettler, Marc Zvi, 4, 335n40

Buber, Martin, xix, xxi, 232–38, 239, 271, 300, 326

Buddhism, xxiv

Cain, 2, 10–13, 33, 53, 56

Charles, Robert H., 54

Chmelniecki, 171, 277, 291

Christ, Carol P., 266

Christianity, xxv, 52, 90, 95, 99, 100, 212, 232, 239, 273, 275, 296, 297, 312–14

Cohen, Arthur, 276, 295, 301–2

Cohen, Hermann, xxi, 225–30, 259, 266, 325, 327

correlation, 64, 227–28, 230

Corrington, Robert, 270

cosmogony, 3, 147, 348n10

covenant, 96, 142, 248, 251, 252, 293, 309, 317

creation, 54, 92, 111, 116, 119, 147, 148, 149, 160, 165, 199, 215, 223, 267, 272; as act of God, 168, 216, 255, 302; Biblical epic of, 2, 4, 5, 121, 152, 155, 166, 260; of first woman, 7, 182; in Plaskow, 268, 269; as process, 169; purpose of, in Mendelssohn, 218–19

Crescas, Hasdai, xx, 137–39, 324

Dan, Joseph, 146, 155

Dead Sea Scrolls, xx, 95–99, 324, 339n50, 341n106

death, xxiv, 6, 7, 13, 14, 15, 16, 29, 33, 35, 47, 48, 50, 52, 54, 55, 59, 63, 64, 76, 87, 102, 120, 159, 162, 164, 165, 184, 202, 203, 204, 212, 219, 249, 253, 255, 256, 260, 268, 288, 289, 314, 315, 318, 320, 323, 327, 335n48, 361n22; as benefit, 81, 82–85, 202, 216–17, 265; in Buber, 237; correlation with wickedness, 64, 68–69, 183, 276, 280, 285, 286, 292, 295, 297; of God, 296, 298; in Kaplan, 243; in Mendelssohn, 213, 216–17; as part of life, 68, 124, 160, 219, 243, 303; as solution to problem of disparity of wealth, 28, 29

demons, 98, 147, 151, 340n83

De Vaux, Roland, 341n106

Dinur, Benzion, 350n1

Donat, Alexander, 295, 299–300
Dubnow, Simon, 350n1
dysteleology, 227

Edels, Samuel, 288, 343n9
Eden, garden of, 2, 5, 6, 7, 10, 11, 17, 21, 151, 182, 183–84, 203, 242
Ehrenreich, Shlomo Zalman, 280, 284–89, 292, 293, 294
Eichmann, Adolf, 246–47, 297, 319
Ein Sof, 146–47, 168
Elazar of Worms, 350n57
Elman, Ya'akov, 83, 87
emanations, 148–50, 152, 169, 325
emergentism, 230
Erblich, Moshe Leib of Sassov, 173, 185, 327
Ettinger, Elzbieta, 358n110
Ettinger, Shmuel, 361n22
eupathy, 103
Eve, 120, 127, 151, 167, 169, 220, 325, 331
evil, xvi, xvii, xx, xxi, xxiii, 7, 8, 32, 33, 35, 42, 46, 47, 51, 52, 53, 56, 57, 61, 64, 67, 78, 83, 90, 91, 93, 95, 98, 103, 122, 124, 148, 164, 178, 191, 209, 210, 218, 220, 226, 231, 238, 242, 245, 257, 265, 279, 281, 291, 309, 311, 314, 315, 316, 321, 323, 330, 331, 332, 351n11; allowing for attainment of good, 143, 158, 160, 176–77, 178, 180, 182–84, 289, 324, 326; altruistic, 357n72; ambiguity of, 64–65; as archetypal sin, 242; astral cause of, 134, 324; banality of, 247; cannot come from God, xxiii, xxiv, 89, 99, 101, 116, 123, 134, 138, 147, 149, 177, 187, 189, 216, 271; cannot exist, 122, 178, 325; cause of, in Zohar, 155, 166; confused with good, 18, 160, 325; created by God, 154, 158, 160, 172–73, 222, 269, 324;
as defect of matter, 123, 130, 138, 143, 325; and different meanings of *ra'*, 1–2, 20, 90; discovered by reason, 15, 121; equated with death, 16, 202, 237, 243; equated with good, 173, 177, 178, 193, 325; forces, 172, 193, 324; frequency of word in Bible, 1; gaining the righteous perspective, 181–82; in good, 173–76, 190; in ibn Daud, 115–16; indiscriminate, 86; induces holiness, 178–79, 181; inherited, 134, 135; as illusion, 176, 184, 260, 302, 325, 329; is avoidable, 33, 35, 36; is real, 43, 44, 122, 154, 184; is unavoidable, 53; leads to good, 134, 143, 160, 190, 218, 266, 326; as less frequent than good, 117, 130, 134, 135, 192; logical difficulty with, xxii, 122; Mendelssohn's definition of, 215–16; as mode of thought, 199–201, 223, 353n18; moral, 12, 30, 31, 60, 89, 122, 124, 142, 143, 156, 217, 219, 220, 224, 245, 247, 250, 253, 304, 308, 345n63; natural, 24, 32, 75, 86, 122–24, 136, 142, 202, 217, 231, 239, 244, 245, 341n105; ontology of, in Philo, 99–101; origin of, 103, 149–50, 151, 155, 167, 168, 169, 172, 193, 236; overcoming, 113, 153, 154, 160, 169, 180, 206, 218, 265, 266, 325; as part of human nature, 250; as part of universe, xxiv, 90, 139, 152, 155, 159, 167, 169, 198, 206, 215, 217, 218, 223, 266, 269, 272, 302, 307, 321, 325, 331; personified, 89, 90; as privation, xxii, 116, 123, 244, 354n58; problem of, xv, xvi, xviii, xix, xxiii, xxv, xxii, 29, 47, 57, 88, 89, 104, 105, 111, 115, 122, 125, 129, 139, 144, 169, 170, 176, 185, 193,

evil (*continued*)
231, 236, 266, 267, 303, 328; radical, xxiv, 229, 279, 295; as result of chance, 243, 326; as result of emanations, 150, 152, 169, 325; in Sa'diah, 105–11; self-induced, 12, 13, 16, 86, 124, 133, 324; spirits, 98, 147, 150, 153; as suffering, 43; unjustified, 134, 198; as violation of the Torah, 21. *See also* good

evil inclination, xx, 62, 74, 89–95, 340, 341n102; in Baḥya, 113, 144; in Borowitz, 250; in Dead Sea Scrolls, 96, 99; as a good, 92, 181, 182, 184; in Hasidic thought, 174, 175, 179, 180, 181, 182; in Luzzatto, 206; in Maimonides, 119; in Mendelssohn, 218; origins of, 90, 91; overcoming, 93, 95, 184; in Philo, 343n151; power of, 92, 93, 94; similarity to, in Philo, 103; in Talmud, 65, 92, 93, 94, 104; in Zohar, 160, 161, 170

Fackenheim, Emil, 229, 300, 307, 312–14, 316, 317, 318, 321
Feldman, Seymour, 131, 136, 137
Fishbane, Michael, 337n87
Fox, Marvin, 120, 122, 345n47
Fox, Michael, 47
free will, xv, xvi, xxiv, 7, 16, 53, 54, 73, 119, 121, 122, 124, 206, 218, 224, 232, 253, 295, 300, 304, 308, 316, 330, 345n63
Friedman, Richard E., 8, 17

Garfinkel, Stephen, 47
Geertz, Clifford, 253, 358n136
Gelernter, David Hillel, 306
Gelman, Ezra, 190

Gersonides, xx, 116, 130–37, 138, 143, 144, 195, 211, 260, 325, 326, 327
Gillman, Neil, xiii, xxi, 48, 49, 76, 252–56, 272, 324, 327
Ginzberg, Louis, 341n106
Ginzburg, H. L., 46
Gnostics, 149, 167, 172
Goldhagen, Daniel, 277
Goldstein, Rebecca Newberger, xv, xvi, xvii, xxii, 333n1
good, xi–xxv, 2, 4, 12, 99, 150, 156, 167, 173, 281, 282, 285, 300, 323, 328, 329, 330, 331, 332; absolute, 143, 302, 316; appreciated only in contrast with evil, 181–82, 325; attained through evil, 182–84, 326; in Baḥya, 112; in Berkovits, 290; in Bible, 5; in Buber, 236–38; as choice, 15–17, 18; concept implied, 15; conduct, 12; deeds, 165, 166, 287; discernable through human reason, 14; in Ecclesiastes, 45–48; errors in determining, 18; in Ezekiel, 21; frequency of word in Bible, 1; in Hasidism, 173–76, 181–82; in Heschel, 308; in ibn Daud, 116; in Isaiah, 19; in Jeremiah, 22–23; in Luzzatto, 206; in Maimonides, 119, 121–22; meanings of, 1; in Mendelssohn, 223; in Micah, 24; as mode of thought in Spinoza, 199–201; in Philo, 102–3; in Proverbs, 33; in Psalms, 24–32; in Sa'adiah, 109–10; Tree of Knowledge of, 5–10; unclear in Prophets, 17; as universal standard, 15; of universe, 5; in Ya'avetz, 143; in Zohar, 158–60. *See also* evil
Goodspeed, Edgar, 51
Gordis, Robert, 9, 47, 292, 307, 314–16, 321
Green, Arthur, 157, 349n29
Greenberg, Irving, 292

Greenberg, Moshe, 38, 41
Greenberg, Uri Tzvi, 275
Greene, Jayson, 249

Habermas, Jurgen, xviii, 225
habitus, 216, 241
Halbertal, Moshe, 117, 123, 125
Halevi, Judah, 9
Halivni, David Weiss, xiii, 292, 293
Hallamish, Moshe, 180
Hapstein, Israel, 179
Hazony, David, 294
Hegel, Georg W. F., 205
Heidegger, Martin, 246, 302, 316
Heschel, Abraham Joshua, xiii, 187,
    307–10, 318, 320, 351n20
ḥesed nigleh/nistar, 282
hester panim, 290, 321
Hick, John, xvi, 333
Hirsch, Samson Raphael, 16
historicization, 83
Holocaust, xi, 142, 189, 190, 289, 291,
    292, 294, 295, 301, 305, 307, 308, 312,
    313, 314, 315, 317, 318, 319, 321, 323,
    328, 352n49, 360n5, 361n22, 362n53,
    364n110; challenge posed by, xii, xv,
    xvi, xvii, 229, 245, 248, 249, 253, 278,
    279; exceptionality of, 277–79; origin
    of word, 273–76
Horowitz, Ya'akov Yitzhak Halevi, 176
Hume, David, 136
ḥurban, 273, 275–76, 286, 360n8, 361n9
Husik, Isaac, xviii, 115, 117, 137, 139
Hutner, Isaac, 275, 361n9
Hyman, Aaron, 103

ibn Daud, Abraham, xx, 114–17, 129, 130,
    136, 137, 143, 260, 325
ibn Ezra, Abraham, 7

Idel, Moshe, 350n1
injustice, 48, 49, 74, 75, 77, 157, 196, 224,
    322; cannot be ascribed to God, 89,
    125, 340n77; as challenge to God, 13,
    29, 32, 42, 57, 60, 82, 88, 223, 278, 323,
    327; in Gillman, 255; inevitability of,
    88–89, 104, 125; is inexplicable, 69,
    104; in Kushner, 259, 260; lessons
    from Qumran, 98; in Plato, 342n137;
    possible resolution of, 67, 104; as
    problem of perception, 65, 126, 156,
    223–24; in Spinoza, 196; redressed
    in the afterlife, 48, 49, 74–76, 126–27,
    129, 139, 144, 212, 221; resolved by
    Gersonides, 131, 135; against the
    righteous, 28, 29, 40, 58, 63, 64, 78, 101
intellect, xiii; in Baḥya, 113; in Gerson-
    ides, 133; in Maimonides, 118–20; in
    Spinoza, 204
Isaac, Binding of, 2, 13, 14–15, 283
Isaac Israeli, 105
Israel of Rizhyn, 187

Jacob Joseph of Polnoye, 172
Jacobs, Louis, 328, 329, 331
Jaspers, Karl, 246
Job, xx, 4, 34–45, 51, 55, 139, 152, 203,
    238, 252, 258, 323, 324, 330, 335n50,
    346n80; in Borowitz, 252; in Buber,
    238; in Cohen, 227; in Gersonides, 135;
    in Gillman, 253–54, 255; in Kushner,
    258; in Maimonides, 126; message
    of, 57, 62, 68; in Plaskow, 269, 270;
    repudiation of, 49; in Rubenstein,
    296; as source for the concept of
    soul, 77; in Spinoza, 203; as sustained
    investigation of unjust suffering, 2; as
    test of the principle that God cannot
    act unjustly, 14; theme of, 51

Johnson, Paul, 225

Josephus, 96, 277

justice, 20, 31, 88, 104, 106, 134, 135, 143, 169, 209, 211, 223, 259, 271, 272, 322, 332; absolute, 88; as characteristic of God, 31, 47, 48, 51, 52, 63, 81, 126, 128, 131, 144, 329; in Baḥya, 111; in Borowitz, 249; in Donat, 306; in Ecclesiastes, 47; in Ezekiel, 20; in Fackenheim, 313; as feature of the afterlife, 106; in Gersonides, 134, 135; as inevitable, 57; in Job, 38, 39, 41, 42; in Kaplan, 241; in Kook, 193; in Kushner, 256, 262; in Luzzatto, 209; in Mendelssohn, 221; in mysticism, 160; as no longer in force, 325; in Psalms, 25, 26; questions of, in chapter summaries, xxi; as quintessential Jewish value, 332; in Shapira, 281, 283; social, 300; in Spinoza, 196, 197

Kabbalah, xx, 145–70

Kant, Immanuel, xvii, xxv, 212, 225, 226, 229

Kaplan, Aryeh, 348n21

Kaplan, Mordecai, xxi, 239–45, 271, 325, 326, 357n78

Katz, Steven T., 239, 244, 245, 275, 277, 278, 295, 361n22, 367n174

Kaufmann, Walter, 356n40

Kavka, Martin, 265

Kegley, Charles, 239

kelipah, 167, 350n57

Kimḥi, David, 7, 8, 9, 293, 347n125

Kobrin, Moshe, 187

Kook, Abraham Isaac, xx, 190–93, 194, 326, 327

Kushner, Harold, xxi, 255, 256–63, 272, 272, 326, 327

Lacquer, Walter, 360n5

Lamm, Norman, 193, 350n8

Leaman, Oliver, 195, 199, 203, 236

Levenson, Jon D., 255

Levinas, Emmanuel, xx, 307, 316–17, 321

Liebniz, Gottfried Willhelm, xxi, 205, 324

Lilith (Lillith), 98, 150, 151, 152, 342n121

Lizensk, Elimelek, 182, 280, 326

Logos, 100, 149

Luria, Isaac, xx, 166–69, 288, 321, 325, 347n125

Luzzatto, Moses Hayyim, xxi, 205–11, 222, 223, 224, 325, 354n45

Luzzatto, Samuel David, 204–5

Macbeth, 247, 314, 323

Magid, Shaul, 166

Maimonides, 16, 111, 114, 116, 117–30, 138, 143, 144, 241, 244, 306, 335n50, 345n47, 346n70, 346n79; and Albo, 139; and Crescas, 137; and Donat, 306; on evil, 325; on free will, xxiv; and Gersonides, 132, 134, 135, 136, 137; on good, 5; on human reason, 42; on Job, 42; and Kaplan, 241, 244; and Kushner, 260; and Mendelssohn, 217, 223; on origin of moral evil, 16; and Spinoza, 195, 200, 202; on suffering, 327; and Tsimerman, 288

Malbim, Meir Leibush, 335n36, 347n125

mamzer, 162

Manoaḥ, Hezekiah, 8

McTaggart, John M. E., 329

Mecklenberg, Jacob Zvi, 334n13

Meiri, Menaḥem, 338n16

Menaḥem Mendl of Vitebsk, 172, 178, 325

Mendelssohn, Moses, xx, 211–22, 223, 224, 225, 256, 271, 325, 327

merism, 9

Meshullam (Zusya) of Hanipol, 177, 178, 186, 325

Metatron, 147

Mitchell, Stephen, 37, 45

Mittleman, Alan, 252

Monter, E. William, 361n22

Morgensztern, Menaḥem Mendl, of Kotzk, 187, 259, 327

Mullins, R. T., 270

mysticism, xx, 145, 146, 147, 157, 205, 222, 308, 348n4, 350n1

myth, 3, 6, 55, 64, 146, 147, 149, 150, 152, 153, 158, 254, 255, 256, 303, 312

Nadler, Steven, 196, 197, 198, 202

Naḥmanides, 7, 8, 9, 16

Nahman of Breslov, 175, 178, 187, 325, 327, 321

Naḥum of Gamzu (Naḥum Ish Gamzu), 80, 351n15

nature, 32, 97, 131, 132, 136, 138, 196, 198, 199, 202, 202, 203, 223, 240, 243, 245, 253, 255, 260, 267, 268, 270, 272, 327, 354n58; human, xxiv, 52, 89, 95, 120, 174, 199, 204, 250, 261; laws of, 196, 197, 198, 200, 217; and natural disasters, 32, 122, 221, 229, 244

nefesh, 77

Neiman, Susan, xxv, 333n12

Neo-Platonism, 105, 149

neshamah, 77

Nietzsche, Friedrich, 19

Nissim Gaon, 334n19

nisus, 231

Nous, 149

Novak, David, 334n19

Noveck, Simon, 229

Nussbaum, Martha, xix, xxi, 263–66, 271, 272, 325

omnibenevolence, xxii, 131, 252, 257, 304, 305

omnipotence, 60, 304, 305, 307, 329, 330, 331

omniscience, xxii, 44, 79, 122, 211, 305, 331, 332, 333(chap1)n2

ontology, 99, 100, 101, 103, 290

Oz, Amos, 360n6

panentheism, 268, 270

pantheism, 268

Pereira, Vera, 76

Philo, xx, 99–103, 149, 258, 326, 327, 343n151

Piekarz, Medel, 350n1

Pinchess, Charles, 264

Pinhas of Koretz, 181, 325

Plato, 77, 100, 102, 123, 137, 212, 303, 329, 339n50, 342n135, 342n137

pleroma, 149, 152

praecipotent, 331

predeterminism, xxiv, 33, 264

process, cosmic, 240, 241; God as, 241

prosperity, 15, 33, 61, 73, 74, 80, 138, 207, 208; of righteous, 60; of wicked, 22, 28, 29, 34, 41, 60, 62, 63, 74, 75, 88, 140, 141, 209, 335n43

providence, 42, 47, 101; in Alexander, 232; in Altschuler, 42; in Berkovits, 291; in Crescas, 137–38; in Ecclesiastes, 47; in Gersonides, 131–36, 144; in Gillman, 254; in Luzzatto, 206; in Maimonides, 126, 128; in Mendelssohn, 218, 22; in Philo, 101; in Rubenstein, 305

pseudepigrapha, 54, 100, 348n20

qualia, 324

Qumran, 95, 97, 98, 99, 341n107

Raphael, Simcha Paull, 55
Reines, Isaac Jacob, 239
reshimu, 168
reward, 15, 16, 42, 55, 71, 72, 80, 108,
   112, 113, 119, 138, 143, 157, 165, 196,
   207, 210, 327, 343n11, 346n79; for
   Abraham, 79; in afterlife, 75, 90,
   107, 210; in Albo, 139, 140, 141;
   anticipation of, 110; in Bahir, 157; in
   Bahya; in Crescas, 138; in Daniel, 49;
   as different from gift, 110; earned by
   ancestral merit, 66; in Ecclesiastes,
   48; eternal, 108; expectations of,
   unwarranted, 84; in Gersonides,
   131, 132, 135, 137; in Gillman, 254; for
   good conduct, 34, 47, 48, 61, 65, 66,
   70, 81, 106, 126, 156, 196, 208, 279,
   339n58; for Job, 42; in Kushner, 258,
   259; in Luzzatto, 207; Maimonides
   on, 120, 126, 127, 129, 130, 346n79;
   for obedience, 16; opinions of Rava
   on, 75; prerequisite for, 66; in She'ol,
   56; through suffering, 71, 72, 80;
   ultimate, 113; World of, in Sa'adiah,
   107, 129; in Zohar, 163, 165
Robinson, John M., 339n49
Rokeah, Shalom, 184
Roskies, David, 294, 360n8
ruah, 48, 77
Rubenstein, Richard, 276, 295–99, 300,
   302, 303, 305, 315, 364n110
Rudavsky, David, 212, 350n1
Russell, David Syme, 56
Russell, Jeffrey B., 90, 340n84

Sa'adiah, xx, 105–11, 129, 130, 140, 143, 144,
   148, 259, 325, 326, 327, 344n23, 344n25
Sacks, Jonathan, xx, 307, 317–19, 321,
   357n72, 368n197

Samael, 150, 151, 152, 348n16
Sandmel, Samuel, 100, 103
Sarna, Nahum, 3
Satan, 36, 150, 153, 324, 340n79, 341n99,
   348n16, 352n49
Schiendlin, Ray, 37, 38, 39, 44
Schneerson, Menachem Mendel, xx,
   189, 190, 194, 326, 352n49
Scholem, Gershom, 146, 147, 152, 157,
   160, 167, 168
Scult, Mel, 243
secret, 49, 50, 72, 94, 147, 151, 352n45,
   360n5; *Revealer of Secrets*, 172; *Secret
   of the Way Things Are*, 98
Seeskin, Kenneth, xviii
Sefer ha-Bahir, xx, 152–57, 169, 148
Sefer ha-Kabbalah, 114
Sefer Hekhalot, 147
Sefer Yetzirah, xx, 148–50, 169, 325
sefirot, 148, 149, 150, 153, 168, 180
Seforno, Ovadiah, 16, 334n24
Shakespeare, William, 323
Shapira, Kalonymous Kalman, 280–84,
   286, 292, 294, 321, 324, 326, 327
Shekhinah, 153, 268
shelemut, 206
Shem Tov, Israel, xx, 172, 268, 325, 326,
   327, 351n11
She'ol, 55–56, 337n95
shevirat ha-kelim, 168
Shne'ur Zalman of Liady, 180, 326
Shoah, xx, xxi, xxiv, xxv, 171, 273–322,
   360n6, 361n9
sin, 11, 12, 16, 18, 34, 35, 37, 38, 44, 52,
   53, 54, 80, 82, 84, 90, 91, 92, 96, 98,
   103, 109, 134, 135, 143, 152, 174, 179,
   180, 197, 204, 220, 248, 285, 288, 294,
   349n43; accountable for own, 84, 211;
   of Adam and Eve, 151, 167, 204, 220,

242, 325, 337n93; of Golden Calf, 175; human propensity for, 99; inherited, 161–62, 165; personified, 96; and repentance, 108, 180, 288, 294, 311; as reason for suffering, 68–69, 126, 130, 140, 142, 178, 208, 227, 242, 248, 254–55, 263, 276, 280, 283, 285, 287, 289, 292–93, 294, 295, 297, 346n79, 352n49, 362n53; of Sodom, 13; unavoidable, 82, 95, 211

sitra aḥra, 163, 164, 179

snake and serpent, 5, 7, 63, 118, 120, 151, 157, 158, 159

Sodom, 2, 13–15, 52, 88, 331, 335n29

Solomon ibn Gabirol, 105

Soloveitchik, Joseph, 307, 310–12, 320, 366n169

Songs of the Sage, 98, 324

Sophia (wisdom), 149

soul, xx, 103, 108, 156, 157, 161, 183, 241, 283, 337n93, 339n50; in Apocrypha, 91; in Bahir, 155, 156; in Baḥya, 113; and body, 48, 56, 113, 283, 339n50; in Buber, 236, 237, 238, 271; concept of, 76; immortality of, 77, 183; in Kaplan, 241; in Levinas, 316; in Maimonides, 127; noble, 24, 56; nonmaterial, 48, 62, 333n1; in Philo, 102, 343n151; Plato on, 77; making, xv; transmigration of, 170, 210, 211, 224, 288; world of, 48, 76; in Ya'avetz, 143

Speiser, Ephraim A., 9, 12, 334n23

Spektor, Yitzḥak Elḥanan, 239

Spero, Shubert, 254

Spinoza, Barukh, 195–205, 222, 223, 262, 271, 325, 327, 353n18

Stone, M. E., 55

Strauss, Leo, 18

suffering, xi, xv, xvi, xix, xx, xxiii, 2, 29, 71, 74, 86, 103, 112, 126, 143, 144, 171, 202, 206, 228, 242, 245, 251, 257, 265, 280, 282, 284, 288, 289, 290, 294, 304, 311, 312, 316, 317, 321, 326, 327, 344n25, 350n1, 361n31; arbitrary, 35; of babies, 161–62; of children, xv, xvi, 110, 130, 136, 161–62, 173; of collective, 188–93; as consequence of God's wrath, 87; as corrective, 265; as evil, 16, 43; as form of sacrifice, 282–83; God as partner in, 282, 304; as good, 177, 178, 208, 227, 327; hastening redemption, 188–89; of innocents, 31, 110, 123, 143, 162, 165, 196, 198, 255, 287, 290; is a blessing, 37, 57, 71, 79, 102, 104, 110, 112, 165, 174, 176, 187, 194, 210, 211, 221, 226, 227, 238, 258, 259, 271, 282, 288, 294, 327; is a mystery, 255, 258, 283, 311, 316, 326, 327, 328, 329, 330; is transformative, 227, 282; of Jewish people, 227–28, 271; of Job, 34, 35, 37, 135, 203, 238, 269; Judaism on, xxiv; leading to compassion, 229; leading to faith, 80, 187, 227, 271, 283, 294, 327; origin of, 235; as part of God's plan, 31, 37, 45, 87, 186, 188, 190, 253, 327; as part of life, xxiv, 32, 37, 192, 226, 327; personal, 185–88, 193; physical, 71; of the poor, 229; problem of, 43, 104, 111, 193, 228, 249; as punishment, 34, 35, 38, 44, 60, 68, 69, 140, 142, 208, 227, 248, 254, 255, 263, 280, 285, 287, 289, 292, 295; question of origin, 51, 249; reality of, xxv, 45, 57, 192, 311; a reason for, 67, 247, 260; rectified by repentance, 311; redemptive, 70–71, 80, 87, 108, 112, 163, 284, 291, 327;

suffering (*continued*)

   as result of astral influence, 74; as
   result of human freedom, 255; as
   result of violation of the Torah, 112;
   of the righteous, 34, 49, 60, 63, 64, 67,
   69, 70, 72, 74, 79, 80, 84–85, 88, 90,
   109, 128, 133, 135, 140, 156, 164, 166,
   237, 339n58; as sign of God's love,
   71, 327; as special recognition, 72; as
   test, 31, 79, 80, 97, 109–10, 112, 187,
   188, 327; unjust, 31, 34, 38, 43, 44, 45,
   72, 84, 109, 112, 156, 165, 243; useless,
   317; value of, 227; vicarious, 84–85,
   109, 135, 156, 163–64, 165, 170, 210,
   211, 227, 327

Sumerian myths, 6

summum bonum, 120

Talmon, Jacob, 278

Targum Onkelos, 5

Targum Yonatan, 334n13, 336n51

teiku, 328

Teitelbaum, Yoel, 284, 362n53

Testament of Amram, 98, 325

Testament of the Twelve Patriarchs, 91

theodicy, xx, 2, 98, 104, 139, 140, 202,
   204, 223, 229, 236, 252, 263, 271, 272,
   279, 284, 288, 309, 315, 332; in Albo,
   139, 140; in Apocrypha, 52, 54, 57;
   in Berkovits, 289; in Borowitz, 250,
   252; in Buber, 236; in Cohen, 229; in
   Daniel, 49; in Gersonides, 135, 137; in
   Gillman, 253, 254; in Gordis, 315; in
   Heschel, 309; as intractable problem,
   332; in Judaism, xxiii–xxv; in Kaplan,
   241, 243; in Kook, 192; in Kushner,
   263; in Levinas, 316, 317; in Luzzatto,

206; in Maimonides, 125, 127, 128; in
   Mendelssohn, 213, 222; in Philo, 100;
   in Plaskow, 267; in Psalms, 24, 26, 31;
   in Qumran, 98; Rabbinic approaches
   to, 63–69; as Rabbinic preoccupation, 62, 99; in Rubenstein, 297; in
   Sa'adiah, 106–10; in Sacks, 318; and
   Shoah, 279, 284, 288; in Spinoza,
   202, 204; understanding the term,
   xxi–xxv; in Zohar, 162

theology, 49, 55, 76, 90, 95, 140, 249, 250,
   252, 259, 266, 276, 296, 298, 302, 321,
   322, 331, 332; in Borowitz, 249, 251;
   changed by the Shoah, 292; Christian, 52; in Cohen, 301; contradiction
   to, 90; Ecclesiastes as transition in,
   48; in Jonas, 303, 304; in Kaplan, 241,
   245; moral, 69; of mitzvah, 251; in
   Plaskow, 267; Rabbinic, 62; reviled
   by Kushner, 257; revolutionary, 56;
   in Rubenstein, 297; as unsystematic
   in Bible, 1

tikkun, 168

Trachtenberg, Joshua, 340n83

transmigration, 155, 156, 170, 210, 211,
   224, 288

Treblinka, 281, 300, 365n126

Tree of Knowledge, 2, 5–10, 17, 52, 118,
   119, 121, 153, 183, 204, 215, 219–20,
   242, 331, 334n13, 334n24, 345n51

tremendum, 276, 301, 302

trials of the righteous, 78–82, 102, 109,
   110, 112, 129–30, 143, 339n52, 346n79

Tsimerman, Hayyim Yisrael, 280,
   286–88, 292, 294, 327

tzaddik, 181, 187, 188. *See also* zaddik

tzimtzum, 167, 321

Urbach, Efraim, 74, 91, 99

virtue, xv, 26, 32, 92, 100, 101, 103, 133,
   185, 191, 196, 197, 201, 204, 221

wealth, 28, 29, 43, 46, 50, 73, 101, 102, 116,
   135, 141, 173, 206–7, 227, 231, 253, 328
Weisblum, Eliezer of Lizensk, 182
Weizmann, Chaim, 274
Whitehead, Alfred North, 225
Wiesel, Elie, 274, 307, 319–20, 321

Williams, Bernard, 265
Wolfson, Harry A., 100, 343n151

Ya'avetz, Joseph, 142–43, 259, 327

zaddik, 176. *See also* tzaddik
Zionism, 362n53
Zohar, xx, 152, 157–66, 167, 169, 170, 177,
   324, 325, 326, 327, 348n20, 349n32,
   350n57
Zoroastrianism, xxiii, 89

INDEX OF TEXTS

IN THE JPS ESSENTIAL JUDAISM SERIES

Thinking about Good and Evil: Jewish Views from Antiquity to Modernity
Rabbi Wayne Allen

Thinking about the Prophets: A Philosopher Reads the Bible
Kenneth Seeskin

Thinking about the Torah: A Philosopher Reads the Bible
Kenneth Seeskin

Thinking about God: Jewish Views
Rabbi Kari H. Tuling

Justice for All: How the Jewish Bible Revolutionized Ethics
Jeremiah Unterman

To order or obtain more information on these or other
Jewish Publication Society titles, visit jps.org.